D1106087

PAUL TILLICH'S THEOLOGY OF THE CHURCH A CATHOLIC APPRAISAL

by
RONALD MODRAS

With a Foreword by Hans Küng

WAYNE STATE UNIVERSITY PRESS·DETROIT 1976

Library of Congress Cataloging in Publication Data

Modras, Ronald
    Paul Tillich's theology of the church.

    Bibliography: p.
    Includes index.
    1. Church—History of doctrines—20th century.
2. Tillich, Paul, 1886–1965.   I. Title.
BV598.M6   230'.2   76–6082
ISBN 0–8143–1552–6

Publication of this book was assisted by the American Council of Learned Societies under a grant from the Andrew W. Mellon Foundation.

To my mother and father

CONTENTS

Foreword

I am delighted to accept the invitation of Ronald Modras, a former student, to write the foreword to his book, which I have read with the greatest satisfaction. I think the best way to do justice to his book is to offer some fundamental observations on the present theological situation as it is presented in light of the theology of Paul Tillich.

Christian theology has the permanent task of translating the New Testament message of Jesus as the Christ for each new generation. Nothing may dispense the theologian from that task. Throughout the history of the Church, every century has had theologians who provided example and direction, winning for themselves the distinction of being called "great theologians." Paul Tillich together with Karl Barth, Rudolf Bultmann, Dietrich Bonhoeffer, and the Niebuhrs were among the most significant Protestant theologians of our century. Without their exemplary "work of interpretation," contemporary Christian theology would be inconceivable.

In this respect Paul Tillich achieved two things in his theology: he succeeded in taking up the traditions and cultures of two "worlds," Europe and America; he succeeded also in creating a synthesis from the traditions and cultures of the two great contrasting Christian confessions, Protestantism and Catholicism. This is what makes reading his work fascinating and fruitful even today.

In our present situation, the scope of problems for theology has shifted appreciably from that of Tillich's day. Tillich maintained a low estimate of the significance of the "historical Jesus" for systematic theology, and refrained from making use of the historical-critical method of interpreting the biblical evidence. Contemporary theology, however, confronted by

11

fundamental controversies about historical biblical criticism and demythologization, cannot ignore these issues any longer. And it is remarkable that, despite all the differences with regard to details, there is arising a broad ecumenical consensus in the discussion of the basic question of theological method.

Nonetheless, with his particular emphasis on St. Paul's Spirit Christology, Tillich exemplifies a theologian with the courage to break not with the living faith of the past but with its dated formulas, in order to relate the Christian message to contemporary questions and concerns. Obviously, Tillich's theology is not definitive. No theologian can provide final answers. But the answers Tillich did provide to the questions of his day, his scholarship, his willingness to live "on the boundary" between Church and society, philosophy and theology—all this can serve as an example to theologians today.

This work by Ronald Modras will be of great help for readers, both in Europe and the United States. It demonstrates a firm command of Tillich's theology and the literature surrounding it. The discussion which follows, focusing on Tillich's central ecclesiological *problematik*, ranges broadly in both matter and method but masters proficiently the abundant material on the issue of Church reform. His interpretation of Tillich's theology is convincing, just as is his discussion of the various kinds of reform, the possibility of radical reform in the Catholic Church, and thus the elimination of opposition between the Protestant "alone" and the Catholic "and." Avoiding lazy compromises, Modras's judgment is balanced, grounded on a first-rate knowledge of European and American theology of the Church. His call to a radical reform in the Catholic Church is matched by a criticism of the elevation within Protestantism of protest into a principle. In both its presentation and appraisal, the work constitutes an important contribution to ecumenical understanding.

This book comes at the right time. The situation of ecumenism in the United States as elsewhere is one in which little excitement or activity can be detected on the level of Church authority. Practical ecumenical reconciliation, however, continues visibly at the grass roots. Catholics and Protestants are learning to value each other's traditions. The principal division today is not simply that between Catholics and Protestants, but between those on both sides who would absolutize their church structures and traditions in contrast to those who are ready to accept the need of their church for reform and to realize it.

Modras makes clear where Tillich himself saw the essential ecclesiological elements of a truly Christian church: in the polarity between

"Catholic substance" and the "Protestant principle," between the priestly element and the prophetic. God's sacramentally mediated presence is constitutive for the Church of Jesus Christ. The decrease of substance within Protestantism can only be deplored. Yet one must also protest the claims for absoluteness raised so often in the Catholic Church in behalf of its doctrines, sacraments, and institutional structures. The ecumenical encounter of Catholics and Protestants is opening up the possibility in our day of bringing the sacramental, constitutive element and the prophetic, corrective element into a new unity.

The author deserves to be congratulated for a work superlatively written. Given the difficult phase in which the ecumenical movement finds itself both in Europe and the United States, one may well wish that both in theory and practice its objective may be achieved. We must get out of the present ecumenical stagnation at the top too, and the sooner the better!

Hans Küng

Tübingen
July 1975

Note to Reader: In those sections devoted mainly to a discussion of a particular work, the page numbers in parentheses in the text refer to that title. When English translations are not available, the translations are the author's.

Introduction

"*Today there is* rather too much than too little said about the Church."[1] Coming from Karl Barth, such a statement gives good reason to pause. What justifies another book on the Church? Certainly there are more pressing issues confronting theology today: the reality of God, the significance of Jesus, the possibility of faith in an age confronted by famines and dwarfed by IBM's and ICBM's. A glance at the bibliographical catalogues is enough to see that, since World War I, we have been inundated with books and articles on some aspect or other of ecclesiology. So why another? Because, although there are areas of theology more important, few areas are still so problematic today for Christians of every tradition. Few areas of theology provoke so many questions, pose so many difficulties. In search of at least a direction toward answers and solutions, we turn to the theology of Paul Tillich. To quote one of his critics, "No one who reads Tillich can fail to learn from him."[2] Here is justification enough for a work such as this.

The temper of the times has changed considerably since Otto Dibelius spoke of the "century of the Church" or Romano Guardini envisioned the Church awakening in the souls of men. Today book jackets tell of an outdated Church, the end of conventional Christianity; they ask if the Church is necessary. Forged as it was on the anvil of compromise, Vatican II's Dogmatic Constitution on the Church did not create a consensus of theological opinion among Catholics, let alone between Catholics and other Christians. If anything, it was a source of ferment and frustration. While persuading sizable numbers of Catholics that there is a validity in describing the Church as the people of God, Vatican II did not always instill a comparable conviction in pastoral authorities still inclined to identify the Church with their own hierarchic offices. The upshot has been a tension within the Catholic Church between critics and apologists of the status quo, a polarization which has been described in less discreet moments as bordering on schism. The problems confronting the Catholic Church today are by no means exclusively theological. But they do tend to be most abrasive precisely in those areas which pertain to the nature and function of the Church, its structures and institutions.

There is something to be said in favor of yet another study in the theology of the Church, provided that it has something to say to the questions confronting Christians today: Is the Church necessary? What makes the Church different? How can the Church claim to be one, when it is obviously disunified? How can the Church claim to be catholic, when it has so often shown itself to be particularist? What does the nondescript group of Jews who became convinced that Jesus of Nazareth rose from death as Christ and Lord have to do with the massive, bureaucratic institutions that have since identified themselves with his name? What is the connection between the Church and the kingdom of God which Jesus preached as imminent? What is the nature and function of authority in the Church? Of dogmas? Of offices? How can they claim for their origins someone like Jesus who championed freedom? What is the relationship of the Church to the world religions, to the social and political movements in today's society? What does it mean to be a Catholic, to be a Protestant? What does it mean to be a Christian at all? These are some of the questions that a study of the Church must confront. And these are the questions that we put to Paul Tillich and his theology of the Church.

And why Paul Tillich? Certainly ecclesiology was not a central issue for him. Tillich's primary interests lay elsewhere, as evidenced by the comparatively scant comment his theology of the Church has evoked. The Church was by no means an ultimate concern for him. Despite this fact, though, he had more than a little to say about the Church, as the first part of this study demonstrates.

Why Paul Tillich? Because in questions related to the doctrine of God, the attitude toward world religions, and the task of translating religious symbols to answer contemporary questions, Tillich has become a powerful influence upon the Catholic Church since Vatican II. He is not always cited directly and his name does not always appear in the footnotes, but his spirit and thought loom large behind much of the theology that has arisen and is being taught in Catholic seminaries, colleges and universities, both in the United States and Europe. He has become in many ways the anonymous father of post-conciliar Catholic theology.

If Tillich has been of enormous influence and benefit to Catholic theology in other areas, there is good reason to seek his counsel in questions pertaining to the Church. The wake of Vatican II has brought with it challenges with which Protestants have been compelled to cope for some time—biblical and historical criticism of traditional doctrines, the meaning and significance of religious experience, Pentecostalism, and the social implications of the gospel are a few. Tillich had a genius for synthesis. He was able to cull from the most disparate sources, many of them familiar to Catholic scholars, others deserving new, unbiased consideration. He possessed a command not only of Augustine and the medieval scholastics but also of the syntheses constructed by Hegel, Schleiermacher, and nineteenth-century liberal Protestantism. He recognized their strengths as well as their excesses and weaknesses, warning us against making the same mistakes.

Tillich's significance as an ecumenical theologian also merits mention here. His elaboration of the priestly and prophetic elements of religion, Catholic substance and the Protestant principle as he called them, has served to illuminate both Catholicism and Protestantism, even to their adherents. He thus provided a basis for ecumenical discussion which has yet to be adequately explored.

There is at least one more reason, though, which justifies another book on the Church, another book on Paul Tillich, and it is in many ways the most compelling one. Tillich had a prophet's zeal for seeing God alone as absolute. No doctrine, no institution, no structure, no matter how ancient or sacred, could be raised up above criticism or reform without incurring Tillich's censure of idolatry. He was not an iconoclast; he believed traditional doctrines, institutions, and structures were deserving of honor. But he would not abide their being absolutized. The Grand Inquisitor for Tillich was symbolic of an ominous reality ready to reappear in different guises at any time. No longer here to fight the Grand Inquisitor himself, Tillich left behind, incarnate in his theology, an ideal that continues to challenge Christians of every tradition, the ideal of a Church where God alone and nothing else claims ultimate concern. Such is certainly not a Church without God, but it is a Church without idols.

17

PART ONE

Paul Tillich's Theology of the Church

1

A Community of Ultimate Concern

Margareta: *Then you don't believe?*

Faust: *Nay, darling girl, no need to misconceive.*
For who can say that name
And claim
A very certain faith?

Is not life teeming
Around the head and heart of you,
Weaving eternal mysteries
Seen and unseen, even at your side?
Oh, let them fill your heart, your generous heart,
And, when you lose your being in that bliss
Give it what name you will—
Your joy, love, heart, your God.
For me, I have no name
To give it: feeling's surely all.
Names are but noise and smoke,
Obscuring heavenly light.

Goethe, Faust

Not without reason, Goethe's Faust has become in these last centuries a symbol of Western man. An heir of the Enlightenment, he is skeptical of the supernatural, yet driven on by a hunger for the infinite, striving, probing, questioning, searching for new horizons, restless for new experiences, never quite content with yesterday's answers. It was for the Fausts of our day that Paul Tillich labored. His theological endeavors were directed toward the questions, doubts, and needs of modern secular man, for those who decline to speak of God or to claim a very certain faith. He sought to demonstrate how, locked within the symbols of Christian tradition, there are meanings and answers which speak to the striving and concerns of today. In doing so, he was able to draw ties between such disparate entities as atheism and religion, anxious doubt and quiet faith. He dared to relate the staid Sunday churchgoer with the fervidly convinced Marxist. And to both Tillich presented his vision of the Church. He was a mediator, a reconciler, trying to do justice to the demands of both ends of the spectrum. His theology of the Church attempted to remain true to the Church's New Testament origins while confronting at the same time the revolutionary situations characteristic of our age. This was certainly no mean enterprise. The question for the reader as for the critic is, did he succeed?

Tillich's theology of the Church "cannot be understood apart from the total context of his thinking."[1] It is woven into the entire fabric of his theology. There is a pattern to his thought, though, a coherence that becomes increasingly more apparent with closer study of his system. To aid in abstracting the thread of his theology of the Church without misrepresenting it or distorting its context, I propose Tillich's doctrine of religious symbols. It has been said of Tillich that his entire theology is one of symbol,[2] which he substantiated: "The center of my theological doctrine of knowledge is the concept of symbol" (KB, p. 333). "You cannot understand theology without understanding symbols."[3] Nowhere is this more the case than in Tillich's theology of the Church. It provides the material from which he fashioned his thinking about the polarity between the priestly and prophetic elements in the Church, Catholic substance and the Protestant principle. Here is one of Tillich's most original contributions to theology. It is also the very heart of his theology of the Church.

Ultimate Concern

Basic to understanding both Tillich's theology of the Church and religious symbol is his concept of ultimate concern. Revelation, religion, and faith are all related and defined in terms of it. Ultimate concern for Tillich is the abstract translation of the great commandment: the Lord, our God, the Lord is one; you shall love the Lord your God with all your heart, and with all your soul, with all your mind, and with all your strength. Because it excludes all other concerns from ultimate significance and makes them preliminary, it is an ultimate concern. Because it is independent of any conditions of character, desire, or circumstance, it is an unconditional concern. It is total, in that no part of ourselves or our world is excluded from it. And it is infinite, in that no moment of relaxation and rest is possible in the face of it (ST1:11).

Although rooted in Kierkegaard's concept of "infinite interest," ultimate concern is even more closely related to Schleiermacher's "feeling of absolute dependence." At a time when it was popular to debunk Schleiermacher, when Barth attacked liberal theology precisely for its "Schleiermacherei," Tillich defended both Schleiermacher and his definition of religion. He admitted that ultimate concern was "rather near" to the feeling of absolute dependence, but insisted that the word *feeling* was not to be given a psychological interpretation or attributed to a psychological function. Instead, it refers to the "awareness of that which transcends intellect and will, subject and object" (ST1:42). Tillich did not hesitate to equate this "awareness" with "experience," an experience of the Absolute. He saw himself doing so within the tradition of Augustine and the early Franciscans. "In the Augustinian tradition the source of all philosophy of religion is the immediacy of the presence of God in the soul or, as I prefer to say it, the experience of the unconditional, of the ultimate, in terms of an ultimate or unconditional concern."[4] It means "having the divine within ourselves, not necessarily by nature, but yet given and felt within our own being" (PPT, p. 216). Whether labeled as ultimate concern or as the feeling of absolute dependence, this religious experience is prior to any reflection or action. Knowledge and action are consequences of ultimate concern, not its constituents (PPT, p. 108).

Unlike ultimate concern, all other concerns are finite, even the most passionate. They emerge and disappear, governed by the "melancholy law of transitoriness" (NB, p. 157). Ultimate concern, not only quantitatively but even qualitatively, is different. It is not simply the top of a pyramid of concerns, but rather embraces the entire lot. Nothing compares with it in importance, because it alone provides the answer to the ultimate meaning of life. It promises ultimate fulfillment and thereby so "grasps" a person that he will not give it up, indeed, cannot give it up except with a bad conscience (UC, pp. 8, 11).

Ultimate concern eludes strict definition precisely because it is an experience. Perhaps its meaning can be further clarified by seeing it in relation to three other concepts essential for any understanding of Tillich's theology of the Church: revelation, religion, and faith.

Revelation is not a deposit of truth. It is not a complex of information, whether guarded in a Church structure, as Catholics tend to view it, or preserved in biblical texts, as Protestants are accustomed to believe.

"Revelation is first of all the experience in which an ultimate concern grasps the human mind."[5] It is an event in which the absolute becomes manifest in an ultimate concern as the ground of our being (DF, p. 79). Although revelation mediates knowledge, it is not information about the nature of things or their relation to one another. It is not information about nature, history, or man so it cannot enter into conflict with empirical knowledge. "Knowledge of revelation is knowledge about the revelation of the mystery of being to us. . . . Therefore, the knowledge of revelation can be received only in the situation of revelation, and it can be communicated—in contrast to ordinary knowledge—only to those who participate in this situation" (ST1:129).

Ultimate concern can be mediated through anything whatsoever—through a person or an event, through history or words. These media are not revelation in themselves; they point beyond themselves to ultimate concern. Usually revelation grasps an individual, and through an individual it grasps a group; this group can then become a medium of revelation for other groups. Thus the prophets were media of revelation to Israel. The apostles were media of revelation to the early Church. And both Israel and the Church have been media of revelation for others. To Tillich's mind, "the Christian Church always has been conscious of its vocation to be the bearer of revelation for nations and individuals" (ST1:120). Implied here is a distinction between original revelation and dependent revelation. An individual receiving an original revelation mediates it to a group which in turn becomes a bearer of that revelation to others, but now as dependent revelation. Thus the history of a revelation-bearing group begins with an original revelation and becomes the locus of continuous revelation. The history of the Church is one of continuous dependent revelation (ST1:126). Before it can mediate revelation, however, the Church must first receive it. This constitutes the correlate to revelation, namely, religion.

Religion is the reception of revelation, the state of being grasped by ultimate concern. Tillich stood in forthright opposition to Karl Barth and those theologians who oppose religion to revelation by regarding it simply as man's futile attempt at self-salvation. He likewise rejected Dietrich Bonhoeffer's vision of a "religionless Christianity." Revelation must be received, Tillich contended, by a particular person or by a particular group, and in a particular environment. It is this reception which constitutes religion, a state of being grasped by an ultimate concern, colored by all the circumstances in which it is received (PPT, p. 241).

Tillich's distinction between two meanings for the word *religion* is of prime importance here. In the narrow sense religion refers to the realm of the concrete and conditional. It supposes a community with clergy, scriptures, dogmas, and symbols, organized for the worship of God. Religion in the narrow sense is an expression, however, of religion in the broad sense, the state of being grasped by an ultimate concern. Tillich preferred this broader description of religion over the narrower one, because it permits inclusion not only of churches and groups which worship God but also of religions, such as Zen Buddhism, in which there is no god. It also permits inclusion of secular movements like Fascism and Communism, which Tillich regarded as quasi-religions in that they possess characteristics of religions proper and claim the same loyalty and veneration (CEWR, p. 4). The point of identity among all religions and quasi-religions is ultimate concern. Whether they intend to do so or not, they offer an answer to the question of the intrinsic aim of existence, to the *telos* of all existing things (CEWR, p. 63).

The broader sense of religion is the state of being ultimately concerned about the question of one's existence, its meaning, estrangement, and finitude. Viewed in this way, religion cannot be confined to a particular realm of life or to a particular function, whether of knowledge, morality, aesthetics, or feeling. It permeates all the aspects of life both for individuals and for groups. Religion is the depth dimension in all the creative functions of the human spirit. It is the substance, ground, and depth of man's spiritual life (TC, pp. 3–8). This broader concept of religion is of obvious significance to the theology of the Church, since it relates the Church not only to other religions but also to secularism, to which it gives a positive religious meaning. It views the Church as participating in a reality far broader than itself. This has been described as Tillich's most influential idea, "the idea of his that will doubtlessly endure longest, that religion is not something to be confined to a single institution, the church, but rather something that must express an entire culture, and be embodied in all its institutions."[6]

Faith, like religion, is defined by Tillich as "the state of being grasped by an ultimate concern" (ST3:131). Since only that which is the ground of our being and meaning should concern us ultimately, it is also described as "the concern about our existence in its ultimate 'whence' and 'whither' " (BR, p. 51). True to his Lutheran heritage, Tillich understood faith more as confidence, as *fiducia*, than as belief. Faith is not a good work, whether of the mind, will, or emotions. It cannot be forced. *Nihil facere sed tantum recipere:* faith does nothing, it simply receives. While revelation for Tillich emphasizes the manifestation of ultimate concern, and religion in the broader sense emphasizes its reception, faith emphasizes its acceptance.

But ultimate concern has an objective side as well. It points not only to a centered act of the personality but also to that toward which the act is directed, namely, the ultimate itself (DF, p. 10). There is no revelation, religion, or faith without content. The predominant religious name for the objective side of ultimate concern, for its content, is God. In non-theistic religions ultimate concern is directed toward a sacred object, an all-pervading power, or a highest principle. In secular quasi-religions it is directed toward a nation, science, or a highest ideal of humanity (CEWR, p. 5). The one thing which all of these contents have in common is that they require materialization in symbols, rituals, and doctrines. The unconditional can never be an object of concern as such. The unconditional can appear only in connection with the conditioned. It "can become a matter of ultimate concern only if it appears in a concrete embodiment" (TC, p. 28). Like everything else in the life of the human spirit, revelation, religion, and faith depend upon language. For Tillich the language of revelation, religion, and faith, the language of ultimate concern, is that of religious symbols.

Religious Symbols

To speak of ultimate concern, to speak of God, a person must speak in symbols. There is simply no other human way to express the infinite. Tillich could not have been more adamant. Demythologizing the New Testament, or any other religious statement for that matter, means interpreting religious symbols, not replacing them. The different dimensions of reality require different approaches. It is the power and mission of religious symbols to express precisely that which will not submit to scientific conception. The language of mathematical science does not suffice for the religious dimension of man's life, the dimension of depth. Here symbolic language is both unavoidable and universal (ST1:131).

In support of his contention that symbolism is inherent to religion, Tillich pointed to the incident (Exod. 33:18–23) in which Moses was not permitted a vision of God's face, only his back (UC, p. 14). Goethe's *Faust*, part 2, which is replete with symbolism, expresses much the same view. Faust cannot look directly into the blinding brilliance of the sun and must be satisfied with a rainbow:

Let then the sun remain at my back behind me!

This bow will serve to image man's endeavor.

Think on it and you grasp what lot is ours.
Reflected color forms our life for ever.[7]

Like Goethe, Tillich was convinced that reflected color is our lot. We see no more than God's back. We approach ultimate concern only through symbols, through a glass darkly.

There are few areas of Tillich's theology that have given rise to so much study and critical evaluation as his thinking on religious symbols.[8] Catholics in particular have given it serious consideration, since Tillich expressly viewed it as within the tradition of scholastic thinking regarding the analogy of being.[9] It has been called Tillich's closest link with Catholic theology.[10]

Tillich's thinking on symbols can be summarized briefly as follows:

1) It is of the utmost importance that symbols be differentiated from signs. A symbol is much more. Signs merely point to something else beyond themselves, like the signs in mathematics. They are harmless. The power of symbols, however, should never be underestimated. Like signs, symbols too represent. But unlike those signs which merely represent, symbols also participate in that to which they point. Although they are not to be identified with that to which they point, symbols do participate in its meaning and power. A flag, for example, is not only a sign but also a symbol; it participates in the power and dignity of the nation it represents.[11] Participation differentiates a symbol from a sign and expresses "what was rightly intended in the medieval doctrine of *analogia entis*, namely, to show a positive point of identity."[12] In virtue of such participation, symbols have an integrating power, a healing power, an elevating, stabilizing, quieting power. They can also have a destructive power, producing restlessness, fanaticism, and disintegration.[13] One should never speak of something as being "only a symbol."

2) It is the function of symbols to open up a level of reality which otherwise would remain closed to us. Like music and painting, symbols unlock levels of reality for which non-symbolic language is inadequate. At the same time they unlock dimensions of the human soul which would remain hidden, dimensions corresponding to the levels in exterior reality opened up by symbols. "Every symbol is two-edged" (TC, p. 57).

3) Unlike signs, symbols cannot be produced arbitrarily. Neither can they be consciously invented. They are created by the collective unconscious of a group, or at least accepted by the collective unconscious of a group in which they appear. A symbol must be affirmed by a group in that the group recognizes in this symbol something of its own being (TC, p. 58).

27

4) Unlike signs which are consciously invented and removed, symbols are born and die. They are born when a situation is ripe for them, when they are able to produce a response in a group. They die when the situation changes, when they are no longer able to open up either reality or the soul (TC, p. 58).

These foregoing points Tillich made with regard to symbols in general and to religious symbols in particular. Religious symbols focus upon ultimate concern and thereby unlock a dimension of reality which otherwise would remain unopened, the dimension of depth. This is the dimension fundamental to every other, the dimension of being itself. Religious symbolism accomplishes this by appropriating the material of ordinary experience and then transcending it. Religious symbolism affirms itself in self-transcending meaning, becoming transparent, or perhaps better, translucent to the infinite.[14] In accomplishing this, however, it must negate itself in its literal meaning.

Tillich was resolute in insisting upon symbolism as the primary expression of religion: although religion can express itself in theological concepts and artistic creations, symbolism is the only language in which religion can express itself directly. For all his insistence, though, Tillich was equally emphatic in maintaining that religious symbols are not to be taken literally. They should not be interpreted literally, because they are taken out of finite reality and applied to that which transcends it infinitely. "To say anything about God in the literal sense of the words used means to say something false about him" (LPJ, p. 109). Although he refused to take religious symbols literally, Tillich did take them seriously. He contrasted himself to Protestant Hegelianism and Catholic Modernism, both of which he saw as interpreting religious language symbolically in order to dissolve its realistic meaning and weaken its seriousness (ST1:241). Such was not Tillich's intention. For him the symbolic does not imply the unreal. The de-literalization of symbols (a term he preferred to demythologizing) is not meant to weaken symbols. On the contrary, it is meant to enhance their reality and power precisely by eliminating their superstitious interpretation (ST1:241).

The interpretation of religious symbols brings up the question of their truth. Tillich saw no essential conflict between religious symbols and reason because religious symbolism pertains to ultimate concern, whereas reason is concerned with matters of preliminary, finite concern. Existentially, however, conflicts do arise, so that criteria are needed to determine the truth of symbols. These criteria have nothing to do with the factual correctness of a symbol; religious symbols are independent of empirical criticism. They cannot be impaired by the criticism of natural science or historical research (TC, p. 65). In language worthy of William James, Tillich embraced a method of verification which was pragmatic rather than cognitive. Symbols are open to distortion. For this reason, the truth of religious symbols is determined by their adequacy and ultimacy. A religious symbol is *adequate* when it is able to communicate the ultimate in such a way that it evokes a reply, when it promotes a genuine religious experience, when it moves to action. When it ceases to create such a response, a religious symbol is dead. A religious symbol is *ultimate* when it is truly translucent, when it negates itself in its concreteness and expresses ultimate concern. A symbol which does not negate itself becomes idolatrous; it becomes elevated to absolute validity. It is the idolatrous tendency of every religion to elevate its concrete symbols to absolute validity. A symbol is true, however, when it expresses not only the ultimate but also its own lack of ultimacy (DF, pp. 96–97).

Tillich distinguished between primary and secondary religious symbols (TC, p. 64). Secondary symbols are of a supporting nature, such as poetic symbols, or water, light, oil. Primary symbols point directly to the referent of all religious symbolism. On the transcendent level this refers to God. On the immanent level this refers to incarnation, to the sacramental presence of the holy in concrete persons, actions, and things. Of all these symbols, all of which point to ultimate concern, the most basic and universal is that of God. "God is the symbol for God" (DF, p. 46). The intent of this paradoxical statement is to distinguish two elements in the notion of God: one is the element of ultimacy, a matter of immediate experience not symbolic in itself,[15] the other is the element of concreteness which is taken from ordinary experience and is symbolically applied to God. There was for Tillich only one non-symbolic statement possible about God: "God is being-itself" (ST1:239). This was the basis for everything else in Tillich's understanding about God, the basis for all religious symbolism. This is the reality toward which all religious symbols point—being-itself, or, as he put it, the God beyond God.

"God is the answer to the question implied in being" (ST1:163). In part 2 of his *Systematic Theology*, Tillich treats the question of God in correlation to being and to the ontological question being implies: why is there something and not nothing? The question of being leads to the question of non-being, the threat of finiteness. This in turn leads to the question of God.

Placing himself in the tradition of Augustine, Tillich denied the very possibility of an argumentative knowledge of God. An immediate knowledge of God is the only kind possible, and for this he preferred the word *awareness*. Without this awareness, without an experience of God in the center of a man's personal existence, God is simply an empty word. It was Rudolf Otto's book *The Idea of the Holy* that convinced Tillich that it is the experience of the holy which leads to God and not an idea of God which leads to an experience of the holy (KB, p. 6). Otto's *mysterium tremendum et fascinosum* inspired Tillich's description of God as the ground and abyss (*Grund* and *Abgrund*) of all being. The metaphor of *ground* points to the power of being, from which all other beings receive their existence. Its roots are fundamentally neo-platonic.[16] The metaphor of *abyss* points to the unbridgeable distance between the finite and the infinite, between beings and the creative ground in which they exist (ST1:235).

In opposition to Heidegger, Bultmann, Barth, Niebuhr, and anyone else who rejected classical metaphysics, Tillich championed an ontological understanding of God. He equated his description of God as the ground and abyss of being with the *esse ipsum* of scholasticism (HCT, p. 189), admitting at the same time, however, the process character of being. The ground and abyss of being is not a static, lifeless *actus purus* (ST1:241). More important, though, is Tillich's conviction that the God who is *esse ipsum (Sein-Selbst)* cannot be *a* being *(Seiendes)*. The power of being itself is not *a* being alongside other beings. God does not exist in the sense of a being found within the whole of reality, not even in the sense of a Supreme Being above all other beings, since the above is but one direction of the "alongside of." If God could be situated as a being within reality, he would then be subject to the structures of reality. Like Zeus in Greek mythology, he would be determined like other beings by fate.[17]

The God beyond God is the God of theism, the God beyond the God who is *a* being. The God beyond God is the God to whom all symbols point, the God who overcomes the subject-object structure of reality and is closer to a person than that person is to himself. He is the Ultimate, the Unconditioned *(das Unbedingte)*.[18]

At this point, a word might be said regarding Tillich's thinking on atheism. The God who is *a* being is the first step to atheism, in that it reduces God to an object beside other objects, whose existence and nature are matters of argument. Such a God, to Tillich's mind, is justifiably rejected by modern atheism.[19] But what of the God beyond God? Can the atheist successfully escape him? Can he rid himself of all faith? If faith is defined formally, as ultimate concern, the answer is no.

Ultimate concern, as mentioned previously, has more than a subjective side, referring to a centered act of the personality. It also has an objective aspect, referring to that toward which the act is directed. Taken objectively, it is the abstract translation of the gospel saying, "Where your treasure is, there will your heart be also" (Matt. 6:21).[20] Defining faith formally as ultimate concern, Tillich was convinced that all men have faith, some ultimate concern which in the final analysis becomes God for them (ST1:211). Ultimate concern was Tillich's phenomenological description of God. It implies that atheism can consist only in an attitude which rejects any ultimate concern whatever, and remains utterly indifferent to the meaning of existence. Because religion pertains to the dimension of depth in man's life, atheism demands being able to say in all honesty that life has no depth, that being itself is shallow. Tillich regarded the possibility of such an attitude of total indifference as highly problematic. He denied the title of atheist even to Marx and Sartre, regarding them instead as humanists who tried to develop answers to the question of existence from hidden religious sources, answers which are matters of faith even though garbed in secular gown (ST2:25). Tillich was convinced that "genuine atheism is not humanly possible."[21] Even the atheists stand in God—that power out of which they live, that truth for which they grope, the meaning in which they believe.

This is not to say that the problem of atheism is solved by verbal sleight of hand. Although faith cannot be rejected altogether, it can be attacked in the name of another faith. God can be denied only in the name of another god. This means that, even though mankind is never without God, it can and does pervert the picture of God. A faith defined formally as ultimate concern is universal. But the contents of that faith may be unworthy to be called ultimate in so far as they are finite, preliminary, or conditioned. This means that the real problem for religion is not atheism but idolatry (DF, pp. 126–27).

Idolatry is a faith that is misdirected, in that it bestows ultimacy upon a finite object. By its very definition, ultimate concern must pertain to something that is not transitory (BR, p. 59). True ultimacy must be a criterion for the proper object of ultimate concern. As Tillich saw it, the entire history of religion can be described as an attempt to find that which may be justifiably regarded as the object of man's ultimate concern. "The continuing struggle through all history is waged between a faith directed to ultimate reality and a faith directed toward preliminary realities claiming ultimacy" (ST3:131).

Tillich's doctrine of the God beyond God and his distinction betwee atheism and idolatry lay important foundations for understanding his thought on the relationship of the Church to the world religions and the quasi-religions, as he styled them, the secular, humanistic faiths of our day.

Different as they are in content, the ultimate concern of the Christian is not totally unrelated to that of the Hindu, the Buddhist, or the Marxist revolutionary. They are all responses, religious or quasi-religious, to the experience of being grasped by an ultimate concern.

Communities of Ultimate Concern

Religion in the broad sense of ultimate concern ordinarily expresses itself through religions, through visible communities discernable by their scriptures, their dogmas, organization, institutions, leaders, and regulations. It has been a vogue in recent years to attack such organized religion in the name of personal religiousness. Tillich regarded such attacks as "nonsense." To be sure, one can and even should attack the forms within religion and the way it may be organized. But to attack organized religion in itself indicated to Tillich a lack of serious thought. Just as in any other realm, so too in religion, absolute autonomy is impossible. The would-be social drop-out neglects to realize that society is the very basis of his existence. Kierkegaard, in his attack against the Church, forgot that without the tradition of the Church, there would be neither the Bible nor the Church of today, and any individual relationship with God would be impossible (PPT, pp. 181–82).

The necessity of communities of ultimate concern can be approached from all three vantage points of ultimate concern: revelation, religion, and faith.

Revelation, as noted, is originally manifested to an individual, but it is always destined for a group. The prophet exists not only for himself but for the community also:

> God calls families, nations, groups within the nation, the group which transcends all nations, the "assembly of God," the church. And God's purpose in history is to save individuals, not as individuals, but as participants in his kingdom, in the unity of all beings under God. Therefore, the message of the prophets and apostles is given to groups. They are called individually, but their message is destined for the nation to which they belong or for the church of which they are members. [BR, p. 47]

Such groups or communities of ultimate concern are not only receivers of revelation. They are likewise bearers, media of revelation for others. They represent and interpret a revelatory event, pointing to that which transcends them and thereby permitting new generations to enter into a dependent revelation, to be grasped by ultimate concern. Such communities of ultimate concern are the locus of continuous dependent revelation (ST1:125–27).

As the response to revelation, religion too, like all things spiritual, requires a community to be its bearer. Both community and tradition follow from the grace character of the holy. So much so is this the case that mystics and monastics, even hermits, live from the substance, from the traditions and symbols, of the broader religious community from which they have withdrawn themselves (GW1:362). A community of ultimate concern is "an assembly where we speak about God . . . the place where the mystery of the holy should be experienced with awe and sacred embarrassment" (EN, p. 83). It is for the sake of religion in the broad sense that religions in the narrow sense exist.

> Without the concreteness of the religious experience in terms of specific symbols and devotional activities, and community participation in them, there results in the long run a disappearance of the substance of religion. It becomes thinner and thinner. It is reduced to occasional feelings that one might or might not experience. Its power is gone. [UC, p. 176]

It would be an ideal for God so to live in us that we would have no need of temples or services. It is precisely an indication of our human condition of estrangement that we do need temples and services, sacred times and sacred places. We are not able to experience the divine as fully present in every moment. We all tend toward the secular, toward flight from God. Religions, and this includes the Church, provide a restraining, a counter-balancing influence. In Tillich's view, "they are not necessary in the ultimate sense, the essential sense of the word; but they are necessary in the existential sense because of man's existential estrangement" (UC, p. 177).

Like revelation and religion, faith too is dependent upon community. It is real only within a community of faith. Tillich provided two reasons for this—language and love. Like every act in man's spiritual life, faith is dependent upon language. Without language there can be no act of faith, no religious experience. Only within a community is language alive. As noted above, the language of faith consists primarily of symbols. A community expresses its ultimate concern through two kinds of symbols: rituals and doctrines. It constitutes itself through ritual symbols and interprets itself through doctrinal symbols. Without these two modes of self-expression, there is no faith. And without communities there are no symbols, since communities are needed not only to maintain symbols but

33

also to interpret them. Outside a religious community, its symbols cannot be fully understood. Within it, religious language provides the act of faith with a concrete content (DF, pp. 24, 117–18, 121).

Love is the second reason why faith implies community. If faith is understood as being ultimately concerned, then it cannot be separated from love. Love is the urge to unite the separated, to unite that which essentially belongs together. One can be concerned ultimately only about that to which one belongs essentially and from which one is existentially separated. Thus, faith implies love, a love which tends toward community. From love and its drive toward community with God on the vertical level there is derived on the horizontal level the love and drive to community with one's neighbor. It is this love which serves as the mediating link between faith and works. Faith implies love; love lives in works; and works too tend toward community:

> Faith is real only in the community of faith, or more precisely, in the communion of a language of faith. The consideration of love and faith has pointed in the same direction: Love is an implication of faith, namely, the desire toward reunion of the separated. This makes faith a matter of community. Finally, since faith leads to action and action presupposes community, the state of ultimate concern is actual only within a community of action. [DF, p. 117]

Religion in the broad sense of ultimate concern expresses itself in communities of ultimate concern. But ultimate concern, that which is experienced as holy, is comprised of two elements. Remember that Tillich was led to his description of God as the ground and abyss of being by Rudolf Otto's phenomenology of the holy as the *mysterium tremendum et fascinosum*. Related to the element of *mysterium fascinosum* is the experience of the holy as present, as here and now.

> It consecrates the place and the reality of its appearance. It grasps the mind with terrifying and fascinating power. . . . The holy must be present and felt as present in order to be experienced at all. [DF, p. 56]

At the same time the holy is experienced as *mysterium tremendum*. To this is related a judgment upon everything that is.

> It demands personal and social holiness in the sense of justice and love. Our ultimate concern represents what we actually are and—therefore—ought to be. . . . Holiness cannot be experienced without its power to command what we should be. [DF, p. 56]

A *Community of Ultimate Concern*

The first of these elements, the *mysterium fascinosum*, may be called the holiness of being *(Sein)*. It leads to an ontological type of faith. The second, the *mysterium tremendum*, may be called the holiness of what ought to be *(Sollen)*. It leads to a moral type of faith.

These two elements in the experience of the holy affect the inmost cells not only of personal faith but of communitarian expression of faith as well. They are present in every act of faith, in every religion. But, because man is finite, he can never unite all the elements of truth in complete balance. He can never maintain both aspects of the holy in perfect balance. One will always outweigh the other. This leads to two types of religion, two types of communities of ultimate concern, the ontological and the moral. The ontological type corresponds to the holy as being, as present. It emphasizes the holy as here and now, grasping us through the medium of a person, event, or thing. It has a distinct sacramental orientation, one which is present in all religions, "the daily bread of faith without which it becomes empty, abstract, and without significance for the life of individuals and groups" (DF, p. 58). The moral type of religion corresponds to the holy as demand. To it belong those communities of ultimate concern which emphasize law, for whom God can be approached only by those who obey the law. Sacramental religions also require subjection to law, but these are ritual or ascetic practices. Moral types of religion emphasize moral obedience to a law which is viewed at once as both a gift and a command of God (DF, p. 65).

The distinction between these two types of religion is not absolute. Ontological and moral elements are essentially united in every religion. There is no community of ultimate concern which is purely sacramental without having moral concerns. There is no community which has a purely moral orientation without having sacramental concerns. While there are always elements of the one type within the other, the two types do diverge. They are driven into conflicts and even mutual destruction (DF, p. 69). These divergences will be discussed in greater detail below in terms of Catholic substance and the Protestant principle.

Tillich was convinced of the necessity of religions as communities of ultimate concern. Religions are not essentially necessary but existentially so, because of man's existential estrangement. For the same reason, religions are all necessarily ambiguous.

Every religion is based on revelation ,the state of being grasped by ultimate concern. As such, religion is *un*ambiguous. But every religion also receives revelation, and, in receiving it, religion *is* ambiguous. In receiving and expressing revelation, religion cannot help but distort it. "No religion is revealed; religion is the creation and the distortion of revelation" (ST3:111). Religion distorts the revelation it has received by turning itself into a means for self-salvation. The heart of genuine religion is a personal encounter with God and reunion with Him, turning from all preliminary concerns toward the unconditioned, the ultimate. False religion attempts to accomplish self-salvation, to reach the infinite by way of finite means, whether by fulfilling laws, accepting beliefs, performing ritual or ascetical acts, or stirring up emotional, mystical experiences (ST2:93–100). It is the glory of religion that it gives us an experience of the holy, an experience of ultimate meaning. But it is the shame of religion that it tends to despise the secular; that it tends to regard its doctrines, rituals, and laws, which point to the ultimate, as ultimate in themselves; that it tends to make itself ultimate and persecute those who do not subject themselves to it (CT, p. 9).

> Religion is the highest expression of the greatness and dignity of life; in it the greatness of life becomes holiness. Yet religion is also the most radical refutation of the greatness and dignity of life; in it the great becomes most profaned, the holy most desecrated. [ST3:104]

The two ambiguities with which religion must contend are profanation and demonization. It moves between them like Scylla and Charybdis, dangers ever present, whether openly or covertly, in every act of religious life. Tillich saw them as central to any understanding of religion, a realization necessary for the effectiveness of both theology and the Church.

Profanation reduces religion to a finite thing among other finite things. Religion is meant to manifest the holy. All of its elements, its scriptures, offices, persons, acts, are meant to point beyond themselves to the unconditioned, the absolute, the God beyond God. All are meant to be "translucent" to the holy. When this does not happen, religion becomes profaned. This can happen either institutionally or reductively. Religion is institutionally profaned when it becomes just another object, when, instead of transcending the finite in the direction of the infinite, it becomes simply "a set of prescribed activities to be performed, a set of stated doctrines to be accepted, a social pressure group along with others, a political power with all the implications of power politics" (ST3:99). Religion is reductively profaned when it is reduced to culture and morality, when its symbols are regarded as little more than primitive science and poetry, when all claim to express transcendence is denied. Demeaned in this way, religion is regarded as merely a useful tool for morality, a legitimate expression of culture. It becomes radically secularized. It was Tillich's opinion that the Catholic Church runs the perennial risk of institutional profanation, while Protestantism stands ever in danger of reductive secularization.

Whereas profanation resists self-transcendence, *demonization* distorts it. It does so by elevating that which points to the absolute to absoluteness itself, identifying a particular bearer of holiness with holiness itself. It confuses the medium with its content (ST3:243–45). In mythology demons and destructive powers are not simply negations of the divine; they participate in the power and holiness of the divine, albeit in a distorted way. To Tillich's mind it is not the profane so much as the demonic which most directly contradicts the absolute claims of the holy itself, the God beyond God.[22]

Ultimate concern, as noted above, necessarily expresses itself in religious symbols. The revelation of the unconditioned is possible only in connection with that which is conditioned. The absolute, the holy, expresses itself in contingent forms. But no form as such is holy or absolute. Such a form points to something beyond itself, to something that remains foreign to it even while belonging to it. It becomes the surface and expression of the unconditioned. But, in doing so, it does not cease being conditioned itself.[23] Form, sacrament or symbol, any finite object which is holy because it points to the infinitely holy, is in danger of becoming identified with the ultimate itself, as if it were holy in itself instead of simply being a bearer of the holy. This is the danger, the ambiguity of demonization, the claim of infinity for that which is finite, of absoluteness for that which is relative. Some examples of demonization are provided by the Roman Empire when it vested itself with divine prerogatives; by national states which make demands of unconditional commitment; by fascism, which Tillich saw as a demonic form of nationalism; by communism, a demonic form of socialism; by scientism, a demonic form of humanism (UC, pp. 23,29). In short, demonization occurs whenever conditioned and changing forms, which point to the unconditioned and absolute and which participate in its power, claim to be absolute and unconditioned in themselves.

Although it occurs outside religions, demonization is a particular danger of all religions, Christianity no less than any other. The Catholicism of the Inquisition and the absolutizing of dogmas by Protestant orthodoxy are two examples of the demonization of Christianity, the raising by the Church of claims to absoluteness for itself. Religious symbols, whether dogmas or rituals, are preliminary, conditional. They are not and cannot be ultimate in themselves. They cannot be the object of ultimate concern. To make them so, to make them the object of unquestioning surrender, is to transform them into idols (ST1:216). Religion can become demonic in four ways: 1) politically, by trying to destroy other communal structures; 2) personally, by creating conflicts within individuals who do not accept the absolute claims of religion; 3) cognitively, by claiming absolute truth for its dogmas and suppressing other expressions of truth; and 4) aesthetically, by suppressing authentic expressions of art and literature in the name of a religiously consecrated style (ST3:105–6).

With reference to atheism and idolatry, Tillich saw the history of religion as a continuous struggle between authentic faith, directed to ultimate reality, and idolatrous faith, which is directed toward preliminary realities claiming ultimacy. That same struggle can be described as one between the *civitas Dei* and the *civitas terrena*, the divine and the demonic. It is a continuous struggle in the inner life of the great religions, against the ambiguities of religion for the sake of the holy itself, the God beyond God. For Tillich "the first word . . . to be spoken by religion to the people of our time must be a word against religion" (PE, p. 185).

2

The Community of the New Being

The Church's one foundation
Is Jesus Christ her Lord;
She is his new creation
By water and the Word.
        Samuel Wesley, *"The Church's One Foundation"*

Whenever Christians of differing traditions come to-
gether for dialogue or prayer for unity, Samuel Wesley's hymn of faith in
Jesus as the Church's one foundation invariably finds a place. It fits com-
fortably into an ecumenical milieu. Catholic or Orthodox, Lutheran or
Calvinist, Anglican, Methodist, whatever the tradition, if it bears the name
Christian, its adherents concur that the sole foundation of the Church is
Jesus Christ. But what does that mean? In what way is Jesus the foundation
of the Church? Did he found a new religion, setting forth dogmas to be
accepted, rituals and laws to be fulfilled? To Tillich's mind there could be
no greater distortion of Jesus. "We are all permanently in danger of abusing
Jesus by stating that he is the founder of a new religion" (SF, p. 104). Not
the founder of a new religion but the one who has brought New Being into
an estranged world—this is Jesus. And the Church is the bearer and
transmitter of that New Being through history.

Tillich came the closest to defining the Church when he wrote:

Christianity achieves actuality in a community based upon the appearance of
ultimate reality in a historic person, Jesus Christ. For Christian faith, this
event is in a profound sense the center of history. The community which

39

carries the spirit of Jesus Christ through the centuries is the "assembly of God," the Church. [WS, p. 20]

Two elements can be discerned in this passage. First, there is the historical element: the connection between the Church and the "historic person, Jesus Christ." The liberal consensus at the turn of the century saw no connection whatever between the two: Jesus was considered a mistaken apocalyptic; the Church, a substitute for the kingdom that did not come. Theology today takes a much more dialectical position, recognizing the clearly eschatological themes of Jesus' preaching and viewing the Church as an "eschatological community." But the question remains: what connection does the Church have with the Jesus of history: Tillich contributed to the discussion with his interpretation of the Church as a messianic community and with the proposal that Jesus did not truly become the Messiah until the Church accepted him as such. The second element in the above passage is theological: the nature of the Church and its mission of carrying the spirit of Jesus through the centuries, or, as Tillich eventually came to describe it, the Church as a bearer of New Being.

Existence, Estrangement, and the Quest for the New Being

Tillich's fullest consideration of Jesus as the Messiah and the Church as the Messianic Community is in his *Systematic Theology*, part 3, entitled "Existence and the Christ." Just as the question of being, "Why is there something and not nothing?" drives us to the question of God, so the question of existence drives us to the question of Christ.

Existence is the state of standing out of non-being. It is the logical opposite of essence, which is the true, undistorted nature of things, the original goodness of everything created. But essence is experienced only in a distorted form, only in existence, which is the unity of being with non-being. The result of this unity of being with non-being in existence is estrangement (ST2:19–21).

Estrangement is the result of the transition from essence to existence, a transition expressed universally by the symbol of "The Fall." Estrangement was created as a philosophical term by Hegel, who contended that it was overcome in history by reconciliation. Existentialism adopted the term but not Hegel's notion of reconciliation, and views estrangement as the basic characteristic of man's predicament. Man is cut off from the ground of his being, from other beings, from himself. As he exists in time and space, man is not what he essentially is and ought to be. **Finitude,** alienation, anxiety, loneliness, despair—all describe man's estranged existential state, a state of *Sickness unto Death* (Kierkegaard), *Nausea* and *No Exit* (Sartre), a state in which man turns himself away from the ground of his being and sets himself up as the center of the world and of life, attempting to draw the whole of the universe into himself (ST2:44–55).

Immersed in this intolerable situation, man seeks to overcome estrangement by bridging the gap between essential and existential being. He seeks healing. This is the quest for the New Being. It is a quest made in the sphere of religion. By obeying laws and performing ascetical practices or ritual activities, man strives for self-salvation, self-healing (ST2:80–86). The forms taken vary from religion to religion, from culture to culture, but the quest itself is universal, because the human predicament of estrangement is universal. Two main types can be distinguished among these attempts to find New Being. One type, exemplified by Brahmanism and Buddhism, is predominantly non-historical and views history as a circle, a self-repeating movement which must be transcended. In this conception the New Being must be found above history. The second type, exemplified by Judaism, Christianity, and Islam, is predominantly historical and views history as a line, a unique, unrepeatable, irreversible historical process, the end and aim of which is a transformation. This conception sees New Being as found in and through history (ST2:86–88). It is the conviction of Christianity that the New Being has been actualized in a decisive event in history, in an event which has given history a center. That event is the appearance of Jesus of Nazareth as the Christ, the bearer of the New Being in its final manifestation.

Jesus the Messiah and the Messianic Community

The symbol of the Messiah, the "Christ," transcends both Judaism and Christianity. It expressed the hope that out of the royal house there would be born one who would conquer all enemies and become the king of peace and justice. He would usher in a "new eon," a new period in history in which the old world would experience a new birth, in which the "old eon" of estrangement would be overcome (ST2:27, 88).

The symbol of the Christ has been used both by Judaism and Christianity. Tillich saw it as an apt symbol for the universal quest of mankind for the New Being, since it unites the horizontal direction of the quest (the historical) with the vertical direction (the trans-historical). It is the claim of

41

Christianity that the different forms of the universal quest for the New Being are all fulfilled in Jesus as the Christ (ST2:89).

The assertion, that New Being has appeared in Jesus as the Christ, is paradoxical. This does not mean that it is irrational or nonsensical, but rather that the claim does not follow from reflective thinking. A paradox is that which contradicts the *doxa*, the common opinion based on ordinary human rational experience. The assertion that New Being has appeared in Jesus as the Christ "contradicts the opinion derived from man's existential predicament and all expectations imaginable on the basis of this predicament" (ST2:92). This for Tillich was the fundamental paradox of Christianity and the basis for all other paradoxical statements within it.

"Christianity was born, not with the birth of the man who is called 'Jesus' but in the moment in which one of his followers was driven to say to him, 'Thou art the Christ.' And Christianity will live as long as there are people who repeat this assertion (ST2:97). To Tillich's mind, the confession of Jesus as the Christ sums up the entire Christian gospel. It recognizes Jesus as the one who brings the new state of things, the New Being. To affirm Jesus as the Christ is to be a Christian. To deny it is to be outside of the Christian Community (SF, p. 123).

Corresponding to his view of religion as a receiving of revelation, Tillich saw the Church as based upon an *event*, an event comprised of two sides. One aspect of the event is the fact called "Jesus of Nazareth." The other is the reception of this fact by those who received him as the Christ. Both sides are indispensable:

> Jesus as the Christ is both an historical fact and a subject of believing reception. One cannot speak the truth about the event on which Christianity is based without asserting both sides. Many theological mistakes could have been avoided if these two sides of the Christian event had been emphasized with equal strength.[1]

To ignore the fact to which the name of Jesus of Nazareth points is to run the risk of docetic-gnosticism and deny that there was a personal life in which existential estrangement was overcome. If there were no such personal life, the New Being would remain a quest and would not be a reality.

Equally to be emphasized, on the other hand, is the believing reception of Jesus as the Christ. Here perhaps Tillich startles us. "Without this reception the Christ would not have been the Christ, namely, the manifestation of New Being in time and space" (ST2:99). In other words, there can be no Christ, Christ cannot heal, unless there is also a Church. Jesus is the

Christ only if he is accepted as the Christ. Jesus can heal only if his healing is accepted.

> If Jesus had not impressed himself as the Christ on his disciples and through them upon all following generations, the man who is called Jesus of Nazareth would perhaps be remembered as an historically and religiously important person. As such, he would belong to the preliminary revelation, perhaps to the preparatory segment of the history of revelation. He could then have been a prophetic anticipation of the New Being, but not the final manifestation of the New Being itself. [ST2:99]

At this point the distinction can be made between the broad formal definition of faith, discussed in chapter 1, and the material definition of Christian faith, which differentiates the Christian Church from other communities of ultimate concern. Formally, faith is the state of being grasped by an ultimate concern. For a Christian, however, faith is the state of being grasped by New Being as it is manifest in Jesus as the Christ (ST3:131).

The Church was born the first moment someone was grasped by New Being as manifested in Jesus, the moment that Jesus was first accepted as the Christ. Early tradition names Simon Peter as the first to express this recognition. But when did it take place? When did the Church first come to be? Was it before Jesus' death or after? And what of those of us who accept Jesus as the Christ today? Do we go back to the Jesus of 30 A.D., to the historical Jesus? On what basis do we accept him as the Christ?

The Christian Church is based on the historical witness that Jesus is the Christ. Although they may differ considerably in other respects, in this affirmation all the books of the New Testament are united. In witnessing to the factual side of the Christ-event, the New Testament also represents the receptive side, the acceptance in faith of Jesus as the Christ. Hence, any attempt to sift fact from faith in the New Testament by historical research is bound to failure. Ever since confronting Albert Schweitzer's *The Quest for the Historical Jesus* as a student, Tillich remained convinced of the inadequacy of the kind of biblicism which does not take historical questions seriously. He also became convinced, though, that we cannot get behind the picture of Jesus given in the New Testament. He rejected Schweitzer's attempt to recreate the factual Jesus behind the image of faith, maintaining that, if Schweitzer's apocalyptic interpretation of Jesus is not correct, then we must admit that we are in a position of not knowing very much about the historical Jesus (PPT, pp. 225, 227).

Tillich's position in regard to the historical Jesus was based upon that of his teacher, Martin Kähler:[2]

1) Jesus of Nazareth happened. The Christ-event had a factual element which could have been photographed. Indeed, "if the factual element in the Christian event were denied, the foundation of Christianity would be denied" (ST2:107).

2) But, although Jesus of Nazareth was a historical event, no one had a purely historiographical interest in him. No uninterpreted facts about him were recorded and handed down to us. The only record we have of him comes from those who accepted him as the Christ and portrayed him as such. Nothing can be known with certainty about him aside from the faith portrait we have of him in the New Testament (ST2:105).

3) Getting at the fact of Jesus of Nazareth, behind the acceptance of him as the Christ portrayed in the New Testament, requires sifting the factual element of the Christ-event from the receiving-element. The results of such sifting cannot give us any more than a probable picture of Jesus of Nazareth, a picture which, like all historical knowledge, is fragmentary and hypothetical. Whether a New Testament critic is conservative or radical makes no difference. "Our knowledge of the historical Jesus never gets beyond probabilities of one kind or another" (PPT, p. 227).

4) Faith, however, cannot rest upon probabilities. Our acceptance of Jesus as the Christ today is independent of the historical results of New Testament criticism. Faith guarantees what research never can. And what is that? Certainly not historical facts:

> Faith cannot even guarantee the name "Jesus" in respect to him who was the Christ. It must leave that to the incertitudes of our historical knowledge. But faith does guarantee the factual transformation of reality in that personal life which the New Testament expresses in its picture of Jesus as the Christ. [ST2:123]

As early as 1911, Tillich phrased the question most radically before a group of theological friends: Though it is unlikely that it will ever happen, what if historical research could demonstrate as historically probable the non-existence of Jesus of Nazareth? His answer:

> The foundation of Christian belief is the biblical picture of Christ, not the historical Jesus. The criterion of human thought and action is the picture of Christ as it is rooted in ecclesiastical belief and human experience, not the shifting and artificial construct of historical research. [OB, p. 50]

Faith rests not upon a scientific reconstruction of the facts behind the New Testament witness but upon the Church and upon the personal experience within the Church of the power of the New Being as a healing and creative reality. Faith does not guarantee historical facts but it does guarantee that something has happened in history which in turn is the basis for something which has happened to the individual, namely, the transformation of his estranged existence.[3] "No historical criticism can question the immediate awareness of those who find themselves transformed into the state of faith" (ST2:114). It is this immediate awareness, this present inner experience with its ability to transform and heal the believer, which guarantees the reality of the Christ-event of two thousand years ago (PPT, p. 211).

The following conclusions can, therefore, be drawn with reference to the Church and the historical Jesus:

1) The faith of the Church today is based upon the faith of the apostolic Church. We cannot get behind it. We accept Jesus as the Christ because the apostolic Church did, and do so for the same reasons they did (ST2:115).

2) Furthermore, contemporary Christianity cannot leap over two thousand years and subject itself to the Christ-event. Such a leap would be an illusion; we are dependent upon two millennia of Church history. The very fact that a man is a Christian and accepts Jesus as the Christ "is based on the continuity through history of the power of the New Being. No anti-Catholic bias should prevent Protestant theologians from acknowledging this fact" (ST2:136).

3) When was the Church born? We do not and cannot know with complete historical certitude when Jesus was first accepted as the Christ, whether it was during his life or only after his death. Even if it were before his death, the Resurrection was nevertheless necessary to convince the disciples that the bringer of the "new eon" did not succumb to the powers of the "old eon." It was the experience of Easter which proved decisive for the foundation of the Church. "In the days in which the certainty of his Resurrection grasped the small, dispersed, and despairing group of his followers, the church was born" (ST2:154).

4) And, finally, what of us today? To Tillich's mind, it is only the certainty of one's own victory over the death of existential estrangement which creates the certainty of the Resurrection of Jesus as the Christ. This faith "is based on the experience of being grasped by the power of the New Being through which the destructive consequences of estrangement are conquered" (ST2:155).

In surveying Tillich's thought on the historical connection between Jesus and the Church, some consideration has already been given to the concept of the New Being as the object of the quest to overcome existential estrangement. At this point, however, the theological implications of the concept of the New Being, particularly as embodied and transmitted through the Church, need to be explored more fully.

The New Being, Brought by the Christ, Transmitted by the Church

The concept of New Being was normative for Tillich, the organizing principle around which he built his entire theology. He saw it as the summing up of the Christian message for our time. "Christianity is the message of the New Creation, the New Being, the New Reality, which has appeared with the appearance of Jesus who for this reason, and just for this reason, is called the Christ" (NB, p. 15). He appealed to St. Paul as the basis for his theology of New Being. "For neither circumcision counts for anything nor uncircumcision" (Gal. 6:15), "If anyone is in union with Christ, he is a new Being; the old state of things has passed away; there is a new state of things" (2 Cor. 5:17) (HCT, p. 21). This "new state of things," this New Being overcomes the old eon by overcoming the estrangement which exists between man and God, man and the world, man and himself. It is the power which heals estrangement, or, in more traditional language, the power of salvation. Jesus as the Christ embodies the New Being. In him the New Being has become history, a visible and tangible individuality (ST2:97).

An obvious objection, of course, to the very idea of New Being is that the new eon does not look particularly different from the old one. So how can Jesus be the embodiment of New Being? This is Judaism's question to the Church. Using eschatological symbolism, the Church answers the objection by distinguishing between the first and second coming of the Christ. The new state of things will be created with the second coming; in the meantime, in the period between the "already" and the "not yet," estrangement is conquered "in principle, i.e., in power and as a beginning." New Being is present in Jesus as the Christ. He is the fulfillment of eschatological expectation in principle. "Those who participate in him participate in the New Being, though under the condition of man's existential predicament, and, therefore, only fragmentarily and by anticipation" (ST2:118). "Principle" and "fragmentarily" are the key words here. Only in Jesus as the Christ has estrangement been totally healed; hence he is the criterion of all healing. All other men, even those who receive him as the Christ, are not totally healed, only fragmentarily (ST2:167).

In Jesus as the Christ, the split between essence and existence is overcome. He is the embodiment of the New Being. This is Tillich's translation of the Incarnation. Or, as he otherwise expressed it, "the Incarnation is the manifestation of original and essential Godmanhood within and under the conditions of existence."[4] Tillich's doctrine of religious symbolism likewise elucidates his understanding of the Incarnation. Note, in the following, his use of words like *picture, manifest,* and *represent.*

> The New Being, manifest in the picture of Jesus as the Christ, represents the essential unity between finiteness and infinity, or the undisrupted unity between man and God. It represents the essential unity between individuality and universality, or the undestroyed community of love and knowledge. It represents the essential unity between contingency and creativity, or the unhampered transition from anxiety to courage and from mortality to eternity. All this is embodied and represented in the picture of Jesus as the Christ.[5]

But Jesus as the Christ is not only the embodiment of the New Being, he is also the bearer of New Being to the Community of the New Being. He imparts New Being to the Church.

> The New Being, which is the quality of his own being, is not restricted to his being. This refers to the community out of which he comes and to the preparatory manifestations of the New Being within it; it refers to the community which he creates and to the manifestations of the New Being in it. [ST2:135]

By accepting Jesus as the Christ, the Church becomes a new creature "in" Christ. It participates in the New Being, so that the characteristics of estrangement are overcome, even though it does so only under the condition of man's existential predicament and therefore only fragmentarily. As such, "the Church is the Community of the New Being, ... the place where the New Being is real" (TC, pp. 212–13). The Church is the communal and historical embodiment of the New Being, the bearer of the New Being in history. This is not a claim which can be empirically verified by detached observation or experiment. The claim is based upon the Church's power to overcome existential estrangement, at least fragmentarily. Overcoming such estrangement is prior to any religious decision or activity. It is grace.

> The term New Being is . . . of particular importance for the interpretation of the Church as the realm in which existence is overcome before any religious activity begins. It is not religious activity which creates the Church, since such activity strengthens the power of existence and consequently prevents

the coming of the Church, if it is done with the purpose of creating the Church. The Church is the historical embodiment of the New Being created by the Incarnation. The very term New Being therefore excludes any doctrine of the Church which conceives it to be brought into existence by religious decisions. The New Being is the prius of the Church just as it is the prius of Christian experience.[6]

In receiving Jesus as the Christ, the Church not only becomes the communal embodiment of the New Being, it also receives the mandate to impart the New Being to others. Every Christian receives the charge to heal estrangement, to be a mediator of the New Being. This is the priestly function of the Church, a function in which every Christian shares, a responsibility which every Christian bears for everyone else (EN, pp. 47–48, 69).

As the Community of the New Being, the Church is more than a religion, more than hierarchical authority or a social organization. "It is all this, of course, but it is primarily a group of people who express a new reality by which they have been grasped. It is the place where the power of the New Reality which is Christ, . . . moves into us and is continued by us" (TC, p. 212). Christianity as a religion is not important. No religion as such produces the New Being. Tillich was emphatic on this. Circumcision, sacrifices, baptism—all these rites do not matter. Jesus does not impose a new theology or a new religious law on us. He does not call us to Christian doctrine or Christian morals. The Church does not call men to Christianity. It calls them rather to the New Being to which the Church serves as a witness. Remember here Tillich's doctrine of religious symbol, pointing, participating, mediating, but never to be identified with that to which it points. The Church points to and transmits the New Being. But the Church must not be confused with the New Being itself. "It would not be worthwhile to teach Christianity, if it were for the sake of Christianity" (SF, p. 108).

What should be our ultimate concern? The New Being, the New Creation. "This matters; this alone matters ultimately. In comparison with it everything else, even religion or non-religion, even Christianity or non-Christianity, matters very little—and ultimately nothing" (NB, p. 19). The significance of the Church lies not in what it is but rather in what it points to and what it mediates:

> If the Church which is the assembly of God has an ultimate significance, this is its significance: That here the reunion of man to man is pronounced and confessed and realized, even if in fragments and weaknesses and distortions.

> The Church is the place where the reunion of man with man is an actual event. [NB, p. 23]

The Church of itself is of no avail. Indeed, "It is the greatness of Christianity that it can see how small it is" (NB, p. 19). "The message of Christianity is not Christianity, but a New Reality" (NB, p. 24).

The Church is not important in itself. The New Being to which it points and which it transmits—this is all-important, a matter of "infinite passion." Here we have, in essence, Tillich's answer to the questions: What is the Church's relationship to other communities of ultimate concern? Is the Christian Church unique as the exclusive bearer of the New Being in history? Is it superior to other religions? The premises have already been laid. Now it is necessary only to bring them together to see that, for Tillich, it is not the Christian Church which is unique or superior but only that on which it is founded, only that to which it points.

The Church's Claim to Uniqueness

If a group is convinced that it possesses a truth, it implicitly denies those claims which conflict with that truth. Even a skeptic, in affirming his skepticism, contradicts anybody who denies the validity of skepticism. What is permitted to the skeptic cannot be denied to the Church. It is natural, therefore, and unavoidable that when Christians affirm Jesus as the Christ, they thereby deny whatever would contradict this assertion. As a consequence, the Church rejects other religions insofar as they contradict explicitly or implicitly the principle that Jesus is the Christ. But a rejection need not be total. It can be partial and even dialectical, uniting exclusion with acceptance. Tillich's conviction was that precisely such a dialectical viewpoint has characterized Christianity's attitude toward other religions. Although there has been a tension between universalism and particularism in Christianity, the predominant attitude has been on the whole decidedly universalist.[7] Tillich was willing to demonstrate the basis for his conviction by going into historical detail.

The universalism of Christianity has its roots in the Old Testament. The covenant between Yahweh and Israel did not give Israel a claim to protection if it violated justice, since justice is a principle which transcends every particular religion and makes the exclusiveness of any particular religion conditional. In the New Testament Jesus confirmed this principle of conditional exclusiveness in his characterization of the Last Judgment

(Matt. 25:31–46), the parable of the Good Samaritan, and in his defense of those outside his circle who performed miracles similar to his. St. Paul asserted that both Jews and pagans are equally under the bondage of sin and equally in need of salvation, "a salvation which comes not from a new religion, the Christian, but from an event in history which judges all religions, including Christianity" (CEWR, pp. 32–33). The Fourth Gospel identified Jesus with the most universal principle of divine self-manifestation. It thus freed the interpretation of Jesus from a particularism through which he would become the property of a particular religious group (CEWR, pp. 31–33).

The early Church Fathers took up the Logos theme of the Fourth Gospel and judged other religions in the light of it. They emphasized the universal presence of the Logos in all religions and cultures, acknowledging their preparatory character for the central appearance of the Logos in the person of the Christ. The Church's dialectical attitude toward other religions was demonstrated by its willingness to borrow from them—theological concepts from Hellenism, moral principles from stoicism. But its universalism was always balanced by one criterion to which all else was subjected, the principle that Jesus is the Christ. This is why St. Augustine could say that the true religion had always existed and was called Christian only after the appearance of the Christ (CEWR, pp. 34–36).

The Church's universalism continued undisturbed until Christianity encountered Islam in the seventh century. This encounter led to defensiveness and to an inevitable narrowing down which finally reached a point of radical exclusiveness. The Crusades were the expression of this new self-conscious exclusiveness. The Church came to regard even Judaism as just another religion, and the relative tolerance which existed prior to this time was replaced by a fanatical anti-Judaism (CEWR, pp. 38–39).

A particularist attitude, which affirmed the exclusiveness of salvation through faith in Christ, held sway from that time until the Renaissance and Enlightenment. In the fifteenth century Cardinal Nicholas of Cusa in his *De Pace Fidei* proposed that the struggle between religions was not necessary since the Logos is present in every religion (PPT, p. 79). Reacting to the destructiveness of the Religious Wars, the Enlightenment assumed a position of toleration, according Christianity superiority but not exclusiveness. Lessing gave classical expression to religious relativism in his drama, *Nathan the Wise*. Kant accorded Christianity an exalted position by interpreting its symbols in terms of his *Critique of Practical Reason*. Fichte accorded Christianity a superiority as a representative of mysticism. Hegel and Schelling regarded Christianity as the fulfillment of all that is positive in other religions and cultures (CEWR, pp. 41–43).

Closer to our day, Troeltsch maintained that any absolutist claims would have to be given up by Christianity; it has been relativized in being limited to the Western World and its culture (PPT, p. 233). The contrary position was upheld by Karl Barth, who rejected the very application of the concept *religion* to Christianity and regarded the Church as being based upon the only revelation that has ever occurred. For him all human religions are but futile attempts by man to reach God by himself.[8]

Viewed in its totality, the present attitude of Christianity to the world religions is indefinite, unsettled, even contradictory. There are elements both of particularism and universalism, struggling against each other. The universalist strain, however, is not to be denied. The Church is not based on a simple negation of other religions. Its attitude is profoundly dialectical, an attitude which constitutes not a weakness but a distinct strength (CEWR, pp. 4, 6, 51, 78).

Tillich claimed St. Paul as an exemplar in that he did not exempt the Church from criticism. He did not put Christianity over against other religions.

> Rather, he puts Christ against every religion. . . . Actually, the absoluteness of Christianity . . . is not the absoluteness of the Christian religion, but of the Christ over all religion. The superiority of Christianity lies in its witnessing against itself and all religions in the name of the Christ. [PPT, p. 107]

Tillich's theology of the Church is decidedly universalist. Biblical revelation offers not an exclusive but a normative knowledge of God. As religion is to revelation, so is the Church to the Christ-event. No claim to final truth can be raised for the Church but only for the event on which Christianity is based, an event which is both received by the Church and necessarily distorted by it.[9]

Tillich linked this universalism with the very word for the Church in the New Testament. *Ecclesia* (from *ek – kalein*, "to call out") originally referred to the calling out of all free citizens in the Greek city-states to the assembly of free citizens. The New Testament used the term to refer to those called out of all nations, those who had been "freed" from the powers of evil and thus constituted the "assembly of God." In early Christianity those who did not come to the *ecclesia* were by no means regarded as being without God. They were simply not yet liberated from demonic influence.

"The idea of the godlessness of people, in the sense of being left alone by God, did not exist at that time" (UC, p. 111).

The primary basis for Tillich's universalism is the doctrine of the Logos.[10] The Logos is the principle of God going out and manifesting himself, the principle of divine self-manifestation. As the universal structure of being, it participates in creation. For this reason the early Church regarded the Logos as *spermaticos,* as present everywhere in the world from the very beginning, like a seed. It is at work in all structures of human existence and is grasped, at least partially, by all men in all religions and cultures. The paradox of Christianity is that the Logos became flesh. The principle of universal revelation appeared as an empirical, historical person, in Jesus as the Christ. That appearance did not contradict prior revelation or put an end to all others. Revelation was operative through the Logos before Jesus and it continues now after him. But that appearance became the criterion of all revelation, both prior and subsequent, and thereby became the criterion of all religions, including Christianity.[11]

Remember that revelation, for Tillich, as the manifestation of ultimate concern, is universal. This conviction was based upon the universal presence of the Logos. "There is a history of concrete revelatory events in all periods in which man exists as man" (ST2:166). These revelatory events are the basis upon which all religions are based. Revelation, however, is not restricted to religion. There is considerable revelation outside religion, as demonstrated by the universal quest for the New Being. Revelation is universal, not as a structural element of reality or a constant occurrence but in the sense that "there is a universal revelatory power going through all history and preparing for that which Christianity considers to be the ultimate revelation" (HCT, p. 2).

Although God reveals himself operatively in the existence of every person, yet revelation has found its ultimate and complete expression in the person and action of Jesus as the Christ. Tillich did not see how the Church could claim anything less: the New Testament picture of Jesus as the Christ has revealing power par excellence. It is not isolated; the Christ-event is not the only revelation. But it is the final revelation. This does not imply that the Christ-event is the last revelation; there is a continuous albeit dependent revelation in the history of the Church. But the Christ-event may be regarded as the last genuine revelation insofar as there can be no subsequent revelation in the history of the Church whose point of reference is not Jesus as the Christ. The Church would lose its foundation if it accepted any other point of reference. Even more than the last genuine revelation, though, the Christ-event is the final revelation because it is the decisive, unsurpassable, universally valid revelation, the criterion of all the others.

> The final revelation, the revelation in Jesus as the Christ, is universally valid, because it includes the criterion of every revelation and is the *finis* or *telos* (intrinsic aim) of all of them. The final revelation is the criterion of every revelation which precedes or follows. It is the criterion of every religion and every culture, not only of the culture and religion in and through which it has appeared. It is also valid for the social existence of every human group and for the personal existence of every human individual. It is valid for mankind as such, and, in an indescribable way, it has meaning for the universe also. Nothing less than this should be asserted by Christian theology.[12]

As the final revelation, the Christ-event stands at the center of revelation history. It is a center with a line leading up to it, by way of preparatory revelation, and a line leading out from it, by way of receiving revelation. All religions and cultures outside the Church are still in the period of preparation. Judaism, Islam, all the non-Christian religions, and even the quasi-religions have been and continue to be media of preparatory revelations. As such they are also media of New Being, means by which men find healing from estrangement. But religions are not the exclusive media. "In some degree all men participate in the healing power of the New Being. Otherwise they would have no being. The self-destructive consequences of estrangement would have destroyed them" (ST2:167). In other words, New Being is not limited to religions anymore than it is limited to the Church. The most that can be said for religions is that they are means ordained by God for preparatory revelation and for the healing of estrangement (GW1:383).

Whereas other religions are bearers of preparatory revelation, the Christian Church, as the receiver of the final revelation, is the bearer of what Tillich called receiving revelation. The period of receiving began with the Christian Church, which "is based on the final revelation and is supposed to receive it as a continuous process of reception, interpretation, and actualization" (ST1:144). Despite this, there are groups and individuals within the Christian Church who are still in the stage of preparation. They have never received the message of the final revelation in its full meaning and power. In fact, the various Christian churches themselves in their institutions and actions are in constant danger of relapsing into the preparatory stage. It is a danger which time and again has become a reality: Christianity, no less than the other religions, is susceptible to the ambiguities of religion, to profanation and demonization. (ST2:167).

The Church, as such, is neither absolute nor unique. It is the Christ-event which is absolute and unique, the event by which the Church was created and by which, like all religions, it is judged. A religious symbol is not to be identified with that to which it points. "Christianity, without being final itself, witnesses to the final revelation. Christianity is neither final nor universal. But that to which it witnesses is final and universal" (ST1:134). We have not yet made clear, though, why Tillich sees the Christ-event as unique, universal, and absolute; the Christ-event, is what "elevates" the Christian Church above other religions. It does not make the Church better than other religions, but does provide the Church with a better criterion by which to judge itself and others (ST3:381). That criterion constitutes the uniqueness of the Christ-event and at the same time destroys, at least in a fragmentary way, the ambiguities of religion. The one advantage Tillich would admit that the Church has over other religions is the cross.

The Christ-event, on which the Church is based, is absolute and unique because Jesus, the bearer of the New Being, is unique. As the Christ he maintained unity with God, even though subject to finitude, anxiety, and conflict. In spite of his participation in all the ambiguities of life, Jesus' being was united without separation or disruption to the ground of all being and meaning. His being was determined every moment by God, and to such an extent that he became completely transparent to the divine mystery. It was this presence of God in Jesus which made him to be the Christ, the bearer of the New Being (ST1:135).

Implied in Jesus' maintainance of unity with God is another prerequisite for his messiahship, namely, his victory over every temptation to exploit his unity with God as a means of advantage for himself. Tillich goes so far as to say that, if Jesus had given in to the temptation to exploit this unity for himself, it would have deprived him of his messianic function. Jesus' acceptance of the cross was the decisive test of his unity with God, of his complete "translucency" to the ground of being. As the medium of the final revelation, Jesus is still simply a medium. Like all media of revelation, like everything else which points to and participates in the holy, so Jesus too was tempted by demonic forces to claim ultimacy for his finite nature. Idolatry perverts revelation by elevating the medium of revelation to the dignity of the revelation itself. Jesus conquered the temptation to become an object of idolatry by accepting the cross, by sacrificing that which was finite and conditional in himself to that which was infinite and unconditional. In his cross Jesus sacrificed the medium of revelation to that to which the medium points. As TIllich put it enigmatically, Jesus is the medium of the final revelation, the bearer of the New Being, only because he sacrificed what is merely "Jesus" in him to that which is Christ (ST1:136).

> Jesus could not have been the Christ without sacrificing himself as Jesus to himself as Christ. Any acceptance of Jesus as the Christ which is not acceptance of Jesus the crucified is a form of idolatry. The ultimate concern of the Christian is not Jesus, but the Christ Jesus who is manifest as the crucified. [DF, p. 98]

In sacrificing himself as Jesus to himself as Christ, Jesus became the bearer of the New Being. He created the new reality of which the Church is the communal and historical embodiment. At the same time he gave the Church a symbol which is superior to any other religious symbol precisely because it is the radical negation of all idolatry, a means to counteract the ambiguities of religion and overcome the demonic. A symbol of faith is true only if it points to ultimacy while at the same time expressing its own lack of ultimacy. Christianity has such a symbol in the cross, for it symbolizes the conquest of the demonic temptation to power, to self-elevation, and to self-absolutization.

> If Christianity claims to have a truth superior to any other truth in its symbolism, then it is the symbol of the cross in which this is expressed, the cross of Christ. He who himself embodies the fullness of the divine's presence sacrifices himself in order not to become an idol, another god beside God, a god into whom the disciples wanted to make him. And therefore the decisive story is the story in which he accepts the title "Christ" when Peter offers it to him. He accepts it under the one condition that he has to go to Jerusalem to suffer and to die, which means to deny the idolatrous tendency even with respect to himself. This is at the same time the criterion of all other symbols, and it is the criterion to which every Christian church should subject itself. [TC, p. 67]

The Church is finite and conditional, like any other religion. It is subject to the same ambiguities, to the same temptation to make itself into an idol, to make its dogmas, rituals, and symbols into absolutes. But in the cross it has the criterion by which it can judge itself and overcome this demonic temptation. Here is the fundamental meaning of the cross. It is a singular expression of the Protestant principle (see chapter 5). Tillich saw it as the primary justification for conversion to Christianity from another religion; in the cross, the ultimacy of ultimate concern is better preserved than in any other symbol (DF, pp. 123–24).

In the cross the Church has a criterion of universal validity for judging itself and all religions. At the same time the cross provides a basis for the universality of the Church and for its ability to approach other religions and cultures dialectically, with a yes as well as a no. In sacrificing the Jesus in himself to that which was the Christ, Jesus crucified the particular for the sake of the universal. His image was liberated from bondage to any particular religion, indeed from bondage to the religious sphere altogether. With this freedom from particularity, the Church is able to say yes—to accept any truth of faith in whatever form it may appear—yet at the same time, it is compelled to say no—to reject any truth of faith as being ultimate (DF, p. 98).

Because of the cross, Christianity has been able to become, as Harnack described it, a compendium of the history of religion. Because of the cross, "Christianity has in its very nature an openness in all directions, and for centuries this openness and receptivity was its glory" (CEWR, p. 83). Polemics raised by dogmatic questions and subsequent dogmatic decisions unfortunately served to narrow down the Church. Christianity ceased to be a center of crystallization for all positive religious elements after they had been subjected to the criteria in its fundamental principle that Jesus is the Christ. "Much of the criticism directed against Christianity is due to this failure" (CEWR, p. 84). For a religion to be universal, it must be aware of the conditional, non-ultimate character of its symbols. Christianity expresses this awareness in the symbol of the cross, even if Christian churches often neglect its full implication by attributing ultimacy to their own particular expressions of the ultimate. "The radical self-criticism of Christianity makes it most capable of universality—so long as it maintains this self-criticism as a power in its own life" (DF, p. 125).

Tillich's consideration of the Church as the Community of the New Being remains abstract, perhaps, until brought into correlation with life. Within this correlation he studies at great length the individual and social embodiment of the New Being, no longer simply in terms of the New Being. Insofar as it first became visible in Jesus as the Christ, the New Being is Christ. But insofar as the New Being is a reality in the spirit of every Christian, constituting the assembly of Christians in every time and place, the New Being is Spirit. Both names designate the same reality.

Christ is the Spirit, and the Spirit is the Spirit of Christ. A Christian is one who participates in this new reality, that is, one who has the Spirit. . . . To be a Christian means to have the Spirit, and any description must be a description of the manifestations of the Spirit. [SF, p. 134]

The Community of New Being

The Spirit is the actuality of the New Being (ST2:180). As the Community of New Being in history, the Christian Church is the visible expression of the Spirit in historical mankind. Besides being the Community of the New Being, the Church is Spiritual Community made manifest.

3

Spiritual Community Made Manifest

The Priest was still on his way, and finally I was bound to voice my deep regret that such delay threatened to deprive my comrade of the final consolations of our Church . . . He then uttered these words almost in my ear. And I am quite sure that I have recorded them accurately, for his voice, though halting, was strangely distinct. "Does it matter? Grace is everywhere."
I think he died just then.

Georges Bernanos, The Diary of a Country Priest

In practically every section of Tillich's theology, there echoes the faith of George Bernanos's country priest that "Grace is everywhere." For Tillich this meant not only grace but also ultimate concern, revelation, faith, and healing. They are all universal, owing to the universal presence of the divine Logos and New Being. In as much as New Being is created by the presence and activity of the divine Spirit in the spirits of men, the universality of New Being points to the universality of Spiritual Presence. The Spirit is free to work in the spirits of men in any and every human situation, secular as well as sacred.

For Tillich the fundamental paradox of Christianity was that the universal Logos became particular, New Being became embodied in the person of Jesus as the Christ. As the community which receives Jesus as the Christ, the Church is the historical, social embodiment of New Being. Or to put it otherwise: the Church is the historical embodiment of Spiritual Community. Let no equation be made here. The Spirit is free. Grace is everywhere, and Spiritual Community is everywhere. The Church is not

Spiritual Community in any exclusive sense. It contains Spiritual Community without confining it. Tillich's thinking on religious symbols must be kept in mind here once again. The Church expresses Spiritual Community and serves it, even while participating in its reality. But the Church is not to be identified with it. The Church is Spiritual Community, yes, but Spiritual Community made manifest.

In his *Systematic Theology,* Part 4, "Life and Spirit," Tillich developed at length his theology of the Church. He did so within the framework of the divine Spirit and Spiritual Community created by the Spirit. It is patently the most complex and intricate part of his entire system, ranging over such diverse fields as politics, medicine, technology, and art. It does so while presenting Tillich's doctrine of Spiritual Presence, Spiritual Community, and the Church in correlation to life.

Life, Its Ambiguities, and the Quest for Unambiguous Life

Tillich's definition of life is an ontological one, the "actuality of being," a mixture of essence and existence, of actualized potentiality and existential distortion (ST3:11). Tillich preferred an ontological concept of life so as to free it from "bondage" to the organic realm and thus render it universal. As a result, the growth and decay of rocks and stars may be considered life processes no less than the growth and decay of plants and animals. All are various aspects of the diversity of life.

Confronted by the diversity of life, the human mind seeks unifying principles in order to understand it. One of the most common is hierarchical order. Tillich rejected it, however, because it divides life into watertight compartments and loses sight of life's essential unity. He suggested that the metaphor *dimension* should replace that of hierarchical levels or grades of being. A plurality of dimensions expresses the differences in life without precluding their unity, since dimensions can meet at a point without excluding one another. Such an approach permits description of the "multidimensional unity of life," the inorganic and the organic, the spiritual and the historical. It permits description in particular of the multidimensional unity of man, in whom all the dimensions of life are actual. Of all these dimensions, though, there is one peculiarly proper to man, the dimension of spirit. Man is "that organism in which the dimension of spirit is dominant" (ST3:26).

As the actualization of potential being, life is a process, a movement out and away from a center and then back toward it. There are three functions which can be discerned within this process. The self-integration of life is a circular movement within the polarities of individualization and participation in which the center of self-identity is established. The self-creation of life is a horizontal movement within the polarities of dynamics and form in which new centers are actualized. The self-transcendence of life is a vertical movement within the polarities of freedom and destiny in which life drives itself toward the sublime. Essentially, these functions are unified and harmonized. Existentially, however, their unity is disrupted by estrangement, driving life to one or the other direction. The result is ambiguity: "self-integration is countered by disintegration, self-creation is countered by destruction, self-transcendence is countered by profanization" (ST3:32). Within every life process, positive elements are so mingled with negative elements that a definite separation of the two is impossible. "Life is neither essential nor existential but ambiguous" (ST3:32).

The ambiguities of life are to be found in all of its dimensions, including the one already designated as proper to man, the dimension of spirit. Tillich defined spirit as the "unity of power and meaning" (ST3:24). It is the power that perceives meaning, and the perception of meaning imparts power. Within the dimension of spirit, the functions of life are as operative as they are in all dimensions: self-integration is actualized as morality; self-creation is actualized as culture; and self-transcendence is actualized as religion, although strictly speaking religion is not a separate function but a quality of the others.

All three functions of the spirit, morality, culture, and religion, are inexorably subject to the law of ambiguity. Morality is subject to the ambiguities of applying the categorical imperative to concrete circumstances, the ambiguities of moral norms and motivations. Culture is subject to the ambiguities of language and art which falsify as well as express, the ambiguities of a technology which transforms means into ends, and the ambiguities of forming community on the basis of exclusion. Religion, as discussed above, is subject to the ambiguities of profanation and demonization.

Because all the dimensions of life are a mixture of the essential with the existential, all are subject to ambiguity. They all yearn likewise for a resolution of ambiguity. This is particularly true of man.

> The question of unambiguous life is latent everywhere. All creatures long for an unambiguous fulfillment of their essential possibilities, but only in man as the bearer of the spirit do the ambiguities of life and the quest for the unambiguous life become conscious. [ST3:107]

Driven by the ambiguities he experiences in all the dimensions of his life, man searches for unambiguous life. He makes this quest primarily in the realm of religion, since it is religion which is the self-transcendence of life in the realm of spirit. "The answer to this quest is the experience of revelation and salvation; they constitute religion above religion, although they become religion when they are received" (ST3:109). Both the quest for unambiguous life and the answer received underlie all religions, giving them their greatness and dignity. Both quest and answer inevitably become ambiguous themselves, however, when expressed in a concrete religion.

As Tillich saw it, the answer to the quest for unambiguous life has been expressed within religion by three symbols: the Spirit of God, the Kingdom of God, and Eternal Life. The first, the Spirit of God, or as Tillich preferred to express it, Spiritual Presence, is the answer to the quest for unambiguous life and the basis for understanding the Church as the manifestation of Spiritual Community.

The Spiritual Presence

Although the concept of the New Being is normative for Tillich's theology and is the principle around which all else is built, the New Being is created in man by the Spiritual Presence. The Spirit therefore shares this centrality.

> The Spirit beareth witness with our spirit that we are children of God. Something new has come, a new reality, a new being, a spirit distinguished from our spirit. . . . The whole message of Christianity is contained in this statement. [SF, p. 137]

Because of the centrality which the Spiritual Presence enjoys in his theology, Tillich has been called a "theologian of the spirit."[1] The point is well made. Tillich saw his as a "theology of experience and inwardness," in the tradition of St. Paul.

> Paul was the great theologian of the Divine Spirit. It formed the center of his theology. The classical Protestant view was held, along with Luther, Melanchthon, Calvin, and Bucer, that Paul was a theologian of justification of grace through faith. That certainly is not wrong. But this was a defensive doctrine for Paul. He developed this doctrine in his fight against the so-called Judaizers. . . . At the center was his experience and doctrine of the Spirit. . . . [PPT, p. 20]

61

> Although I am not a mystical theologian, I would say that I am more on the side of the theology of experience and inwardness, for I believe that the Spirit is in us. In the concept of the Spirit the highest synthesis is given between the Word of God which comes from the outside and the experience which occurs inside.[2]

Tillich admitted that using the almost forbidden word *spirit* (with a small *s*) in this day and age practically demanded an act of courage. He dared to do so, however, in order to give an adequate name to that function of life which characterizes man as man, the function which is actualized in morality, culture, and religion. He did so also in order to provide the empirical material which is used in the symbol *Divine Spirit* (with a capital *S*).

> Man, in experiencing himself as man, is conscious of being determined in his nature by spirit as a dimension of his life. This immediate experience makes it possible to speak symbolically of God as Spirit as of the divine Spirit. [ST3:111]

Tillich usually preferred to speak of Spiritual Presence rather than Holy Spirit in order to make it clear that the Spirit of God is not a separated being. The divine Spirit is "God present," the "presence of the Divine Life within creaturely life" (ST3:107).

> Spirit is not a mysterious substance; it is not a part of God. It is God himself; but not God as the creative ground of all things and not God directing history and manifesting himself in its central event, but God as present in communities and personalities, grasping them, inspiring them, and transforming them. [EN, pp. 69–70]

The relation between spirit and Spirit is expressed by the metaphorical use of the preposition *in;* the divine Spirit dwells and works in the human spirit. But in breaking into the human spirit, the divine Spirit does not rest there. It drives the human spirit out of itself and into successful self-transcendence. The human spirit is grasped by something ultimate and unconditional. The classical term for this state of being grasped by the Spiritual Presence is ecstasy.

Tillich took pains to emphasize that, in driving the human spirit beyond itself, the Spiritual Presence does not destroy man's rational structure. "Ecstasy does not destroy the centeredness of the integrated self" (ST3:112). But the ecstatic character of the experience of the Spiritual Presence does do something which the human spirit cannot do by itself. It creates unambiguous life. Driven by the ambiguities of life, man searches in quest for unambiguous life, but he can never attain it of himself. The finite cannot compel the infinite; the human spirit cannot compel the divine Spirit to enter the human spirit. Man cannot grasp unambiguous life unless he is first grasped by it. When he is grasped in this way, however, the subject-object structure between God and man is dissolved. "A union of subject and object has taken place in which the independent existence of each is overcome; new unity is created" (ST3:119). The best example of this transcendence of the subject-object structure is prayer. In prayer God is not merely an object but a subject at the same time, so that God prays to himself through us.

Tillich admitted that great care must be taken to avoid confusing ecstasy with chaos or subjective intoxication. But he believed just as strongly that the Church must avoid profaning the Spirit. He accused the Catholic Church of institutional profanation, in that it replaces the charisma of the New Testament with office. He accused Protestantism of secular profanation, in that it replaces ecstasy with doctrinal or moral structure. Tillich regarded his *Systematic Theology* as "a defense of ecstatic manifestation of the Spiritual Presence against its ecclesiastical critics; in this defense, the whole New Testament is the most powerful weapon" (ST3:118).

The ecstatic state created when the human spirit is grasped by the divine Spirit is the transcendent union of unambiguous life. This union manifests itself by faith and love. Faith is "the state of being *grasped* by the transcendent unity of unambiguous life"; love is "the state of being *taken into* that transcendent unity" (ST3:129). The distinction between the two is logical, not real. In faith one is grasped by God, whereas in love one adheres to him. In relation to God, though, the distinction disappears. "Being grasped by God in faith and adhering to him in love is one and the same state of creaturely life. It is participation in the transcendent unity of unambiguous life" (ST3:138). Tillich summarized it this way:

> The Spiritual Presence, elevating man through faith and love to the transcendent unity of unambiguous life, creates the New Being above the gap between essence and existence and consequently above the ambiguities of life. [ST3:138]

But the invasion of the human spirit by the divine Spirit does not occur in isolated individuals. Since all the functions of the human spirit are conditioned by the social context of I-Thou encounters, the Spirit invades the human spirit in and through social groups, through communities.

Spiritual Community

The unambiguous life created within communities by the Spiritual Presence was represented in the New Testament under the image of the Body of Christ. The sixteenth-century Reformers described it as the Invisible Church. For our own day Tillich proposed the term *Spiritual Community.* [3]

Spiritual Community, it must be emphasized, is not a group existing alongside other groups. Rather, it is a power and a structure inherent and effective within groups (ST3:162). Spiritual Community is not to be identified with any one religious community, not even the Christian Church. It is the quality in the churches which makes them to be churches, their inner *telos*, their invisible Spiritual essence (ST3:165). Spiritual Community is spiritual in that, although it is unconquerably real, nevertheless it is hidden, open to the eyes of faith alone. Because it is a creation of the Spirit, it can be seen only with the aid of the Spirit: only Spirit can discern Spirit. Even though it is hidden, Spiritual Community is not simply an ideal, which actual religious communities strive to approximate. Neither is it a community of so-called spiritual beings, angelic hierarchies, saints, or the saved from all periods and nations. It is the invisible essence of all visible religious communities.

Spiritual Community is *un*ambiguous. It is a manifestation of unambiguous life. But an important distinction needs to be made between ambiguity and fragmentariness. Like Spiritual Presence and the New Being which it creates, Spiritual Community is, in itself, unambiguous; in its manifestation in time and space, however, Spiritual Community is fragmentary.

> The fulfilled transcendent union is an eschatological concept. The fragment is an anticipation (as Paul speaks of the fragmentary and anticipatory possession of the divine Spirit, of the truth, of the vision of God, and so on). [ST3:140]

The unambiguous life is present in mankind as a whole, in preparation for the central manifestation of divine Spirit, but it is present only fragmentarily, that is, by way of anticipation. It was present without distortion in Jesus as the Christ; but it was still fragmentary in that he was still subject to the ambiguities of existence, exhaustion, loneliness, and death. The unambiguous life is present in the manifestation of Spiritual Community, created under the impact of Jesus as the Christ; but again it is only fragmentary, "appearing under the condition of finitude but conquering both estrangement and ambiguity" (ST3:150). So long as it is subject to time and space, to the condition of finitude, unambiguous life can be only fragmentary, anticipatory. Integral possession of unambiguous life will come only beyond time and space. But even though fragmentary and anticipatory now within time and space, the unambiguous life present within Spiritual Community still possesses distinguishing marks.

Tillich delineated the character of Spiritual Community in terms of the story of Pentecost. The ecstatic experience of the Spiritual Presence at Pentecost grasped the followers of Jesus in such a way that it reestablished their faith. It inflamed them with a love which expressed itself immediately in mutual service. It united diverse individuals, nationalities, and traditions, as was symbolized by the miracle of tongues, and overcame the disruption of mankind, symbolized by the Tower of Babel. It created a missionary drive within the community, a universal openness to all men. The Pentecost story teaches that there is no Spiritual Community without faith, love, unity, universality, and holiness (ST3:151).

Spiritual Community is a community of faith. "The term 'community of faith' implies the state of tension which exists between the faith of the individual member and the faith of the community as a whole. But it follows from the nature of the Spiritual Community that this tension does not lead to a break" (ST3:155). There is no break, because it is open in all directions. Spiritual Community contains an indefinite variety of expressions of faith without excluding any of them. Based on the central manifestation of the Spiritual Presence, it overcomes the gap between infinite and finite and is the criterion for the faith of all religious communities, for the faith of all churches.

Spiritual Community is a community of love. As it is able to contain the tension between the faith of the community and that of the individual member, so too Spiritual Community "contains the tension between the indefinite variety of love relations and the *agape* which unites being with being in the transcendent union of unambiguous life" (ST3:156). Love within Spiritual Community unites its individual members despite the variety of their love relations. Spiritual Community is thus the criterion for love within all religious communities, within all churches.

The unity of Spiritual Community follows from its character as a community of faith and love. There is tension among the diverse conditions of faith within the community, as well as among the indefinite variety of love relations. But Spiritual Community is able to withstand these tensions without a break. As such, it is the criterion for unity within all religious communities, within all churches (ST3:156).

The universality of Spiritual Community likewise follows from its character as a community of faith and love. "There is no Spiritual Community without openness to all individuals, groups, and things and the drive to take them into itself" (ST3:152). Although universality within Spiritual Community is unambiguous, it is only fragmentary and anticipatory. "The limits of finitude restrict the actual universality in every moment of time and at every point of space" (ST3:157). Nevertheless, it is the criterion for the universality of all religious communities, for the universality of all churches.

The holiness of Spiritual Community follows from its other marks. Through its faith, love, unity, and universality, Spiritual Community participates in the holiness of the Divine Life. As the spiritual essence of all religious communities, of all churches, it communicates to them its holiness and becomes the criterion of their holiness as it is received by them (ST3:155–57).

Besides faith, love, unity, universality, and holiness, there is a final characteristic of Spiritual Community. As a fragmentary expression of unambiguous life, Spiritual Community is marked by the fragmentary union of the three functions of life under the dimension of spirit, a unity of morality, culture, and religion. It anticipates the biblical vision of the holy city in which there are no tables of commandments, no aesthetic detachment, no temple as a separate entity (ST3:157–61).

The most important distinction, however, with regard to Spiritual Community is yet to be made. Spiritual Community is not to be identified with any one religious community, not even with the Christian Church. What then is its relation to the Church? The answer is dialectical: it is a relation of identity and non-identity. Spiritual Community embraces two stages. It is both latent and manifest.

Tillich's distinction between latent and manifest Spiritual Community is a trademark of his theology of the Church. Stated simply, it is the difference between "before" and "after" encounter with Jesus as the Christ, "before" here meaning not before 30 A.D., but before any existential encounter with him (ST3:147). The distinction, which Tillich earlier though less accurately phrased as "latent and manifest Church," goes back to the early days of his theological career and his experiences in the Religious Socialism Movement after World War I.

The problem of Church and Society prompted me, in an essay entitled "Kirche und humanistische Gesellschaft" [Church and humanistic society], to draw a distinction between a "manifest" and a "latent" Church. This was not the old Protestant distinction between the visible and invisible Church, but was concerned with a duality within the visible churches. The kind of distinction I suggested in that essay seems to be necessary in order to take into account the Christian humanism which exists outside the churches. It is not permissible to designate as "unchurched" those who have become alienated from organized denominations and traditional creeds. In living among these groups for half a generation, I learned how much of the latent Church there is within them. I encountered the experience of the finite character of human existence, the quest for the eternal and unconditioned, an absolute devotion to justice and love, a hope that lies beyond any Utopia, an appreciation of Christian values and a very sensitive recognition of the ideological misuse of Christianity in the interpenetration of Church and State. It has often seemed to me that the "latent Church," as I call what I found among these groups, was a truer church than the organized denominations, if only because its members did not presume to possess the truth.[OB, p. 67]

Another motive for making the distinction are the riddles posed by the history of the Christian churches: Why are the Christian churches so overwhelmingly limited to one section of mankind, to one particular civilization, to one particular culture of this civilization? Why, for almost five hundred years, have secular movements, such as scientific humanism and naturalistic communism, arisen within Christian civilization? Why have these secular outgrowths succeeded far more impressively in non-Christian lands than Christianity itself, despite the considerable missionary efforts that Christianity has made in those lands? (ST3:378).

In attempting to answer these questions, Tillich's distinction follows quite logically from the foundations he has already laid: the universality of revelation as ultimate concern; the distinction between preparatory and receiving revelation; the designation of the appearance of Jesus as the Christ as the central but not unique revelation within a continuing history of revelation. It follows also from the universal presence and and operation of the divine Spirit.

The assertion that Jesus is the Christ implies that the Spirit, which made him the Christ and which became his Spirit (with a capital "S"), was and is working in all those who have been grasped by the Spiritual Presence before he could be encountered as an historical event. This has been expressed in the Bible and the churches by the scheme of "prophecy and fulfillment." . . . The Spirit who created the Christ within Jesus is the same Spirit who prepared and continues to prepare mankind for the encounter with the New Being in him. [ST3:147]

As was intimated in the consideration of universalism and particularism in Church history, the distinction between a latent and manifest

Church is able to appeal to a long and impressive tradition. As early as the end of the first century at Rome, the *Shepherd of Hermas* (*Vision* II,4.1) described the Church as already being a venerable, old woman: "She was created the first of all things. For this reason she is an old woman." St. Irenaeus, writing in the second century, maintained: "Where the Church is, there too is the Spirit of God; and where the Spirit of God is, there is the Church and every grace" (*Adversus Haereses* III,24.1). The anti-Gnostic Fathers were cited by Tillich as describing the history of salvation in terms of a number of covenants; the covenants given at creation and at Mount Sinai are not negated but affirmed by the New Covenant given in the revelation of Jesus as the Christ (HCT, p. 44). Tillich appealed as well to St. Clement of Alexandria for the opinion that all nations are in some way prepared for the revelation of Jesus as the Christ, the Jews by the Law, the Greeks by their philosophy. The Logos is never absent from people (HCT, p. 55).

One of the most influential sources for Tillich's distinction is St. Augustine (HCT, p. 121). The city of God is present within the Church. But the Church is a *corpus mixtum*, a mixed body, embracing some people who belong to it essentially and spiritually and others who do not. For Augustine there is a dialectical relation between Spiritual Community and the visible church, a yes and a no. Tillich accused the Catholic Church of identifying Spiritual Community and visible Church to the extent that the Church becomes absolutized. Sectarian movements and Protestantism, on the other hand, emphasize the differences between them.

> According to Catholic doctrine the first (the Church) is the condition of the second (the spiritual community of the faithful); according to sectarian beliefs the second, if anything, is the condition of the first. These two concepts of the church have been in conflict throughout the history of the church. [HCT, p. 133]

Reference to Protestant and sectarian interpretations of St. Augustine's theology of the Church brings up the relationship of Tillich's distinction between the latent and manifest Church to the traditional Protestant distinction between the visible and invisible Church. They are not the same. Although they have sometimes been confused, the two distinctions overlap (OB, p. 67). "The qualities invisible and visible must be applied to the Church both in its latency and in its manifestation" (ST3:153). Tillich's is not John Calvin's radical distinction between a visible church and an invisible church, wherein the invisible church is the body of those who are predestined (HCT, p. 272). Neither is it the distinction, emphasized by

Pietism, of a small church within the large church, an *ecclesiola in ecclesia* (HCT, p. 285). Tillich built instead upon Luther's concept of the invisible church, which he interpreted not as a separate church but rather as the spiritual quality of the visible church, corresponding to the whole concept of Spiritual Community, not just its latency (HCT, pp. 252–53). But Tillich broadened Luther's concept. The latent Church is both visible and invisible, and the manifest Church is both visible and invisible.

From all that has preceded, it would seem that the latent Church, as Tillich saw it, is visible when its ultimate concern is expressed in an organized system of ritual and symbols. Non-Christian religions participate in the latent Church and are certainly visible. Individuals who are grasped by Spiritual Presence but do not articulate their ultimate concern by adopting the symbols and rituals of organized religion participate in the invisible latent Church. The visible manifest Church consists of those who accept Jesus as the Christ and participate in the life of the Christian churches. The invisible manifest Church consists of those who consciously and explicitly accept Jesus as the Christ but do not identify themselves with any of the Christian churches.[4]

Despite the considerable differences between the latent and manifest churches, Tillich regarded them as essentially one. They are not entirely separate, let alone opposed, communities. "The church is *one* historical reality starting with the promise of God to Abraham, centered in the appearance of Christ, and moving toward the final fulfillment" (PE, p. 31). It "follows upon an age-long preparation—a general preparation in all religions and cultures throughout the world and a special preparation in an 'elect people'. Accordingly, we must recognize not only the manifest church but also a 'latent' or 'potential' church existing everywhere and at all times" (WS, p. 20).

The prototype of latent Spiritual Community are the ancient people of Israel and the Judaism of today. There is latent Spiritual Community as well in Islamic mosques and devotional communities, in Asian mysticism and the monastic groups to which the mystical religions give rise. It is present in all the many and varied manifestations of community discernible in the history of religion, which, in most cases, is identical with the history of culture (ST3:154). Tillich's experience with Christian humanism led him to make the distinction in the first place. There is latent Spiritual Community not only outside the Church but also outside all forms of organized religion. It can be found in youth alliances and friendship groups, in educational, artistic, and political movements. It can be found too among individuals "without any visible relation to each other in whom the

Spiritual Presence's impact is felt, although they are indifferent or hostile to all overt expressions of religion" (ST3:153). Even the secular opponents of the churches, such as communism, are not excluded from Spiritual Community. Tillich regarded them as representing Spiritual Community in its secular latency.

Latent Spiritual Community is characterized by both a negative and a positive element. Latency is the state of being partly actual, partly potential. Its potentiality consists in the fact that it has not yet existentially encountered the New Being in Jesus as the Christ. But mere potentiality is not enough; there must be actualized elements as well. The actuality of latent Spiritual Community is the impact of the Spiritual Presence in faith and love. Within latent Spiritual Community "there are elements of faith in the sense of being grasped by an ultimate concern, and there are elements of love in the sense of transcendent reunion of the separated" (ST3:154). Recognition of these elements, of the essential unity between the latent and manifest Spiritual Community, serves as a protection against ecclesiastical arrogance. Religion in latent Spiritual Community may be distorted and its expressions may be primitive, but it is not non-religion. In its ministry and missionary activity, the Church approaches non-Christians as fellow members of Spiritual Community and not as complete strangers (ST3:155).

Despite the essential union between latent and manifest Spiritual Community, there is still one all-important difference between them. Latent Spiritual Community lacks an ultimate criterion for its faith and love. It lacks the transcendent union of unambiguous life as it is manifest in Jesus as the Christ. This means that the latent Spiritual Community is open to the ambiguities of religion, to profanation and demonization, without possessing an ultimate principle of resistance. It lacks that criterion which serves for manifest Spiritual Community as its means of self-negation, reformation, and transformation. It lacks the cross.

Because it lacks the cross as a criterion, latent Spiritual Community is deficient in comparison with manifest Spiritual Community. Latent Spiritual Community may, in some respects, represent Spiritual Community better than the churches, even as it may serve as a critic of the churches in the name of Spiritual Community. Nevertheless, the relationship of the latent stage of Spiritual Community to its manifest stage is teleological. The various expressions of latent Spiritual Community "are unconsciously driven toward the Christ, even though they reject him when he is brought to them through the preaching and actions of the Christian Churches" (ST3:154). This is true even of anti-religious, anti-Christian movements.

"Not even communism could live if it were devoid of all elements of the Spiritual Community. Even world communism is teleologically related to the Spiritual Community" (ST3:155).

Besides lacking the cross as a defense against demonization, latent Spiritual Community also lacks the organization necessary to withstand the onslaughts of modern paganism. This is another reason for the necessity of manifest churches.

> The last few years have shown . . . that only the organized Church is capable of maintaining the struggle against the pagan attacks of Christianity. The latent Church has neither the religious nor the organizational weapons necessary for this struggle. [OB, p. 67]

The Church and the Churches

Spiritual Community is not a religious group existing alongside other groups, but is a power and a structure inherent in all religious communities. If these religious communities are based on a foundation other than the appearance of Jesus as the Christ, they are called synagogues, temple congregations, mystery groups, cult groups, or movements. Only if they are consciously based on the appearance of Jesus as the Christ may they be called churches, in the strict sense of the word.

> The church in New Testament Greek is *ecclesia*, the assembly of those who are called out of all nations by the *apostoloi*, the messengers of the Christ, to the congregation of the *eleutheroi*, those who have become free citizens of the "Kingdom of the Heavens." There is a "church," an "assembly of God" (or of the Christ), in every town in which the message has been successful and a Christian *koinonia*, or communion, has come into being. [ST3:162]

Besides these individual local assemblies, or churches, there is also the overall unity of these local churches in the Church universal. Both local churches and the Church universal are manifestations, existential expressions in time and space, of Spiritual Community.[5] Spiritual Community constitutes the Spiritual essence of the Church and the churches, effective in them through its power, its structure, and its fight against their ambiguities. On the other hand, both the Church universal and the individual churches within it are social groups of individual Christians. As such they are subject to all the ambiguities of religion, morality, and culture. As existential expressions of Spiritual Community, they are at the same time distortions of it. This is the paradox of the Church and the churches—the

71

fact that they are, at the same time, both sociological and theological realities.

Both the Church universal and the churches within it participate in the ambiguities of life, of religious life in particular; on the other hand, they also participate in the unambiguous life of Spiritual Community. They are visible and invisible, sociological and theological. Both aspects must be emphasized equally: first, in order to avoid devaluating the empirical churches as they exist here and now (as certain types of Spirit movements have); and second, in order to avoid indifference to the invisible church or Spiritual Community as an irrelevant ideal (as liberal Protestantism did) (ST3:165).

The Church is a sociological reality, subject to the laws which determine the life of all social groups, to the ambiguities of life in general and to profanation and demonization in particular. Because it is a sociological reality, therefore, the Church is not only an expression of Spiritual Community but also a distortion and betrayal of it.

> The sociologists of religion . . . rightly point to the social stratification within the churches, to the rise and fall of elites, to power struggles and the destructive weapons used in them, to the conflict between freedom and organization, to aristocratic esotericism, and so forth. Seen in this light, the history of the churches is a secular history with all the disintegrating, destructive, and tragic-demonic elements which make historical life as ambiguous as all other life processes. [ST3:165]

Not infrequently, the churches are viewed solely as sociological realities, to the exclusion of their theological aspect. This can be done either for polemical or for apologetic purposes. Critics of the churches, often because of exaggerated expectations and inevitable disappointment, polemize against the churches by comparing their rather miserable concrete reality to their claim to embody Spiritual Community. Apologists for the churches often cite their significance as the largest, most effective social agencies dedicated to enhancing the good life. Viewing the churches solely as sociological realities for apologetic purposes is just as much a distortion as doing so for polemical intent. "A church which is nothing more than a benevolent, socially useful group can be replaced by other groups not claiming to be churches; such a church has no justification for its existence" (ST3:166).

Although there is validity to seeing the Church within the categories of sociology, it requires theological consideration as well. Within the ambiguities of the social reality of the churches, there is embodied unambiguous Spiritual Community, manifested by them in fragmentary fashion, but in reality nevertheless. Here too lies a danger of exclusiveness however. A theological view can hardly be exclusive to the extent that it simply denies the existence of the sociological characteristics of the churches and their ambiguities. But it can deny their significance. Tillich accused Roman Catholicism of taking just such an exclusively theological view of itself by ignoring the significance of the ambiguities of life and submerging the sociological aspect of its character into the theological, identifying its historical existence with that of Spiritual Community (ST3:166).

The Church, because it participates in the unambiguous life of Spiritual Community, manifests the very same marks as Spiritual Community, namely, faith, love, holiness, unity, and universality. But because it participates as well in the ambiguities of life, the Church manifests them fragmentarily. The marks can be ascribed to the churches only with the addition of "in spite of." Here more than anywhere else the paradoxical character of the Church becomes evident.

THE MARKS OF THE CHURCH

Like Spiritual Community, which constitutes its dynamic essence, the Church too is a community of faith, founded on the New Being in Jesus as the Christ. In Spiritual Community, however, the ambiguities of religion are conquered completely, whereas in the Church they are conquered only in principle. (Principle here means, as in the Greek *arche* and the Latin *principium*, the power of beginning, a power which remains the controlling force in an entire process.) In the Church, ambiguity is recognized and rejected, but not removed. As indicated above, there is tension within Spiritual Community between the faith of the individual and the faith of the community as a whole. There is tension, but it does not lead to a break. Not so with the Church: "In the churches a break is presupposed and leads to the ambiguities of religion, but it does so in such a way that these ambiguities are resisted and in principle overcome by the participation of the community of the church in the Spiritual Community" (ST3:173).

A number of difficulties are to be recognized, when speaking of the churches as communities of faith. Originally it was not difficult to speak of the Church as a community of faith, since the decision to enter involved a risk, perhaps even of one's life. When this situation changed and whole civilizations became Christian, active faith, the *fides qua creditur*, became overshadowed by the creedal foundations of the Church, the *fides quae*

73

creditur. Faith became interpreted as an unconditional subjection to these creeds, which were themselves the product not only of Spiritual creativity but also of such ambiguous social forces as hierarchical arrogance and political intrigue (ST3:174). In our own day, characterized by criticism and skepticism, what does it mean for the Church to be a community of faith, when whole communities, as well as individual Christians, are beset by doubt?

When a student at the University of Halle in 1904 and a member of a Christian fraternity there, Tillich faced the question of the compatibility of doubt with adherence to a professedly Christian community. The answer he gave then was the same he maintained throughout his theological career: even if an individual doubts radically, as long as he takes the problem of his doubt very seriously and struggles with it, he remains a member of the community (PPT, p. 154). Remember that, for Tillich, Christian faith is not simply an act of the intellect but rather, the state of being grasped by New Being as it is manifest in Jesus as the Christ. If faith is understood as belief, then doubt is incompatible with faith. But if faith is understood as ultimate concern, then doubt is not only not incompatible, it is a necessary element of faith, a consequence of the risk of faith (DF, p. 18). Insofar as faith is an experience of and a communion with the infinite, it is certain. But insofar as it is the finite act of a finite being, faith suffers all the limitations of a finite act and is subject to doubt. Faith does not demand the suppression of doubt but rather the admission and acceptance of weakness and wavering. "Faith is the courage that conquers doubt, not by removing it, but by taking it as an element into itself" (EN, p. 81).

The basic content of Christian faith is that Jesus is the Christ. Every Christian Church is based upon this assertion. The very name Christian implies it.

> For the individual, this means a decision—*not* as to whether he, personally, can accept the assertion that Jesus is the Christ, but the decision as to whether he wishes to belong or not to a community which asserts that Jesus is the Christ. If he decides against this, he has left the church, even if, for social or political reasons, he does not formalize his denial. [ST3:174]

And what of those who belong to the Church but question their status because of doubts even about the basic assertion that Jesus is the Christ?

> For them it must be said that the criterion of one's belonging to a church and through it to the Spiritual Community is the serious desire, conscious or unconscious, to participate in the life of a group which is based on the New Being as it has appeared in Jesus as the Christ. [ST3:175]

Regarding the more difficult problem of creeds, Tillich saw them as unavoidable attempts to formulate conceptually the implications of the basic Christian assertion that Jesus is the Christ. While it is necessary for the Church to formulate a particular doctrinal tradition, such a tradition is not absolute. It is not the only one possible. As a manifestation of the Spiritual Community, the Church cannot avoid fighting for the community of faith. But it remains subject to the ambiguities of life, so that its creeds are themselves ambiguous. They are not unconditionally valid.

Since it has Spiritual Community as its dynamic essence, the Church is also, as Augustine affirmed, a community of love. Love here is not to be identified with sentiment, feeling, or compassion. Such an emasculated concept of love was rightfully attacked by Nietzsche. Tillich suggested that the very word *love* might best be avoided for a while and the word *agape* used instead.[6] In the sense of *agape,* love includes not only emotions but also justice and power. Love must be viewed ontologically, as a structure rooted in being itself, the drive that unites the separated, not the strange but the estranged, whatever ultimately belong together (LPJ, pp. 18, 25–26).

As a community of love, the Church is a place where the estranged come together in mutual acceptance. It is a presupposition in the Church that every member bears to every other member an attitude of reuniting affirmation in terms of the eternal meaning of their being. This relation of mutual acceptance and affirmation becomes actual in spatial and temporal nearness (the "neighbor" of the New Testament) (ST3:178). "The Church is the place where an act of love overcomes the demonic force of objectification—of making people into objects, into things" (TC, p. 212). This understanding of love makes the Church superior to other religions.

> The highest form of love and that form of it which distinguishes Eastern and Western cultures is the love which preserves the individual who is both the subject and the object of love. In the loving person-to-person relationship Christianity manifests its superiority to any other religious tradition. [LPJ, p. 27]

Although the estrangement among men is healed within the Church as the actualization of Spiritual Community, yet the union is only fragmentary. Because the Church is a sociological reality subject to the ambiguities of life, its members, despite their essential union, remain separated from each other existentially by political, social, economic, and educational differences; by differences of national and racial background; by personal sympathies, antipathies, and preferences. In some churches—for example, the early church in Jerusalem—the concept of the Church as a community of love led to an attempt to remove economic disparities. Such an attitude fails to take into proper consideration the ambiguities within every community of love. "Often it is the ideological imposition of love which produces the most intensive forms of hostility" (ST3:178).

No claim for political, social, and economic equality can be derived directly from the Church's nature as a community of love. But it does follow from its nature that the Church attack and transform those forms of inequality which make actual community impossible.

> This refers to political, social, and economic inequalities and forms of suppression and exploitation which destroy the potentialities for humanity in the individual and for justice in the group. The church's prophetic word must be heard against such forms of inhumanity and injustice. [ST3:178]

While striving to help men attain the material goods which sustain their potentialities as men, the Church needs to be aware of the ambiguity of this particular manifestation of love. Charity is capable of perverting the very purpose of love. "It can be used as a means for maintaining the social conditions which make charity necessary, even a thoroughly unjust social order" (ST3:179). Thus *agape* strives to create the conditions which make love possible in the other.

Besides striving against basic inequality, love also implies judgment against that which negates it. This means that the Church by its very existence continually exercises judgment in the name of Spiritual Community both on its own members and those outside it. Even though the Church must of its nature exercise judgment, it necessarily becomes involved in the ambiguities of judging, namely, authority and power. And precisely because it judges in the name of Spiritual Community, it is in danger of becoming radical in its judging, fanatical, destructive, and demonic. The Church, in exercising judgment, has been given to such ambiguous policies as excommunication within Catholicism or, what can be even worse, social ostracism within Protestantism. It is easy to forget that "the decisive feature of the judging of love is that it has the one purpose of re-establishing the communion of love—not a cutting off, but a reuniting" (ST3:179).

With Spiritual Community as its dynamic essence, the Church is also holy. This holiness is not derived from the holiness of its institutions or doctrines, its ethical principles or devotional activities. On the contrary, these are precisely the aspects of the Church which are subject to the ambiguities of religion. Neither is the Church's holiness derived from the holiness or moral perfection of its members. Rather, it is the holiness of the Church which makes its members holy by leading them to the New Being, on which the Church rests. The churches are holy because of the holiness of their foundation, the New Being as it appeared in Jesus as the Christ. The holiness of the churches and of individual Christians is not a matter of empirical judgment but of faith in the working of New Being within them. Just as individuals are made holy despite their sinfulness, so too the churches are made holy despite their unholiness. The good news of justification by grace through faith is just as valid for the churches as for their members (ST3:167).

The paradox of the Church's holiness, the fact that it is holy "in spite of" its sinfulness, was not, to Tillich's mind, accepted by the Catholic Church in its own case, at least not prior to the II Vatican Council. While Catholicism admitted critical judgment of its members, including judgment of the pope himself, it did not admit critical judgment of itself as an institution, of its doctrinal decisions, ritual traditions, moral principles, or hierarchical structure. "It judges on the basis of institutional perfection, but this basis itself is not judged" (ST3:168). A claim to holiness based on any kind of institutional perfection was for Tillich utterly inadmissible. "The holy church is the distorted church, and this means every church in time and space" (ST3:168). It is not institutional perfection but its regenerative power that constitutes the most conspicuous sign of holiness in the Church. "It is generic to the churches' holiness that they have the principle of reformation within themselves..." (ST3:168). Tillich regarded movements of prophetic criticism and reformation as symptoms of Spiritual Presence at work within the churches, even in their most miserable state. The Spiritual Presence within them works through their ambiguity and creates the fragmentary beginnings of unambiguous life.

Since unity is a mark of Spiritual Community, the Church, as an existential expression of Spiritual Community, also enjoys the predicate of unity. This does not mean that the unity of the churches can be derived from their actual unity. But neither can the predicate of unity be denied them because of their present disunity. The unity of the churches is independent of empirical reality. It is identical rather with their dependence on Spiritual Community as their dynamic essence. The churches are united because of the unity of their foundation, the New Being which is effective in them. Thus, every local church, every denomination, can claim the mark of unity, since it is related to the event of the Christ as its foundation. The unity of the church is real in each of the churches in spite of the fact that all of them are separated from each other. The Church's unity, like its holiness, is paradoxical. "It is the divided church which is the united church" (ST3:170).

Tillich accused pre-Vatican II Catholicism of not recognizing the paradoxical nature of Christian unity when it claimed to represent in its particularity the unity of the entire Church. Because of the ambiguities of religion, the unity of the Church is necessarily paradoxical. Division of the churches is unavoidable. The ecumenical movement is a powerful expression of the Church's awareness of the predicate of unity, but, despite many successes in its struggle against the ambiguities of religion, it will never conquer them altogether. Within time and space, the ambiguities of life and hence the paradoxical nature of the unity of the churches will always remain. Their divisions, however, do not contradict their essential unity with respect to their foundation. Despite their disunity, this essential unity endures.

Because Spiritual Community serves as its dynamic essence, the Church likewise enjoys the predicate of universality. (Tillich replaced the more classic "catholic" with "universal" because "catholic" has come to be reserved exclusively for the Roman Catholic Church or for strongly sacramental churches such as the Orthodox and Anglican.) Universality is what distinguishes the Church from a sect; a sect is characterized by the attempt to protect what it considers unconditional by means of separation and particularism (GW5:16).

Because it actualizes Spiritual Community, the Church, and every church within it, is universal—both intensively and extensively. The Church's intensive or qualitative universality is its power and desire to participate in everything created under all the dimensions of life. It keeps them wide open to all that is created and good. There is nothing in nature, in man, or in history that is excluded from the life of the churches and their members. "This is the meaning of the principle of the *complexio oppositorum*, of which the Roman church is rightly proud" (ST3:170). Universality is violated, though, when one of its many possibilities is elevated to an absolute position and other elements are excluded. Because of the ambiguities of life, the Church's intensive universality is paradoxical. This was exemplified by the Reformation and Counter-Reformation, when both Catholic and Protestant churches largely cut themselves off from the universality of abundance and became mere segments of life. The intensive universality of the churches is paradoxically present in their particularity.

They may include music but exclude the visual arts; they may include work but exclude natural vitality; they may include philosophical analysis but exclude metaphysics; they may include particular styles of all cultural creations and exclude other styles. [ST3:171]

The extensive or quantitative universality of the Church consists of the validity of its foundation for all nations, social groups, races, tribes, and cultures. It follows as an immediate implication of the acceptance of Jesus as the bringer of the New Being. It was exemplified by St. Paul who brought into himself and into the churches to which he ministered elements of Jewish, Greek, Roman, and syncretistic Hellenistic tradition. In accord with its extensive universality, the Church had to separate itself from Judaism. This was necessitated by Judaism's commitment to its national law, a law which could never become the law of all nations. Universality means embracing more than even Law and Prophets. "The assembly of God, namely the Church which gathers from all nations, is the end of all religious nationalism and tribalism, even if expressed in terms of prophetic traditions" (TC, p. 39). Yet the Church's extensive universality is also subject to ambiguity.

Greek Orthodoxy identifies the universal Spiritual Community with the reception of the Christian message by Byzantine culture. Rome identifies the universal Spiritual Community with the church, ruled by canon law and its guardian, the Pope. Protestantism shows its particularity by trying to subject foreign religions and cultures to contemporary Western civilization in the name of the universal Spiritual Community. And in many cases racial, social, and national particularities prevent the churches from actualizing the predicate of universality. [ST3:171]

As with its other marks, so too the universality of the Church, both intensive and extensive, is paradoxical. It is universal, because of its foundation, in spite of its particularity.

These then are the marks of the Church: faith, love, holiness, unity, and universality. They are the signs of the Church's participation in Spiritual Community, but always within the ambiguities of religion, and therefore paradoxically, because the Church is a sociological reality as well as a theological one.

Thus far we have considered the Church only in its relation to Spiritual Community, in its essential character. To its existential character, as a visible, living entity, belong the functions of the Church. Each of these functions follows from the nature of the Church as an immediate and necessary consequence. Because they are involved in the ambiguities of life, particularly of religious life, even though their aim is to conquer them, it should come as no surprise that, like the churches which perform them, the functions of the Church are paradoxical.

THE FUNCTIONS OF THE CHURCH

The first thing to be said about the functions of the Church is that they are distinct from the institutions which serve them. Here is one of Tillich's most important distinctions, an insight pregnant with implications for ecclesiology. The functions of the Church are derived from its foundation, following as an immediate and necessary consequence of the very nature of the Church. They may be more hidden than manifest, and the forms they take may differ greatly one from another, but they are never lacking. They belong to the very essence of the Church. They can appear in different degrees of conscious care, intensity, and adequacy, but, where there is a living church, they must always be present.[7]

Not so with institutions. Institutions serve the functions of the Church and depend on them. But particular institutions are not necessary to the nature or functions of the Church. Institutions may become obsolete and be replaced by new institutional forms which grow up spontaneously and exercise the same function. Thus, for example, worship is a necessary function of the Church, but no particular institution is demanded by the nature of the Church to perform this function. Creating communal holiness within a group is a necessary function of the Church, but no particular institution is required to provide the necessary organization and leadership to create the community. The functions of the churches remain. Their institutions come and go.

> No institution, not even a priesthood or ministry, special sacraments or devotional services, follow necessarily from the nature of the church, but the functions for the sake of which these institutions have come into being do follow from it. They are never completely missing.[8]

Tillich distinguished four categories among the Church's functions— those of constitution, expansion, construction, and relation. Because they are performed by sociological groups as well as in the name of Spiritual Community, they are involved in the ambiguities of life, even though their very aim is to conquer these ambiguities. They participate in the paradox of the churches.

Constitution

The constitutive functions of the Church are related to its foundation in Spiritual Community and follow from its being the Community of the New Being. The Church receives the New Being, responds to it, and mediates it to others. It does so, however, within the polarity of tradition and reformation. Tradition is a necessary element in the life of all churches; it is the link between the foundation of the Church and every new generation which grows into it. Tradition, though, is in danger of making demonic claims unless tempered by the opposite corrective pole of reformation. All churches are tempted to invest their traditions with absolute validity, thereby elevating them into idols. Reformation is a permanent principle which struggles against this demonization and upholds the freedom of the Spirit. Reformation, if left untempered, is in danger of degenerating into merely destructive criticism. But, when reformation is united to tradition, the result is not conflict but living tension (ST3:185).

Under this polarity of tradition and reformation, the Church receives and mediates the New Being. It is the entire Church which receives and the entire Church which mediates. Anyone who receives, mediates; and one who has received did so only because the process of mediation is going on continuously in the Church through the media of Word and sacrament. "In practice mediation and reception are the same: the church is priest and prophet to itself. He who preaches preaches to himself as listener, and he who listens is a potential preacher" (ST3:189).

In receiving and mediating the New Being, the Church likewise responds to it. The response consists of affirming that which is received, a confessing of faith, and the act of turning to the source of that which is received. Faith is confessed not only in expression of creedal formulas but also in prose, poetry, symbols, and hymns. Worship is expressed personally and communally through adoration, prayer, and contemplation, whenever the Church turns to the ultimate ground of its being, the creator of Spiritual Community within it. Whatever the form of worship, though, the most important element is that of transcending the subject-object scheme of ordinary experience. Worship is not a conversation with another being called God. He who is spoken to is he who speaks through us. "It is the Spirit which speaks to the Spirit, as it is the Spirit which discerns and experiences the Spirit" (ST3:192). This is the paradox of prayer—the identity and non-identity of him who prays and Him who is prayed to.

Expansion

Related to the universal claims of Spiritual Community are the expanding functions of the Church. The universality of Spiritual Community is implied in the confession that Jesus is the Christ. Every church making that confession necessarily participates in functions of expansion, namely, missions, education, and evangelism. It does so within the polarity of verity and adaptation.

From its very beginning, in trying to be Jewish to the Jews and Greek to the Greeks, the Church operated and developed under the principle of adaptation. Just as it accommodated itself to Hellenistic culture then, it seeks to accommodate itself today—not only in addressing itself to foreign religions and cultures but, even more immediately, in addressing itself to the civilizations which it helped to form. A danger of adaptation, though, is emptying relativism. It needs to be tempered by the opposite, corrective pole of verity. Verity prevents accommodation from surrendering the content of the Christian message and ultimately disintegrating into secularism. Verity, on the other hand, needs to be tempered by adaptation if it is to be prevented from making absolute claims and throwing religious truths like stones at people's heads, heedless of whether they can accept them or not. The verity of the Christian message can be received only if adapted to the categories of the culture in which it is received (ST3:186).

Under this polarity of verity and adaptation, the Church expands by way of missions, education, and evangelism. Historically and systematically, missions are the first function of expansion of the Church, going back to Jesus' sending the disciples to the towns of Israel. Although after two thousand years of missionary activity, the majority of men are still non-Christian, yet there is no place on earth not touched somehow by Christian culture. This is not accidental. Every church in every moment of its existence is necessarily missionary. Whether voluntary or involuntary, whenever active members of the Church encounter people outside the Church, they are missionaries, even if only implicitly, simply by being Christian and thereby giving witness. Throughout the course of its history, though, the Church has established institutions for missionary activity. The purpose of these institutionalized forms of missionary activity should not be seen as a matter of saving individuals from eternal damnation. This traditionalist rationale must be rejected, since it presumes that the masses of humanity are separated from God and Spiritual Community. This does not imply that the missions are simply a means of cultural cross-fertilization, as nineteenth-century liberal theology proposed, or an attempt to unite the world religions. The missions are an activity of the Church whereby it works for the transformation of its latency into manifestation all over the world. Since the Church's universality cannot be proven theoretically, its missions provide a pragmatic proof by actualizing universality. They provide the test of the assertion that Jesus is the Christ (ST3:193).

The second function of expansion, education, continues the life of the Church from one generation to another. It started the moment the first family came to confess that Jesus is the Christ. It consists of more than simply imparting information about Church doctrine and history, more than awakening subjective piety. Education serves to introduce each new generation into the reality of Spiritual Community, into its faith and love. This happens through understanding and participation. There can be no understanding of the Church's life without participation. Yet, at the same time, to avoid becoming mechanical and compulsory, participation requires understanding (ST3:194).

Evangelism, the third function of expansion, is directed toward the estranged, indifferent members of the Church as well as toward non-Christians within a Christian culture. It operates as practical apologetics and evangelistic preaching. Practical apologetics is the art of answering questions about the nature of the Church and its faith. The most effective answer to such questions is the silent witness of faith and love within the Church, the reality of New Being within it. But apologetics breaks through the intellectual walls of skepticism and dogmatism with which the Church's critics protect themselves against invasion of the Spiritual Presence. Because these walls are constantly being built in all of us, apologetics needs to be cultivated by the churches. "Otherwise they will not grow but will diminish in extension and increasingly become a small, ineffective section within a dynamic civilization" (ST3:195).

Evangelism also operates through evangelistic preaching. It is a charismatic function which depends upon the emergence of people within the Church able to speak to those who may still belong to the realm of Christian civilization but have ceased being active members of the Church, and are now indifferent or hostile toward it. Evangelistic preaching has an impact on its listeners which ordinary preaching lacks. It is not a merely psychological or emotional impact, although this is an ever-present danger always to be kept in mind. It seeks to create a Spiritual impact, an experience of Spiritual Presence transcending the gap between the essential and the existential, conquering estrangement and creating New Being. The criterion for evangelistic preaching is not emotional excitement but the transformation of the listener, grasped through it by the Spiritual Presence (ST3:195).

Construction

The constructing functions of the Church are related to the actualization of its Spiritual potentialities. The Church builds its life by using and transcending the functions of man's life under the dimension of the human spirit. It cannot help but actualize itself by means of cultural creations, doing so in the realm of theory, the aesthetic and cognitive functions, and in the realm of praxis, the personal and communal functions. All of these constructing functions operate within the polarity of form-affirmation and form-transcendence. The Church, when engaging in aesthetic, cognitive, personal, or communal self-expression, takes material, whether styles, methods, norms, or relations, and then transcends them.

> The churches do not act as churches when they act as a political party or a law court, as a school or a philosophical movement, as patrons of artistic production or of psycho-therapeutic healing. The church shows its presence as church only if the Spirit breaks into the finite forms and drives them beyond themselves. [ST3:187]

It is a constant and dangerous tendency of form-transcendence that it be demonically repressive, that it bend authentic expressiveness, truth, humanity, and justice in order to build them into the life of the Church. For this reason, form-transcendence needs to be tempered by the opposite, corrective pole of form-affirmation. In spite of the form-transcending character of religious art, aesthetic rules must be obeyed. In spite of the form-transcending character of religious knowledge, the cognitive rules must not be broken. Form-affirmation prevents form-transcendence from becoming demonic repression, while at the same time form-transcendence prevents form-affirmation from degenerating into empty formalism, from substituting the impact of the Spiritual Presence with the self-creative acts of the human spirit (ST3:187).

The aesthetic function expresses the meaning of the Church's life through artistic symbols, poetic, musical, and visual. It takes as its content the religious symbols given by the original revelation and the traditions based upon them and attempts to express them anew in ever-changing styles. In doing so, the aesthetic function does more than provide a beautifying addition to the Church's devotional life. Artistic expressiveness has the power to stabilize and transform as well as give life to what is expressed. Expression cannot help but affect what it expresses. Because of this the churches have tried to influence and control those who produce religious art; the Eastern churches in the visual arts, the Catholic Church and Protestant churches in music and hymnal poetry.

The polarity of form-transcendence and form-affirmation in the aesthetic realm results in a tension between the two principles which control religious art: the principle of consecration, the justified request of the churches that the religious art they accept express what they confess; and the principle of honesty, the justified demand of artists that they be permitted to use the styles to which their artistic conscience drives them. Through consecration the Spiritual Presence makes itself felt in liturgical music and language, pictorial and sculptural representations, and architectural space. Honesty, however, puts a limit to the demands that can be made on an artist in the name of consecration. It militates, for example, against the repetition of styles which have lost their expressiveness for an actual situation, such as pseudo-Gothic imitation in church architecture.

Although some artistic styles may lend themselves more readily to expressing ecstatic transcendence—expressionism, for example—the Church may not force any particular style upon the autonomous development of the arts. Neither is one facet of the arts better suited to expressing transcendence than another. Protestantism's iconoclastic fear of idolatry has led it to prefer music and hymnal poetry over the visual arts, but, in Tillich's opinion, this has impoverished it. The very nature of the Spirit stands against exclusion of the visual from the experience of its presence. The lack of the visual arts in Protestant churches is "systematically untenable and practically regrettable" (ST3:201).

The cognitive function appears in the Church's life as theology. Its subject matter, like that of the aesthetic function, are the symbols given by the original revelation and the traditions based on them. But theology interprets these symbols and relates them to the general categories of knowledge, expressing them in concepts determined by the criteria of rationality. This gives rise to doctrine, established dogmas, and further theological speculation. Like the aesthetic function, so too the cognitive function is never lacking in the life of the Church. "The statement that Jesus is the Christ contains in some way the whole theological system, as the telling of a parable of Jesus contains all artistic potentialities of Christianity" (ST3:201).

The polarity between form-transcendence and form-affirmation appears in the cognitive realm too as the meditative act, which penetrates the substance of religious symbols, and the discursive act, which analyzes and describes the form in which the substance can be grasped. The meditative element of cognition is directed toward the symbols of the original revelation; the Church has a right to reject a theology in which its symbols are lacking. The discursive element is infinitely open in all directions and cannot be bound to a particular set of symbols. Discursive thought does not exclude a theological sector within itself, so long as the theological sector does not claim a control over the other sectors.

As expressionism, in the aesthetic function, lends itself more readily to transcendence than other modes of artistic expression, so too in the cognitive realm Tillich believed that existentialism lends itself to form-transcendence, that is to say, those philosophies which ask the question of human existence and of man's predicament. But here too, as in the arts, the Church may not force a particular philosophy or style of thought upon its theologians (ST3:204).

The communal function of the Church works to create and express communal holiness within a historical group, to actualize within them manifest Spiritual Community. Under the polarity of form-transcendence and form-affirmation, this becomes an effort to actualize and maintain communal holiness while preserving the principle of form-affirmation within a group, namely, justice. Communal holiness contradicts justice whenever a church commits or permits injustice in the name of holiness. Communal life in any form, not merely religious community, is in constant tension with the principle of justice and results in the ambiguities of exclusiveness, equality, leadership, and legal form. Because it participates in Spiritual Community, the Church struggles against these ambiguities, but it can never fully conquer them.

The ambiguity of inclusiveness achieves community by excluding certain persons on principle from participating in it. The Church overcomes this ambiguity by claiming to be all-inclusive beyond any social, racial, or national limitations. Although this claim is unconditional, its fulfillment certainly is not, as the racial tensions present within the churches demonstrate. On principle, the churches must reject any set of symbols which compete with their own, excluding anyone who confesses a faith other than their own. Without this exclusion a church could not exist. Yet in exercising such exclusion, a church becomes guilty of idolatrous adherence to its own historically conditioned symbols (ST3:204).

The ambiguity of inequality is overcome by the churches in their acknowledgment of the equality of all men before God. This does not entail the demand for social and political equality, but should create a desire for equality in the life of the Church. This has not been the case, however, particularly in the Church's treatment of "public sinners." The equality of all men under sin and forgiveness has been acknowledged by the Church, but by no means always practiced (ST3:206).

The ambiguity of leadership belongs to every historical community. It is one of the inescapable ambiguities of life, from which the churches are not exempt. Every system of religious hierarchies is conducive to social injustice. Even where there are no formal hierarchies such as the papacy and episcopate, there are degrees of importance in the churches, there are dominating forces and power groups. Examples of the ambiguity of leadership range from the medieval alliance of ecclesiastical and feudal hierarchies to the dependence of today's parish pastors on the economically and socially influential families in their congregations. From the Old Testament to our own day, prophets continue to rise up and attack a religious leadership which is susceptible to the ambiguity of tyranny as much as any other leadership. These continuous attacks do not injure the Church but save it from itself (ST3:207).

Like the other ambiguities which affect the communal functions of the Church, the ambiguity of legal form cannot be avoided either, so long as people exist in time and space. Every individual, even the most creative, requires given structures that embody the experience and wisdom of the past and thereby liberate him from having to make innumerable decisions on his own, structures that show him a meaningful way to act in most situations. For Tillich, nothing in human history has reality without legal form. No community can escape the sociological necessity of laws and some form of organization. This includes a community which centers itself around a set of religious symbols and traditions. As suggested earlier, an attack on organized religion is basically an attack upon the communal element of religion in the name of private or personal religion. It is self-deceptive. A man or woman can become a person only in person-to-person encounter. The language of religion is dependent upon community. Dissatisfaction with organized religion is ultimately rooted in discontent with the ambiguities of life, discontent with man's estrangement from his essential unity with God. Such dissatisfaction is really a complaint that eschatological reunion has not yet arrived (ST3:208).

The personal function of the Church works to create and express personal holiness within its members, a saintliness which makes the individual transparent to the Spiritual Presence within him. Under the polarity of form-transcendence and form-affirmation, this becomes an effort to actualize such transparency while preserving humanity at the same time. Personal saintliness has long been made dependent upon an asceticism which negates many human potentialities. As a consequence, it has often come into tension with the ideal of humanity. The question arises as to whether such tension necessarily becomes conflict.

The asceticism often characteristic of traditional Catholic monasticism, which resigns from the material in order to reach the Spiritual, contradicts the ideal of humanity. It implicitly denies the goodness of creation. Equally objectionable is the asceticism of self-discipline which developed into Puritanical repression within Protestantism and which rejects most forms of pleasure or entertainment. There is an asceticism, though, which Tillich regarded as completely in harmony with the ideal of humanity, that is, the ascetic discipline without which no creative work is possible, the conquest of that subjective self-affirmation which prevents a person from fulfilling as many human potentialities within himself as possible (ST3:210).

Relation

The relating function of the Church arises from its nature as a sociological reality as well as a manifestation of Spiritual Community. As a sociological group the Church cannot avoid entering into continuous encounters with other sociological groups, acting upon them and receiving from them. It does so by way of silent interpenetration, critical judgment, and political establishment. These correspond to the priestly, prophetic, and royal offices of the Church.

By the priestly function of silent interpenetration, the Church radiates the Spiritual Presence into all groups of the society in which it lives. The rapid secularization of modern life obscures this influence, but if the churches were to disappear suddenly, the impoverishment within society would immediately become evident. There is a mutual exchange between Church and society. In silently giving Spiritual substance to the society in which they live, the churches silently receive an influx of developing and changing cultural forms. The Church draws from society the forms in which it preserves and conveys its substance (ST3:212).

By the prophetic function of critical judgment, the Church exposes and protests against the negative qualities of the society in which it lives. Its success may be modest, but even a society which rejects prophetic criticism is transformed by it. Here too, though, the relation between Church and society is mutual. Society is justified in exercising a form of "reverse prophetism" by criticizing a communal holiness within the Church which contradicts justice or an individual saintliness which contradicts the ideal of humanity (ST3:213).

By the royal function of political establishment, the Church attempts to influence other social groups from the local to the international level in such a way that the right of the Church to exercise its priestly and prophetic functions is acknowledged by these groups. But even when they act politically, the churches do so in the name of Spiritual Community. This means that they must do so without resorting to military force, intoxicating propaganda, the arousing of religious fanaticism, or any other means which contradicts the character of Spiritual Community. Once again there is a reciprocity between Church and society, a justified political impact on the churches from the side of society. Even the churches are subject to the law of political compromise, and they must be ready not only to direct but also to be directed. The one limit on the political establishment of the churches is that their character as expressions of Spiritual Community remain manifest. This would exclude the Church's assumption of totalitarian control over all realms of life; it would exclude as well the subjection of the Church to the role of servant to the state, as if the Church were just another department or agency (ST3:214).

As is the case with its other functions, so too the relating functions of the Church operate under a polarity: in this case, one of mutuality and opposition. Insofar as they labor under the same ambiguities of life as other sociological groups, the churches share an equality of predicament, a mutuality which should preclude any arrogance, pseudo-spiritual will to power, or demonic interpretation of their paradoxical holiness as absolute holiness. On the other hand, insofar as they strive against the ambiguities of life, the churches are bound to oppose the society in which they live, to maintain a radical otherness and exercise prophetic criticism against the evils in society. A church which loses this radical otherness becomes little better than a benevolent social club. It has been the history of Catholicism to emphasize the otherness of the Church and fall prey to demonic hubris. It has been the history of Protestantism to emphasize the mutuality of the Church's predicament and fall prey to a radical secularity. The principle of "the Church against the world" properly determines the relating functions of the Church only if balanced by the principle of "the Church within the world" (ST3:216).

These then are the constitutive, expanding, constructing, and relating functions of the Church. But there remains one more aspect of Spiritual Community to be considered. Important as the marks of the Church and its functions are, neither constitute the Church as such. The Church is people, and Spiritual Community is made up of people who are grasped by the Spiritual Presence and determined by it, even though fragmentarily. Viewed from this perspective, Spiritual Community is the communion of saints. It is a community of persons transparent toward the divine ground of being, determined by faith and love, and, in that faith and love, united to God. Because Spiritual Community is the dynamic essence of all the Christian churches, this may be predicated of every active member of the Church, although paradoxically. Every individual in the Church participates in Spiritual Community. As such he is a saint, in spite of his lack of saintliness. Every member in the Church shares in the priesthood which is common to all who belong to Spiritual Community.

> Although for the sake of order and adequacy to the situation, special individuals may be called to a regular and trained performance of priestly activities, . . . their functioning as experts does not give them a higher status than is given by participation in the Spiritual Community. [ST3:217]

In considering the individual member within the Church, the question arises as to which is ontologically prior, the Church or the individual member. The objective interpretation emphasizes the predominance of the Church over the individual. It sees the individual as entering a church which always precedes him, and points to the fact that the faith which constitutes Spiritual Community is a reality which precedes the ever becoming, changing, disappearing, and reappearing acts of personal faith. The subjective interpretation of the Church, on the other hand, emphasizes the precedence of the individual over the Church. It sees the decision of the individuals to form a covenant as the act which creates a church. Tillich believed that duality between the objective and subjective interpretation of the Church was largely overcome by the concept of Spiritual Community. Even the subjective interpretation of the Church presupposes that when individuals decide to form a covenant and create a church they are already determined by the Spiritual Presence. They form the covenant as members of Spiritual Community. Spiritual Community precedes any local church and any covenant, and, from the second generation on, individuals are drawn by the atmosphere of family and society into a church whose actual presence precedes their voluntary decision to join it (ST3:218).

The moment at which an individual openly becomes a member of the manifest Church can usually be stated exactly. But it cannot be determined when an individual essentially becomes a member of Spiritual Community.

Conversion in most cases is a gradual process, going on unconsciously long before it breaks into the consciousness of faith. Conversion to a church is something quite relative. It is simply a transition from the latent stage of Spiritual Community to the manifest stage. Men are never completely without faith or healing. The Church in its missionary and evangelistic activity does not address itself to "lost sheep," since, ultimately, there are no men who are totally without God. On the contrary, the Church, as manifest Spiritual Community, builds upon latent Spiritual Community (ST3:219).

The dimensions of life were enumerated above as inorganic, organic, spiritual, and historical. The historical dimension of life presupposes the spiritual, embraces it and adds to it. Considered under the dimension of spirit, the quest for unambiguous life was answered by Tillich with the symbol of Spiritual Presence creating Spiritual Community. Considered under the dimension of history, the same quest for unambiguous life was answered with the symbol of the kingdom of God. Viewed from this vantage point, the Community of the New Being and Spiritual Community made manifest take on a different light—the kingdom of God represented in history.

4

Representing the Kingdom of God in History

One day, the Gospel tells us, the tension gradually accumulating between humanity and God will touch the limits prescribed by the possibilities of the world. And then will come the end. Then the presence of Christ, which has been silently accruing in things, will suddenly be revealed - like a flash of light from pole to pole. Breaking through all the barriers within which the veil of matter and the watertightness of souls have seemingly kept it confined, it will invade the face of the earth. . . . Such will be the consummation of the divine milieu.
Pierre Teilhard de Chardin, The Divine Milieu

Tillich did not share the optimism of Teilhard de Chardin (ST3:5). Teilhard's vision of evolutionary progress was alien to him. Tillich was too true to his Lutheran heritage, too sensitive to the pervading presence of sin, estrangement, and ambiguity in life, too convinced of the fragmentary nature of the healing that is possible in time and space. But Tillich could share Teilhard's ideas about the dimensions of life and its evolutionary processes. And, though the language and categories differed considerably, he shared Teilhard's transhistorical vision as well. Teilhard saw the consummation of history in terms of the "divine milieu." Tillich saw it in terms of penetrating and appreciating the meaning of the biblical symbol of the kingdom of God.

History became a central problem for Tillich very early in his theological career, particularly amid the chaos ensuing after World War I. He was led to the rediscovery of the concept of *kairos* as the breakthrough of eternity into time, of the kingdom of God into history.[1] This proved to be a major theme of his theology for many years, some would even say the central theme, until World War II when the *kairos* theme was supplanted by the more transhistorical concept of New Being.[2] Both as philosopher and theologian, Tillich belied the accusation of Cardinal Newman that "to be deep in history is to cease to be a Protestant."[3] Tillich was deep in history, and there is no doubt but that he remained a Protestant.

From all that has already been considered, it comes as no surprise that Tillich saw the relationship of the Church to the kingdom of God as dialectical; and, once again, it is Tillich's concept of symbol that best explains the dialectical nature of that relationship. Perhaps more explicitly than anywhere else, this is demonstrated in the propositions which Tillich distributed privately among his students before publication of his *Systematic Theology*. They were to provide the skeleton from which he developed his magnum opus. According to these propositions, the Church cannot be equated with the kingdom of God. The Church can at best represent it in history, for "the Kingdom of God is a symbolic expression of the ultimate fulfillment in which the contrast between essence and existence is overcome universally and completely."[4] The Church is a symbol of the kingdom of God in history. It points to the kingdom, participates in its reality, and serves it. But the Church cannot identify itself with the kingdom of God without demonically elevating itself into an idol.

History, Its Ambiguities, and the Quest for Its Meaning

The historical dimension of life for Tillich is a continuation of the dimension of spirit. The most embracing of all, the historical dimension presupposes the others but adds a new element to them, the note of finality. The spiritual dimension is characterized by the actualization of power and meaning; it describes the process of actualization (ST3:25, 297). The historical dimension, on the other hand, looks to fulfillment of power and meaning; it describes the direction of the process of actualization. "History exists where meaning is realized by freedom" (IH, p. 273). It unites factual occurrences with their interpretation by historical consciousness, a consciousness maintained not by individuals but by communities, by history-bearing groups (ST3:302, 308).

Life under its historical dimension, no less than under its other dimensions, is subject to ambiguity. "History, while running ahead toward its ultimate aim, continuously actualizes limited aims, and in so doing it both achieves and defeats its ultimate aim. All ambiguities of historical existence are forms of this basic ambiguity" (ST3:339). Thus there arises from this basic ambiguity the drive within history-bearing groups to build empires, to wield power and become all-inclusive. This drive is counteracted in turn by a reaction in the direction of isolation and the defense of a limited unity. Within the realm of historical creativity, that which is new struggles ambiguously with the old. Revolution seeks to produce the new, but at the expense of destroying the old. Reaction, on the other hand, seeks to preserve past creations and thereby create a barrier toward advancement. In the realm of religion, the sacred old struggles with the prophetic new. Some groups claim to represent the aim of history in terms of an actual fulfillment in the past, while others claim to represent the aim of history in terms of an anticipated fulfillment in the future (ST3:344).

Amid these ambiguities, man searches in quest of the meaning which history provides for existence. All interpretations of history attempt to provide in some way the answer to this quest. They are of two general classes, corresponding to the general types of attempt to discover the New Being: the non-historical and the historical.

The negative, non-historical interpretations see time as having no goal either within or above history. History is a circle or simply a series of happenings. It is merely the place in which individual beings live their lives, bereft of any *telos* (ST3:350–53).

The positive, historical interpretations see time as running toward an end, but one which is fulfilled in history itself. They take various forms. Progressivism is a belief in progress, as an infinite process without a definite end. The inadequacies of this interpretation were revealed by the catastrophes of the twentieth century. Utopianism is progressivism but with a definite aim, namely, the arrival at that stage of history in which the ambiguities of life are conquered. It is the force which drives the proponents of revolutionary movements to believe that some present revolutionary action will bring about the final transformation of reality. The fatal error of utopianism is that it disregards the ever-present estrangement of essence and existence and the subsequent ambiguities of life within time and space. It makes unconditional what is conditioned and inevitably results in disillusionment and cynicism. Transcendentalism sees the aim of history as a static supernatural order into which individuals enter after their death. It holds that the aim of history has been revealed in the past, and that nothing essentially new can be expected until the hereafter. The chief inadequacy of this interpretation, exemplified by traditional Catholicism and orthodox Lutheranism, is that it limits salvation to the individual. It claims ultimacy for the present ambiguous historical situation, and excludes culture as well as nature from historical transformation and healing (ST3:352–56).

For Tillich, these answers, both the exclusively non-historical and exclusively historical, are inadequate to the quest for the meaning of history. They stand in contrast to the answer provided by Christianity in the symbol of the kingdom of God. Here is a most adequate answer to the question of the meaning of history, precisely because it is as broad as the dimension of history itself. It embraces both an inner-historical and a transhistorical sense.

The Kingdom of God

It was as a member of the Religious Socialism Movement in the 1920s, when confronted by the collapse of nineteenth-century progressivism and the growth of utopian revolutionary movements, that Tillich found the non-historical interpretations of history irrelevant, the historical interpretations inadequate. He developed his own interpretation in terms of the kingdom of God as Christianity's answer to the ambiguities of history. Just as God is the depth of being, the kingdom of God is a symbol pointing to the depth and meaning of history. The kingdom of God is the ground and aim of social life, of that which we take seriously without reserve in our moral and political activities (SF, p. 65). It is the transcendent unity and fulfillment of the meaning of our existence, but with a special relationship to our historical existence here and now.[5]

> It has an inner-historical and a transhistorical side. As inner-historical, it participates in the dynamics of history; as transhistorical, it answers the questions implied in the ambiguities of the dynamics of history. In the former quality it is manifest through the Spiritual Presence; in the latter it is identical with Eternal Life. [ST3:357]

This double character renders the kingdom of God most apt as a symbol for the aim of history. Its aptness is demonstrable from its connotations. First, the kingdom of God has a political connotation, corresponding to the political character of history-bearing groups. Even after being transformed into a cosmic symbol, this political connotation was not lost. The kingdom of God is not simply to be awaited until the other side of the grave. Second, the kingdom of God has a social connotation of peace and justice. For this reason it meets legitimate utopian expectations, but adds the qualification "of God" so as to imply the impossibility of any earthly fulfillment. It is not achieved solely by man's activity. Third, the kingdom of God has a personalistic connotation. No individual is obliterated within it but rather is given eternal meaning. Finally, the kingdom of God connotes universality. It involves the fulfillment not only of individual man but of all life under all dimensions (ST3:358).

The most important characteristic of the kingdom of God, though, is its double quality of being both immanent and transcendent at the same time. Its fulfillment transcends history yet occurs through history. The kingdom of God is in our midst, and yet we pray "Thy kingdom come." Both aspects must be kept in mind if it is to be a positive and adequate answer to the question of the meaning of history. "Any one-sided interpretation deprives the symbol of its power" (ST3:359). It is normal that one side or another will predominate at various periods. Unfortunately the course of Christianity has shown that one or the other element can become overemphasized to such an extent that the other element becomes practically submerged. The result is a distortion.

Such a distortion of the symbol of the kingdom of God was for Tillich the conservative ecclesiastical interpretation of history expounded by Augustine. Although Tillich admitted to standing within the Augustinian tradition in many areas of his theology, ecclesiology was not one of them (HCT, pp. 104, 111). Augustine was forced to contend with the chiliastic revivals of the early Christian belief in the imminent coming of the kingdom of God in history, the thousand-year reign of Christ. He reacted by adopting a conservative-absolute form of interpreting history, one which looks to the past for the definitive event. Nothing essentially new can happen; history has already reached its last epoch. In this way Augustine left his mark on the next thousand years by removing the dangerous, revolutionary consequences of the idea of the thousand-year reign of Christ and assuming that it is fulfilled in the Christian Church, that is, in the sacraments and, as the administrators of the sacraments, in the Church's hierarchy.[6]

> The new is victoriously established in history, although it is still attacked by the forces of darkness. The church in its hierarchical structure represents this new reality. There are still improvements, partial defeats, and partial victories to be expected and, of course, the final catastrophe, in which the evil is destroyed and history will come to an end. But nothing really new can be expected within history. A conservative attitude toward the given is demanded. [PE, p. 36]

The upshot of such an interpretation, of course, is that radical criticism of the Church becomes impossible. "There is no historical goal before us from which the critique could be launched. The expectation of one's individual death has replaced the expectation of the end of history" (PE, p. 23). The Church is set up as absolute. The monarchy of Christ is defined as the monarchy of the Church. Forgotten completely is the fact that the Church still exists in time and space and is therefore subject to the ambiguities of existence, a prey to profanation and demonization.

> When Augustine equates the Kingdom of God with the Church and the Kingdom of Satan with the great world empires, he is partly right and partly wrong. He is right in asserting that in principle the church is the representative of the Kingdom of God; he is wrong in overlooking the fact—which as a Catholic he could scarcely help overlooking—that the demonic powers can penetrate into the church itself, both in its doctrines and institutions.[7]

Augustine's interpretation of history corresponds in principle with the inner feelings and self-consciousness of all predominantly sacramental churches. It depreciates all other historical realities, and views the history of a particular church as being supremely significant.

> Her inner conflicts and their resolution, her fights against external enemies—these are the viewpoints under which all other events are envisaged and estimated. The fight for God and against the world, which is the present historical task, means, in practice, a fight for the church, for pure doctrine, for a hierarchy. [PE, p. 36]

At the opposite pole from Augustine and his emphasis upon the kingdom of God as immanent, is the revolutionary-absolute concept of history typified by the medieval Italian abbot, Joachim of Floris. Joachim renewed the idea that the thousand-year reign of Christ is still lying ahead in the inner-historical future, a period in which both hierarchy and sacraments will come to an end and everything will be directly related to God spiritually. The Church is relative; the ideal for Christianity is not in the past but the future. Joachim's ideas had an explosive, revolutionary power. They were, in Tillich's opinion, at least indirectly responsible for the tradition of revolutionary thinking in Western Europe, a tradition which in the past inspired both the sectarian movements of the Reformation and American utopianism, a tradition which continues to inspire the socialist movement today. The thousand-year reign has given rise to dreams not only of the "Age of the Spirit" but of the "Age of Reason" and the "Classless Society" as well (HCT, pp. 175–80).

For Tillich both "conservative ecclesiasticism and revolutionary utopianism are alike idolatry" (PE, p. 38). They identify the unconditional with a given reality, whether an existing church or an expected revolution;

ultimately both prove to be erroneous extremes. There is no absolute church. Neither will there ever come an absolute kingdom of reason and justice within history. As a middle way between these two distortions of the kingdom of God, Tillich proposed his concept of *kairos*, not limited to the past but raised to a general principle of history and therefore relevant also to the present (PE, p. 36).

Tillich introduced his doctrine of *kairos* into philosophical and theological discussion after World War I in connection with the Religious Socialism Movement. He adopted it from the New Testament concept of "the fulness of time" or "the right time," used by Jesus with respect to the time of his suffering and death, used by both Jesus and John the Baptist with respect to the kingdom of God which is "at hand." In contrast to *chronos*, which in Greek refers to the measured, quantitative side of time, *kairos* refers to the qualitative side of time. It approximates the English word *timing*. *Kairos* describes a turning point in history, a "moment in which the eternal breaks into the temporal, and the temporal is prepared to receive it" (PE, p. xv). It is a time of revelation and salvation, a time of genuine progress in which there is created something that has not only temporal but also eternal meaning.

Tillich distinguished between "the *kairos*" or "the great *kairos*" and "relative *kairos*." The great *kairos* refers to "the moment at which history, in terms of a concrete situation, had matured to the point of being able to receive the breakthrough of the central manifestation of the Kingdom of God."[8] The great *kairos*, the unique *kairos*, for a Christian is the appearance of Jesus as the Christ, whereby he becomes the center of history. *Center* here does not imply quantitative measurement. Neither does it describe a particular historical moment in which the cultural process came to a point where the lines of the past were united and thereby came to determine the future. Rather it expresses a moment in history for which everything before is preparation and everything after is reception. Jesus as the Christ is the central manifestation of the kingdom of God in history (ST3:364).

> The only historical event in which the universal center of the history of revelation and salvation can be seen—not only for daring faith but also for a rational interpretation of this faith—is the event on which Christianity is based. This event is not only the center of the history of the manifestation of the Kingdom of God; it is also the only event in which the historical dimension is fully and universally affirmed. The appearance of Jesus as the Christ is the historical event in which history becomes aware of itself and its meaning. [ST3:368]

But what happened in the unique *kairos*, the appearance of Jesus as the Christ, may happen again and again in the process of time in a derived form. These are relative or secondary *kairoi*. They too are a "breakthrough" of the kingdom of God into time, an invasion of the finite by the infinite,[9] but they depend upon the great *kairos* for their criterion and source of power. These dependent *kairoi* have occurred and continue to occur in all the preparatory and receiving movements in the Church, both latent and manifest (ST3:370).

> The Old Testament manifestation of the Kingdom of God produced the direct preconditions for its final manifestation in the Christ. The maturity was reached; the time was fulfilled. This happened once in the original revelatory and saving stretch of history, but it happens again wherever the center is received as center. [ST3:365]

The process of maturing toward the central manifestation of the kingdom of God in history continues in the latent Church. But there is also a process of receiving from this central manifestation. There is "an original history of reception from the center, derived from its appearance in time and space: and this is the history of the church" (ST3:366). Within this history, the kingdom of God, like the Spiritual Presence, is never absent. But the experience of the presence of the kingdom of God as determining history is not always given. "The Kingdom of God is always present, but the experience of its history-shaking power is not. *Kairoi* are rare and the great *kairos* is unique, but together they determine the dynamics of history in its self-transcendence" (ST3:372).

The doctrine of *kairos* maintains both the transcendent and the immanent aspects of the kingdom of God, and thus avoids both ecclesiastical conservatism and revolutionary utopianism. Tillich saw it as a basis for reading the "signs of the times," for interpreting the present moment as the bearer of a demand and a promise, breaking through out of eternity into time.[10]

> The concept of the fullness of time indicates that the struggle for a new social order cannot lead to the kind of fulfillment expressed by the idea of the Kingdom of God, but that at a particular time particular tasks are demanded, as one particular aspect of the Kingdom of God becomes a demand and an expectation for us. The Kingdom of God will always remain transcendent, but it appears as a judgment on a given form of society and as a norm for a coming one. [OB, pp. 78–79]

It is readily evident from the above that the Church cannot be identified with the kingdom of God any more than it could be identified with Spiritual Community. Identification would be tantamount to idolatry. The relationship of the Church to the kingdom of God is not one of equation but rather of representation, participation, and service.

The Church and the Kingdom of God in History

Just as the historical presupposes, builds upon, and embraces the spiritual dimension of life, so too the kingdom of God presupposes, builds upon, and embraces Spiritual Community. But it embraces more than Spiritual Community. It includes not only persons able to enter into Spiritual Community but also all elements of reality, all realms of being under the perspective of their ultimate aim (ST3:375). With this univer- salist conception of the kingdom of God, it is obvious why Tillich denied so emphatically the claim that the Church "is" the kingdom of God. On the contrary, the kingdom of God is independent of any form, of any church or confession. Everywhere and at all times it breaks into the world of rela- tivities, where the absolute is experienced through relative forms. Al- though the kingdom of God is communicated through groups and churches, no group, no church can claim absoluteness. No church can be identified with the kingdom of God.

> This is not even Augustinian (and far less is it Reformation) theology. The Church represents the Kingdom in history, but the Kingdom transcends the Church not only in terms of an unambiguous perfection, but also in terms of an all-embracing universality. When Church and Kingdom are identified, Roman Catholic aspirations are not far away.[11]

As it manifests Spiritual Community, so too the Church represents the kingdom of God in history. "The Church itself is not the Kingdom of God, but it is its agent, its anticipation, its fragmentary realization."[12] Furthermore, like its manifestation of Spiritual Community, so too its representation of the kingdom is ambiguous. "In both functions the churches are paradoxical; they reveal and hide" (ST3:375). They misrepre- sent as well as represent. The root of this ambiguity is the fact that the Church exists in an "intermediate situation." The Church lives in a period between *kairoi*, between an "already" and a "not yet." It is the Church's faith that, in the person of Jesus, the center of history, the Christ, *has come*. This is implied in the sacramental element in the Church. But the Church

5 6 3 7 2

also professes that the Christ, as the end of history, *is coming.* This is implied in the prophetic element in the Church (IH, p. 264). In this way the Church answers the Jewish criticism that Jesus could not have been the Messiah, that the new eon has not yet come, that the old state of things remains unchanged and we must still wait for the coming of the Christ. Christianity agrees that we are still in a period of waiting. But, in contrast to Judaism, it asserts that the might of the demonic is broken in principle, in power and beginning, because the Christ has appeared in Jesus of Nazareth. Although the demonic, disruptive forces of history have not disappeared, and even grow stronger and more destructive with the increase of the power of the kingdom of God, nevertheless, the conquest of the old eon has taken place in the person of Jesus as the Christ. This is the conquest of New Being, shared by all those who participate in the Christ and in the Church insofar as it is based on him as its foundation (ST2:163–64).

In representing the kingdom of God in history, the Church performs a two-fold task, a two-fold service corresponding to the dual nature of the kingdom as immanent and transcendent, as "already" and "not yet." For one, the Church witnesses to the kingdom of God as present and all-embracing. The sacramental element in the Church manifests the holy as present under the multidimensional unity of life.

> To the degree in which a church emphasizes the sacramental presence of the divine, it draws the realms preceding spirit and history, the inorganic and organic universe, into itself. Strongly sacramental churches, such as the Greek Orthodox, have a profound understanding for the participation of life under all dimensions in the ultimate aim of history. The sacramental consecration of elements of all of life shows the presence of the ultimately sublime in everything and points to the unity of everything in its creative ground and its final fulfillment. It is one of the shortcomings of the churches of the "word," especially in their legalistic and exclusively personalistic form, that they exclude, along with the sacramental element, the universe outside man from consecration and fulfillment. But the Kingdom of God is not only a social symbol; it is a symbol which comprises the whole of reality. And if the churches claim to represent it, they must not reduce its meaning to one element alone. [ST3:377]

The second task of the Church is to witness and prepare for the kingdom as coming. "The churches have been and always should be communities of expectation and preparation. They should point to the nature of historical time and the aim toward which history runs" (ST3:376). This is the Church's prophetic role, in which it actively contributes to the

pursuit of the aim of history and struggles against the forces of demonization and profanation militating against this aim. Drawing upon the power of
the New Being, its foundation, the Church serves as a tool for the kingdom
of God, as a "fighting agent" of the kingdom. It is a leading force in the drive
toward the fulfillment of history (ST3:376).

> The Church, represented by the churches, is the fighting side of the King-
> dom of God in history. And the objective of the fight (priestly as well as
> prophetic) is always the creation of faith and love, that is, reunion with God
> and man and world.[13]

But not only the Church as manifest Spiritual Community serves as a
leading force in the drive toward the fulfillment of history. Latent Spiritual
Community serves this task as well. Here is a realization which calls the
churches to humility in their function as representatives of the kingdom of
God in history.

> The Kingdom of God in history is represented by those groups and individu-
> als in which the latent church is effective and through whose preparatory
> work in past and future the manifest church, and with it the Christian
> churches, could and can become vehicles of history's movement toward its
> aim. [ST3:376]

In fighting prophetically against the forces of demonization and profanation, the Church is itself subject to these same ambiguities. This means
that the Church's prophetic criticism of the demonic and profane must be
directed first and even foremost against itself. Such self-criticism leads to
reformation movements. As Tillich saw it, "it is the fact of such movements
that gives the churches the right to consider themselves vehicles of the
Kingdom of God, struggling in history, including the history of the
churches" (ST3:377). Given the estrangement of essence and existence,
these ambiguities are never really completely conquered. Church history
is rife with examples of profanation, for example, superstition in Catholic
and Orthodox churches, and secularism in Protestant churches. Church
history is filled likewise with examples of demonization, such as Catholic
claims to infallibility, the Inquisition, the tyranny of Protestant orthodoxy,
the fanaticism of many Christian sects, and the stubbornness of fundamentalism (ST3:381).

Such examples make it obvious that Church history cannot be regarded as "sacred history" or a "history of salvation." "Church history is at
no point identical with the Kingdom of God and at no point without
manifestation of the Kingdom of God" (ST3:378). Sacred history is to be

found in Church history but is not limited to it. Salvation history is both manifest and hidden by Church history. But Church history has one quality which no other history possesses. It has the ultimate criterion by which to judge itself—the New Being in Jesus as the Christ. The presence of this criterion "elevates" the Church above any other religious group, not because it is better but because it has a better criterion by which to judge itself and other groups (ST3:381).

With this criterion, the Church struggles not only against ambiguity within its own history, against profanation and demonization, it also struggles against ambiguity within world history. It judges the world while judging itself. And its struggles have not been in vain. The Church has had a transforming influence on world history. For example, the Church can point to the fact that, wherever it has been accepted, Christianity has changed person-to-person relations in a fundamental way.

> This does not mean that the consequences of this change have been practised by a majority of people or even by many people. But it does mean that whoever does not practise the new way of human relations, although aware of them, is stricken by an uneasy conscience. Perhaps one can say that the main impact of church history on world history is that it produces an uneasy conscience in those who have received the impact of the New Being but follow the way of the old being. Christian civilization is not the Kingdom of God, but it is a continuous reminder of it. [ST3:383–84]

Thus the Church, representing the kingdom of God in history, shares in the struggle of the kingdom of God against the ambiguities of history. Within the ambiguous struggle between isolationism and all-inclusiveness, Tillich believed that the Church must try to find a middle way between a militarism which believes in achieving the unity of mankind through conquest and a pacifism which overlooks or denies the necessity of power and compulsion. Within the ambiguous struggle between revolution and tradition, the Church must seek to build revolution into tradition so that, despite tensions, a creative solution in the direction of the ultimate aim of history can be found. Within the ambiguous struggle between the sacred old, which emphasizes exclusively the kingdom of God as realized in history, and the prophetic new, which emphasizes exclusively the kingdom as expected, the Church must keep alive the tension between the consciousness of presence and the expectation of the coming.

> The danger for the receptive (sacramental) churches is that they will emphasize the presence and neglect the expectation, and the danger for the activistic (prophetic) churches is that they will emphasize the expectation and

neglect the consciousness of the presence. The most important expression of this difference is the contrast between the emphasis on individual salvation in the one group and on social transformation in the other. Therefore it is a victory of the Kingdom of God in history if a sacramental church takes the principle of social transformation into its aim or if an activistic church pronounces the Spiritual Presence under all social conditions. [ST3:391]

The Church has the important but difficult task of trying to unite horizontal and vertical dimensions, to unite the social with the individual demands of religion. To concentrate exclusively on the vertical is to forsake society and its needs, ignoring the problems of justice and equality, and leaving them to movements like fascism and communism. To concentrate exclusively on the horizontal and believe in an inner-historical fulfillment of the kingdom of God "leads to metaphysical disappointment—not only psychological disappointment, but a much more fundamental disappointment, namely, disillusionment with any belief in something finite which was expected to become something infinite" (UC, pp. 123–24). It is this which determines whether a church is alive or not—the power with which it unites the vertical with the horizontal, the power with which it awaits the kingdom of God and seeks at the same time to make it real in history.[14]

The Kingdom of God beyond History

Tillich's Lutheran awareness of sin and his personal sensitivity to the ambiguities of life did not permit him to consider the possibility of an inner-historical fulfillment of the kingdom of God. Fulfillment is possible only beyond history. This is the other aspect of the kingdom of God, that which embraces the symbol of Eternal Life. "Eternal Life is identical with the Kingdom of God in its fulfillment, it is the non-fragmentary, total, and complete conquest of the ambiguities of life—and this under all dimensions of life . . ." (ST3:401). Creation is essentialized, liberated, healed. Essence and existence are reconciled. History attains its goal.

The fulfillment of the kingdom of God beyond history spells the end of ambiguity and hence the end of religion in the narrow sense of a particular sphere of man's life. Insofar as the Church necessarily connotes the ambiguities of religion, fulfillment spells the end of the Church. Spiritual Presence, Spiritual Community, and the kingdom of God become identical with Eternal Life. With Eternal Life, morality comes to an end; there is no longer an ought-to-be. There is no culture, because there is no truth that is not also done. And there is no religion. The kingdom of God beyond history is dominated by the vision of the "Heavenly Jerusalem," a city which has no temple because God is there as all in all.

> Religion is the consequence of the estrangement of man from the ground of his being and of his attempts to return to it. This return has taken place in Eternal Life, and God is everything in and to everything. The gap between the secular and the religious is overcome. [ST3:403]

The question of history and the kingdom of God brings to a close both Tillich's *Systematic Theology* and the broad outlines of his ecclesiology. Three areas still remain which deserve particular consideration. They flow as corollaries from all that has been said, particularly regarding religious symbolism. They are: Tillich's concept of Catholic substance and the Protestant principle; authority in the Church; and the relationship of the Church to the modern world.

5

Catholic Substance and the
Protestant Principle

The Chaplain: *She asked for a cross. A soldier gave her two sticks tied together.*

Ladvenu: *I took this cross from the church for her that she might see it to the last: she had only two sticks that she put into her bosom . . . When I had to snatch the cross from her sight, she looked up to heaven. And I do not believe that the heavens were empty.*

George Bernard Shaw, Saint Joan

In the preface to his *Saint Joan,* George Bernard Shaw described Joan of Arc as a "Protestant saint," as a heretic who preferred her own interpretation of God's will to that of the Church. Shaw is not alone in the opinion, and a creditable amount of argument can be marshalled in its defense. But even though persuaded of the Maid's Protestant inclinations, Shaw did not neglect to recognize her Catholicism as well, particularly her very Catholic need when at the stake to have a cross. She could not bear to face the flames until some tangible sign of faith and grace was thrust into her hands. The symbol gave her strength, even though it was no more than two sticks tied together.

Shaw's portrayal of Joan of Arc as a Protestant saint with Catholic needs strikes a sympathetic chord with Tillich's theology of the Church. The convergence of Catholic and Protestant principles posed no contradiction for Tillich. On the contrary, he was convinced that the priestly and the prophetic, that word and sacrament are more than simply complementary modes of communicating Spiritual Presence within the Church. Tillich regarded them as indispensable to each other. "The Spiritual Presence is effective through the Word and the sacraments. Upon these the church is founded and their administration makes the church the church" (ST3:120). Furthermore, the priestly element is more fundamental to religion than the prophetic. Sacraments are older than the word, although the word is implicit in the silent sacramental material (ST3:121).

In the discussion of religious symbolism, it was pointed out how strongly Tillich stressed the necessity of religious symbols as the means by which the transcendent infinite finds finite human expression. Yet, to avoid becoming idolatrous, a symbol must negate itself in its concreteness and point beyond itself. Here in essence is the raw material which Tillich developed into his theology of the priestly and prophetic elements of the Church, Catholic substance and the Protestant principle.

Catholic Substance

Catholic substance is Tillich's designation of the sacramental as a medium of the Spiritual Presence (ST3:122). From the very beginning it has presented difficulties for Protestantism as no other question. And no other question within Protestantism has received such uncertain answers.

> The whole protest of the Reformation was in fundamental opposition to the sacramental system of Catholicism. Indeed, all sides of the Protestant criticism may be interpreted as an attack of the Protestant spirit upon the Catholic tendency to a sacramental objectivation and demonization of Christianity. [PE, p. 94]

Tillich regarded the sacraments as perhaps the most important feature of the Church in the Middle Ages. He agreed with Ernst Troeltsch that the Catholic Church is the greatest sacramental institution in all of world history (HCT, p. 154). In Tillich's estimation, though, the *ex opere operato* notion of sacraments identifies a finite reality with the divine to such an extent that the sacraments no longer serve as pointers to the divine but as powers which contain the divine in themselves (HCT, pp. 147–48, 157). Moreover, the sacraments constitute the basis for an authoritarian system of church hierarchy, since only the hierarchy can administer the sacraments, without regard to their intellectual and moral qualifications.[1]

The Protestant Reformation, to Tillich's mind, rightly objected to the superstitious use of sacraments, and emphasized the prophetic word. In doing so, however, it wrongly permitted its sacramental foundation to erode, almost to the verge of disappearance. The sacraments are dying within Protestantism, Tillich wrote in 1950. Protestant criticism has led to the reduction of the sacraments to two, and in some areas even these have lost their significance. They are being maintained only by the power of custom. Systematically it is difficult for Protestants to give a theological reason for sacraments.[2]

Tillich viewed this situation with alarm. "The decrease in sacramental thinking and feeling in the churches of the Reformation and in the American denominations is appalling" (PE, p. xix). The reason for his alarm was the conviction that this decrease in sacramental thinking endangers the very basis of Protestantism and its prophetic protest. The sacramental is the one essential element of every religion. A complete disappearance of it would lead to the disappearance of cult and finally to the dissolution of the visible Church itself.[3] The weakening of the sacramental power within Protestantism is responsible, at least partly, for the intellectualization of the Christian message and for the phenomenal growth of secularism in Protestant countries. It constitutes a challenge on which the very destiny of Protestantism depends (PE, pp. xix, 112).

Tillich did not find any particular sacrament or sacraments essential to the Church, but the sacramental element in general. Sacraments should not be restricted to two or seven. Number does not matter. What does matter is the universal concept of sacrament, the experienced presence of the holy (HCT, pp. 155–56). Tillich defined sacrament along the broadest lines. "The sacramental is nothing else than some reality becoming the bearer of the Holy in a special way and under special circumstances" (TC, p. 64).

> The largest sense of the term denotes everything in which the Spiritual Presence has been experienced; in a narrower sense, it denotes particular objects and acts in which a Spiritual community experiences the Spiritual Presence; and in the narrowest sense, it merely refers to some "great" sacraments in the performance of which the Spiritual Community actualizes itself. [ST3:121]

A sacrament is any object or event in which the transcendent is perceived to be present, in which the infinite is present to the finite. If this larger sense is disregarded, sacraments in the narrower sense lose their significance.[4] He saw that significance precisely in pointing to the universal sacramental principle.

Their holiness is a representation of what essentially is possible in everything and in every place. The bread of the sacrament stands for all bread and ultimately for all nature. This bread in itself is not an object of sacramental experience but that for which it stands. In Protestantism every sacrament has representative character, pointing to the universality of the sacramental principle. [PE, p. 111]

Coming under the genus of religious symbols, the sacraments fulfill the functions and follow the laws of religious symbols. The most important aspect to be remembered about them is that they are more than mere signs which point to something beyond themselves. Because they are symbols and not mere signs, they are intrinsically related to that which they express. They participate in what they symbolize and thereby become bearers of the Spirit (ST3:123). As symbols and media of the Spirit, the sacraments unite two essential factors: a relationship to nature and a participation in salvation history.

In the sacraments, nature participates in the process of salvation.[5] "The Spirit 'uses' the powers of being in nature in order to 'enter' man's spirit" (ST3:123). Although in principle anything may convey the Spiritual Presence, certain elements such as water, bread, wine, fire, and oil have certain inherent qualities which make them not only adequate to their symbolic function but even irreplaceable. Water, for example, has a power which makes it especially apt to become sacramental material, in that it symbolizes both the origin of life and the return to that origin in death (PE, p. 104). The twentieth-century rediscovery of the unconscious by psychology permits us to realize anew the necessity of using the powers of nature in order to mediate the Spirit to the total man. Words may appeal to our intellect and move our will, but the sacramental grasps our unconscious as well as our conscious being. It is a neglect of this aspect of the sacraments within Protestantism which has led to either an intellectualization or a moralization of the Spiritual Presence (ST3:122).

But the intrinsic power of nature alone does not suffice to constitute a sacrament. A purely natural sacrament is unacceptable for a Christian, because nature in itself is ambiguous. It is subject to demonization (PE, p. 110). This necessitates the other essential factor of the sacraments, their participation in salvation history. Only insofar as nature is related to the events of the history of salvation is it liberated from the demonic and made capable of becoming sacramental. Every sacramental reality within Christianity must be related to the New Being as it appeared in Jesus as the Christ. There is reason, therefore, to regard Jesus as the *Ursakrament*, the fundamental Sacrament of Christianity and the source of all sacramentalism in the Church. No sacrament can be understood apart from him.[6]

To Tillich's mind, however, the relationship of the sacraments to the history of salvation does not imply that any particular sacrament can claim a divine prescription as the basis for its right to existence. "The Christ has not come to give new ritual laws. He is the end of law" (ST3:124). Grace is not bound to any finite form, not even to a religious form (GW7:61). Tillich made this most explicit in the unpublished theses distributed for his class lectures: "The freedom of the Church from and for every sacramental action is a result of the fact that the new being in Christ has repealed the Ritual Law and stands in accord with the creative power of the divine Spirit in the Church."[7]

Tillich's important distinction between functions in the Church and the institutions which serve these functions needs to be kept in mind here (cf. Chap. 3). No institutions, and therefore no special sacraments or devotional services, follow necessarily from the nature of the Church. The functions of receiving and mediating Spiritual Presence and the function of worship follow from the nature of the Church, but the same cannot be said for any particular sacrament or form of worship (ST3:189).

> The concrete organization of the sacramental symbols is a matter of tradition and a problem of determining their adequacy to the present situation. It cannot be derived systematically from the nature of the New Being in Jesus as the Christ.[8]

If this be so, the question necessarily arises: is the Church bound to any definite sacramental media? Yes, Tillich answered, insofar as all sacramental acts must be subject to the criterion of the New Being in Jesus as the Christ and must somehow refer to the historical and doctrinal symbols which have emerged within Christianity, to the crucifixion, for example, or to eternal life. But the answer is no, insofar as the Church is free within these limits to appropriate new sacramental symbols, so long as they are adequate and possess symbolic power (ST3:123).

Remember that religious symbols for Tillich, and therefore individual sacraments as well, are quite capable of dying, of losing their ability to grasp the human spirit. Tradition and not divine institution constitutes the basis for any individual sacrament.

> The definitive selection of great sacraments from the large number of sacramental possibilities depends on tradition, evaluation of importance, and criticism of abuses. However, the decisive question is whether they possess

and are able to preserve their power of mediating the Spiritual Presence. For example, if a large number of the Spiritual Community's serious members are no longer grasped by certain sacramental acts, however old they are and however solemn their performance, it must be asked whether a sacrament has lost its sacramental power. [ST3:124]

As he emphasized New Being and had little to say about Jesus, so Tillich emphasized the sacraments in general but neglected them in particular. He sought to justify his neglect of the individual sacraments in the *Systematic Theology* with the excuse that it is a system and not a summa (ST3:5). His most extensive treatment of Baptism and the Eucharist were little more than parenthetical attempts to exemplify the realistic interpretation of the sacraments, which he offered as an alternative, to merely metaphoric or ritualistic interpretations.[9]

Tillich did not neglect, though, to make strong recommendations to Protestant churches regarding sacraments. Although they have been disappearing within Protestantism, a renaissance of the sacraments is not beyond the range of possibility. "But the one thing needful is that the whole Protestant attitude toward the sacraments be changed" (PE, pp. 111–12). This does not imply that Protestantism must revert to a "magical sacramentalism," which separates the sacramental object from an active faith turning toward God. "Apart from the correlation between faith and sacrament, there can be no sacrament" (PE, p. 110). But it does mean that Protestant worship, which has traditionally centered around the preaching of the word, should not limit the word merely to that which is spoken or written. The word of God is his self-communication, and this can occur through actions, gestures, and forms as well as through sounds and syllables (PE, p. 218).

> The usual opposition between word and sacrament is no longer tenable. We must recognize the inadequacy of "Protestant personalism" and overcome the tendency to focus attention on the so-called "personality" of Jesus instead of on the new being that he expresses in his person. We must consider the unconscious and subconscious levels of our existence so that our whole being may be grasped and shattered and given a new direction. Otherwise these levels will remain in a state of religious atrophy. The personality will become intellectualistic and will lose touch with its own vital basis. [PE, p. 112]

For all his insistence upon the importance of preserving the sacramental element within the Church, Tillich also maintained that "every sacrament is in danger of becoming demonic" (ST3:122). There is the ever-present danger that ritual actions, which represent the holy, will claim holiness for themselves. Because of their beauty or sacred tradition, certain expressions of grace tend to become identified with grace itself (PE, pp. 111, 218). To counteract this tendency to distort the sacramental element within the Church, Catholic substance needs to be maintained in polar tension with the Protestant principle.

The Protestant Principle

To overestimate the importance of the Protestant principle to Tillich's theology is practically impossible. It runs through his writing like a leit motif, giving it the coherence and unity that has become a hallmark of his thought. Tillich has been credited with making all of Protestantism luminous, successfully reducing it to one, essential, far-reaching principle.[10] Because of this principle of unification, one not always friendly critic of Tillich has gone so far as to call him "the liberator of American Protestantism."[11]

It was from his teacher, Martin Kähler, that Tillich first received an insight into the existential power and all-embracing character of the Pauline-Lutheran doctrine of justification. This new awareness of its relevance led Tillich to drive the doctrine of justification to further conclusions and thereby develop it into the Protestant principle, a decisive criterion for all theological interpretation.

> On the one hand, the doctrine of justification denies every human claim before God and every identification of God and man. On the other hand, it declares that the estrangement of human existence, its guilt and despair, are overcome through the paradoxical judgment that before God the sinner is just.[12]

The Protestant principle can be described as "the divine and human protest against any absolute claim made for a relative reality . . . the judge of every religious and cultural reality" (PE, p. 163).

> It is the guardian against the attempts of the finite and conditional to usurp the place of the unconditional in thinking and acting. It is the prophetic judgment against religious pride, ecclesiastical arrogance, and secular self-sufficiency and their destructive consequences. [PE, p. 163]

One can see why this principle of radical prophetic criticism deserves to be called Protestant; it draws from and unites both the *sola fide, sola gratia* of Luther and the *soli Deo gloria* of Calvin.

The Protestant principle is grace as well as judgment. God affirms man in spite of his sinfulness. Tillich regarded the Lutheran concept of justification as the fundamental principle of the Reformation. It maintains that, when it comes to forgiveness, all we can do is receive; our act of turning to God and receiving his grace is unambiguously a receptive act.[13] Tillich was not convinced that justification was as central to St. Paul's theology as it was to Luther's. He saw it as the third of three main centers that make up a triangle in St. Paul's thought: his consciousness of realized eschatology; his doctrine of the Spirit; and justification by grace through faith, which constituted Paul's critical defense against legalism (HCT, pp. 230–31).

In the spirit of John Calvin, the Protestant principle insists upon the radical transcendence of God, the "infinite qualitative distinction," as Kierkegaard put it, between God and man, time and eternity, the finite and the infinite. The prophetic tradition is keenly aware of this distinction, of the exclusively unconditional character of the unconditioned, traditionally designated as the "majesty of God." It demands that the priestly element in religion, that all symbols of the unconditional, be recognized as conditional in themselves, as momentary, evanescent, and self-negating, expressing the presence of the divine not only by what they are but even more by what they are not.[14]

Tillich viewed the early Protestant reformers as being in the tradition of the Old Testament prophets. "Propheticism is first of all attack against the distortions of the priestly religion, and the heart of every theological distortion is always the idea of God."[15] "The divinity of the Divine, the ultimacy of the Ultimate, the unconditional character of the Unconditioned. That is the point where the Reformation starts."[16] Tillich shared Calvin's conviction that the human mind is a "perpetual manufacturer of idols," insofar as it makes absolute claims for the relative and demands unconditioned loyalty to the conditioned. In opposition to this idolatrous tendency, Tillich appealed to the Protestant principle as an embodiment of the prohibition of the first commandment against idols, a defense of the godliness of God.[17]

The Protestant principle also reflects the influence of Classicism upon Tillich. Like Goethe, Tillich was convinced that the reason of man and the reason of Divinity are very different, and there is nothing sadder to see than the unreconciled striving after absolutes within this thoroughly conditioned world.[18] Tillich also shared Albrecht Ritschl's neo-Kantianism, at least to the extent that he saw Kant as very much the philosopher of Protestantism in his insistence that we are finite and bound to accept our finitude.[19] The struggle and, even more, the failure of Ernst Troeltsch and his generation to find absolutes within history also convinced Tillich of the correctness of the Protestant principle. In Tillich's estimation, Troeltsch's failure to find absolutes amid the relativities of history was more significant and more productive than any apparent success of those who create idols and thereby permit themselves false and at best painfully fragile absolutes.[20]

The Protestant principle is pervasive throughout Tillich's theology; although expressly treated here for the first time, it has appeared in different guises from the very beginning of this study. Its roots are sunk into the very foundations of Tillich's theology and his view of God as the *mysterium tremendum et fascinosum* (PE, p. 163). God is not *a* being alongside other beings, but rather the ground and abyss of all being and meaning; as a result, God cannot be contained in or confined to any finite form. The Protestant principle takes cognizance of this distance between the finite and infinite by reserving ultimacy to God alone.

The Protestant principle proceeds likewise as a consequence of the human predicament, an outcome of man's estrangement from his true being and his subjection to the ambiguities of life (TC, p. 68). It follows, therefore, that the cross constitutes the foremost symbol of the Protestant principle, in that it "expresses not only the ultimate but also its own lack of ultimacy" (DF, p. 97). When Jesus sacrificed himself as Jesus to himself as the Christ, the cross became the criterion which judges the Church, its dogmas, symbols, sacraments, and members. "No finite being can attain the infinite without being broken as He who represented the world, and its wisdom and its power, was broken on the cross" (NB, p. 112).

Considered in reference to faith, the Protestant principle declares that the estrangement between God and man is overcome solely on the basis of God's grace without any good works on man's part, either moral or intellectual. Not only the sinner but also the doubter is justified by faith, so long as he takes his doubt seriously, for faith is involved in every doubt which is taken seriously. One cannot reach God by right thinking, by submitting the intellect to the Bible or to the doctrine of the Church. Works of the intellect, like works of piety and morality, follow from union with God but cannot establish it (PE, pp. x–xi).

Applied to the Church, the Protestant principle means *Ecclesia semper reformanda*. "No human group can claim a divine dignity for its moral achievements, for its sacramental power, for its sanctity, or for its doctrine" (PE, p. 226). "The Protestant principle denies that there can be any human institution, including a church with its doctrines and ethical demands, above the dynamics of history."[21]

It implies that there cannot be a sacred system, ecclesiastical or political; that there cannot be a sacred hierarchy with absolute authority; and that there cannot be a truth in human minds which is divine truth in itself. Consequently, the prophetic spirit must always criticize, attack, and condemn sacred authorities, doctrines and morals. [PE, p. 226]

One can see in the light of the Protestant principle why Tillich did not permit any unqualified identification of the Church with the kingdom of God or with the Pauline concept of the Body of Christ. One also sees how the Protestant principle is related to Tillich's doctrine of *kairos* and its protest against the absolute claims of either ecclesiastical conservation or revolutionary utopianism (PE, p. 226). The Protestant principle judges as demonic any attempt to identify a sacrament or religious symbol with that toward which it points and in whose power it participates. It raises a prophetic protest against any claim to absolute truth or authority within the Church, or, for that matter, any absolute law. Laws, including the ten commandments, provide us with the wisdom of the ages; but, because they are necessarily interpreted and applied by individuals to specific instances, they cannot bind absolutely. Human reason is always open to error and distortion. For this reason, laws "guide the conscience in concrete situations, but none of them, taken as law, has absolute validity."[22] Armed with the Protestant principle, Christians have the task to protest and resist the idolatry of raising ultimate claims for any civilization or any Church (EN, pp. 122–23).

In view of the radicalness of the Protestant principle and the ruthlessness with which Tillich wielded it, especially in regard to the Church, he might seem at first glance to be hypercritical if not destructively negative. Tillich recognized clearly, though, that there is no "absolute" negation or protest. "Negation, if it lives, is involved in affirmation; and protest, if it lives, is involved in form" (PE, p. 206). The Protestant principle is a corrective and not in itself a constructive principle. Thus Tillich disagreed with those movements which deny that the Spirit requires mediation and hold that the Spirit speaks through the inner word. Even the inner word must first come from outside. Mediation is necessary (ST3:127). Worship, preaching, and instruction presupposes a substance. "No church can be founded on a protest" (RS, p. 192). The no of the Protestant principle must be conjoined to the yes of Catholic substance, for without the creativity of Catholic substance, the Protestant principle would fall into nothingness. Earlier in his writings, Tillich called this union of protest and creation "the Gestalt of grace" (PE, 207).

Tillich used the German word *Gestalt* to refer to "the total structure of a living reality" (PE, p. 206n1). A Gestalt of grace embraces both itself and the protest against itself, both form and the negation of form. Tillich distinguished the Gestalt of grace from Roman Catholic teaching, which he believed objectifies and paves the way for sacred hierarchies, infallible authorities, and automatic sacraments. The key concept here is that of transparency, or better, translucency. "A Gestalt of grace is a 'transparent' Gestalt. Something shines through it which is more than it. . . . The saint is a saint, not because he is 'good', but" because he is transparent for something that is more than he himself is" (PE, p. 212). Tillich contrasted the transparency of a Gestalt of grace to what he described as the Catholic teaching of transmutation.

> In the Catholic view the finite form is transmuted into a divine form; the human in Christ is received in his divine nature (the monophysitic trend in all Catholic Christology); the historical relativity of the Church is sanctified by its divine character (the exclusiveness of the Roman church); the material of the sacrament is as such filled with grace (the dogma of transsubstantiation). . . . Protestantism asserts that grace appears *through* a living Gestalt which remains in itself what it is. The divine appears *through* the humanity of the Christ, *through* the historical weakness of the church, *through* the finite material of the sacrament. The divine appears through the finite realities as their transcendent meaning. Forms of grace are finite forms, pointing beyond themselves. . . . The Protestant protest prohibits the appearance of grace through finite forms from becoming an identification of grace with finite forms. [PE, p. 211–12]

The Gestalt of grace is present, but not tangible, (*Gegenwart* but not *Gegenstand*), perceptible only to the eyes of faith (GW7:41). As such, the Church is a Gestalt of grace, not a "transubstantiated" community but a "transparent" one, a bearer of grace without being identified with it. The Protestant principle does not admit any identification of grace with a visible reality, not even the Church in its visibility. The Church in its spiritual quality, though, is an object of faith, a Gestalt of grace. This includes the latent Church, since the Church as a Gestalt of grace is older and larger than the manifest Christian churches (PE, pp. xvii, 213). Grace is not bound to any finite form, not even to a religious form. Although it is the Church's nature to be transparent to the unconditioned, it is quite capable of being false to that nature. Furthermore, a secular group or movement may likewise be called to become a bearer of grace, although latently (PE, p. 213).

Catholic substance and the Protestant principle find their concrete historical embodiment in the Catholic and Protestant churches. A complete picture of Tillich's theology of the Church requires consideration of his thought in regard to Catholicism, Protestantism, and their contemporary confrontation with each other in ecumenical encounter.

Catholicism

Because of the all-inclusiveness and broad synthesis of his system, above all in drawing together Catholic substance with the Protestant principle, Tillich has been called an ecumenical theologian par excellence.[23] This is not to imply, though, that he always displayed an irenic attitude, at least not in regard to Roman Catholicism.[24] Tillich wrote for the most part before the ecumenical "thaw" between Catholics and Protestants, so he may be accused of failing more than once to display the tendency, which he praised in American theology, to interpret one's adversary *in meliorem partem* (PPT, p. 97). Tillich admitted that he once had seriously entertained the idea of becoming a Catholic, but that was in 1933, before German Protestantism woke up to the true nature of Nazism; being a Christian in Germany then seemed to offer no alternative other than Catholicism or "nationalist paganism in Protestant dress" (OB, p. 39). He was grateful to have been spared making the choice. Catholicism, as Tillich saw it, is characterized by priesthood, sacrament, and law, all combining into an authoritarianism which he viewed as no less than demonic (HCT, p. 218).

Tillich was persuaded that the early centuries of Church history offer no support to a Protestant in criticizing the Catholic Church. With Harnack, he saw in the Church's defense against the onslaughts of Gnosticism the development of all the formative principles of later Catholicism—the closing of the canon, the defining of apostolic tradition, the replacement of charism with office, the rise of the episcopate (HCT, pp. 39, 49). He believed it important for Protestants to realize how early the fundamentals of Catholicism were present in the Church: "Whatever we say against the Roman Church, we should not forget that the early developments in Christianity led this way" (HCT, p. 101). The age of the Apostolic Fathers preserved what was needed for the life of the young Christian congregations, even though, like any second generation, the period lost some of the spiritual power which characterized the preceding era of the apostles (HCT, pp. 17–18). Even the rise of the monarchical episcopate was a natural development.

117

If the authority which guarantees truth is embodied in human beings, it is almost unavoidable that there will be a tendency to narrow down upon one individual who holds the final decision. In Clement of Rome we already find traces of the idea of apostolic succession, that is, that the bishop represents the apostles. This shows clearly how early the problem of authority became decisive in the church and started a trend toward its fuller development in the Roman Church. [HCT, p. 19]

Recognition of the earliness of Catholicism, however, in no way implies an acceptance of its principles.

The so-called agreement of the first five centuries is by no means an agreement with the principles of the Reformation. Therefore, if someone says that we should unite by going back to the development which runs from Irenaeus to Dionysius the Areopagite, I would say that he had better become a Catholic, because Protestantism cannot do that. In these first centuries there are many elements which Protestantism cannot accept. [HCT, p. 50]

The most unacceptable aspect of the Catholic Church for Tillich was its claim to absolute validity and ultimate truth; the Catholic Church identified itself with Spiritual Community, with the thousand-year reign of Christ, with the kingdom of God "from the point of view of the sacramental graces present in the hierarchy" (HCT, p. 149).

This makes it impossible to criticize the Roman church in essentials—in doctrine, ethics, hierarchical organization, and so forth. Since the Roman church identifies its historical existence with the Spiritual Community, every attack on it (often even on non-essentials) is felt as an attack on the Spiritual Community and consequently on the Spirit itself. This is one of the main roots of both hierarchical arrogance and, in opposition to it, of anti-ecclesiastical and anti-hierarchical movements. [ST3:167]

This claim was, to Tillich's mind, demonic; it leads Catholicism to regard itself as the criterion for every other church (GW3:108). It also leads to Romanism, the heritage of a universal monarchy which Catholicism inherited from the Roman Empire. "If we are tempted to evaluate the Roman Church more highly than we should, we ought to ask ourselves: how many Roman elements are in it, and to what extent are they valid for us in our culture" (HCT, p. 2). For Tillich, as for Harnack, Catholicism is very much the Church of "empire."

The demonic claim to being absolute was the chief criticism Tillich had of Catholicism and in many ways, the source of all his other objections. He criticized the abuse of the figure of Mary in much popular Catholic piety. He attacked Catholic legalism, the unimpeachability of the papacy, and the attitude which placed tradition on the same par as Scripture and then equated tradition with the latest decision from the Vatican. He attacked the authoritarianism exemplified by the encyclical *Humani Generis* (1950), when it presumed the competence to declare existentialism unsound as a philosophy.[25]

Sometimes Tillich's criticism of Catholicism transgressed historical accuracy, to say nothing of moderation in expression. Such, for example, are his accusations that the practice of indulgences in the sixteenth century constituted a "marketing of eternal life," or that the papacy came so to dominate the Church that it virtually abolished the authority of the other bishops. A similar exaggeration was his claim that the condemnation of Jansenism served to drive out the best in Catholic tradition, namely, St. Augustine's doctrine of grace, faith, and love; that any Catholic who adopted Augustianian principles was in danger of excommunication (HCT, pp. 72, 220–23, 232). The Jesuits, in particular, came in for Tillich's ire, in that "they turned the consciences of the Catholic princes toward all the cruelties of the Counter-Reformation," were "completely devoted to the power of the church," undercut the authority of the bishops, and, by fostering the principle of moral probabilism, are responsible for "a tremendous ethical relativism, laxity, and chaos" (HCT, pp. 220–23).

Catholicism and its theology fared no better at Tillich's hands when he compared them to Protestantism. Lutheranism, in his estimation, sees religion as a personal relationship with God, whereas Catholicism "is a system of divine-human management, represented and actualized by ecclesiastical management" (HCT, p. 228). Grace for a Protestant is ethical, personal community with God, whereas, for a Catholic, it is the transmission of divine substance. Catholicism creates a religion of the masses and a supra-personal mysticism, whereas Protestantism creates individual personalities and personal community.[26] Protestantism regards sin as separation from God; Catholicism emphasizes sins as individual acts. Protestantism sees the secular world as immediate to God; Catholicism sees the secular world as needing mediation through supernatural substance which is present in the hierarchy and its sacramental activities (HCT, pp. 193, 212–13).

Tillich was not always negative in his critique of Catholicism. He defended the Middle Ages against the charge that they were dark ages of terrible superstition, and considered them instead as a time of spiritual substance, both intellectual and religious, a spiritual substance which Protestantism has lost to a great extent.

> The Catholic Church... has manifestly been able to preserve a genuine substance that continues to exist, although it is encased within an ever hardening crust. But whenever the hardness and crust are broken through and the substance becomes visible, it exercises a peculiar fascination; then we see what was once the life-substance and inheritance of us all and what we have now lost, and a deep yearning awakens in us for the departed youth of our culture. [27]

Tillich admired Catholicism for its *complexio oppositorum*, particularly as it existed up to the time of the Council of Trent. He acknowledged sympathetically that it was a defensive attitude against Protestantism and Humanism which caused the Catholic Church to lose much of its openness and to narrow down, even as Protestantism did in its period of orthodoxy. He held that Catholicism "should be judged first in its glory as exemplified by the early and medieval church, and only secondly in its narrowness as revealed since the Council of Trent."[28]

The *aggiornamento* inaugurated by Pope John, together with the Second Vatican Council, came as a surprise to Tillich. It served to ameliorate considerably his attitude toward the Catholic Church.

> Pope John's recognition of this [the narrowness of the Counter-Reformation] was a really great experience for me after seventy-six years. He realized that this narrowness cannot be maintained, or the Catholic church would become completely irrelevant. [UC, p. 93]

Although he adopted a "wait and see" attitude toward the Second Vatican Council, Tillich was much heartened by the Catholic view expressed at that time, that, even though doctrines are unchangeable, their interpretation can change (ST3:168). He was amazed to see the Catholic Church apply to itself the principle of *ecclesia semper reformanda* and went so far as to admit that the Catholic Church appears more open to reform today than the churches of the Reformation (ST3:4). Tillich acknowledged that the power of the papacy could be used for good and expressed a feeling both of admiration and of kinship for Pope John:

> He was able to criticize the church, his own church, and could declare publicly how the church had become irrelevant for many people in our time. He has shown us that the spirit of prophetism which can criticize the religious group in which the prophet lives has not completely died out in the Roman Church. It is still there and surprisingly has been voiced from the top of the hierarchy from where one would least expect it. The other thing that he has done is to make it possible to reach out to those outside the churches, not only to the "separated brethren" outside the Roman Catholic Church, but to the

secularists and even to those who are enemies of the church and Christianity. On the basis of my own religious socialist past I feel a kinship with him. He shares the prophetic self-criticism which is open to the truth which has been forgotten in the church and which is now represented against the church by the secular and the anti-religious movements of our time.[29]

The efforts of the Catholic Church to renew itself came, unfortunately, toward the end of Tillich's life. Before these efforts at renewal, however, and the more positive attitudes they awoke in him, Tillich could not help but view the conversion of a Protestant to Catholicism as anything other than a falling or slipping back, a relapse into the security of an authoritarian system (ST3:176). It was just such a relapse that he feared, when he analyzed the Protestantism of his day. He did not hesitate to ask if ours was not indeed the end of the Protestant era.

Protestantism

As Catholic substance is expressed by Roman, Byzantine, and Anglo-Catholic churches, so are the Protestant churches the special historical embodiment of the Protestant principle. The two, however, are not to be identified. The Protestant principle enjoys a universal validity which transcends Protestantism. It was announced in the Old Testament by the prophets, and was singularly manifested by the New Testament in its picture of Jesus as the Christ. It was established as the sole foundation of the churches of the Reformation in their protest against a Catholicism that had, to Tillich's mind, become demonic in its claim to absolute authority. But, although the Protestant principle is meant to be a "living, moving, restless power" within them, the Protestant churches too have proven unfaithful to it. Protestantism has not always remained true to its prophetic protest. After its attack against the embodiment of God in the institutions of the Catholic Church, God became once again enclosed in institutions and doctrines—more in institutions with Calvinism, more in doctrines with Lutheranism. In the period of Protestant orthodoxy, the prophetic witness about the divinity of the Divine became a matter of disposition and organization. Thus history demonstrates that the Protestant principle not only informs and inspires the Protestant churches, but judges them as well, even as it judges every religious and cultural reality.[30]

As pointed out above, no church can be founded merely upon a protest. Yet Protestantism became a church. Here is the inner contradiction that constitutes at once the greatness and the tragedy of Protestantism.

121

> The inner dilemma of Protestantism lies in this, that it must protest against every religious or cultural realization which seeks to be intrinsically valid, but that it needs such realization if it is to be able to make its protest in any meaningful way. [RS, p. 192]

Tillich characterized the Protestant element within Protestantism as the radical proclamation of "the human boundary-situation," the ultimate threat confronting human existence (PE, pp. 195–202). In its awareness of the human boundary-situation, Protestantism reaffirms man's autonomy and refuses the temptation of religious safety. It recognizes that existence cannot in any way be made secure—not through intellectual or spiritual activity, not through sacraments, mysticism, asceticism, right belief, piety, or any aspect belonging to the mundane substance of religion. The serious acceptance of the boundary-situation was for Tillich the primary differentiating factor between Protestantism and those churches in which Catholic substance predominates.

> Mystical-sacramental religion easily gives the impression of lacking seriousness, of presuming to possess a human guaranty against the ultimate threat to everything human. The lesser importance which the Protestant attributes to the church, to the service of worship, and to the religious sphere in general is at bottom bound up with this awareness of living on the boundary.... Because religion and the church are in themselves no guaranty to the Protestant and must not be allowed to become such, he confronts them with the same independence with which he confronts every human possibility, not with the proud independence of one who makes himself superior to everything else but rather with the independence of one who finds himself in a situation in which he shares the lot of everything human to be subject to the ultimate threat of not-being.... On this plane alone is the opposition between the two Christian confessions to be understood, not on the basis of the clash between subjectivism and ecclesiastical allegiance. The choice lies between either the radical acceptance of the boundary-situation or the attempt by means of church and sacrament to secure man against the unconditional threat.[31]

This awareness of the human boundary-situation gives Protestantism its unique relationship to secularism, a secularism which Tillich regarded not as irreligion but rather as the expression of latent religion in nonreligious forms.

> Protestantism, by its very nature, demands a secular reality.... The formative power of Protestantism is always tested by its relation to the secular world. If Protestantism surrenders to secularism, it ceases to be a Gestalt of grace. If it retires from secularism, it ceases to be Protestant, namely a Gestalt that includes within it the protest against itself. [PE, pp. 213–14]

Tillich realized the danger of constantly trying to live on the human boundary-situation. He admitted the tendency of Protestantism to become secular, to become empty of substance in its surrender of all that claims to be holy in itself. Strengthened by the symbol of the cross, though, this is the risk Protestantism must take. It is a risk Tillich deemed preferable to the danger which stands opposite to secularism. Protestantism is just as capable as Catholicism of seeking security in absolutes, whether that absolute be the Bible, or, as in the case of Protestant orthodoxy, "pure doctrine." "To stand at the boundary means to stand not only in unrighteousness but also in error" (PE, p. 200).

Striving to live constantly on the human boundary-situation is a difficult endeavor, so difficult that Tillich could forsee the possibility of the virtual end of Protestantism, as it is historically embodied in the Protestant churches.[32] The Protestant churches grew up in a historical period marked by liberalism, a period which championed individualism and autonomy. This period is now passing. The wars and revolutions of the twentieth century are symptomatic of a radical transformation taking place in Western civilization, a transformation in which traditions and ancient symbols are forgotten, in which mass disintegration fosters a pervasive attitude that life is meaningless. This mass disintegration is driving modern men to seek security in a common ideology and common symbols, in a centralized power and authority. Autonomous thinking is increasingly being rejected as leading to a sense of meaninglessness.

Protestantism stands in complete contradiction to these tendencies toward centralization and collectivity. It protests against absolute authorities and sacred systems, be they ecclesiastical or political. Even though men seek for security, Protestantism cannot and will not provide it. The Bible cannot provide it, since it must be interpreted. Protestant authority cannot provide it, since it is only an intellectual authority, based on skill in logical and scientific argument. As a result, more and more individuals have become "unable to endure the tremendous responsibility of permanently having to decide in intellectual and moral issues" (PE, p. 228).

Writing considerably before the Catholic Church had exhibited an openness to reform, Tillich viewed Catholicism as exerting an attraction for the autonomous man who had become insecure in his autonomy. He saw Catholicism as offering an emancipation from autonomous responsibility. After the World Wars, "many people out of a sense of meaninglessness or lack of any contents which are normative, binding, and productive of community, etc., returned to the Roman Catholic Church as the embracing and protecting mother" (PPT, p. 90). Tillich was not surprised that

Catholicism exerted such an attraction, but that the attraction was not greater than it was. He became convinced that modern man still stands in the liberal tradition of recent centuries and is unwilling to surrender the autonomy that is his (PE, pp. 193–95). He himself was determined to remain on the boundary, and he offered proposals as to how Protestantism might do the same (OB, p. 45).

Even should the Protestant era of liberalism come to an end, the Protestant principle would not be invalidated. As the permanent criterion of everything temporal, the Protestant principle would survive (PE, pp. viii, xxv). As for the Protestant churches, they can continue to exist only if they succeed in undergoing a fundamental change. They must become aware of the seriousness of the situation and obtain a new understanding of the symbols by which they live. They must provide a message which a disintegrated world seeking reintegration will accept. In all of this, the mere imitation of Catholicism will not suffice. Ultimately the most important contribution the Protestant churches can make to the world is to protest prophetically against every power which claims absolute and hence divine power for itself, whether that power be church or state, party or leader. In view of the urge toward a new collectivism, this message is more necessary today than at any time since the Reformation (PE, pp. 204, 229–30). But the message is not the unique possession of the Protestant churches. "Protestantism lives wherever, in the power of the New Being, the boundary-situation is preached, its 'No' and 'Yes' are proclaimed" (PE, p. 205). It lives in the Protestant principle, and this principle can operate not only in the Protestant churches but also in Catholicism, in orthodoxy, and in secular movements outside the churches (PE, p. 232).

The transformation taking place in Western civilization necessitates a transformation in the Church. We do not, as yet, see the whole picture of the coming age, but Tillich looked into the future and wrote in 1948:

> The end of the Protestant era is not the return to the Catholic era and not even, although much more so, the return to early Christianity; nor is it the step to a new form of secularism. It is something beyond all these forms, a new form of Christianity, to be expected and prepared for, but not yet to be named. [PE, p. xviii]

Christianity in the coming era must be expressive of an "evangelical Catholicism," uniting the Catholic, sacramental element, the Protestant, prophetic element, and the profane, contemporaneous element.[33] This insistence upon maintaining both Catholic substance and the Protestant principle makes Tillich uniquely valuable for ecumenism in our day and for the movement toward Christian unity.

Ecumenism

Tillich credited the development of his theological thought regarding Catholic substance and the Protestant principle to his experience in the United States. He found its interdenominational situation capable of liberating one from a Protestant provincialism. His encounter with the Episcopal church proved particularly rewarding in this regard, demonstrating that many Catholic elements could be preserved together with a basic Protestant theology (TC, p. 169).

As early as 1941, Tillich established his worth as an ecumenical theologian with an article entitled "The Permanent Significance of the Catholic Church for Protestantism".[34] In it he criticized Roman Catholicism for its legalism, but admitted that Protestantism needs a new approach to authority. If men are to listen, even the prophetic message must be supported by authority. Tillich praised Catholic theology for its formal clarity, logical consistency, and philosophical exactness. He believed Protestantism could learn from the Catholic attempt to bring reason and revelation into correlation with each other, particularly in apologetics and ethics. Protestantism could also learn from Catholic mysticism, its recognition of the importance of meditation, contemplation, and mystical union. No religion can last long if it emphasizes only the distance between God and man and neglects the presence of the divine.

In this same vein, the chief contribution that the Catholic Church makes to Protestantism is to remind it of its sacramental foundations. Tillich denied any visible Church the claim to divine, absolute authority or to any identification of itself with the holy. But Protestantism does need the Catholic Church to remind it that, before an individual can experience the holy, the Church must first represent the presence of the holy. Tillich admitted quite frankly that Protestantism, in great part, lacks an understanding of the nature and meaning of the Church. The ecumenical movement, however, has awakened in Protestantism an awareness of the importance of a doctrine of the Church. Tillich looked to the Catholic Church to aid Protestantism in coming to a new understanding of the Church in order to formulate such a doctrine.

Tillich greeted the more affirmative relations between Catholicism and Protestantism warmly. As firmly as he believed that the sixteenth-century Reformation was necessary, he admitted too that, besides being a religious gain, it was also a religious loss (ST3:6). The priestly and the prophetic spirit, which were for the most part separated then, must be reunited. Christianity needs expression today in a Church which has the power to integrate the masses of people through recognized authority, effective symbols, and sacramental actions—but under the criticism of the Protestant principle (RS, p. 218). He formulated the task of ecumenism pointedly with the question: "How can the radicalism of prophetic criticism which is implied in the principles of genuine Protestantism be united with the classical tradition of dogma, sacred law, sacraments, hierarchy, cult, as preserved in the Catholic churches (TC, p. 169)?

This question, which constitutes the challenge confronting the ecumenical movement, could not be answered by Tillich alone, or by any other single theologian. Tillich did more than most, though, to move in the direction of an answer by analyzing the impact of Catholic substance and the Protestant principle upon the churches which embody them. Both elements are present in every religion and every church. They are ultimately rooted in the basic relation of God and man. But there are tendencies in every church to emphasize one element over the other, and these tendencies constitute the considerable differences between Christian churches.

Tillich likened the sacramental churches, which embody Catholic substance, to an embracing mother. They look upon the holy primarily as incarnate, as a given, present reality, represented by persons, objects, and functions which enjoy a holiness, that is to say, a consecration, independent of their individual character or moral worth. A person is born into such churches without being asked. Because holiness is viewed as a present reality and not a demand, sins do not negate membership (GW3:110, 151–52).

On the other hand, prophetic churches, embodying the Protestant principle, are rather like a demanding father. They look upon the holy primarily as demanded, as dependent upon a decision. The Church is regarded as founded by a covenant, freely entered into. Membership depends not only upon such a decision but also upon a certain degree of moral and religious perfection. Such churches tend to become theocratic, to strive to bring personal morals and social institutions into conformity with the laws of God (GW3:111–12).

It bears repeating that Catholic substance and the Protestant principle are not mutually contradictory. The prophetic does not attack the priestly as such, inasmuch as the prophet himself arises from the sacramental substance of the Church. The prophet does not attack tradition; rather he turns tradition against itself. He raises his no not against the sacramental but against any claims the sacramental makes for itself, as well as against any social injustices overlooked or excused by the sacerdotal (GW3:153).

Catholic substance and the Protestant principle are not contradictory but correlative, existing in polarity with one another. Arising from the priestly tradition, Catholic substance is constitutive of the Church. Arising from the prophetic tradition, the Protestant principle is the corrective of the Church. Catholic substance views the holy primarily as *mysterium fascinosum*, the ground of all being; the Protestant principle views the holy as *mysterium tremendum*, the abyss of all being. For Catholic substance, holiness is being, *Sein*, a gift, a consecration. For the Protestant principle, holiness is what-ought-to-be, *Sollen*, a demand, a striving for perfection. Catholic substance looks to the past and tradition, emphasizing realized eschatology and the "already present." The Protestant principle looks to the future, emphasizing apocalyptic eschatology and the "not yet."[35]

Just as the Church must live within the tension of two *kairoi*, between the kingdom of God within history and the kingdom of God beyond history, so too must the Church live within the tension between the priestly and the prophetic, between the constitutive and the corrective, between the incarnational and the eschatological. Both elements of the polarity need each other, if the priestly is to avoid becoming demonic and if the prophetic is to avoid becoming profane (OB, p. 42). In emphasizing one, much to the exclusion of the other, both Catholicism and Protestantism have lost in great measure the Pauline experience of the Spirit as the unity of all types of faith. "Only if Christianity is able to regain in real experience this unity of the divergent types of faith can it express its claim to answer the questions and to fulfill the dynamics of the history of faith in past and future" (DF, p. 73).

Tillich viewed the contemporary encounter and cooperation between Catholic and Protestant churches as a *kairos*, "a moment full of potentialities" (ST3:6). But not for a moment did he forget the estrangement that marks human existence and results in the ambiguities of life. The ecumenical movement powerfully expresses the unity of the churches both as a gift and as a task. It replaces fanaticism with cooperation, and conquers denominational provincialism. It produces a new vision of the unity of all churches in their foundation (ST3:169). It assists the churches to recognize Spiritual Community in each other, a community of love which constitutes their dynamic essence, joins them together, and affirms their particularities even as it judges them (ST3:182). But let no illusions be harbored. Although it may serve to heal divisions which are historically obsolete, the ecumenical movement will never be able to overcome within history the paradox of the churches. Within space and time, unity can be predicated of the Church only "in spite of" disunity.[36]

> Neither the ecumenical nor any other future movement can conquer the ambiguity of unity and division in the churches' historical existence. Even if it

were able to produce the United Churches of the World, and even if all latent churches were converted to this unity, new divisions would appear. The dynamics of life, the tendency to preserve the holy even when it has become obsolete, the ambiguities implied in the sociological existence of the churches, and above all, the prophetic criticism and demand for reformation would bring about new and, in many cases, Spiritually justified divisions. The unity of the churches, similar to their holiness, has a paradoxical character. It is the divided church which is the united church. [ST3:169–70]

Just as everything in Tillich's ecclesiology leads up to Catholic substance and the Protestant principle, so too everything else follows from it. His understanding of the priestly and prophetic provided Tillich with a clearer insight into the Church and its ecumenical task; it also offered him a solid base for approaching the problem of the Church's confrontation today with the great historical religions, as well as with secularism and the quasi-religions born of secular faith, with liberal humanism and socialism. It is a confrontation which Tillich considered as significant for the Church as the contemporary encounter between Catholicism and Protestantism (ST3:6). Here is the whole complex question of the Church in its relationship to today's world.

Before going on to that final aspect of Tillich's ecclesiology, though, special consideration should be given to a particular application Tillich makes of the Protestant principle, namely, to the question of authority. This has always been an explosive issue in the Church, and our own day is no exception. From all that has preceded, Tillich's position comes as no surprise. Armed with the Protestant principle, there was no area in which Tillich was more determined to fight against idolatrous absolutes than that pertaining to authority within the Church.

6

Authority in the Church

But with us all will be happy and will no more rebel nor destroy one another as under thy freedom. Oh, we shall persuade them that they will only become free when they renounce their freedom to us and submit to us. And shall we be right or shall we be lying? They will be convinced that we are right, for they will remember the horrors of slavery and confusion to which thy freedom brought them. . . Too, too well they know the value of complete submission! And until men know that, they will be unhappy.
Fyodor Dostoyevsky, "The Grand Inquisitor" in The Brothers
Karamazov

Tillich's thinking was to a remarkable degree autobiographical.[1] Nowhere is this more the case than in his approach to authority in the Church. A personal struggle for intellectual autonomy made such an impression upon Tillich that Karl Barth, in an early polemic, accused him of "still fighting against the Grand Inquisitor."[2] Tillich would not deny the accusation. He regarded Dostoyevsky's Grand Inquisitor as the most impressive symbol of the demonic for our time—the elevation of religion, or of anything else relative and finite, to the level of the absolute. The Protestant principle was Tillich's chief weapon in a struggle which he was convinced would always be necessary. "History has shown that the Grand Inquisitor is always ready to re-appear in different disguises, political as well as theological."[3]

It was Tillich's father who proved chiefly responsible for his lifelong struggle against claims to absolute authority. He was a man who embodied the traits of Prussian authoritarianism, "a conscientious, very dignified, completely convinced and, in the presence of doubt, angry supporter of the conservative Lutheran point of view" (KB, p. 8). The fact that his father was a pastor and a superintendent in the Lutheran church compounded the difficulty, for it inclined the young Tillich to identify parental with divine authority.

> I was able to reach intellectual and moral autonomy only after a severe struggle. My father's authority, which was both personal and intellectual and which, because of his position in the church, I identified with the religious authority of revelation, made every attempt at autonomous thinking an act of religious daring and connected criticism of authority with a sense of guilt. [OB, pp. 36–37]

The one avenue of escape permitted Tillich was philosophy. His father was convinced that there could be no conflict between philosophy and revealed truth, and Tillich went on from there.

> From an independent philosophical position a state of independence spread out into all directions, theoretically first, practically later. It is this difficult and painful break-through to autonomy which has made me immune against any system of thought or life which demands surrender of this autonomy. [KB, p. 8]

The scars left upon him by this personal struggle account for Tillich's often strident attitude toward Catholicism as well as his radical use of the Protestant principle (OB, p. 39). He would not tolerate the least encroachment upon the autonomy he had won at so great a price.

> An autonomy won in hard struggle is not surrendered so readily as one that always has been accepted as a matter of fact. . . . Freedom that has not been fought for and for which no sacrifices have been made is easily cast aside. [OB, pp. 38–39]

But if Tillich was determined to struggle against any form of absolutism in authority, this does not imply that he denied the necessity of authority, or that he chose the supremacy of purely autonomous reason. Tillich affirmed the need and place of authority in the Church, but his affirmation was dialectical. To a yes to authority he joined a no to authoritarianism. Neither heteronomy nor autonomy was his solution to the question of authority, but a theonomy that transcends them both.

A Church which points to the absolute, even though it participates in its meaning and power, cannot be identified with the absolute. A Church which is itself conditioned cannot claim unconditioned authorities, and any authority within the Church which does claim to be absolute is no less than demonic. Structures no less than symbols are open to idolatry. Rarely has the Grand Inquisitor found an adversary as determined in his opposition as Tillich.

Authority in General

For Cardinal Newman, "the essence of all religion is authority and obedience."[4] No attitude toward authority could be more at variance with such a notion than Tillich's. In this respect, at least, Tillich was a product of the Enlightenment. Not that he argued for a religion of pure reason, but he was convinced that no attack on religion is more frequent, more successful, or more justified than the attack upon its authoritarian character. It was from Kant, whom he regarded as "the prophet of human reason and dignity,"[5] that Tillich took up the assault on authoritarianism. Tillich agreed with Kant that it is more comfortable to live under the authority of guardians, be they religious, political, or philosophical. But opting for security constitutes immaturity, lack of resoluteness, and refusal to use one's own reason. Christian maturity means preferring truth over safety, "even if the safety is consecrated and supported by the churches" (CB, p. 140). "The decisive step to maturity is risking the break away from spiritual infancy with its protective traditions and guiding authorities. Without 'no' to authority, there is no maturity" (EN, p. 134). Such a stance should not be mistaken for an attack against all authority, but rather against heteronomy.

Heteronomy imposes a strange (*heteros*) law (*nomos*) upon the intellect by issuing commands from "outside" as to how reason should grasp and shape reality. It asserts that man is unable to act according to universal human reason and must be subjected to a law which is superior to him.[6] Moral commandments are regarded as expressions of a divine will which is sovereign and without criteria, a will which cannot be measured in terms of adequacy to human nature and hence must be obeyed as something coming from outside through revelation (LPJ, p. 76). Heteronomy is thus "the authority claimed or exercised by a finite being in the name of the infinite" (ST1:148). Its basis is "the claim to speak in the name of the ground of being and therefore in an unconditional and ultimate way (ST1:84). Heteronomy describes the attempt of religion to dominate autonomous cultural activity from the outside (PE, p. xii). Two examples of such attempts at domination were the Catholicism of the late Middle Ages and Protestant orthodoxy.

Heteronomy imposes an alien law, religious or secular, on man's mind. It disregards the logos structure of mind and world. It destroys the honesty of truth and the dignity of the moral personality. It undermines creative freedom and the humanity of man. Its symbol is the "terror" exercised by absolute churches or absolute states. [PE, p. 46]

Tillich's chief criticism against heteronomy was that, in demanding unconditional obedience to finite authorities, it threatens man's very being. Heteronomy splits his conscience, his inner life, by denying his rational structure and appealing indirectly to the pleasure principle, to man's desire to escape fear and doubt and attain security. Heteronomy reduces the laws of God to the commands of a tyrant like Zeus, representative of an archaic demanding divinity, an arbitrary willfulness who stands as an object outside of man and is to be obeyed solely out of fear of destruction (PPT, p. 26). Tillich's sympathies were clearly on the side of Prometheus.

No outside command can be unconditional, whether it comes from a state, or a person, or God—if God is thought of as an outside power, establishing a law for our behavior. A stranger, even if his name were God, who imposes commands upon us must be resisted. . . . We cannot be obedient to the commands of a stranger even if he is God. [TC, p. 136]

The will of God is not a command imposed on us from outside, however; it is not an arbitrary law laid down for us by some heavenly tyrant. God is strange to us only when we are estranged from ourselves. We can be commanded unconditionally only by that which springs from our own essential being. The will of God for us is precisely that—our own essential being with all its potentialities. The will of God manifests itself to us in our essential nature, not as a "strange law" but as the "silent voice" of our nature as human beings. For this reason alone is it binding upon us.[7] This being the case, God's will can be seen as constituting the very foundation for man's autonomy.

Autonomy is the law (*nomos*) of self (*autos*), but not in the sense of lawless willful subjectivity or the arbitrariness whereby a man becomes a law unto himself. Autonomy is "the obedience of the individual to the law of reason, which he finds in himself as a rational being. . . . It is the law of subjective-objective reason; it is the law implied in the *logos* structure of mind and reality" (ST1:84). Autonomy is the very opposite of willfulness. It is obedience to the law of reason, which is the law of nature as well as the divine law, rooted in the ground of being-itself.

Autonomy operates in the theoretical, as well as in the practical, spheres of

132

culture. It replaces mystical nature with rational nature; it puts in the place of mythical events historical happenings, and in the place of the magical sense of communion it sets up technical control. It constitutes communities on the basis of purpose and morality on the basis of individual perfection. It analyzes everything in order to put it together rationally. It makes religion a matter of personal decision and makes the inner life of the individual dependent upon itself. [PE, p. 44]

Man's autonomy does not stand against the will of God or necessarily turn away from the unconditional. It does, however, see cultural forms only in their finite relationships. As a result, it cuts the ties of a civilization from its ultimate ground and aim. To the measure that it succeeds, a civilization becomes empty of spiritual substance.

Autonomy is able to live as long as it can draw from the religious tradition of the past.... But more and more it loses this spiritual foundation. It becomes emptier, more formalistic, or more factual and is driven toward skepticism and cynicism, toward the loss of meaning and purpose. The history of autonomous cultures is the history of a continuous waste of spiritual substance. [PE, p. 46]

Twice in history, autonomy has disintegrated into an outspoken secularism—once when Greek philosophy and drama criticized the figures of the gods and the symbols of religion; and once again in the modern era, when religious heteronomy provoked first the Renaissance and Enlightenment, and now naturalism and revolutionary movements (UC, pp. 32–33). The decline of Greek philosophy from rational autonomy into skepticism constituted for Tillich conclusive historical evidence of the inability of autonomous reason to create by itself a world with real content. "Free-wheeling intelligence was suspect to me. I had scant confidence in the creative power of purely autonomous thought" (OB, p. 37).

Unmitigated autonomy results in a spiritual bankruptcy, that invariably succumbs to a new heteronomy. As an alternative to the two, Tillich raised a call to what has been described as "his greatest challenge to modern thought."[8] His answer to the need of today's secularism as well as to the question of authority in the Church is an autonomy informed by religious substance, in other words, theonomy.

Theonomy recognizes God (*Theos*) as the law (*nomos*) for both the structure and the ground of reason. This does not imply the acceptance of a divine law imposed on reason by a supreme authority. Rather, "it means autonomous reason united with its own depth. In a theonomous situation reason actualizes itself in obedience to its structural laws and in the power of its own inexhaustible ground" (ST1:85). Theonomy overcomes the contradiction between empty autonomy and imposed totalitarian heteronomy, in that it is ontologically prior to either one of them, constituting instead a higher unity of the two. Theonomy describes a situation which avoids the emptiness of pure autonomy by permitting the ultimate meaning of existence to shine through all finite forms of thought and action. At the same time, it avoids the destructiveness of heteronomy by asserting that man's essential nature is the law that is given him by God. Theonomy is "self-transcending autonomy," autonomy driven to its depths, and as such an expression of the Protestant principle. Theonomy unites the demand that everything relative become the vehicle of the absolute with the insight that nothing relative can ever become absolute in itself.[9]

Because of the estrangement which marks existence and gives rise to the ambiguities of life, there is no complete theonomy within history (ST1:85). There are periods in history, though, which are marked, at least fragmentarily, by theonomy. In such periods, "reason is neither subject to revelation nor independent of it."[10] "Rational autonomy is preserved in law and knowledge, in community and art," while at the same time there is an awareness of the "depth of reason," the ground of autonomy (ST1:149). Examples of such periods for Tillich were the early and high Middle Ages, when Catholicism was less heteronomous than in the late Middle Ages.

As a sociological group laboring under the ambiguities of life, the Church is subject to the almost irresistible temptation of becoming heteronomous and suppressing autonomous criticism, yet it is never completely bereft of theonomous forces. As Spiritual Community made manifest, the Church is the place where theonomy becomes actual. The Spiritual Presence is experienced personally as witnessing to the truth and authority of both the Bible and the Church (PPT, p. 26). Clearly, Tillich was not on principle opposed to authority within the Church. "Authority can be natural and factual, without involving a break within ourselves, disrupting our autonomy and subjecting us to a foreign law of heteronomy" (HCT, p. 139). But in order to be acceptable to Tillich, authority had to be theonomous.

The Authority of Offices

One of the most informative indications of Tillich's thinking concerning offices in the Church is his published sermon, "By What Authority" (NB, pp. 79–91). In it he described authority in terms of being started and increased, being guided by those who have more than we do. Because we are finite and therefore dependent on one another, we need authority to help shape our lives. "Our daily life would be impossible without traditions of behavior and customs and the authority of those who have received them and surrendered them to us" (NB, p. 84). The real question is not one of authority but rather of valid authority. Tillich contrasted the authority of the priests and scribes, that is, the authority of office, with the authority exemplified by John the Baptist, the authority of charism, of spirit, and of native ability. For Tillich, the authority of the prophet, legitimated by the power of what he has to say, is much more acceptable than that of established office. Although he granted the legitimacy of established authorities, he determinedly denied them ultimacy.

> The place where God gives authority to a man cannot be circumscribed. It cannot be legally defined. . . . You cannot derive it. You must be grasped by it. You must participate in its power. This is the reason why the question of authority never can get an ultimate answer. Certainly there are many preliminary answers. . . . The God who cannot answer the question of ultimate authority because He is Spirit does not remove the preliminary authorities with whom we live our daily lives. . . . He does not deprive us of the protection of those who have more wisdom and power than we have. He does not isolate us from the community to which we belong and which is a part of ourselves. But he denies ultimate significance to all these preliminary authorities, to all those who claim to be images of His authority and who distort God's authority into the oppressive power of a heavenly tyrant. [NB, pp. 88–90]

The contrast which he drew between Jewish officialdom and John the Baptist, Tillich delineated elsewhere as the distinction between established authority, or authority in principle, and factual authority. Established authority, the authority of office or position, is one-sided and exercised by a select number of persons or groups. Because of the absolute character of what they stand for, such persons tend to claim absolute authority and immunity from criticism. Examples of such authority are parents who wish to remain authorities to their children throughout their lives, teachers who refuse to liberate their pupils from their tutelage, and, of course, the Pope insofar as he is regarded as an ultimate authority for every Catholic. To Tillich's mind, "all this 'authority in principle' is unjust authority. It disregards the intrinsic claim of human beings to become responsible for ultimate decisions."[11]

Quite different from authority in principle is authority in fact, which is both exercised and accepted by everyone at every moment. It is a rational authority, originating out of experience and wisdom. Everyone shares in it, even the least educated person, since everyone has had some unique experience or acquired some bit of wisdom which is lacking to most others. "It is an expression of the mutual dependence of all of us on each other; it is an expression of the finite and fragmentary character of our being, of the limits of our power to stand by ourselves. For this reason it is a just authority."[12]

With regard specifically to authority in the Church, Tillich viewed early Christianity as a religion of the Spirit. But the Church soon had to defend itself against the quasi-religious self-deification of the Roman Empire, and, in doing so, had to accept elements of legalism and authoritarianism into itself (CEWR, pp. 10–11). Representing the sacramental reality upon which the existence of church, state, and culture depended, the hierarchy, with the papacy at its head, eventually became the fundamental religious force of the Middle Ages. It was against the demonic identification of the hierarchy's authority with that of Christ that the Reformation rose up in protest. When Luther attacked the pope as the Antichrist, he did so not merely polemically but theologically, because of the papal claim to represent Christ by divine right (HCT, pp. 145, 208, 234). In rejecting the claims of a sacramental priesthood, however, the Reformation created an authority vacuum, a vacuum quickly filled by the leading lay members of the churches, the princes or the more prominent members of the congregations. It was an emergency solution to an emergency situation, but it eventually came to assume a certain permanence.

> In this way the Protestant churches became subjected to the earthly powers, and to this day they have this problem. In Lutheranism it was the problem of the church's relation to the princes, their cabinets, and authoritarian governments. In the Calvinist countries, and also in America, it is the socially ruling classes which are decisive for the church and make up its administrative backbone.[13]

Assuming a position like Luther's, Tillich denied the infallibility of either pope or councils. So long as they raise no absolutistic claims, though, he was willing to accept the authority of both of them on purely pragmatic grounds: "The pope and councils are both human, and can fall into error. The pope can be tolerated as the chief administrator of the church on the basis of human law, the law of expediency" (HCT, p. 234). Again, Tillich's distinction between function and institution needs to be remembered here. The functions of the Church, among them the communal constructive functions of leadership and legal form, follow necessarily from the nature of the Church. But none of the institutions which serve these functions, including priesthood and ministry, follows necessarily (ST3:189).

> Nothing in human history has reality without a legal form, as nothing in nature has reality without a natural form, but the legal form of the churches is not a matter of an unconditional command. The Spirit does not give constitutional rules, but it guides the churches toward a Spiritual use of sociologically adequate offices and institutions. It fights against the ambiguities of power and prestige which are effective in the daily life of the smallest village congregations as well as in the encounter of the large denominations. No church office, not even those which existed in the apostolic churches, is a result of a direct command by the divine Spirit. But the church is, and its functions are, because they belong to its nature. The institution and offices serving the church in these functions are matters of sociological adequacy, practical expediency, and human wisdom. [ST3:207]

Thus, while accepting the authority of offices within the Church, Tillich denied them the claim to divine establishment. A foremost expression of the Protestant principle for him was the priesthood of all believers.

> Everyone who belongs actively to a church is a "priest" by the fact of his belonging to the Spiritual Community, and he is able to exercise all the functions of a priest, although, for the sake of order and adequacy to the situation, special individuals may be called to a regular and trained performance of priestly activities. But their functioning as experts does not give them a higher status than is given by participation in the Spiritual Community. [ST3:217]

Tillich thus inclined toward a radical laicism in the Church. A layman can become a minister at any time, and a minister is no more than a layman with special training to fulfill a special function. In virtue of the priesthood of all believers, there remains the function of the minister to preach the Word and administer the sacraments; but the hierarchical position of the ministry, the concept of priesthood as a special, sacramentally consecrated degree in the Church, Tillich rejected. Every Christian layman can perform "in principle" the duties of preaching and administering the sacraments, although not in the regular life of the Church. As soon as he does so, however, he is acting as a minister.[14] "I . . . believe the dynamic dimension of the religious is betrayed when certain institutions and personalities are considered to be religious in themselves. To think of the clergyman as a man whose faith is a professional requirement borders on blasphemy" (OB, p. 72). The clergyman's gown of today is the professor's gown of the Middle

Ages, symbolizing an authority that appeals not to obedience but to the intellect. "Protestantism is a highly intellectualized religion," one in which theological faculties, in interpreting the Bible, have become the highest, although not always most effective, authority in the Church (PE, p. 227).

In virtue of the Protestant principle, Tillich accepted the authority of office within the Church. He granted that, like all authority, it rightfully wields a power which is founded upon love and takes as its task the fostering of union among persons and within persons (LPJ, pp. 49, 120). But he refused to recognize any "objectivation" of authority which would see divine authority embodied in certain human persons to whom "a kind of divine reverence" is to be given. If authority is not regarded as such an embodiment, then a decisive element of authority is re-established, and autonomy lies open to the possibility of becoming theonomy, "directed, without being sacrificed, by the divine Spirit".[15]

The Authority of Scripture

In replacing the authority of the hierarchy with the authority of the Bible, the reformers, Tillich admitted, changed the meaning of authority. Unlike a living authority, a book requires interpreters. This applies to the Bible as much as to any book. There is no such thing as an abstract Christian message; it is always embodied in a particular culture. Separating the permanent Christian message from the transitory cultural forms found in the Bible necessarily requires interpretation (ST3:193).

As he admitted that the Bible needs to be interpreted, so Tillich also acknowledged the risk which this involves for a Protestant. Since the time of Origen, there has been a plurality of Christian interpretations of Scripture. The authority enjoyed by theological faculties in interpreting the Bible, while eminent, is not binding, and only rarely does it produce unanimity. This gives autonomy a wide field, and runs the danger of relativism. But this is the "Protestant risk." It is inseparable from the Protestant principle, rooted in the awareness of Spiritual freedom.

> It is the prophetic Spirit which creates the courage for such a risk. Protestantism takes this risk—even if it may mean the disintegration of particular churches. It takes the risk in the certainty that the Spiritual Community, the dynamic essence of a church, cannot be destroyed. [ST3:184–85]

It is a risk which not only the Church but also every Protestant must take.

Each Protestant, each layman, each minister... has to decide for himself whether a doctrine is true or not, whether a prophet is a true or false prophet, whether a power is demonic or divine. Even the Bible cannot liberate him from this responsibility, for the Bible is a subject of interpretation: there is no doctrine, no prophet, no priest, no power, which has not claimed biblical sanction for itself. For the Protestant, individual decision is inescapable. [PE, p. 226]

Tillich recognized that not all Protestants were as willing as he was to take the "Protestant risk": Protestant orthodoxy rejects it partly, Protestant fundamentalism completely. Tillich decried the "intellectual distortion" of faith by Protestants who equate faith with the acceptance of the literal authority of the Bible.

They fall into the absurdities of biblical literalism, and elevate, often unknowingly, the dogmatic theology of the late sixteenth and early seventeenth centuries to unconditional authority, identifying this theology with the meaning of the Bible and, consequently, with the Word of God.[16]

Such biblicism contradicts the Protestant principle, reducing faith to "self-salvation," to the intellectual good work of sacrificing one's critical powers to the letter of the Bible. Biblicism elevates the Scripture into a law book of truth dictated by the Holy Spirit, with authority which is absolute. This for Tillich was "more suppressive than anything in Catholicism."[17]

Protestant theology protests in the name of the Protestant principle against the identification of our ultimate concern with any creation of the church, including the biblical writings insofar as their witness to what is really ultimate concern is also a conditioned expression of their own spirituality. [ST1:37]

Ironically, Tillich blamed Calvin for leading Protestants into elevating the Bible into an idol. Although Calvin upheld the guidance of the Holy Spirit for the interpretation of Scripture by the pious reader, yet he limited this operation to the biblical content. He reduced the biblical writers to mere scribes of the Holy Spirit. The Bible for him was the oracle of God (HCT, p. 275). Over Calvin's interpretation of biblical authority, Tillich preferred the early liberal belief in the principle of harmony, which held that, in religion as well as in culture, economics, and politics, there is a providence directing everything in history toward ultimate fulfillment. In spite of denominational differences, diverse trends, and conflicting purposes, Tillich believed that behind the backs of the individual Bible-readers there works a providence which creates a kind of meaningful unity.

On the basis of this principle of harmony there is founded the Protestant notion of the Bible interpreting itself. (ST1:265).

The most extensive treatment which Tillich accorded the authority of Scripture falls within his consideration of the sources and norm of theology. The Bible is the original document about the events upon which the Church is founded. It contains the decisive manifestation of ultimate concern for Christians, the picture of Jesus as the Christ. For this reason, the Bible is the basic source and criterion of all Christian theology, the judge of the Church's tradition. Tillich denied, however, that the Bible is the only source.

> The biblical message cannot be understood and could not have been received had there been no preparation for it in human religion and culture. And the biblical message would not have become a message for anyone, including the theologian himself, without the experiencing participation of the church and of every Christian. [ST1:34–35]

The Bible contains not only the manifestation of Jesus as the Christ but also the reception of this manifestation in the apostolic Church. The writers of the New Testament gave witness both to the new reality in Jesus as the Christ and to the way in which they and the first Christian communities received that new reality. In this sense, the New Testament authors are the beginning of the Church's tradition. Tillich disagreed with Barth's idea of tradition or church history as simply "the auxiliary science in theology."[18] Church history and the history of religion and culture are also sources of theology, although Scripture is the primary source.

But even as the primary source for Christian theology, the Bible is not sufficient of itself. The breadth and variety of the material within Scripture require a norm, a principle of interpretation. Tradition cannot be normative, since there is always an element in it which must be judged and cannot be the judge itself. Steering a path between traditional Catholicism and orthodox Protestantism, Tillich regarded tradition as guiding but not normative. It is a permanent task of Christian theology to elaborate a norm out of the whole of the biblical material and apply it equally to Scripture and to tradition.[19]

The question of a norm for Christian doctrine arose early in the Church. A creed, centered around the baptismal confession of Jesus as the Christ, became the material norm; the Church hierarchy became the formal norm. With the Reformation rejection of hierarchic authority, though, the Bible became the formal norm for Protestants. The Pauline principle of justification by grace through faith became the material norm for Lutherans. In Calvinism justification as the material norm came to be replaced more by predestination (ST1:47).

Tillich found material norms for interpreting Scripture implicit throughout Church history. Although they do not exclude each other in content, they do differ with each other in emphasis. In the early church the doctrine of Jesus as the Christ was normative. For the Eastern churches it became the Johannine concept of the liberation of finite man from error and death by the Logos, who is incarnate truth and life. For the Roman church it became salvation from guilt and disruption by the sacrifice of the God-man and the sacramental representation of that sacrifice. For Luther justification was normative; for Calvin, predestination. For liberal Protestantism it was the "synoptic" picture of Jesus, representing the ideal of human existence; for recent Protestantism, the prophetic message of the kingdom of God in the Old and New Testament. As a norm for our own day, Tillich offered his concept of the New Being as a contemporary expression of the formula that Jesus is the Christ, the bringer of the new reality of reunion which overcomes estrangement (ST1:48).

The most important characteristic of a norm for interpreting Scripture is that it is not the work of one individual. Rather than being the opinion of a private theologian, it is "a product of the collective experience of the Church," resulting from the encounter of the Church with the biblical message (ST1:52).

> This encounter is different in each generation, and its difference becomes visible in the successive periods of church history. The norm grows; it is not produced intentionally; its appearance is not the work of theological reflection but of the Spiritual life of the church. [ST1:48]

Here is another indication of the importance Tillich accorded the Church.

The Authority of Dogma

In the light of the foregoing, a reader certainly does not expect Tillich to regard dogmas and creeds as anymore absolute than he did Church offices or the letter of Scripture. One is perhaps surprised, though, at the high esteem in which he held tradition, the ancient councils, and their dogmatic decisions, and the importance which he attached to them. "I believe that the developments in ancient Christian theology are really foundations, foundations that must be considered immediately after the biblical foundations" (HCT, p. 89). Church history is a source of theology together with the Scriptures. Tradition, although not of itself normative, is the expression of the continuous reception of the New Being in history. Without it, no theological existence is possible.

Radical biblicism is a self-deception. "Becoming contemporaneous with the Bible," as Kierkegaard put it, or, as Tillich himself put it in less complimentary terms: "the jumping theory" of Protestantism—cutting one's self off from any connection with the past except for the Bible—is simply impossible. Even though Protestantism may not recognize tradition in its life, it is operative nevertheless.

> No one is able to leap over two thousand years of church history and become contemporaneous with the writers of the New Testament, except in the Spiritual sense of accepting Jesus as the Christ. Every person who encounters a biblical text is guided in his religious understanding of it by the understanding of all previous generations. [ST1:36]

Dogma, derived from the Greek *dokein*, "to think, to hold an opinion," originally constituted the doctrinal basis of various philosophical schools, differentiating them one from another. To become a member of such a school, one first had to accept its basic presuppositions. Christianity followed this model in establishing as its central dogma belief in Jesus as the Christ.[20] This dogma together with other dogmas that follow from it and support it are expressions of the life of the Church. As such, they are inevitable. In religion, as in all other areas of life, there is no human existence without thought. "Man cannot repress his cognitive function in dealing with the content of his religious devotion" (ST3:288). Methodological thought in religion produces theological doctrines. These doctrines are expressed not only in formal dogmas and creeds but also in poetry, hymns, symbols, and rituals. "A church is not quite consistent when it avoids a statement of faith in terms of a creed and at the same time is unable to avoid expressing the content of its creed in every one of its liturgical and practical acts" (ST3:190).

The function of dogmas and creeds is two-fold: to preserve the substance of the Christian message and to interpret it. Both functions point to the necessity of dogmas and creeds. Almost as soon as it confronted the non-Jewish world, the early Church found it necessary to interpret the Christian message by translating it from Jewish into Hellenistic concepts and categories. This Hellenization was not the introduction of foreign elements into Christianity, as Harnack contended, but was the *sine qua non* for the spread of the Church into the pagan world. This process is already apparent in the pages of the New Testament. Although it is problematic whether or not these Hellenistic categories were adequate for translating the biblical message, it is unfair to criticize the Church Fathers for using them. They had no others at their disposal (ST2:139).

The second function of dogma is preservative, to protect the substance of the Christian message against distortions and destructive heresies. Dogmatic development should not be viewed as something unfortunate or lamentable. On the contrary, it was the necessary means by which the Church maintained its identity. Without such definitions of faith, many elements would have undermined the entire Church, threatening its very existence (ST1:32). Thus, for example, to preserve the particular character of Christianity, the Church had to protect itself against the Gnostic attempt to render meaningless its unique basis in the person of Jesus (HCT, p. 36). Similarly, it had to protect itself against the Arian attempt to render Jesus as the Christ into an incarnate half-god, a creature who would be unable of himself to bring eternal life (ST2:169).

The tragic aspect of dogma is that the Christian message, while being defined, is also narrowed; valid elements, too valuable to be lost, become excluded. Theologians have the task, therefore, of preventing dogmatic formulations from becoming rigid. They must strive to recover valuable elements lost through the self-reduction which invariably accompanies self-definition. "The theological work we have to do is to illuminate the original meaning of what was done in this or that dogma, and also what was lost by it, and then reformulate it" (UC, p. 66). Tillich's own attempt to recover elements lost through dogmatic self-reduction was exemplified by his Christology and his answer to those who criticized it as being Adoptionistic or Nestorian.

> My task in answering these accusations cannot be an attempt to deny them. From the point of view of the accepted dogma they may be correct. But, theologically, ideas rejected by the ancient theologians and their successors may contain a truth which must be expressed in contemporary categories and concepts.[21]

As important and necessary as dogmas may be, they are not absolute. Christian revelation cannot be defined into sharply formulated dogmatic propositions. Dogmas point to the truth, but they are not to be regarded as laws of truth or as the truth itself. When absolutized in this way, dogmas become demonic and heteronomous. They become tools of suppression which prevent the honest search for truth and arouse the rightful opposition of anyone who is sincerely engaged in that search. This is particularly the case when dogmas are supported by civil law, as they were in medieval society. Precisely this absolutizing of dogmas has given them such negative connotations.[22]

In formulating and defending its creedal and dogmatic foundations, the Church needs to be aware of its own ambiguity. In the light of the Protestant principle, it must acknowledge that its judgment, whether in pronouncing a dogmatic judgment or applying it to a concrete case, is itself conditioned and ambiguous. In struggling to preserve the Christian message, the Church must recognize the possibility of falling "into disintegrating, destructive, or even demonic errors" (ST3:176). Dogmas can be esteemed without being absolutized. "We should estimate the dogma very highly; there is something great about it. But it should not be taken as a set of particular doctrines to which one must subscribe. This is against the spirit of the dogma, against the spirit of Christianity" (HCT, p. xvii).

The refusal to absolutize dogmas renders them compatible with doubt. Dogmas can provide a confessional foundation to the Church even while allowing room for criticism and uncertainty.[23] For theology this means that all the materials of Church history can be used in interpreting the biblical message—Greek, Roman, and modern concepts, the teaching of the Fathers, and the ecclesiastical decisions of popes and councils. But theology is not bound to any of these concepts or decisions any more than it is bound to the letter of the Bible. "God is in heaven and man on earth," and being on earth within time and space means being historically conditioned. There can never be an unconditioned theology (ST1:37). Dogmatic decisions of the Church, therefore, while normative, are only indirectly so.

> Every period of church history . . . unconsciously or consciously contributes through its special situation to the establishment of a theological norm. Beyond this, however, church decisions have no directly normative character. . . . The indirectly normative character of ecclesiastical decisions consists in their function as signposts, pointing to dangers for the Christian message which once have been overcome by such decisions. They offer a very serious warning and a constructive help to the theologian. But they do not determine authoritatively the direction of his work. [ST1:51–52]

In refusing to identify the transcendent with any particular form, the Protestant principle frees theology from identifying the Christian message with Hellenistic concepts and permits the expression of that message with any tool which proves more adequate. The Protestant principle points to the historical contingency of dogmas and creeds and to the struggles which gave rise to them. Dogmas are not valid for all cultures and all times, since, like all human concepts, they are essentially inadequate for expressing the substance of the Christian message (ST2:139–42). The dogmas of the Church should not be idolized but interpreted. "It is always through interpretation that the divine Spirit manifests itself, transforming the original point of reference again and again in many ways" (UC, p. 79). Greek elements need not be rejected in favor of Old Testament language. Christianity is no nearer to the Jews than it is to the Greeks. The concepts of the Old Testament prophets and Church Fathers both need to be translated into symbols and language capable of speaking to our own culture (PPT, p. 222).

Tillich's application of the Protestant principle to Church dogma obviously affects the concept of heresy. To take tradition and the Church's dogmatic decisions seriously demands taking heresies seriously. A theologian should not lightly promote a view regarded as heretical by the Church as a whole. He must, however, follow his theological conscience, a conscience sharpened by tradition and dogma.[24] But an important distinction needs to be made among the dogmas themselves. The fundamental and decisive dogma of the Church is that Jesus is the Christ. All other dogmas are protective and supportive of this one fundamental belief. These supportive dogmas are, of themselves, not of the utmost importance. Heresy arises with the unavoidable attempt to formulate conceptually the implications of the basic Christian assertion that Jesus is the Christ. Rejection of the dogma that Jesus is the Christ is not heresy but a separation from the Church, since it is upon this assertion that the Church is based (ST3:176). Not so, however, with the supportive, protective dogmas implied by it.

> Certainly, a church's decision to base its preaching and teaching on a particular doctrinal tradition or formulation is necessary; but if the decision is accompanied by the claim that it is the only possible one, the Protestant principle is violated. [ST3:177]

The Authority of Jesus

Tillich was convinced that the conflicts between Church and State, canon law and civil law, religious society and secular society would end as soon as religious communities and personalities with sacred books and truths would recognize that they point to the absolute and participate in it but are not absolute in themselves (GW1:264). This is the Protestant principle applied to authority in the Church. The extent to which Tillich carried the Protestant principle, though, is best seen in its application to the person of Jesus as the Christ. "The Lord is the Spirit." We do not "know" him according to his historical existence (flesh) but only as the

Spirit who is alive and present. Basing his position on St. Paul's Spirit-Christology, Tillich regarded the Church as exempted from a Jesus-theology which makes the man Jesus into an object of faith. The Christ is Spirit and not law. In consequence of this, Christianity is preserved from a heteronomous subjection to an individual.[25] No special trait given us by the New Testament picture of Jesus as the Christ can be used as an absolute law.

> The final revelation does not give us absolute ethics, absolute doctrines, or an absolute ideal of personal and communal life. It gives us examples which point to that which is absolute; but the examples are not absolute in themselves. . . . The New Being in Jesus as the Christ is the paradox of the final revelation. The words of Jesus and the apostles point to this New Being; they make it visible through stories, legends, symbols, paradoxical descriptions, and theological interpretations. But none of these expressions of the experience of the final revelation is final and absolute in itself. They are all conditioned, relative, open to change and additions. [ST1:151]

But Jesus is not so much an application of the Protestant principle as a source of it. It is an abuse of the name Jesus to make it the basis for transforming witnesses to him into ultimate authorities, whether Bible, creeds, reformers, or popes. One need simply remember Jesus' struggle with those in authority. He rejected even the term *good* when it was applied to him in isolation from God. "There is something in the Christian message which is opposed to established authority. There is something in the Christian experience which revolts against subjection to even the greatest and holiest experiences of the past" (NB, p. 87). This "something," as indicated before, is best symbolized by the cross, for Tillich "the greatest symbol of which I know for the true authority of the Church and the Bible. They should not point to themselves but to the reality which breaks again and again through the established forms of their authority and through the hardened forms of our personal experiences" (NB, p. 88).

The authority of Jesus as the Christ is not the consecrated image of one who rules as a dictator, but of one who emptied himself of all authority. And on this is modeled the authority of the Church, "not the consecrated earthly image of the Heavenly Ruler" but "a medium through which the Spiritual substance of our lives is preserved and protected and reborn" (NB, pp. 90–91).

7

The Church in the Modern World

*The joys and the hopes, the griefs and the anxieties of the men
of this age, especially those who are poor or in any way
afflicted, these too are the joys and hopes, the griefs and
anxieties of the followers of Christ. . . . United in Christ, they
are led by the Holy Spirit in their journey to the Kingdom of
their Father and they have welcomed the news of salvation
which is meant for every man. That is why this community
realizes that it is truly and intimately linked with mankind and
its history.*
Second Vatican Council, On the Church in the Modern World

Tillich died less than two months before the Second
Vatican Council gave its final approval to the Pastoral Constitution on the
Church in the Modern World. He never saw the completed document.
Although he would have taken exception to many of the statements in it, he
undoubtedly would have endorsed its intent. The relationship of the
Church to the world was a concern which, in a very real way, consumed his
entire professional career. Tillich looked upon his life and work as existing
on the boundary between Church and society, theology and philosophy,
religion and culture. With Dietrich Bonhoeffer, he saw the Church as
finding its salvation within the world, not in withdrawal from it. He called
the Church out of its ghetto, challenging it to take today's secular culture
into itself and transform it, even as the early Church absorbed and transformed the values of classical Greek and Hellenistic society. To refuse this
task would be to pay the price of hopeless irrelevance (FR, p. 55).

The challenge he extended to others, Tillich took up himself. Most of his writings, he affirmed, were an attempt to relate Christianity to secular culture (TC, p. v). Church and culture exist not alongside each other but within each other, and although existentially they tend to establish themselves as separate, essentially the religious and secular realms belong together. Religion is the depth dimension of culture. By defining religion and culture according to their broadest meaning, as ultimate concern and all the productions of man's creative spirit, respectively, Tillich viewed culture as the form of religion and religion as the substance of culture.[1]

In his attempt to relate Christianity to secular culture, Tillich sought not only to make the Church and its faith intelligible to today's world, but also to make more intelligible the situation of the world today to the Church. In both *The Religious Situation* (1926) and *The World Situation* (1945), Tillich analyzed Western society as characterized by the breakdown of the capitalistic spirit of self-sufficient finitude. Capitalistic society had attempted to establish human control over the world of nature and mind. But a breakdown of confidence in the complete rationality of science, technology, and capitalistic economy has led to a pervasive sense of meaninglessness and emptiness in our day, followed in turn by revolutionary movements and a search for new absolutes based upon secularism. The proper attitude which the Church should take to this situation is one of "belief-ful realism." It is a vision which unites the vertical with the horizontal dimension, one in which the Church, rather than merely opposing or surrendering to it, relates the world to the ground and source of its being and meaning.[2]

Tillich wrote extensively on three main areas concerning the Church in the modern world, areas in which he participated personally, and which determined the direction of much of his thinking on other questions of theology. Although oriented toward the practical, pastoral aspects of Church life, his thought in these areas flows logically from his more theoretical theology of the Church. All three are related to the polarity between Catholic substance and the Protestant principle. They are: the Church's task of interpreting Christian symbols for today; the question of the Church and social justice; and the relationship of the Church to the world religions.

Interpreting Christian Symbols for Today

Because symbols are the only language in which religion can express itself directly, the Church is perforce a symbol-creating community (GW1:277). Tillich's doctrine of religious symbols should be kept in mind here. Religious symbols appropriate empirical matter and transcend it, pointing to the absolute and participating in its meaning and power without being absolute in themselves. They are not true or false in the sense of cognitive judgments, but adequate with respect to their expressive power. And most important, because they are not absolute in themselves, symbols live and die. They live when they are able to produce a response in a group, when they are able to grasp people and thereby to unlock for them an otherwise closed aspect of reality and of the soul; and they die when the situation that produced them changes and they are no longer able to open up either reality or the soul. Whether a religious symbol within Christianity is alive or not can be judged only by the consciousness of the living Church.

Tillich was convinced that the Church today is faced with a grave hermeneutical problem. Its religious symbols have lost much of their power. The language and categories of the biblical prophets and Church Fathers are too far removed from our historical situation. They no longer speak to modern man nor do they move him. Merely echoing the past and parroting its formulas has become futile. Tillich asked, therefore, if symbols like original sin, salvation, the kingship of Christ, the Body of Christ, have died for our day or if they can be revived through interpretation. Because symbols cannot simply be replaced at will, he believed attempts must be made to revive them through interpretation. Tillich directed his entire theological work to this purpose, to the interpretation of religious symbols in such a way that secular man—and, living in secular society today, we are all secular men—can understand and be grasped and moved by them (ST3:4–5).

To interpret the symbols of Christianity and make them live is proper to the apologetic tradition of the Church. It is not a matter of defending God by having him fill in the gaps left by science. This kind of approach to apologetics has given it pejorative connotations. Apologetics, rather, should be seen in terms of mediation. It is an answering theology, in the tradition of Aquinas, Augustine, and the second-century apologists who answered the polemical attacks of pagan philosophers.[3] Apologetics must be distinguished from kerygmatic theology, in which the Church's message is reproduced and organized either in predominantly biblical terms or language taken from classical tradition. Apologetic theology attempts to answer questions and criticism of the Christian message. That which is customary or self-understood does not need apology or call for an answer. Anything that is new and unexpected, though, does need apology; it does owe an answer.[4]

To Tillich's mind, a theology of mediation is almost a tautology, since all theology implies mediation between mystery (*theos*) and understanding (*logos*). Theology speaks a rational word about God. God, however, is not directly the subject matter of theology; symbols are. Theology presupposes religion and the symbols with which religion expresses its ultimate concern. Thus Christian theology has the task of mediating the traditional symbols of Christianity, explaining and translating them, making them meaningful in terms of changing experiences, new questions, and different categories.[5]

Tillich related the question of translating Christian symbols to the very contemporary problem of the relevance of the Church, and in particular of the ministry, to today's world. It is regrettable but undeniable that the ministry of preaching has become largely irrelevant in our day, in spite of the fact that there are many highly educated, theologically learned, socially aware, and religiously devoted men and women in the ministry. The fault is not necessarily theirs. "It is history which has created the problem of the irrelevance of the minister, and not the inevitable deficiencies and failures of ministers, theologians, and Church authorities."[6] The problem lies at the root of secularism and its consequent search for the conquest of meaninglessness. The ministry and its message are of themselves quite pertinent. "Nothing could be more relevant for man than what concerns him ultimately."[7] But the Church and the preachers of its message have not yet learned to speak to people in a largely secularized world in such a way that those who hear them experience the ultimacy of the message.

Tillich did not deny the danger of mediating theology. Deviating from biblical language and ecclesiastical formulas obviously entails an accommodation which runs the risk of surrendering the substance of the Christian message.[8] But the risk must be taken. "Dangers are not a reason for avoiding a serious demand" (ST3:4).

The first task of theology in interpreting Christian symbols is deliteralizing them. To demythologize religion in the sense of removing symbols as a vehicle of its expression would be to deprive religion of its language. Not demythologization is needed, but deliteralization—a removal of literalist distortions which tend to make the symbols absurd. A literalist interpretation of Genesis in particular has proved responsible for reducing Christianity to the level of legend and superstition. The symbols connected with the ascension, second coming, and last judgment have been the victims of literalism as well. We all can be grateful to historical criticism of the Bible for liberating Christian truth from so many such distortions.[9]

Besides the negative task of deliteralizing Christian symbols, the Church has the positive task of translating them, of developing a new terminology which makes their original meaning clear. Words and expressions need to be found which are adequate to our own situation. Unfortunately, attempts thus far to translate the language of Scripture, tradition, and liturgy into a contemporary idiom have been less than successful. If symbols are dead, they should be discarded, Tillich held, no matter how long or glorious their tradition. Or at least they should not be used until transformed and reborn into their original power.[10] Symbols can be transformed from within, but only if we first ask ourselves what they mean for our existential situation, in other words, if we correlate them with life.

Correlation was the primary method Tillich used to revitalize Christian symbols. It has been called the "nerve" of his system.[11] Correlation first analyzes the human situation out of which existential questions arise; then it proceeds to show that the symbols of the Christian message provide answers to these questions (ST1:62–66). The symbols which embody the truths of Christianity are not simply derived from man's natural state; they are not merely creations of man's religious self-realization. But neither are they "strange bodies" fallen from a strange world, to be thrown at people's heads like stones. They should be seen instead as offering answers to the human predicament. In this way Tillich took a middle path between neo-orthodoxy, which holds for no point of contact between Christian faith and man's more general human thought and activity, and the nineteenth-century liberal idea that there is a simple relation between the two. Tillich correlated revelation with the question of reason; God with being; the Christ with existence; the Spirit with life; and the kingdom of God with history. In such a scheme, the God of Abraham, Isaac, and Jacob is by all means the God of the philosophers.

In order for correlation to succeed in revitalizing symbols, it should be remembered that a person cannot receive an answer to a question he has not asked yet. The Church must first know the questions that are being asked by people today before it can answer them. Before it can offer its symbols in answer to the questions of the human predicament, the Church must first participate in that predicament. Only after it has participated in finitude, anxiety, and estrangement can it appreciate the answers and healing which it has to offer (ST2:14–16).

Of particular assistance and advantage to the Church in making its symbols meaningful for our day is the existentialism which characterizes much of today's philosophical consciousness. In analyzing the human situation, existentialism asks questions about being and non-being and expresses concern about the meaning of existence and the problems of guilt and death. Its literature speaks of *The Wasteland, No Exit,* and *Man against Himself.* Within this framework, the Church can make its religious symbols more intelligible to people today.[12] Sin can become meaningful in terms of estrangement and inner conflict, salvation in terms of healing and the fulfilling of ultimate meaning in a person's existence. Justification makes new sense as accepting yourself as accepted. Jesus as the Christ acquires a new significance when viewed as the bearer of the New Being, which overcomes ambiguity and estrangement.[13]

In interpreting its symbols for our day, the Church removes unnecessary stumbling blocks to faith and allows the depth dimension of meaning to shine through its symbols and to offer light and certitude to a world harassed by unrest and chaos. The Church thus provides an inestimable service to the modern world.[14] But this alone is not enough. "The Christian answer must be at the same time both theoretical and practical. It will have reality only if it is the answer in action as well as in interpretation of men and women deeply involved in wrestling with the times" (WS, p. 49). The Church must not only speak to the world with its symbols, but also join with it in grappling with the problems of social justice.

The Church and Social Justice

Tillich was no "ivory tower" theologian. From almost the very beginning of his professional career, his theological principles propelled him into the arena of socio-political involvement. The chaotic condition of Europe at the end of World War I convinced him of the bankruptcy of the bourgeois world of self-sufficiency and easy satisfaction. Tillich took his stance with the political left and became one of the founders of Religious Socialism.[15]

Religious Socialism was neither a political party nor a religious organization but an unstructured attempt to understand socialism in a religious way. It accepted the analysis of capitalistic society made by Karl Marx and endeavored to place the struggle for social justice and the unity of mankind upon a Christian foundation. German Lutheranism, with its traditional anti-revolutionary bias, was estranged from the revolutionary spirit of the labor movements. The Church had allied itself with the *petite bourgeoisie* and found itself alienated from the working masses. Religious Socialism attempted to mediate between the two, between the individualism and transcendentalism of the Church and the secular utopianism of the socialist movements. It worked to convince the Church that there is a Christian humanism present in the labor movement and to convince socialism that Christianity is not simply otherworldly. To Tillich's mind, Religious Socialism was "the necessary form of Christian activity and apologetics among the working classes."[16]

Socialism continues to pose a serious challenge to the Church today, not the challenge of an enemy voice, but the challenge to cease absolutizing itself or identifying itself with the traditional forms of the past. In virtue of the Protestant principle, it is quite possible that God speaks more directly through the Church's antagonists than its representatives.[17] We need to recognize the quasi-religious character of socialism, its power to unite men in common cause, to evoke enthusiasm and even heroic sacrifice. The Church needs to ask itself whether, under the guise of secular theory and practice, socialism does not represent a special type of religion, originating in Jewish prophetism (PE, pp. 175–81).

Tillich did not advocate by any means that the Church should sub-scribe unconditionally to socialism. Jesus was not a socialist, and the prophetic message he preached was hardly an economic program. The New Testament gives neither law nor advice regarding concrete political behavior. Christianity is independent of every particular cultural form and every particular political and economic order. This has been demonstrated time and again by the Church's ability to exist either in the slave system of late Rome, the agrarian system of the Middle Ages, or the capitalistic system of today. Despite this independence, though, given the ethics of love established by Jesus, Christianity does have more affinity for some socio-economic systems than for others. Christian ethics cannot help but raise objections to any ordering of society which is based fundamentally upon political and economic egoism, which leads to a division of society into privileged and underprivileged classes, and thereby robs millions of people of meaningful lives. Socialism cannot become a doctrine of the Church, but it can be viewed as a demand of the concrete situation of contemporary late industrial society.[18]

Tillich believed the Church should maintain a positive attitude to-ward socialism, not simply to win over the laboring classes but because of the ethical ideal which socialism presents. The Church should recognize that organization of security against the devastation of atomic warfare or of permanent unemployment requires collectivist measures. The Church should affirm the socialist hope of a new world and perceive Marxism, even in its communist form, as a secularized expression of Christian hope in the realization of the kingdom of God in history.[19] To its positive affirmation, though, the Church must join a negative critique as well. The Church must struggle against the tyranny and dehumanization present in communism, as it must struggle against the demonic elements in every political movement. This is the prophetic mission of the Church in its relation to the world today, to attack the demonic, absolutist claims made by any political party, by any movement or government.[20] The Protestant principle protests against the consecration of ideologies and political power structures as much as against ecclesiastical absolutes.

Although the Church can criticize a given social reality prophetically by invoking the Christian principles of justice and love, it is not equipped to decide about the concrete application of those principles. It cannot outline perfect social structures or suggest concrete reforms. This must be left to the courage, intuition, and risk of individuals and voluntary groups (TC, pp. 50, 197–98). In the area of economics, even though it cannot offer technical advice, the Church "can insist that the virtually infinite productive capacities of mankind shall be used for the advantage of everyone, instead of being restricted and wasted by the profit interest of a controlling class" (WS, p. 23). In the political realm, without offering detailed or legal suggestions, the Church "must declare that . . . those political forms are right which are able to produce and maintain a community in which chronic fear of a miserable and meaningless life for the masses is abolished, and in which every man participates creatively in the self-realization of the community, whether local, national, regional, or international" (WS, p. 27).

If the Church through its ministers does address itself to matters of political organization, it must do so as the Church and not as a pseudo-political agency.

> The relevance of the ministry lies not in its political utterances, nor in their possible value, but in its representation of the source from which such utterances should come. If churches work as political pressure groups under the leadership of their ministers, they do what other groups also do, while no other group can replace the Church. Only by embodying and preaching the new reality on which it is based can the Church and its ministry be relevant for our time.[21]

In other words, the Church's message to the world today must be both judging and transforming. Otherwise the Church becomes just another servant of public opinion, just another contributor to what is already accepted. The Church must combine the vertical, trans-historical dimension and its transcendent concerns, with the horizontal, historical dimension and its concerns for peace and justice here and now. The dual character of the kingdom of God as both within history and beyond it should always be kept in mind in this effort. The Church must be both the city on the mountaintop and the leaven in the meal, both separated from the world and involved in it. The vertical dimension points to eternal meaning and saves the horizontal from an empty activism that inevitably resolves itself into cynicism and despair. The horizontal dimension points to the temporal realization of the eternal and prevents the vertical from becoming an escapist gnosticism, indifferent to a world it considers evil. "If religion is to speak a transcending, judging, and transforming word to the people of our time, it must do so in both directions, the vertical and the horizontal, and this in mutual interdependence" (PE, p. 186).

In combining the vertical and horizontal dimensions, the Church in its relation to the world must combine "religious obligation" with "religious reserve." It must be more than an agency safeguarding accepted moral standards, a servant to a social, cultural system. The Church must point to the transcendent meaning of life. Hence, its religious reserve. But the Church represents this transcendent meaning of life in the midst of history and for the sake of history. It serves to anticipate as well as point to the kingdom of God and its justice, to be the "fighting side" of the kingdom of God in history. Hence, its religious obligation (GW10:158, 214). This then is the word the Church must speak to the world today, not a political or economic word but a religious word, "the word of those who know something about man and history; who know the tragedy and the hope involved in the temporal because they know about the eternal . . ." (PE, p. 191).

The Church and the World Religions

The challenge posed in our day by socialism is one which vexes not only Christianity. All the world religions are confronted by the invasion of modern technology, an invasion usually followed by a secularization which destroys old traditions both of culture and religion. Religious indifference inevitably accompanies secularization, but only as a transitory phase. The vacuum it produces is subsequently filled by the appearance of such quasi-religions as socialism, communism, nationalism, or liberal humanism— secular movements which make as their ultimate concern not God but rather such concerns as science, a nation, a particular form of society, or a highest ideal of humanity. The world religions have proved no more prepared than the Christian churches to meet the challenge of secularization and the quasi-religions. The common need to meet this challenge, together with the conquest of distance by modern technology, has brought about a *kairos* for creative dialogue between the Church and the world religions. This is an opportunity which the Church cannot ignore, if it is to cease being provincial (ST3:6).

Tillich's interest in the world religions dated back to the mid-1920s and Marburg, where he discussed the problems of Christianity and the world religions with Rudolf Otto. His interest was rekindled many years later when he spent ten weeks in Japan in dialogue with Buddhist priests and scholars. This dialogue resulted in Tillich giving a series of lectures in 1961 at Columbia University, later published under the title, *Christianity and the Encounter of the World Religions.* But even Tillich's earlier writings demonstrate the significance of other religions for the Church. His concept of universal revelation, the importance of the Logos idea in his theology, his development of latent Spiritual Community, all stemmed from and contributed to the high esteem Tillich had for the revealing and saving powers he believed to be inherent in all religions.[22]

With regard to Judaism, Tillich admitted to a unique relationship between the Synagogue and the Church. He called for the replacement of any mission of conversion toward Jews with attitudes of openness, affirmation, and dialogue. Such affirmation rests upon the foundation of the New Testament, in particular the epistle to the Ephesians, which allows for the interpretation that Jews and Christians live together under the same covenant (UC, p. 105). Tillich characterized Judaism as upholding the God of time over the gods of space. It represents the spirit of prophetic criticism against tendencies toward idolatry that exist within the Church as well as within Jews themselves and other national groups. The Church needs this prophetic criticism as well as the Jewish reminder of its pagan roots. It needs the Jewish reminder of the "not yet," of the fact that the work of the Christ is not yet finished. Together with believing Jews, the Church awaits the coming of the Messiah, although for Christians it is the second coming. The bond between Judaism and Christianity requires of the Church not only the rooting out of Anti-Judaism but also the affirmation of the Old Testament as an integral ingredient of Christian existence.[23]

With regard to the religions of the East, the basis for affirmation and dialogue exists not in a common covenant as with Judaism but in those elements which are common to all religions. Catholic substance and the Protestant principle are constituents in all religion. "None of the various elements which constitute the meaning of the holy are ever completely lacking in any genuine experience of the holy, and, therefore, in any religion" (CEWR, p. 67). These elements belong to the very nature of man, the universe, and the Logos as the revelatory self-manifestation of the divine. Examples of such elements are sacrifice, miracles, and concepts of holiness, of the divine, and of the demonic. There are sacramental, prophetic, and mystical elements in every religion. The decisive point for dialogue between Christianity and the world religions is not the historically determined, contingent embodiment of these elements but rather the elements themselves.[24] In the light of these analogies and of the Protestant principle, Tillich took critical exception to the attitude which views all religions other than one's own as false and futile human attempts to reach God. The people outside Judaism and Christianity are not outside God. They participate in latent Spiritual Community and are grasped by God on the level at which they can be grasped—in their experience of the Divine, in the realm of holiness in which they are living and in which they perform acts of faith, adoration, prayer, and cult, even though the symbols with which they express the holy may seem primitive and idolatrous. It may be distorted religion, but not non-religion. It is the reality of the Divine preparing within the latent Church for the manifest Church.[25]

> It is regrettable and altogether unconvincing if Christian apologetics begins with a criticism of the historical religions without attempting to understand the typological analogies between them and Christianity and without emphasizing the element of the universal preparatory revelation which they carry within them. [ST1:221]

Tillich did not hesitate to offer suggestions for conducting dialogue between Christianity and the world religions. By way of beginning, such interreligious discussions should not concentrate on contrasting concepts of God, man, history, or salvation. Rather, they should begin with the question of the intrinsic aim of existence, the *telos* of all existing things. Whether intentionally or not, all religions and quasi-religions attempt to give an answer to this question. Another valid point for discussion, and one which would avoid the hazards of dogmatic subtleties, is secularization and the confrontation of religion with secular quasi-religions (CEWR, p. 63). No matter what the questions discussed, though, dialogue between representatives of the Church and the world religions makes certain presuppositions:

> It first presupposes that both partners acknowledge the value of the other's religious convictions (as based ultimately on a revelatory experience), so that they consider the dialogue worthwhile. Second, it presupposes that each of them is able to represent his own religious basis with conviction, so that the

> dialogue is a serious confrontation. Third, it presupposes a common ground which makes both dialogue and conflicts possible, and, fourth, the openness of both sides to criticism directed against their own religious basis. [CEWR, p. 62]

Tillich regarded this last point, an openness of both sides to criticism, to be of special importance. In its dialogue with the world religions, the Church must be open to judgment and criticism. First, however, it must criticize itself—by the event upon which it is based—the appearance and reception of Jesus as the Christ, "a symbol which stands for the decisive self-manifestation in human history of the source and aim of all being" (CEWR, p. 79). With Jesus as the Christ as its criterion, the Church judges not only itself but other religions as well.

> What is particular in him is that he crucified the particular in himself for the sake of the universal. This liberates his image from bondage both to a particular religion—the religion to which he belonged has thrown him out— and to the religious sphere as such; the principle of love in him embraces the cosmos, including both the religions and the secular spheres. With this image, particular yet free from particularity, religious yet free from religion, the criteria are given under which Christianity must judge itself and, by judging itself, judge also the other religions and the quasi-religions. [CEWR, pp. 81–82]

Once again the Protestant principle manifests itself in Tillich's theology, attacking any claim to absolute validity raised by any religion as well as by any church. No absolute symbols, no absolute political systems, no absolute religions. The claim of a religion to absoluteness can be no more than a claim to witness to the absolute in a relative way. The more a religion implies this in its essential nature, the more compelling its claim to truth (SA, pp. 140–41).

Because the Protestant principle denies absoluteness to any religion, an attitude of mutual self-judgment between the Church and the world religions serves to prevent Christianity from any mission of "conversion" in the traditional sense of the word. To Tillich's mind, not conversion but exchange, mutual giving and receiving, should be the aim of dialogue between the Church and the world religions. Missionary success has been very limited in a nation like Japan, where superior civilizing forces have shaped society. But dialogic encounter can make inroads into the spirituality of the world religions, breaking through mutually to the point at which the vision of the holy liberates us from bondage to any particular manifestation of the holy (CEWR, pp. 60–61). "A particular religion will be lasting to the degree in which it negates itself as a religion" (CEWR, p. 97).

The aim of interreligious dialogue, therefore, is not to make converts but to drive other religions to their own depths, to that point where they realize that they are witnesses to the absolute without being absolute in themselves (SA, pp. 140–41). This does not demand that the Church or any religion relinquish its particular tradition but rather that it evaluate it properly.

> In the depth of every living religion there is a point at which the religion itself loses its importance, and that to which it points breaks through its particularity, elevating it to spiritual freedom and with it to a vision of the spiritual presence in other expressions of the ultimate meaning of man's existence. This is what Christianity must see in the present encounter of the world religions. [CEWR, p. 97]

On October 12, 1965, Tillich presented a public lecture at the University of Chicago entitled, "The Significance of the History of Religions for the Systematic Theologian." In it he credited two years of seminars with Mircea Eliade on world religions as providing him with new and fresh insights into the Christian message. "Every individual doctrinal statement or ritual expression of Christianity receives a new intensity of meaning" (FR, p. 91). He told his audience that, had he the time, he would write another *Systematic Theology*, this time not oriented toward twentieth-century Western society, so totally involved in the secular world of science and technology, but about a theology oriented toward and in dialogue with the whole history of religion (FR, p. 91). Tillich did not have the time, however; that lecture on the history of religions proved to be his last. He suffered a severe heart attack the next morning and died ten days later. His last expressed hope for the future of theology, in dialogue with the world and the religions of the world, may well be regarded as his hope for the future of the Christian Church.

Tillich died as he had lived, situated on a boundary, searching out new and distant boundaries—between East and West, between the twentieth century and twenty-first, between a two thousand year old Church and a new world aborning. His open and forthright appraisal of world religions and the secular quasi-religions of our day was dialectical, but essentially affirmative. To the end he countered Catholic substance with the Protestant principle. The polarity between them provides an apt conclusion to an exposition of his theology of the Church, even as it constituted a fitting conclusion to a lifetime spent in theological service to that Church.

PART TWO

A Catholic Appraisal

8

On Venturing a Critique of Paul Tillich

Catholic theologians engaged in ecumenical dialogue, while standing fast by the teaching of the Church and searching together with separated brethern into the divine mysteries, should act with love for truth, with charity, and with humility.
Second Vatican Council, Decree on Ecumenism

It is no little thing to venture a critique of Paul Tillich, either about the Church or any other aspect of his theology. But, like the mountain that has to be climbed simply because it is there, Tillich's thought provokes scaling.[1] Few who have essayed it would deny it was worth the effort. His less sympathetic readers may conclude that the proper function of his theology is to arouse constructive criticism,[2] yet even they admit that no theologian had more to say to our day concerning the vital issues of faith and understanding than Tillich.[3] Certainly, together with Barth, Bonhoeffer, and Bultmann, Tillich belongs among the giants who have stamped their imprint upon Protestant thought in this century. That imprint is increasingly being felt in Catholic theology as well.

Difficulties

Even for the theologically sophisticated, "to think with Tillich requires arduous, repeated and continuous effort."[4] He poses difficulties which complicate not only criticism but even comprehension.

First, there is the depth, complexity, and obscurity of his profoundly

163

dialectical thought. For Tillich, "the undialectical No is as primitive and unproductive as the undialectical Yes."[5] Not without good reason did he entitle his intellectual biography *On the Boundary*. He saw it as his fate "in almost every direction, to stand between alternative possibilities, completely at home in neither."[6] His theological career encompassed not only two continents and two eras marked by two world wars but spanned as well the polarities of theology and philosophy, religion and culture, Church and society, the history of ideas and the challenge of today's need. Because of his firm rejection of fundamentalism, he stood much closer to the tradition of nineteenth-century liberal theology than most of his contemporaries. Yet he defies the label *radical* or *conservative*. Like all systematic thinkers who have produced a large corpus of material over a lifetime, Tillich transcends simple analysis, or at least any analysis simpler than that of a philosophical idealist, working within a phenomenological framework and maintaining an existentialist approach to life as he sought to understand and explain Christian symbols.[7]

Second, compounding the difficulty is the problem of Tillich's language, its lack of classical categories and vocabulary, whether biblical or theological.[8] The result is an elusiveness which sometimes arouses the suspicion of being studied. Conspicuous in their absence are references to Scripture, tradition, and the usual scholarly apparatus of bibliography and footnotes. Often enough his system redefines terms by giving them new nuances. And, when traditional terms would not do, Tillich felt perfectly free to employ new terms, which have since become part of the theologian's stock in trade, for example, ultimate concern, Spiritual Community, *kairos*, Catholic substance, the Protestant principle. His language alone explains how he can be both attacked and claimed by theological camps ordinarily opposed to one another.[9]

A third difficulty with Tillich's theology is its terse style. His *Systematic Theology* comprises only three volumes, quantitatively a modest achievement compared to Barth's *Church Dogmatics*. But Tillich's style is so compact, and the questions he considers in the *Systematic Theology* are so numerous and complex, that even an informed reader often finds it necessary to reread passages several times in order to grasp all the implications fully. It has been estimated that the three volumes might easily have encompassed three times the number of pages.[10]

And finally, the breadth of his thought poses yet another difficulty for the Tillich reader and critic. No dimension of human life was foreign to his philosophical or theological interest, whether depth psychology, modern art, architecture, or contemporary political and social issues. Regardless of what area of human life to which he addressed himself, Tillich brought to it

an almost awesome command of the history of ideas. The many epigramma-
tic allusions sprinkled throughout his writings indicate indirectly what is
more amply demonstrated by the authorized transcriptions of his lectures
on the history of Christian thought (HCT; PPT).

Tillich was a confessed Lutheran by birth, education, and experience,
and he maintained that the substance of his theology remained Lutheran
(OB, pp. 74–75). His coreligionists were sometimes hard pressed, however, to recognize him as within the Lutheran family.[11] His thinking was
drawn from the whole sweep of Christian tradition. The deep concern of
early Greek thought for the question of being;[12] the writings of the Greek
and Latin Fathers, especially Origen and Augustine;[13] the scholastics and
mystics of the Middle Ages; the Renaissance humanists; the sixteenth-
century reformers; the theologians of the Enlightenment and of
nineteenth-century liberalism with its quest for the historical Jesus; the
syntheses of Hegel, Schleiermacher, and Ritschl,[14] their neo-orthodox
critics; and Karl Marx—all of them provided Tillich with the raw material
which he worked into his own original synthesis. He quarried for theological gold in some of the most unlikely places, in both familiar and sometimes
forgotten mines.[15] German speculation (TC, p. 163) in particular left its
mark upon Tillich—the idealism of Schelling and through him the mysticism of Jacob Boehme,[16] the anti-rationalism of Schleiermacher, the ill-
fated quest of Troeltsch to find absolutes within the contingencies of history,[17] the phenomenology of Rudolf Otto,[18] the existentialism of Heidegger.[19] Without citing it explicitly, Tillich's writing indicates a more than
casual familiarity with the work of modern critical biblical exegesis; he held
that its impact was in every part of his system.[20] A list of other influences
indicating the breadth of his thought would have to include Nicholas of
Cusa, Calvin, Spinoza, Kant, Kierkegaard, Nietzsche, Dilthey, Kähler,
and Buber. To these Tillich himself added the historical developments
which had made an impact upon his system, that is, the encounter of
religion with secularism, the exchange between Christianity and the world
religions, and the ecumenical rapprochement between Catholics and Protestants (ST3:6–7). In the face of such catholicity of competence, his critics
often found it difficult to restrain expressing their admiration: "Professor
Tillich's thought is vast; his erudition, amazing; his breadth, dazzling."[21]

Catholic Affinities

If Tillich's thought, language, style, and breadth prove formidable
for Protestants, a Catholic might well regard himself as all the more

handicapped. Words are often used differently in Catholic theology and there is a long history of differing questions, categories, and philosophical orientation. Protestant theology often moves on an entirely different niveau.[22] Yet there are affinities which permit a Catholic to feel quite at home with Tillich.

Remarkable consistency is a feature not only of Tillich's *Systematic Theology* but also of his other writings, including the earlier ones in which the themes of his system are found in germ.[23] Unlike Barth's *Church Dogmatics,* in which the thought evolves from one volume to the next, Tillich's system has been compared to those of Aquinas, Calvin, and Schleiermacher. Tillich has been called Thomist, not because of his subscription to Thomistic theses, but because "he is moved by the same feeling for unity and completeness in his vision of the real."[24] Tillich himself maintained that Protestant theology could well learn from the medieval tradition of systematic thinking: "The medieval thinkers knew that in order to think consistently, you must think systematically" (HCT, p. 159).

The willingness to pursue philosophical theology and thereby seek a synthesis also renders Tillich congenial to Catholic theology. It likewise served to make Tillich something of an anomaly among his Protestant contemporaries who emphasized the estrangement between philosophy and theology, the diastasis between Christianity and the modern mind.[25] Tillich believed that "synthesis can never be avoided" (HCT, p. 293). He admitted that it was "a driving force in all my theological work."[26] It was the method of correlation which provided him the *via media* for a synthesis that avoided either identification or estrangement of philosophy and theology (HCT, p. 293).

Not only the medieval system and synthesis but medieval ontology as well relates Tillich to Catholic theology. Ontological concepts like "being itself," "essences," and "universals" may have fallen strangely upon American Protestant ears but they strike familiar chords in Catholic theology. The distinction between essence and existence is central to Tillich's ontology, and his use of the analogy of being has been regarded as his closest link with Catholic theology.[27] On the basis of his "comparatively medieval realistic kind of thinking," Tillich admitted that "there is hardly a day that I do not fight against nominalism" and therefore logical positivism (HCT, p. 143).

His consistent, synthetic, and ontological thinking substantiates the opinion that "there is much Catholicism in Tillich . . . ."[28] His command and use of Catholic theological tradition certainly exempted him from Harnack's complaint against Protestants who know more about Gnosticism than the Catholic Church.[29] Indeed, he can be credited with familiarity with phases of Catholic thought usually ignored by Catholic theologians.[30] But these affinities do not suffice to explain the growing interest in Tillich manifested by the increasing number of Catholic books, dissertations, and articles on his theology, or the popularity of courses on his theology at Catholic colleges and universities. Not his antinominalism explains the importance his theology is assuming within post Vatican II Catholicism but his attempt to seek a solution to the conflicts between religious tradition and the modern mind, his attempt to translate the Christian message and give it new relevance.

Throughout his theological career Tillich wrestled with the apologetic question formulated by Schleiermacher: "Shall the knot of history be thus loosed: Christianity with barbarism and learning with unbelief?"[31] Unlike Schleiermacher, however, it was not to the "cultured despisers of religion" that Tillich directed his writing but to the "lost souls of modern men."[32] For this reason he has been called the Origen of our day, "seeking to relate the Gospel message to the disciplines of our culture and to the whole history of culture."[33] Tillich struggled to reconcile the tension between religious and humanist traditions, between Christian faith and modern technological Western society. By his own admission Tillich's entire theological endeavor was aimed at making the Christian faith mean something for people today, especially for young people. He sought to make faith possible by removing unnecessary obstacles and searching into the depths of the Christian tradition to find positive answers to their questions. To this end he pointed to the timeless elements within Christianity, too often unwittingly rejected along with those aspects of the Christian tradition which science and technology have rendered unacceptable.[34]

> The church never took seriously the problem of finding a union of tradition with the modern mind and of showing the significance of the traditional symbols to modern man. [PPT, pp. 63–64]

> I presuppose in my theological thinking the entire history of Christian thought up until now, and I consider the attitude of those people who are in doubt or estrangement or opposition to everything ecclesiastical and religious, including Christianity. And I have to speak to them. My work is with those who ask questions, and for them I am here. [UC, p. 191]

In the light of the dialogue he conducted with modern philosophy and culture, post-conciliar Catholicism is finding in Tillich a forerunner, if not always a model. His avowed loyalty to the Christian tradition yet his freedom from its forms exerts a profound fascination upon Catholics bent upon renewal and caught up in the twin tasks of critical reinterpretation and reevaluation which renewal implies. The undertaking he assumed explains not only Catholic interest in Tillich, but also the extremes of reaction which his work aroused, whether by way of acclaim or critical rejection.

The Critics and Their Contradictions

Superlatives are rarely accorded by theological critics. Yet the difficulty of the challenge Tillich took up and the competence he brought to it inspired a degree of positive approval often hard put to express itself short of enthusiasm. Tillich was hailed by his critics as: "the outstanding Protestant theologian of our time";[35] a modern Thomas Aquinas;[36] "the most enlightening and therapeutic theologian of our time";[37] an apostle to the skeptics, the intellectuals, the disillusioned of our era;[38] a "landmark and turning point in the history of modern theology";[39] "a modern Renaissance man in the best possible sense of that term";[40] "daring, learned, urbane, tolerant, massive, and sharply critical . . . a figure in whom the present dominates all his knowledge of the past."[41] As the "most philosophical of the theologians of our century,"[42] Tillich has been regarded as a stroke of good fortune for our day (*ein Grenzfall, ein Sonderfall, ein Glücksfall*).[43] He was able to join philosophical eros to Christian agape.[44] The advent of his system has been described as something to celebrate,[45] as one of the most significant religious accomplishments of our century.[46]

> Paul Tillich has spoken to modern man with a penetration which is perhaps unequaled by any other man of thought. It is the honesty with which he approaches reality and the freshness with which he discusses the perplexities and joys of our individual and collective lives which make his writings fascinating.[47]

> He was a mystic in a pragmatic culture, a biblical theologian and preacher in a technological age, an existentialist in a functional society, an ontologist and in a way a rationalist in a positivistic era, a philosopher of religion in a time when many theologians as well as secularists scorned both philosophy and religion.[48]

> The adjective "great" . . . can be applied to very few thinkers of our time, but Tillich, . . . stands unquestionably amongst these few.[49]

Despite the acclaim he received, Tillich, unlike Barth, never founded anything like a movement or school of theology. Although he disavowed the Death of God theologians as "going too far,"[50] they claimed him as "the modern father of radical theology."[51] The Death of God movement has already waned, though, whereas Tillich's influence is just beginning to make itself felt, not only within Catholic theology as already suggested but also in Germany, where his works have been translated and collected (GW). It is this mounting impact beyond American Protestant circles which may yet prove Tillich to be not only "the most influential theologian in America,"[52] or "the most profound and far-reaching among contemporary theologians"[53] but also "beyond our day—the voice of the theological ages."[54]

As extravagant as the praise Tillich often received was, by no means was it unanimous. Strong negative criticism was also his lot, proving him no more exempted from the *rabies theologorum* than any other creative religious thinker. Because of his lack of traditional terminology, his willingness to seek a synthesis, and his attempt to reinterpret the Christian message, Tillich has been variously labeled as an atheist, a communist, a nihilist, and a liberal.[55] He has been accused of such sundry and ordinarily incompatible heresies as Sabellianism, Docetism, Adoptionism, Nestorianism, and Manichaeism.[56] His method of correlation has been attacked from one side for forging the questions in the light of predetermined answers,[57] and from the other side for subordinating religious faith to ontology.[58]

The criticisms against him range widely—from overlooking the divine element in Scripture and minimizing its historical element,[59] to diluting the gospel with non-biblical elements, falsifying pneumatology, and explaining the clear with the obscure.[60] Tillich has also been reproached for giving the impression of being the first to discover the full meaning of the cross.[61] He has been denied the mantle of traditional Protestantism, let alone traditional Christianity. "A Protestantism that has come to light only in the twentieth century can no more be Protestantism than a Christology discovered in the twentieth century can be the Christology of Revelation."[62] For allegedly forsaking transcendence as a reality and accepting it only as transcendent meaning, Tillich has even been called "the most dangerous theologian" of his day.[63]

One of the most frequent criticisms leveled against Tillich is ontologism, reducing Christianity to philosophy by stripping it of its specifically Christian elements and converting its doctrines into universal philosophical concepts.[64] This is not simply a complaint that Tillich's language or categories are too philosophical, impersonal, or abstract; the accusation is that he approaches more closely the impersonal world of the East and the Vedanta than the personalist world of ideas found in the Bible.[65] At those points where he is too close for comfort to Hegel or

Schleiermacher, Tillich has been rejected as putting aside the kerygma in favor of a logos philosophy.[66] His theology has been dismissed as incompatible with both Scripture and Christian tradition.

Tillich was not without his critics, nor was he without his defenders. Against the charge there was too little of the kerygmatic in his theology, Tillich himself countered with the claim that the influence of historical-critical biblical theology was present throughout his system (ST3:4). Tillich saw himself as a mediating rather than as a kerygmatic theologian like Barth (ST1:4–6). But, as one of his apologists pointed out, Tillich would be the last to claim finality for his views,[67] or, it might be added, exclusiveness. Tillich never claimed that correlation was the only method of theologizing. Moreover, Tillich admitted that he personally leaned to conservatism in New Testament exegesis. He believed there is a more accurate portrayal of Jesus in the gospels than many extreme critics allow. But he refused to permit Christian faith to rest on the vagaries of biblical scholarship.[68] In contrast to those critics who accuse him of unfaithfulness to Scripture, Tillich's theology has also been judged as "wholly and finally determined by the revelation of God recorded in the Bible."[69]

Against those critics who classified Tillich simply as a nineteenth-century liberal, it has been countered that, although he keeps some liberal principles, Tillich is no liberal theologian.[70] He recognized the powerful historical-critical leadership of liberal theology, but, along with neo-orthodox theologians, reacted against its tendency to reduce Christianity to simply a consciousness of history. He explicitly refused to align himself with a theology which replaced a crucified Christ with a historical Jesus, or which resolved with moral categories the paradox of justification by grace.[71] Tillich also rejected the optimistic liberal doctrine of progress. As he wrote to Thomas Mann:

> We found it impossible to agree with the theological position of the liberals. It seemed to us that they lacked insight into the "demonic" character of human existence. . . . We concluded that the conservative tradition had preserved more of the true understanding of human nature and of the tragedy of existence than had the liberal progressive bourgeois ideology.[72]

Tillich's attitude toward liberalism must be judged as dialectical. While he accepted its historical-critical methodology, he attacked any scheme of self-salvation, emphasizing grace alone as the means for justification. He attacked liberalism's rejection of mysticism as well as its anti-metaphysical bias. He criticized as well its attempt to strip religion of symbols, choosing instead deliteralization and reinterpretation.[73]

Against those who charged him with novelty and heterodoxy, Tillich's theology has been defended as being "in intention and achievement, conservative."[74] His basic categories and concepts are not without precedent in Christian tradition. His favorite ideas and terms, which may sound novel, often enough in actuality have time-honored ancestors.[75] His originality lay not in new concepts but in "his depth of insight, the systematic consistency with which he developed the internal relations of the various elements of his philosophy and theology, and the daring he displayed in crossing borders into new fields."[76] Against those who accused him of pantheism, because of his doctrine of the God beyond God, Tillich has been described as being "on the side of the angels," or, more specifically, on the side of the Angelic Doctor; with Aquinas, Tillich saw God as transcending all categories, as the *ens realissimum,* the *summum bonum.*[77] Against those critical of his Christology, it has been pointed out that Tillich asserts that Jesus is in fact the Word of God made manifest in human life and that this manifestation makes a difference.[78] Even one who found it difficult to accept Tillich's notion of Symbol as an adequate basis for Christology, instead of incarnation, has admitted that Tillich sees Christ as making Christianity what it is. Christ is the center of history for Tillich, the end of the beginning and the beginning of the end.[79] Another critic has put it more succinctly, "the general tenor of Tillich's theology seems . . . to stand within the classical dogmas."[80]

The late Jesuit theologian, Gustave Weigel, who has been frequently cited here, was not only an enthusiastic admirer of Tillich but also a staunch apologist. Tillich credited him once with "the best analysis of my thought I ever have seen. It is incisive, clear, and benevolent at the same time."[81] Weigel refused to be convinced by those critics who accused Tillich of being a fifth columnist, wittingly or unwittingly destroying Christianity from within.[82] In Weigel's estimation, Tillich had no scorn or contempt for the past. He was no adolescent iconoclast. But he refused to be tied down to the errors of the past, just because they belonged to his heritage. He was neither a disdainful rebel nor a servile repeater.[83]

Tillich stressed, overstressed, or understressed those parts of the Christian tradition he believed needed to be stressed, overstressed, or understressed, in order to interpret it for our day.[84] And this, together with other difficulties cited above, explains why Tillich was so frequently misunderstood. "He seems neo-orthodox to the liberal theologian, liberal to the neo-orthodox, modernist to the fundamentalist, indiscriminately biblical to the modernist, historicist to the idealistic philosopher, and idealistic to the historicist."[85]. It becomes apparent that the only way to approach a

171

critique of Tillich's theology is not only with care but also with an open mind. The dialectical subtlety of his thought, the elusive ambiguity of his language, the terseness of his style, and, above all, his avowed intention to reinterpret the gospel for our day by freeing it from outdated forms expose Tillich to misunderstanding. Just how often Tillich *de facto* was misunderstood can be seen by examining the critical secondary literature regarding his work, in particular those collections of critical essays in which Tillich had the opportunity to respond (KB; OW).

Tillich needs to be read carefully; he deserves to be judged the same way. Because he was convinced that so many words in the Christian vocabulary have become twisted and falsified by their connotations, Tillich felt compelled to seek new ways to express the traditional Christian message. An evaluation of his work merits a corresponding effort. As one commentator put it: "We must not be content to compare his *expression* of the Christian message with ours; we must go beyond words; we must judge Tillich's theology on the basis of his intention, the *sense* of the totality of his words, and the correspondence of that sense with reality."[86] It has been said that his intention was patently pious.[87] If for no other reason than its intention, Tillich's theology deserves to be read *in meliorem partem*.

If the ecumenical experience of recent years has shown anything, it is that there is some truth in every falsehood and some falsehood in every truth. There is orthodoxy latent in every heresy and heresy latent in every dogma of orthodoxy. The same truth can be approached from different points of view, expressed in different terms and categories. Ecumenical dialogue, both official and otherwise, has succeeded beyond the wildest conjectures of just a few years ago in demonstrating substantial agreement among Catholics and various Protestant churches on such various areas of faith as the Nicene Creed, Baptism, and the Eucharist. Its success has indicated the necessity of being open, of being willing to see and to embrace truth no matter what its sources, no matter how new or alien its forms.

Whether in the name of truth or fairness, there is no other way to attempt a critique of Tillich's theology. To be sure, irenics do not exclude honesty. Judging *in meliorem partem* does not justify misrepresenting Tillich's thought for the sake of superficial similarity. But neither does it permit presumption of error or rejoicing in incompatibility. Reinhold Niebuhr described Tillich's exploration of the boundary between metaphysics and theology as walking on a tightrope. It is "not negotiated without the peril of losing one's balance and falling over on one side or the other. . . . Tillich performs upon it with the greatest virtuosity, but not without an occasional fall. The fall may be noticed by some humble pedestrians who lack every gift to perform the task themselves."[88] Does Tillich lose his balance in his theology of the Church? Judging *in meliorem partem* requires that this be not lightly presumed. And, if it proves he does, the fall should be seen not only as regrettable but all the more as a challenge to learn from him and do better.

9

The Priestly and Prophetic in Polarity

While we are divided in faith, we are divided within the same faith—the same, because and insofar as we and you can believe in the self-same Lord.

Karl Barth, "A Letter to the Author," in Küng, Justification

The first task to be faced in any critique of Tillich's theology of the Church is that of limiting the area of consideration. In attempting an adequate presentation of his ecclesiology, concepts have been introduced from several different areas of Tillich's theology—the nature of revelation and religon, the nature of religious symbols, the God beyond God, Christology and the New Being, Spiritual Presence. Although those concepts may have raised questions and are related, perhaps even intimately, to Tillich's theology of the Church, they have been mentioned only in passing, and cannot constitute a primary concern here.

Even within the proper realm of Tillich's ecclesiology, several avenues of approach might be taken, any number of areas invite questioning and development. There is Tillich's theology of the Church as the Community of the New Being and Tillich's provocative notion that Jesus would not have been the Christ if he had not been received as such by the Church. It has been suggested that "this is, perhaps, the highest view of the theological importance of the church ever held by a theologian. The church is not simply helpful (or beneficial, in older language, part of the *bene esse*) to God's activities, but it is necessary (part of the very being or *esse*) to God's salvatory actions through Christ."[1] There is also Tillich's solution to the question of the Church and the historical Jesus. With his concern to save faith from the ravages of biblical criticism, does Tillich reduce the Church to a mystery religion, cut loose from any historical roots? What does the "New Quest of the Historical Jesus" have to say to Tillich in this regard? What of Tillich's solution to the question as to when and how the Church took its origin from Jesus?

Tillich's concept of Spiritual Community offers another attractive possibility of approach. It has been rightly observed that "the idea of the overlapping quality of the spiritual community is simultaneously one of the most traditional ideas and one of the most liberal and creative concepts in Tillich's theology."[2] Neither Catholics nor Protestants today are satisfied with Luther's emphasis upon the *ecclesia spiritualis,* Calvin's notion of the Church as an emergency creation, or Bellarmine's idea of the Church as visible as the Republic of Venice. Does Spiritual Community help to understand better the relationship of the invisible and visible elements of the Church by seeing them in terms of essence and existence?[3] Can it give a fuller appreciation of the relationship of the Church to the Holy Spirit? Does it clarify the meaning of the marks of the Church within ecclesiology? And what of Tillich's subsequent distinction between the Church as a theological and as a sociological reality? Or the distinction between the necessary functions of the Church and the institutions which serve those functions, without being individually necessary themselves? What are the other implications of the Church as the historical and therefore necessarily ambiguous realization of Spiritual Community under the conditions of existence?

The universality of revelation in Tillich's theology and his concept of latent Spiritual Community offer yet other possibilities for consideration. Tillich follows in the tradition of Clement of Alexandria, Origen, and Nicholas of Cusa in ascribing positive meaning to the non-Christian religions. He reminds both Catholic and Protestant missiologists that grace precedes the Church. He shatters the exclusivist tendencies of post-Tridentine Catholicism as well as Luther's belief that there is only darkness outside of the gospel.[4] What are the implications of latent Spiritual Community for the Church's missionary efforts, for dialogue with non-Christian religions, for the significance of convert-making? Do the prayer and worship of other religions have a relationship to the Christian sacraments? Is the Church to be found in the synagogue, the mosque, the Hindu temple? Latent Spiritual Community respects the wishes of those who prefer not to be regarded as crypto or anonymous Christians. Does it permit us a more favorable, or at least a more dialectical, view of secular society and its humanistic movements?[5]

175

And what of the Church as the "fighting side" of the kingdom of God in history? Does Tillich have anything to say to so-called political theology? How is the Church to combine both vertical and horizontal dimensions in its confrontation with the world? What are the implications of "religious obligation" and "religious reserve"?

These and any number of other questions or topics might well engage a Catholic consideration. As valuable as they may be, though, none deserves more attention than the one which from the very first has been demonstrated as the center of Tillich's theology of the Church. It constitutes one of his primary and most original contributions to theology and ecumenism. It colors and renders intelligible Tillich's dialectical attitude toward Scripture, tradition, dogmas, sacraments, the necessity of the Church, authority in the Church, and the claims of the Christian Church to superiority over other religions. Our consideration will focus on the polarity between the priestly and prophetic in the Church, between Catholic substance and the Protestant principle.

The Heart of the Matter

The Protestant principle has been regarded by some of Tillich's commentators as the root of all his thinking, the principle of his entire system.[6] The claim is not without foundation. Tillich maintained that the substance of his theology was Lutheran and that the Lutheran concept of justification by grace through faith was the one fundamental principle of the Reformation. From his teacher Martin Kähler, Tillich became convinced that justification was a "universally applicable fundamental idea."[7] Furthermore, the Protestant principle was for Tillich an expression of man's lack of ultimacy, his utter finitude. Tillich's whole work as a philosopher and a theologian can be seen as growing out of his insight into the meaning of human finitude.[8] Our concern here, however, is not with Tillich's whole philosophy and theology but simply his ecclesiology. The Protestant principle not only commands the center of that ecclesiology but in fact serves as a decisive influence upon all else—always in polarity, though, with Catholic substance. At the risk of being somewhat repetitious, the following may serve as a brief summary.

Catholic substance describes the concrete embodiment of Spiritual Presence in symbols, sacraments, rituals, and dogmas. It is the priestly element in all religion. The unconditioned or absolute, the God beyond God, can never be an object of ultimate concern in and of itself without mediation. Concrete conditioned embodiment is necessary through religious symbols which point to the absolute and participate in its meaning and power. In the realm of religion, symbolic language is universal and unavoidable, constitutive of the Church as it is of all religions as communities of ultimate concern. It establishes the basis for the necessity of the Church—not ideally or essentially, but existentially—because of man's existential estrangement from the ground of his being. Faith is dependent upon symbols, and symbols are dependent upon communities to keep them alive, to transmit and interpret them (chap. 1).

In this same vein, the Church itself may be described in terms of the sacramental. The Church witnesses to and transmits the New Being, as it was embodied in Jesus as the Christ (chap. 2). It manifests and serves Spiritual Community, its own spiritual essence as well as that of all religions, created by the Spiritual Presence (chap. 3). The church represents the kingdom of God in history, participates in its reality, and serves as its prophetic tool and fighting agent (chap. 4). Catholic substance emphasizes the incarnational, the "already now" aspect of the eschatological tension (chap. 5). It legitimates authority in the Church and necessitates dogmas and creeds (chap. 6). It relates the Church to the world religions and provides an apt basis for dialogue with them (chap. 7).

In constant tension with Catholic substance, however, there stands the Protestant principle, the protest against any absolute claim made for a relative reality, hence for any symbolic, sacramental embodiment of Spiritual Presence, for any conditioned representation of the absolute. This is the prophetic element in all religion, the protest against all idolatry. Only God is God, and nothing—no book, no institution, no sacrament, no symbol, even the most effective—may be put in God's place by according it ultimacy. God is not *a* being but the ground of all being. This requires the rejection of any attempt to absolutize concrete being in any of its manifestations, the protest against any attempt to make divine a visible form of being.[9] It follows that symbols, although the necessary language of religion, are not to be taken literally. Their truth lies not only in their pointing beyond themselves to the ultimate but also in their negating themselves by expressing their own lack of ultimacy. To identify a finite and hence relative symbol of the absolute with the absolute itself is demonic (chap. 1).

In virtue of the Protestant principle, the Church may point to and transmit New Being, but should not be confused with New Being itself. No claims for uniqueness, absoluteness, or final truth can be made for Christianity itself, but only for the event on which it is based (chap. 2). Although the Church manifests Spiritual Community, it is not to be identified with it. It is a sociological reality as well as a theological, subject to the ambiguities of existence. The Church, like its essence, is one, holy, and universal; unlike its essence, it is only paradoxically so, that is, despite its lack of unity, its lack of holiness, its lack of universality (chap. 3). Because the kingdom of God is independent of any form, the Church should not be regarded as the kingdom of God on earth. To do so is to elevate it demonically and set it above criticism or reform (chap. 4).

By emphasizing the apocalyptic, the "not yet" aspect of the eschatological tension, the Protestant principle serves as a corrective, precluding finality for any finite reality, including the Church. The Protestant principle recognizes the Church as translucent to Spiritual Presence, but it does not permit the Church or any of its structures to be identified with grace, with the Spiritual Presence itself. As a consequence, *ecclesia semper reformanda.* No aspect or area of the Church is beyond reform (chap. 5). The Protestant principle affirms authority in the Church, but does not permit that authority to claim absolute obedience or subjection in the name of God. It esteems Scripture, as it does dogmas, as pointing to the truth, but the Protestant principle does not permit either Scripture or dogmas to be regarded as the truth itself, or as infallible laws or formulas of truth (chap. 6). It has a universal character found in all religions and a universal validity which judges all religions, all political systems, all ideologies (chap. 7). All of this is symbolized most strikingly by the cross.

Tillich's primary objection to Roman Catholicism was that it did not understand the meaning of the cross, that it made itself and its structures, its dogmas, sacraments, and hierarchic system, into absolutes. This for Tillich was tantamount to idolatry (chap. 2). The Catholic Church, as he saw it, identified itself with Spiritual Community. It took an exclusively theological view of itself, submerging its sociological character and utterly neglecting its subjection to the ambiguities of existence (chap. 3). The Catholic Church, by identifying itself with the kingdom of God on earth, elevated itself and its structures above criticism. At the same time it distorted the meaning of the kingdom of God by placing exclusive emphasis upon the kingdom as immanent within history, neglecting thereby the kingdom as transcendent beyond history (chap. 4).

Its demonic claim to absolute validity and ultimate truth, the identification of itself with Spiritual Community and the kingdom of God, Tillich saw as the source of hierarchical arrogance and as the basis of all his other objections to Roman Catholicism. This identification leads the Catholic Church to regard itself as the criterion for every other church. It leads to the heritage of universal monarchy, unimpeachable papacy, and absolute authoritarianism (chap. 5). It leads to heteronomous claims to unconditional obedience, to sacred hierarchies, and to infallible dogmas (chap. 6). Tillich admitted that the spirit of prophetic protest was not completely extinct within the Catholic Church. He was heartened by the beginnings of the Second Vatican Council and by the Catholic admission that the interpretation of dogmas could change. The Catholic Church was applying to itself the principle of *ecclesia semper reformanda*, and this, together with Catholic-Protestant dialogue, was a *kairos* for Tillich, a moment full of potentialities. In was a step forward toward the "evangelical Catholicism" which he believed is the only viable form of Christianity for the coming era.

Its Significance

The significance of Tillich's theology of Catholic substance and the Protestant principle can best be gauged by the fact that both the terms and the meaning Tillich accorded them have since become part of the stock-in-trade of systematic theology. It was nothing new to designate the Catholic Church as emphatically sacramental, in contrast to Protestant churches whose emphasis is the Word. But Tillich has helped even Catholics to appreciate more fully the significance of sacramentalism within the Catholic Church and the dominant influence which it bears upon all other aspects of Catholicism.

Even more original and significant, though, is the synthesis Tillich made of Protestantism. By means of the Protestant principle he gave a rational coherence to a phenomenon which, often enough, to Catholics at least, seems indifferent to all coherence.[10] Although Protestant churches are embodiments of it, the Protestant principle transcends them; the Protestant churches have often proved unfaithful to the Protestant principle and have fallen under its judgment. But, as Tillich saw it, the Protestant principle constituted the sole foundation of the Reformation churches in their protest against Catholicism (chap. 5). The historical function of Protestantism is primarily one of protest. Not a merely negative protest; before one can be against anything, he must be for something. Every negation is at the same time an affirmation. Sheer protest is impossible. Negative protest arises out of a positive acceptance of God alone as unconditional, thus constituting an essential element of all valid religion. Even Catholicism, if it is to be authentically Christian, must also be protestant and live a boundary-line existence.

Because of his development of the Protestant principle, Tillich was credited by Gustave Weigel with having "made luminous that strange thing, Protestantism, to which he is passionately attached" (ThSt11:185). He developed an apology for Protestantism, not necessarily one with which Luther would have been happy nor one with which all Protestants today would agree. But neither can it be denied that "Tillich has taken out the basic ideas of Lutheranism and proposed them in the simplest and most trenchant form."[11]

> Tillich's synthesis is the only one at hand that includes all the elements of the Protestant phenomenon, and arranges them organically. The system is coherent and it is rational. So many things in Protestant thought and action which at first sight seem completely unintelligible become logical and consequent in the light of his theory.[12]

But the significance of Tillich's synthesis for the explanation of Protestantism need not rest exclusively on Catholic testimony. An examination of studies by Protestants on the nature, spirit, and meaning of Protestantism indicates considerable similarity and sometimes even dependence upon Tillich, even though his work may not always be explicitly cited. Ernst Wolf, for example, in his article "Protestantismus" in the standard Protestant reference *Religion in Geschichte und Gegenwart*, concurs with Tillich that Protestantism can be understood in terms of a principle (RGG5(1956):648–61). A long list of Protestant theologians may be considered as essentially in agreement with the Tillichian synthesis:

Robert McAfee Brown[13] leans heavily upon Tillich's language as well as his theology when he describes Protestantism from the four perspectives of: a) the unique Lordship of Jesus Christ; b) the Old Testament command that "you shall not have other gods besides me" (Deut. 5:8); c) *ecclesia semper reformanda;* and d) the Pauline principle that "we carry this treasure in vessels of clay, to show that the abundance of power is God's and not ours" (2 Cor. 4:7). "The Spirit of Protestantism involves a willingness to live at risk, not only because the claim to human security is a denial of God, but because when human securities have been destroyed, God can enter in."[14]

Theodore Ellwein[15] sees the genius of Protestantism manifested in the fact that it canonizes no finite form of the Church. In accord with the principle of *ecclesia semper reformanda*, Protestantism is always open to change, even of the Reformation. "It is Protestant to raise a critical protest against any attempt to absolutize and thereby to ideologize a provincial and historically conditioned partial truth."[16]

Kurt Guggisberg[17] emphasizes God's truth as surpassing any of our concepts of it. From its very beginnings, Christianity has exhibited many and various forms and directions; and this same plurality and variety can be maintained today, so long as they attempt to strive for the truth without claiming a full possession of the truth.

Kurt Lesse,[18] in ten theses describing the nature of Protestantism, holds that Protestantism maintains, as its highest religious principle, the union of a Gestalt of grace with prophetic criticism. Consequent is the protest against any absolutization of the relative.

Walther von Loewenich,[19] like Tillich, sees the cross as the primary exemplar of the justification event, and it is by this that Protestantism must be determined. "Protestantism stands and falls with the proposition: The Reformation goes on."[20]

Regin Prenter[21] upholds the term *Protestant* in the face of those who reject it as too negative and prefer instead something more positive like *evangelical Christianity.* He would keep the term precisely because it indicates a protest against anything that would threaten the positive, original witness of evangelical Christianity.

Hans H. Walz[22] sees the Protestant principle as central to and determinant of what is sometimes called the "New Protestantism," in contradistinction to the sixteenth-century Reformation. It struggles against anything historically contingent which sets itself up as absolute. For the sake of the absolute authority of God, it protests against any attempt of the finite and human to claim divine authority for itself.

Heinz Schütte, a Catholic theologian, has surveyed the views of modern German theologians regarding the essence of the Protestant protest. He confirms our contention of the significance of Tillich's synthesis with his summary of the basic affirmation of Protestiantism:

Protestantism witnesses to
1) the Godliness of God, his personal, free, and exclusive action and his exclusive authority,
2) the creatureliness and sinfulness of the creature, his finiteness, dependence, and openness to the threat of error and sin.
Protestantism turns against anything that conflicts with this witness.[23]

Tillich's objection to Roman Catholicism, that it raises itself and its structures above criticism, has also been echoed by other Protestant theologians. Swiss exegete Oscar Cullmann, like Tillich, has contended that the Catholic Church neglects the prophetic "not yet" of the kingdom of God by emphasizing exclusively the priestly "already here."

> It is a fundamental conviction for each believing Catholic that that which I call the eschatological tension between present and future, between already-fulfilled and not-yet-completed, has been in part removed in his church, most particularly in the infallible teaching office.[24]

> On the other hand, it is a firm conviction on the part of Protestants that the eschatological tension between present and future, between "already fulfilled" and "not yet finished" has in no way been removed in the human members of the church in spite of the resurrection and ascension. For this reason they believe that actual infallibility cannot exist in the church any more than actual sinlessness, although she represents the body of Christ and there is nothing higher on earth.[25]

Ernst Käsemann concurs with Tillich's accusation that the Catholic Church elevates itself demonically when it arrogates to itself privileges which belong *solo Deo, solo Christo*.

> With Rome, here is the symbol of the church which chooses to make itself absolute, and which in its tradition, its official capacity, and its legal claims, avoids the judgment of the crucified Lord. We cannot accept that mother and schoolmistress of the faithful, who robs Christ of his titles and remains the opponent of the reforming *particula exclusiva*.[26]

Schütte, in his survey of contemporary German Protestant theology, describes the Protestant protest as primarily a no directed against Catholic absolutes. In Protestant estimation here is where the fundamental difference lies between Catholicism and Protestantism. Protestantism protests against the infallibility and unchangeability of dogmas (General Synod of the Reformed Church of Holland);[27] the identification of the Catholic Church with the kingdom of God (H. Dietzfelbinger; H. Diem);[28] Catholic triumphalism and self-glorification and its neglect of future eschatological fulfillment (K.E. Skydsgaard);[29] the Catholic system of ecclesial securities, for example, the notion of an infallible Magisterium, the concept of the Church as a salvation institution (W. Stählin); [30] the Catholic Church's self-elevation through a *theologia gloriae* instead of standing under a *theologia crucis*, becoming thereby a church triumphant even though it designates itself a church militant (K.G. Streck).[31]

The ecumenical significance of Catholic substance and the Protestant principle, alluded to above, bears repeating here. Tillich has been hailed as an ecumenical theologian par excellence.[32] "Tillich's ecclesiology shows clearly the passionate endeavor of all his theology to overcome the division between Catholicism and Protestantism, in that he comprehends both of them in their truth."[33] Tillich insisted that Catholic substance and the Protestant principle complement rather than contradict each other. In order to avoid distortion, they need to remain in a tension of polarity with each other. It is a polarity which affords an extremely useful framework for ecumenical rapprochement seeing that it indicates the need Catholics and Protestants have of each other.

> The paradox of Catholic substance and Protestant principle . . . is matched by the need of both Protestantism and Roman Catholicism for this very combination. Liturgical reform in Roman Catholicism cannot get its mind off Martin Luther; Protestant studies of worship continually inquire whether the loss of Catholic substance has not impoverished Protestant spirituality since the Reformation.[34]

There is justification, therefore, for concentrating this critique upon Tillich's theology of Catholic substance and the Protestant principle. Not only does it constitute the heart of his ecclesiology but it illuminates both Catholicism and Protestantism. It defines what has been accepted by numerous Protestant theologians as the primary difference between Roman Catholicism and the Protestant churches. And it provides a useful framework for ecumenical dialogue on a theological level between the two Christian traditions.

The question that now arises, however, is, How shall a critique be made? What standard should be used? How can Catholic substance and the Protestant principle be measured? The first answer that immediately comes to mind is by Scripture, of course. But would this really help? Is this really the issue at hand? Do not both Protestants and Catholics appeal to the Bible for their respective traditions? Are not both the priestly and the prophetic elements of Christianity found in Scripture? Tillich did not deny this and neither do the majority of exegetes and theologians, both Catholic and Protestant.

The question raised by Tillich's theology of Catholic substance and the Protestant principle is not how Catholic or Protestant is the Bible but, rather: How catholic are Protestants? How protestant are Catholics? What place does the constitutive, priestly element of Christianity have in Protestant churches today? What place does the corrective, prophetic element have in the Roman Catholic Church today? How catholic can Protestantism become and still remain Protestant? How protestant can Catholicism become and still remain Catholic? Does the Roman Catholic Church absolutize itself and its structures, as Tillich contended? Does this constitute the essential difference today between Catholic and Protestant churches? Does it justify the division which exists between Catholics and Protestants?

These are the questions provoked by Tillich's ecclesiology. But it is a Catholic appraisal that is being essayed here, and that cannot help but make a difference. Although an attempt will be made to give due consideration to both poles of Tillich's dialectic, a Catholic reflection may perhaps be excused for expressing special interest in such matters as: the place of the Protestant principle within the Catholic Church; the extent to which it has been operative and could be operative within Catholicism; the implications which the Protestant principle bears for the Catholic Church and its future. Tillich deplored the waning of the sacramental, priestly element within Protestantism and warned of a decline in the Protestant churches because of it. Protestant theology has not to date attempted a thorough study of the place and implications of Catholic substance within Protestantism. The Roman Church of the sacraments would appear to have made more progress in becoming also a church of the Word than the churches of the Word have made in becoming also churches of the sacraments. But this is a concern more proper to Protestant evaluation than Catholic. Our concern here is to see just how exclusively Protestant is the Protestant principle. Can it be found within Catholicism too, particularly within the post-Vatican II Catholic Church today? Does the Catholic Church necessarily identify itself with the kingdom of God on earth? Does it usurp the Lordship of Christ by identifying itself with Spiritual Community? Does it absolutize itself above the possibility of radical criticism and reform? These are important questions. They deserve a Catholic consideration and honest answers.

10

The Protestant Principle and Catholic Parallels

We should not forget that whatever is wrought by the grace of the Holy Spirit in the hearts of our separated brethren can contribute to our own edification.
Second Vatican Council, Decree on Ecumenism

Catholic substance and the Protestant principle, as Tillich saw them, are complementary to each other, even indispensable. Although one or the other inevitably predominates, no religion or church is utterly bereft of either one. The priestly element, though, is more fundamental to religion than the prophetic. The prophet raises his protest against idolatry in the name of God by arising out of the priestly tradition and turning that tradition against itself.[1] The Protestant principle arises out of Catholic substance. Protestant protest, therefore, is not foreign to Catholic tradition.[2] Tillich saw it as operative in the person and work of Pope John XXIII (PPT, pp. 236–37). But if not alien to Catholicism, to what extent is it present? Can parallels be found between Catholic teaching and Tillich's theology of the Church?

Because of the Protestant principle, the Church for Tillich may not be identified with the kingdom of God. It may not be identified with Jesus as the Christ, with the New Being, the Spiritual Presence, or Spiritual Community. In virtue of its priestly, sacramental element, the Church represents the kingdom of God; it points to and transmits the New Being embodied in Jesus as the Christ; it manifests Spiritual Community. It does so, however, while standing under the cross, a symbol of *soli Deo gloria* and

185

A Catholic Appraisal

justification by grace through faith. The Church is constantly open both to criticism and reform. Can a Catholic agree with these contentions? Can they be found within the Catholic Church and its theology? The answer is yes. Tillich's contentions are paralleled by Catholic theology and by official Catholic teaching today with respect to the kingdom of God and the Body of Christ.

The Church and the Kingdom of God

Tillich accused the Roman Catholic Church of identifying itself with the kingdom of God.[3] He has not been alone in raising the objection. Adolf von Harnack,[4] William Temple,[5] and Theodore O. Wedel[6] raised similar charges, regarding the identification as the fundamental error of Roman Catholicism and the basis for its "exorbitant" demands. They had no difficulty in producing evidence of the Catholic identification. Some of the foremost Catholic scholars have described the Church in terms of the kingdom of God on earth,[7] although they usually qualified the claim by adding that the Church is only the beginning of the reign which will be perfected beyond history. The encyclical of Pope Pius XI, establishing the Feast of Christ the King, explicitly identified the Church with the kingdom of Christ destined to cover the whole world (*Quas Primas*, 1925).

The identification of the Church with the kingdom of God is not one which was made by Roman Catholics alone, however. Some Protestant exegetes have seen the identification as already unmistakable in the New Testament, as implied in Jesus giving the "keys of the Kingdom" to Peter (Matt. 16:19) and in the parables of Matthew's gospel, "some of which are unintelligible unless the kingdom of heaven means the Christian Church."[8] In opposition to the Byzantine imperial theology which saw the Christianized Roman Empire as the fulfillment of the messianic promises, there arose in the West a theology of theocracy which implied an identification of the kingdom of God with the hierarchic church.[9] Augustine maintained the inherited equation in some of his writings (*City of God* VIII. 24;XV.20), identifying the age of the Church with that of the thousand year reign of Christ (*City of God* XX. 9). But he proceeded to purify the theology of the kingdom, making important distinctions between the Church as a mixed kingdom here and now, marked by ignorance and infirmity, and the future kingdom without spot or wrinkle (*City of God* XX. 9; *Retractions* II. 18). Augustine's distinctions were not always kept in mind, however, and the Middle Ages were characterized by a vision which identified the City of God with Christendom.

Like their Catholic opponents, the Protestant reformers also over-looked the decisively eschatological character of the kingdom. Melanchthon equated the kingdom of God with the church of pure doctrine. Martin Bucer's *De Regno Christi* (1557) had its influence not only on John Calvin but on Genevan and English politics. The upshot was a Protestant vision of a reformed church and state, kingdom of God and Christian commonwealth coalescing into a theocracy in which public and private life both were ruled by the Bible and the commandments of God.

At the end of the nineteenth century, while Catholics continued to identify the kingdom of God with the Church, Protestant theology, particularly in Germany under the influence of Albrecht Ritschl, identified the kingdom of God with a universal ethical community, a moral ideal to be achieved by human effort. Both concepts received a severe blow, when Johannes Weiss[10] and Albert Schweitzer[11] demonstrated that the kingdom preached by Jesus in the New Testament was essentially eschatological and transcendental in nature, soon to erupt upon the earth. Schweitzer's emphasis upon the exclusively apocalyptic nature of the kingdom aroused the reaction of Charles Dodd,[12] who placed his emphasis upon "realized eschatology," whereby the kingdom is seen as a primarily present reality. Catholic exegetes today, like most of their Protestant counterparts, prefer to take a position between the two extremes, maintaining, as Tillich does, that the kingdom of God has a two-fold dimension of "not yet" and "already now."[13]

Catholic New Testament exegesis has come today to see the Church and the kingdom of God as distinct, disparate entities.[14] They cannot be identified. This clearly contradicts the notion of the Church being the kingdom of God on earth. "In the New Testament the identification is never made. If we understand the two realities at all, it cannot be made. The Reign is larger than the Church. The Church herself is subject to the Reign; and the establishment of the Church is not the eschatological consummation of the Reign."[15] The kingdom is essentially eschatological, the great intervention of God into history announced by the prophets for the end of time.[16] As such, "it is not the Church but the kingdom of God which is the ultimate goal of the divine economy of salvation. . . ."[17] The Church is not the kingdom itself but has the prerogative and task to lead men into the kingdom. It is the organism through which and in which Christ gathers men into God's kingdom.[18]

187

Catholic theology has followed the lead of Catholic biblical scholarship and has come likewise to emphasize the distinction between the Church and the kingdom of God. The Church is not the kingdom but "the community of those who believe in the kingdom, give witness to it, wait for it and hope for it."[19] The Church is as distinct from the kingdom of God as a pilgrim from his destination. "The Church, if only she be rightly understood, is living always on the proclamation of her own provisional status and of her historically advancing elimination in the coming kingdom of God towards which she is expectantly travelling as a pilgrim."[20]

Hans Küng has been particularly outspoken in criticizing the description of the Church as "God's kingdom on earth," or as "the present form," "the preliminary stage," or "the forerunner" of the kingdom of God. There is no question of identity between the two, since the kingdom, according to the New Testament, is universal, final, and definitive. And there can be no question of a strict continuity between the two, since the kingdom is not the product of an organic development but of a "wholly new and unprepared perfecting action of God." The Church is provisional, belonging to the present. The kingdom is definitive, belonging essentially to the future. The Church embraces sinners and grows from below. The kingdom embraces the righteous and comes from above.[21] "The reign of God cannot be identified with the people of God, the Church, any more than the saving act of God can be identified with man's reception of salvation."[22]

But if Church and kingdom are not identical, neither are they disconnected. "Jesus came to inaugurate the Reign; the immediate effect of his work was the foundation of the Church. The Church in any hypothesis must have a unique position in the Reign. . . ."[23] Far from being unconnected, the Church is bound up very intimately with the teaching of Christ on the reign of God." It continues Jesus' preaching of the kingdom he initiated and stands in its service.[24] It does so, however, not as a bringer or bearer of the kingdom, but as an announcer, a herald; not as a fore-stage (*Vor-Stufe*) but as a fore-sign (*Vor-Zeichen*).[25]

The relationship of the Church to the kingdom of God, therefore, as seen by Catholic theology today, is essentially dialectical, non-identical yet also non-dissociated. This same dialectic is visible in official Catholic teaching. As described by Vatican Council II, the Church is clearly distinct from the kingdom:

> The Church on earth, while journeying in a foreign land away from her Lord (cf. 2 Cor. 5:6), regards herself as an exile. Hence, she seeks and experiences those things which are above, where Christ is seated at the right hand of God,

where the life of the Church is hidden with Christ in God until she appears in glory with her Spouse (cf. Col. 3:1–4). [CE, #6]

The Church . . . will attain her full perfection only in the glory of heaven. Then will come the time of the restoration of all things (Acts 3:21). . . . However, until there is a new heaven and a new earth where justice dwells (cf. 2 Pet. 3:13), the pilgrim Church in her sacraments and institutions, which pertain to this present time, takes on the appearance of this passing world. [CE, #48]

While helping the world and receiving many benefits from it, the Church has a single intention: that God's kingdom may come, and that the salvation of the whole human race may come to pass. [CEMT, #45]

Vatican II's description of the Church as a pilgrim in exile clearly differentiates the Church from the kingdom of God.[26] Because the Church is not disconnected from the kingdom Vatican II sometimes used language which allows for misinterpretation:

The Church, or in other words, the kingdom of Christ now present in mystery grows visible in the world through the power of God. [CE, #3]

The Church . . . receives the mission to proclaim and establish among all peoples the kingdom of Christ and of God. She becomes on earth the initial budding forth of that kingdom. While she grows, the Church strains toward the consummation of the kingdom. [CE, #5]

In the notes which inevitably accompany the translations of the conciliar documents, commentators were not slow to clear up any misunderstanding which might arise from the last two passages. In *The Documents of Vatican II*, Avery Dulles writes:

The kingdom of God, which Jesus inaugurated in His public life by His own preaching and by His very person, is not fully identical with the Church. But since Pentecost the Church has had the task of announcing and extending the kingdom here on earth, and in this way initiating in itself the final kingdom, which will be realized in glory at the end of time.[27]

In the *Lexikon für Theologie und Kirche*, Aloys Grillmeyer writes:

In Christ and the Spirit, the Church has to fulfill the mission of announcing the kingdom of Christ and God among all peoples. At the end of the fulfillment of this mission stands the consummated kingdom. Thus the Church, in Christ and in the Spirit, becomes the agent for the realization of God's reign. [LThK, pp. 12, 162]

189

The Church and the Body of Christ

In attempting to translate biblical and theological vocabulary for today's world, Tillich deliberately avoided terms like *grace, Holy Spirit,* and *Body of Christ.* He described them instead as New Being, Spiritual Presence, and Spiritual Community. In virtue of the Protestant principle, he insisted that none of them were to be identified with the Church. The Church points to grace (the New Being) and mediates it, but is not to be confused with it. The Holy Spirit (Spiritual Presence) creates the Body of Christ (Spiritual Community), which constitutes the essence of the Church, but neither are to be seen as limited to its visible confines. As the Messianic community, the Church may raise claims for the Christ-event upon which it is based, to which it points, and in which it participates; but it may not raise any absolute claims for itself. The Church may not be identified with Jesus as the Christ any more than religion may be identified with revelation.

Tillich accused Roman Catholicism of identifying itself with grace, the Spirit, the universal Church, and the Body of Christ. Again, as with the kingdom of God, he was not alone in raising the objection. Nor was it utterly unfounded. Protestant critics needed only to point to the Mystical Body of Christ theology which held sway over Catholic ecclesiology between World Wars I and II, and, in particular, the official Catholic expression of the theology in the 1943 encyclical of Pope Pius XII, *Mystici Corporis.* Offense was taken at the encyclical's identification of the biblical Body of Christ with the Roman Catholic Church, as if Orthodox and Protestants were not members of the Church, as if non-Catholic Christians were to be regarded as tantamount to non-Christians.[28] Another objection against the Mystical Body theology as a whole was that of identifying the Church with Christ by regarding the Church as *Christus prolongatus* or an *incarnatio continuata.*[29] Consequently there was not only a confusion of the Church with grace, as if grace were not to be found outside the Church, but an ecclesiastical Monophysitism, as if the Church could claim the majesty and authority of Christ for itself.

It would be far beyond the limits of this study to go in depth into the history and development of the Catholic theology of the Church as the Body of Christ, even as it was presented in more recent times.[30] Let it suffice to point out that recent Catholic ecclesiology, prior to Vatican II, was not without its ambiguities and contradictions, even on the official level. On the one hand there was *Mystici Corporis;* on the other hand, there was Canon Law, which regarded all baptized persons as belonging to the Roman Catholic Church and bound by its laws (Canons #12 and #87); furthermore, there was the statement by the Holy Office to Archbishop Cushing of Boston (1949),[31] which condemned the notion that grace and salvation could not be found outside the Roman Catholic Church.

But ambiguity is to be found already within the New Testament. Certainly the notion of the Church as the Body of Christ in 1 Corinthians and Romans is different from that in Colossians and Ephesians. For the Church Fathers, for example, Augustine and Gregory, the Body of Christ is not at first sight an ecclesial notion at all, but rather Christological and soteriological; it includes the just of all ages and corresponds to the notion of the Church from the time of Abel.[32] In the patristic period and early Middle Ages, the Church was the *totus Christus* (Augustine), the *corpus verum* of Christ, the Eucharist was designated as the *corpus mysticum*.[33] In the later Middle Ages the term *mystical* was added to the notion of the Church as the Body of Christ; the term *body* came to be interpreted as a legal body, a juridical person, and reference came to be made to the mystical body of the Church.[34] In rejecting the juridical notion of the Church, the reformers saw in the Pauline concept of the Body of Christ a figurative expression of the hidden inner union of grace between Christ and the individual Christian, one which did not touch upon the visible order at all.[35] Vatican Council I avoided the term altogether; the notion of the Church as the Body of Christ was regarded as obscure and dangerously Protestant.

In reaction to the primatial, hierarchic, juridically oriented ecclesiology, exemplified by Vatican I, the Mystical Body of Christ theology was resurrected once again in Catholic circles, this time out of German romanticism. As expounded originally by Johann Adam Möhler and later by Matthias Scheeben in the nineteenth century, and then in the twentieth century in a classic fashion by Karl Adam, the Mystical Body of Christ theology was intended to provide an antidote to the identification of the Church with the hierarchy. In doing so, however, it confused partially the unbiblical qualification of *mystical* with mysticism. The *ecclesia catholica* of the Fathers was confused with the *ecclesia Romana* of the medieval canon lawyers.[36] The result was the notion of the Church as a mysterious organism of divine grace, a continuation of the incarnation, and the consequent identifications to which Tillich and other Protestant theologians objected.

In the wake of *Mystici Corporis* and the reactions it aroused,[37] Catholic theology was compelled to take a more critical and differentiating look at the biblical and patristic foundations for any valid concept of the Church as the Body of Christ. In doing so, it was able to enlist the aid of

191

Protestant exegesis.[38] The result has been that, even when the Church is viewed as the Body of Christ, both Catholic exegesis and theology have come to reject any notion of an *incarnatio continuata*. Both have come to stress the distinction rather than the identification between the Church and Jesus, not in spite of but because of the Pauline imagery.

Catholic exegesis, like its Protestant counterpart, is far from being uniform in its interpretation of the Pauline Body of Christ concept.[39] There is agreement, however, on certain basic points.[40] In the proto-Pauline letters, (1 Cor. 12:12–31; Rom. 12:4–8; also 1 Cor. 6:12–20; 10:14–22), it is the local church, not the universal Church, which is designated as the Body of Christ. Paul uses a popular Stoic metaphor to emphasize, not the union of Christ and the Church, but rather the union and cooperation of Christians with one another in Christ. "The relation of Christ to the faithful as head to body is not *ex professo* considered."[41] In the deutero-Pauline letters (Colossians and Ephesians), the body and head themes of the undisputed Pauline epistles are joined to express the subordination of the Church to Christ, who is Head and Lord. The emphasis rests not upon any identity of Christ and the Church but rather upon the distinction. The Lordship of Christ and the subordination of the Church to him are expressed by the analogy of Christ as head and the Church as body, in the sense that a husband is the head of his wife (Eph. 5:24).[42]

Catholic theology has sometimes been unmindful of the conclusions of exegesis. Happily this is not the case here.[43] Catholic theology too has come to recognize that the Church as the Body of Christ is "a metaphor which is not to be arbitrarily pressed. . . ."[44] Although one may speak of a divine and human element in the Church, an invisible and a visible element, one may not speak of two natures or one personality in the Church. There is no question of the Church being *Christus prolongatus*.[45] "If one uses an exact manner of speaking, it cannot be said that the incarnation is continued in the Church. It was a singular event which is operative in the Church. But it does not repeat itself in the Church."[46] Christ is present in the Church as its Risen Lord, above all in its worship, but he is not contained in the Church or confined by it. "There is no hypostatic union between Christ and the Church any more than there is between Christ and the individual Christian." The union which does exist between them is not ontic or organic but historic and dynamic. It intensifies in proportion to the Church's obedience to Christ as its Head and Lord.[47]

Together with exegesis and theology, official Catholic teaching today, as expressed by Vatican II, rejects any identification of the Catholic Church with Christ or with the working of the Holy Spirit. Apparently in reaction to the excesses of the earlier Mystical Body of Christ theology of this century, one can detect almost an aversion to the concept at Vatican II. In contrast to the concept of the Church as the People of God, which receives special consideration in a chapter all its own (chap. 2) in the *Dogmatic Constitution on the Church,* the notion of the Church as the Body of Christ is listed as simply one of several biblical metaphors describing the Church in chapter 1. Certainly there is no danger of identifying the Church with Christ when it is considered under the title of the People of God. And even when considering the concept of the Church as the Body of Christ, the Council describes it as "an excellent analogy" (CE #8), implying that, as with all analogies, the differences are greater than any similarities.

Concerning the relationship of the Catholic Church to the working of the Holy Spirit (Spiritual Community) and the question of membership in the Church, Vatican II avoided any claims whatever of exclusiveness or identification. In order not to equate the *Una Sancta* established by Christ with Roman Catholicism, Vatican II does not say that the Church of Christ "is" the Catholic Church but rather "subsists" (*subsistit*) in the Catholic Church (CE #8). It does so without denying that it may subsist in other churches as well. This point is developed in the conciliar *Constitution on the Church* (#15) and in the *Decree on Ecumenism* (#3), which recognize other Christian communities as churches and thus instruments of divine grace. Without giving up claims to a unique fullness for the Catholic Church, Vatican II avoids altogether the static notion of membership in the Church of Christ, employing instead the more dynamic concepts of *incorporation* and *relationship* (CE #14, #15). Not only are Catholics joined in the Spirit with other baptized Christians but all Christians are also related to those outside the Church who accept the grace of God, both those who profess an explicit faith in God and those who do not but nevertheless strive to live a good life (CE #16).

Far removed from the Second Vatican Council were the exclusive identifications which Tillich found so contradictory to the Protestant principle. If not explicitly, then without a doubt functionally, the concept of latent Spiritual Community has become operative within the Catholic Church as a result of Vatican II.

> The Church is beginning to accept the fact that it is not itself the center of all. The Church no longer regards itself as the true center around which the whole of human history circles, although it knows that it has a special and important function to fulfill in this history.[48]

The Church as Sacrament

One of the most striking parallels between Tillich's ecclesiology and modern Catholic theology is a development of the concept of the Church as symbol or *Ursakrament*. The notion is rooted in the patristic understanding of *sacramentum* as *mysterion* and as *sacrum signum*. In light of this broader understanding of the word, Augustine referred to Christ as the one sacrament of God (PL 33: 845); Cyprian regarded the Church as a sacrament of unity (PL 3: 787).

The word *sacrament* has had a long and complicated career, going back to pre-Christian times and uniting juridical elements with notions taken from the Hellenistic mystery cults. Although used in various ways by the Church Fathers, the term gradually took on a more restricted sense. In the twelfth century it came to be applied exclusively to seven sacraments, and the broader understanding of sacrament fell into disuse. Within recent years, however, primarily through the writing and influence of Otto Semmelroth, Karl Rahner, Edward Schillebeeckx, and others,[49] the broader notion has been resurrected. There has developed within Catholic theology a concept of the Church as a primordial sacrament, a concept given prominence by the Second Vatican Council.

Tillich never explicitly referred to the Church as a symbol or sacrament. Indeed, he seems to have avoided making the reference quite deliberately. The fact should come as no surprise, since such a designation would certainly have been open to misunderstanding by his Protestant students and readers. But perhaps his avoidance of the term should give Catholic theologians as well reason to pause and reflect upon the advisability of applying it to the Church. *Sacrament* is not at all biblical. It does not mean a great deal to the average Christian, even to the average Catholic, to describe the Church as a sacrament; in fact, it proves quite confusing. (Is the Church another sacrament? an eighth sacrament? Does this change Catholic teaching on seven sacraments? Is Christ the primordial sacrament or is the Church?) Because the word is complex, perhaps even equivocal, because its history is complicated, there seems to be adequate justification for some hesitation in applying it to the Church. This is not to say, however, that the idea of the Church as a sacred symbol or sign is not valuable.

Although he avoided using the term, Tillich clearly ascribed to the Church all the qualities and functions which Catholic theology ascribes to the word *sacrament* in the broad sense. The Church points to New Being (grace) and mediates it. It manifests Spiritual Community and represents the kingdom of God, participating in their reality, transmitting their healing power. Even if they are not in all respects identical, the affinities between Tillich and the Catholic theology of the Church as sacrament are undoubtedly considerable.

Together with an apologetic interest in emphasizing the sacraments, New Testament exegesis provided one of the strongest incentives to Catholic theology for developing the concept of the Church as sacrament. It has become clear to Catholic exegetes, as to their Protestant counterparts, that the Church cannot be identified with the kingdom of God. The relationship indicated by the New Testament as existing between the kingdom of God and the Church is one of non-identity yet also non-dissociation. How could this dialectical relationship be expressed? The classical data of the treatise on sacraments seemed to provide a possible answer. "The Church is not yet the form or shape of God's reign in its eschatological fulfillment. This transitory character of the Church as the messianic sacrament of the unity of all mankind and the whole world is only too evident in the Church's empirical existence. . . ."[50] The Church "prepares for" and "represents" the future kingdom.[51] Commenting on Vatican II's statement that the Church is the kingdom of Christ, present in mystery (CE #3), A. Grillmeyer explains that means both hidden, like a seed, and sacramental, instrumental and effective of salvation. The Church is the sacrament of the kingdom of God as it realizes itself.[52]

> The Church is the primordial sacrament of this kingdom and, because she is Holy Church, its secret beginning, precisely when she recognizes in her own weakness the manner in which God's redemptive might will come.[53]

> The Church not only does not stand in opposition to the kingdom of God, but it is a *sign* of its presence, made concrete and definitively tangible in Christ. The Church is a sign of the kingdom of God, as were the words which Jesus spoke and the deeds he performed. Furthermore, the Church stands *in service* of the Kingdom of God, as it imparts the advent of God's kingdom fulfilled in Jesus, the dominion of the Risen Lord; as it mediates the work of Christ in word and sacrament, in Baptism and Eucharist. Thus the Church becomes the *ursakrament* of the kingdom of God.[54]

As the concept of sacrament serves to describe the relationship of Church to kingdom, so too can it characterize the relationship of the divine and human, the invisible and the visible elements in the Church, implied by the concept of the Body of Christ (Spiritual Community).

> The place of the Body of Christ concept can be fixed today between the [two] extremes. On the one hand it is not reduceable (*rückführbar*) to the profane pattern of the corporation, as if the Church were visible in the same sense "as

the Republic of Venice" (Bellarmine). . . . Neither, on the other hand, is it merely an image of the purely interior bond of the *gratia capitis* with those who receive grace, a community without direct relation to institutional factors. . . . It is neither a part of the visible order of this world nor a *civitas platonica* of simply spiritual community. Rather, it is a sacrament, a *sacrum signum*, and as such a visible sign, but one which does not exhaust itself in its visibility. With its whole being, it is nothing else than a pointer (*Verweis*) to the invisible and the way thereto.[55]

Taking the lead from exegesis, Catholic theology has developed the notion of the Church as sacrament in various directions. For example, H. Fries: "The Church has the commission to be a sign of god."[56] O. Semmelroth: "We have called the Church a sacrament. With this is included two ideas: first, that the Church in its visible form is an image which portrays the salvific work of Christ in our world of today; and second, that this image not only refers the remembrance of the viewer to the copied reality of Christ's salvific work but, in an objective way, 'contains' it, as the Council of Trent said of the sacraments."[57] G. Weigel: " . . . the action of the Church is as symbolic as its being. The Church symbolically is Christ and her actions will be symbolic by the same reason . . . In symbol she, the great symbol, manifests herself and does her work."[58] E. Schillebeeckx: "The body of Christ in heaven is . . . the enduring sign of the messianic redemption itself in visible form. But for the time being, until the *parousia*, this sign remains invisible to us earthly men. Therefore the Lord gave this external sign of the redemption a visible prolongation on earth: the visible Church."[59]

Like Tillich, Catholic theology too has come today to see the sacramentalism of the Church as a useful means to characterize the relationship of the Church to the broader community of salvation which Tillich described as latent Spiritual Community:

> By the word "Church" we express our faith in a mystery of redemption that is operative wherever people are. Church signifies for us a world-wide Spirit-created communion among men. At the same time, this universal understanding of Church does not devaluate the specific character and role of the Christian Church. . . . The Christian Church is the visible sign and the perpetual pledge of that mystery which works in the whole of human history and leads men into truth and friendship.[60]

The concept of the Church as sacrament was not only taken up by the Second Vatican Council but it was also given singular prominence. In the first paragraphs of the *Dogmatic Constitution on the Church*, the Council stated: "By her relationship with Christ, the Church is a kind of sacrament or sign of intimate union with God, and of the unity of all mankind" (#1). It cited St. Augustine's Enarration of Psalm 138: "For it was from the side of Christ as he slept the sleep of death upon the cross that there came forth the wondrous sacrament which is the whole Church" (*On the Liturgy*, #5). The Church is, to cite St. Cyprian, "the visible sacrament of . . . saving unity" (CE #9). It is "the sign of Christ" (CE #15), "the universal sacrament of salvation" (CE #48). Commenting on this last passage, O. Semmelroth points out that thus the Church functions as an eschatological reality: what will be completed in the "not yet" has broken into this world "already" through the medium of a sign.[61]

Tillich's Protestant principle expresses Luther's *sola gratia, sola fide* as well as his theology of the cross, for Luther as for Tillich the *Urbild* of justification. It combines the Old Testament prohibition against idolatry with Calvin's passion for *soli Deo gloria*. And all this may be summed up in the consuming concern for upholding the godliness of God. As Tillich put it, "the divinity of the Divine, the ultimacy of the Ultimate, the unconditional character of the Unconditioned. This is where the Reformation starts."[62]

But is the godliness of God an exclusively Protestant belief? The first of the Ten Commandments; justification by grace through faith; the "infinite qualitative distinction" between God and man; the concern for God's glory—are these in any way excluded from Catholic faith or practice? The answer, of course, is no. The most unlettered Catholic would answer as much in the light of Catholic piety and practice. *Lex orandi, lex credendi*. Recent Catholic theology has served to demonstrate the same from tradition and official Catholic teaching. The pioneering work of Louis Bouyer, Yves Congar, Hans Küng, and Karl Rahner deserves special mention in this vein; they have helped to lay aside polemical antitheses. There is no need to go into their well-known contributions here. Suffice simply the following Protestant witness. H. Bornkamm: "There are many things we have misunderstood in the life of faith of the Catholic Church, and many things we have overlooked in our bias."[63] The General Synod of the Reformed Church of Holland: "We cannot put aside the theological teaching of the Roman Church thoughtlessly today as evidently false, unbiblical, and unevangelical."[64]

The question was posed in chapter 9—How exclusively Protestant is the Protestant principle? Can it be found within Catholicism today? The answer is that, in certain important respects at least, the Protestant principle is not at all exclusive to Protestantism. It is not at all alien either to Catholic theology or to official Catholic teaching. Theory is one thing though; practice, another. It is in application that a hypothesis is tested.

Does the Catholic Church draw the logical conclusions from the aforestated premises? If it cannot be identified with the kingdom of God, with Christ, or with the working of the Spirit, then by necessity, *ecclesia semper reformanda*. Has the Catholic Church come to adopt this most Protestant application of the Protestant principle?

Here too, at first blush, the answer *seems* to be in the affirmative. One need survey only a small sampling of the literature on Catholic reform which has appeared since the announcement of Vatican II. Writing during the period of preparation prior to the Council, when the word *reform* still sounded uncomfortably Protestant to many Catholic ears, H. Küng was able to state: *"Reformare* . . . is a word with a solid foundation in Catholic tradition."[65] Küng's opinion has come to be echoed by numerous other Catholics. P. Wacker: it is "an ancient Catholic principle" (*urkatholisches Prinzip*).[66] Y. Congar: "The Church has always been active in reforming itself" (VFR, p. 19). H. Fries: "The Church in its concrete form . . . is in constant need of renewal."[67] J. Cardinal Döpfner: Reform is "an essential element of the Church."[68]

If there remained any doubt about the Catholic foundation for a notion of constant reform in the Church, Vatican II has eliminated it: "The Church, embracing sinners in her bosom, is at the same time holy and always in need of being purified (*semper purificanda*), and incessantly pursues the path of penance and renewal (*poenitentiam et renovationem continuo prosequitur*)" (CE #8). "Christ summons the Church, as she goes her pilgrim way, to that continual reformation of which she always has need, insofar as she is an institution of men here on earth" (DOe, #6). And Pope Paul VI:

> The Church is composed of men—imperfect, limited and sinners. The Church is a sacred institution, but built with human material, always inadequate and perishable. It is inserted in the passing stream of history, so it is influenced in its development by the contingencies and changes proper to the times. And so great and authoritative desire was expressed for "aggiornamento," for reform, for authenticity, for "rejuvenation of the Church." . . .
> This is one of the most interesting, most grave, and most urgent topics of our times. And we, who no less than any one else want the correct reform of the Church, consider as a "sign of the times," the possibility which is offered to tht Church today to attend to her proper reform. This is a work which must always be able to acknowledge the frailty of men, even of Christians, and to correct their eventual weaknesses and distortions of the ecclesiastical body. If understood in its genuine sense, we can make our own the program of a continual reform of the Church: *ecclesia semper reformanda*.[69]

It is no exaggeration to say that, since the advent of Pope John XXIII, *ecclesia semper reformanda* has become, for all practical purposes, a

Catholic cliché. Tillich himself admitted that the Catholic Church today appears more open to reform than do the churches of the Reformation (PPT, pp. 236–37). But what kind of reform? Is it the same kind that Tillich had in mind? Certainly the word has been used in any number of different ways—reform of persons, morals, conditions, abuses, the life of the Church, the structures of the Church, *the* structure of the Church. The necessary distinctions are not always made. Pope Paul VI spoke of the "genuine sense" of continual reform. What is that "genuine sense"? What are the kinds of reform that have been and are being advocated within the Catholic Church? What are the kinds of reform that have taken and are taking place within Catholic faith and practice? Do they correspond to Tillich's radical application of the Protestant principle? Here seems to be the point for determining how protestant the Catholic Church can be in practice.

11

Ecclesia Catholica—Semper Reformanda?

In a higher world it is otherwise: but here below to live is to change, and to be perfect is to have changed often.
Cardinal Newman, An Essay on the Development of Christian Doctrine

The history of the Church can easily be written as a chronicle of scandals, abuses, and the need for reform. "The need for reform in the Church . . .extends through many centuries and is perhaps as old as the Church itself."[1] But Church history can also be written as a chronicle of reform. "In the history of the Church there has been hardly a single century when genuine reformist ideals did not seek to prevail."[2] *Ecclesia semper reformanda* as a slogan may have arisen in Dutch Calvinism only within the last few centuries,[3] but its theory and practice go back to the earliest years of Christianity.

It would be out of the question to attempt in one book, let alone one chapter, a detailed description of the various kinds of reform that have been advocated and executed in the course of the Church's two thousand years. Reform poses "a permanent theme in Church history,"[4] " a problem so vast that only a library of books could handle it adequately."[5] After his own fashion, each of the saints has been a reformer. Every ecumenical council, not to speak of innumerable national, provincial, and local synods, in one way or another has had reform as its object.[6]

The concept is a complex one, related to a number of similar ideas. Derived from the Latin *re + formare*, "reform" can mean: "to give an object another form"; "to restore an object to its original form"; "to correct faults, abuses, or conditions that have become disformed"; "to shape a person or object anew according to his own or its own essential being." "The idea of reform takes its meaning at any given moment from concrete historical circumstances and from theories and presuppositions which are by no means constants in the history of thought."[7] Reform is related to such widely diverse ideas as the Golden Age, the eternal return, renaissance, and the myth of the Phoenix; conversion, redemption, Baptism, and Penance; the question of sinfulness in the Church, millenarianism, resurrection, and revolution.[8]

It is necessary here only to sketch a few highlights in the history of Church reform, to describe and exemplify various types of reform that have taken place. More attention is given to examples in twentieth-century Church history, but even here nuances and details can be omitted. A convenient schema is the four types of reform suggested by Yves Congar in *Vraie et fausse réforme dans l'Église*, namely: reform of persons; reform of abuses; reform of the life of the Church; and, finally, the more radical reform of the structure of the Church. Congar's classification is not the only one possible. His categories are not always clearly differentiated and overlap somewhat; some examples of reform fall under more than one heading. But rarely does history lend itself to neat systematization. Congar's categories are adequate for our purposes, however, and if this seems a deviation from Tillich's ecclesiology and the question of the operative presence of the Protestant principle within Catholicism, the purpose is to see both of them within the broader spectrum of history and the development of Catholic thought toward Church reform.

Reform of Persons

Although some references to the idea of reform can be found prior or parallel to Christianity, nowhere did reform assume the importance outside the Church that it did within. "The idea of reform may be considered as essentially Christian in its origin and early development."[9] It arose from the early Latin versions (the Vetus Latina and Vulgata) of St. Paul's epistles: "Jesus Christ who will reform *(reformabit)* the body of our lowliness . . ." (Phil. 3:21) "Be reformed *(reformamini)* in the newness of your mind" (Rom. 12:2; cf. also 2 Cor. 3:18; Eph. 4:23; Col. 3:10). From Scripture it entered into the liturgy, the Fathers, and the medieval theologians.[10] The sense, however, was primarily that of reformation within the interior renewal of the individual, not simply a moral reformation but a new level of existence continuing the rebirth of Baptism. "The belief in man's reformation toward his original image-likeness to God (*reformatio* or *renovatio ad imaginem Dei*) was of central importance for early Christian and medieval thought and life."[11] But it concerned "first and foremost the individual."[12]

In the age of the Fathers,[13] the Church was seen primarily from a mystical point of view, in terms of Christ, the sacraments, and the liturgical communion of the faithful.[14] To describe the Church from this vantage point, both Greek and Latin Fathers borrowed freely from Scripture for images, comparing the Church with special frequency to the moon, which takes its light from the sun (Christ), or to the sinful woman (Rahab, Thamar), who is purified by faith and Baptism. The Greek Fathers emphasized reform as a return to Paradise, a mystical anticipation of a condition of innocence and integrity (Clement of Alexandria, Gregory of Nyssa). This idea developed parallel to the notion of restoring man's "image and likeness" to God (Gen. 1:26). The Latin Fathers developed the reform idea not in terms of restoration to a former condition but rather a renewal for the better, (Tertullian, Cyprian, Augustine). Hence, the Leonine oration: "Deus qui humanae substantiae dignitatem mirabiliter condidisti et mirabilius reformasti . . ." In his conflict with Pelagianism, Augustine opposed the idea that man could reform himself or the world on his own. While insisting on continuous effort on the part of man, he stressed the role of God as the divine reformer over human reformers.

For Augustine, as for the rest of Christian antiquity, "Church reform is personal reform."[15] The Church itself was viewed as a celestial reality, apart from its members and therefore pure and holy, "not having spot or wrinkle or any such thing" (Eph. 5:27). Gradually, however, the idea of reform also became effective as a supra-individual force, primarily, although not exclusively, with the advent of monasticism. "The origins of Christian monasticism in the strict sense coincide approximately with the moment in the history of the Church in which she was confronted by the new tasks and dangers resulting from her having become a power not only in the spiritual, but also in the material order; and from that time onward those who in one way or another followed the monastic, the 'religious,' way of life, were the principle agents of reform in the Christian world."[16] Thus, according to G. Ladner, "the idea of the reform of man to the image and likeness of God became the inspiration of all reform movements in early and medieval Christianity."[17] With monasticism and the movements for monastic reform, particularly that which emanated out of Cluny and reached its apogee in the eleventh-century Gregorian reform, there arose the concept of a reform of the universal Church itself. "Notwithstanding the very ancient and important practice of ecclesiastical councils of renewing the 'old canons' and the 'doctrine of the Fathers'. . . . the idea of a reform of the whole Church itself does not seem to appear before the age of Gregory VII, when the Church begins to be defined also as an eminently sacerdotal, clerical quasi-corporation, in addition to being the liturgical communion of all the faithful."[18]

Once the Church came to be seen in terms of its members, efforts to reform it became not only conceivable but characteristic. Witness the reform efforts of Innocent III, the Reform Councils, the Reformation, and the Counter-Reformation. Although these efforts concentrated on politics and laws rather than on a religious or ethical ideal, yet the reform of persons was never entirely forgotten. At the Council of Constance (1414–18), the reform-minded participants were reminded by an anonymous preacher: "Return to Christ, to the foundation of faith, to truth and a faultless way of life, to faith and doctrine—this is the only true reform."[19] In the opening speech to the V Lateran Council (1512–17), Giles of Viterbo formulated his celebrated reform dictum: "Man must be changed by religion, not religion by men," (*homines per sacra immutari fas est, non sacra per homines.*)[20] A similar attitude was echoed in the last century by J.A. Möhler: "A Christian should not seek to perfect Christianity but should try to perfect himself within it."[21] Whenever it is envisioned primarily as a celestial reality apart from its members and their present condition, the only reform that can be logically sanctioned in the Church is that of the persons within it.

The belief that Church reform is primarily, if not exclusively, a matter of reforming the persons within the Church has also had its exponents in our own century. When certain movements in Germany began advocating a reform of Catholic structures and institutions at the turn of the century, articulate defenders arose to champion the status quo. Structural, institutional reforms suggested by Reform Catholicism were branded as revolutionary by men like Bishop Keppler and Albert Maria Weiss. Church reform for them could be a matter only of personal interior and moral renewal.

Bishop Paul Wilhelm von Keppler of Rottenburg, Germany, was an outspoken exponent of reform primarily in terms of persons. He attacked the ideas of Reform Catholicism with an address (December 1, 1902) subsequently published under the title *Wahre und falsche Reform* [True and false reform]. It deserves to be quoted at length, because of the representative nature of its arguments:

> Is a reform of the Church, of Catholicism possible? Of course; but naturally not in that which is divine in it, not in dogma, in moral law, . . . or in

organization; by all means, however, in what is human. And to this human element belongs above all, and here I emphasize, the character life of Catholics. [P. 3]

The whole Catholic faith, the whole Catholic life, is a matter of the soul, a matter of the heart. For this reason a reform of Catholicism cannot come from the head but only from the heart. It will never appeal one-sidedly to reason and judgment. It will pursue moral goals above all, and only secondarily or not at all intellectual goals. [P. 8]

Weakness and looseness of character is the real sickness of our age. For this reason, every true reform must be a character reform. Mankind today . . . has as good as lost its soul. [P. 9]

The hope to win modern men for Christianity and Catholicism through compromises and concessions is futile. First of all, anyone thoroughly entangled in the modern world cannot be won over. Anyone who has his fill of the modern world can only be won over by something entirely different, by a genuine life of faith, an unfalsified, unspoiled Christianity, not by a modernized Christianity, not by a margarine-Catholicism. [P. 6]

It does not occur to Catholic men to let themselves turn into reform-simpletons. [P. 13]

There is nothing to reform within Catholicism. Among Catholics there is much to reform. It is from this distinction that every genuine reform must proceed. [P. 15]

Keppler's talk was printed and distributed widely, creating a sensation with rhetoric like "margarine-Catholicism" and "reform-simpletons." While it aroused bitter rebuttal from the proponents of Reform Catholicism, the Vatican expressed both pleasure and gratitude. But Keppler was not alone in his attacks upon Reform Catholicism. Albert Maria Weiss made it his life's work to struggle against all forms of liberalism not only outside the Catholic Church but inside as well.[22] He viewed Reform Catholicism as a mortal danger threatening the very existence of the Catholic Church. It was not the Church which required reform but the advocates of reform. More modesty and prayer were needed, less criticism and debate.[23] Reform of persons would obviate the need for any other kind of reform. "For one loses the courage to preach presumptuously the obligation of reform to others, if he recognizes above all his own need for reform."[24] Weiss urged that "the zeal for reform be applied to the renewal of the interior, spiritual life."[25] The call for this type of reform cannot be raised too often or too loudly. It is effected primarily by means of penance and prayer.[26]

Rarely since the time of Bishop Keppler and A.M. Weiss has Catholic reform been seen so exclusively as a matter of reforming persons. Reform continues to be regarded primarily as personal, though, by those who take an exclusively mystical, if not Donatist, approach to the Church and see it as a reality distinct from the members who comprise it. Such a point of view can admit fault, and therefore a need for reform, only in the members of the Church, not in the Church itself. In this vein, there is C. Journet: The Church is not without sinners but it is itself without sin."[27] He was able to appeal to *Mystici Corporis* by Pius XII and its teaching that human weakness can be found among the members of the Church, even the most elevated; but the Church itself is holy in its sacraments, faith, laws, and spiritual gifts (AAS35:225).

The need for personal and moral reform and the interior renewal of those within the Church was a central concern for St. Paul, and it remains so for the Church so long as it exists. Without it all other reform efforts are empty, formalistic, and ultimately useless. There can be no reform worthy of the name without a change of heart (DOe, #7). But is the reform of persons enough? It goes without saying that such a conception of Church reform has little to do with the Protestant principle as Tillich understood it. But neither does interior renewal exhaust the meaning of reform in Catholic tradition. This can be demonstrated by yet another Catholic application of *ecclesia semper reformanda*.

Reform of Abuses

Congar describes reform of abuses in terms of the means taken to correct them, namely, law (VFR, pp. 58, 188, 357). For reform of abuses and disorders in the Church, it suffices to create and apply ecclesiastical ordinances, canons, controls, and sanctions, or simply to restore their good observance. As soon as the Church began to feel the effects of imperial recognition by Constantine, this type of reform began to appear at local levels. At the First Council of Tours (461) we read: "because through long carelessness the rule concerning matters of ecclesiastical discipline has been somewhat corrupted, they [the Council] wished to confirm their definition;"[28] at the Second Council of Toledo (531): "If, however, the decrees of former councils have so far been neglected through the abuse of the times, they must now receive the censure of a revival of order."[29] Only with the age of Gregory VII, however, did the reform of abuses on a broader level become both a possibility and a program. Once it began to be seen as "an eminently sacerdotal, clerical quasi-corporation,"[30] reform of the Church *in capite et membris* became a watchword for the entire Middle Ages.

After the collapse of the Carolingian empire, the decline of both Church and papacy, especially in the tenth century, had become such as to render a reform of abuses indispensable. Out of the monasteries, above all from the Burgundian monastery at Cluny, there emanated a reform movement which eventually was to influence not only two thousand monasteries but also both the papacy and German throne. At the Synod of Sutri (1046), Emperor Henry III, a disciple of Cluny, deposed three rival popes and brought about the rise of a reform papacy. A series of reform synods renewed and generalized decrees against simony and established a new method of electing a pope. Pope Gregory VII (1073–85), however, was the first to give an overriding priority to the reform of abuses in the Church at large. He added heavy sanctions to the reform decrees of his predecessors and saw to it that they were applied. By means of legal measures Pope Gregory effected the reform which bears his name and became the paragon of the reforming pope. "He was convinced that the translation of pure doctrine into reality could be made only through the vehicle of the law. He insisted that the papacy was primarily a governmental institution and, as such, presupposed law; for a government without the law is impotent."[31]

The eleventh-century reforming agent became itself the object of criticism in the twelfth century, as Bernard of Clairvaux attacked the wealth of Cluny and its neglect of the poor (PL182:915). He did not hesitate to criticize the papacy as well for not being more vigilant of discipline (*De Consideratione*, PL182:727–808). Under his influence the Cistercian order affected all of Europe with their asceticism and revitalized piety. The Cistercians, Augustinian canons, and Norbertines in the twelfth century, the mendicant orders of Dominic and Francis in the thirteenth, served the cause of inner renewal by demonstrating evangelical poverty in the midst of an increasingly wealthy and power-conscious Church. The very symbol of that power, Pope Innocent III (1198–1216), convoked the IV Lateran Council (1215) in imitation of the ancient ecumenical councils precisely "for the reformation of the universal Church" (PL216:824). It enacted decrees reforming abuses with regard to preaching, the sacraments, clerical education, pilgrimages, indulgences, relics, et al. Innocent's death a year later, however, prevented any fundamental renewal from ensuing.

Decadence continued, exemplified by the Avignon Papacy (1304–77). When he convoked the council of Vienne (1311–12), Pope Clement V listed reform among its goals, although for him Church reform meant regulation of finances and the protection of the clergy from the secular power. William Durandus, Bishop of Mende, however, presented at Vienne a tract, *"De modo concilii generalis celebrandi,"* in which he accused the Roman Curia of being responsible for the most glaring abuses in the Church, such as permitting bishops to possess more than one benefice (pluralities) and thus neglect residency, infringing upon the rights of bishops, papal centralism, and venality. He charged that the pope himself is not competent to change laws or make new ones without a general council; that such a council should be called every ten years; and that Church reform must begin with the head of the Church. The tract won Durandus only the anger of the Roman Curia, although it was soon to be echoed by the Reform Councils of the fifteenth century, especially the Council of Constance (1414–18), when the spectacle of the Western Schism had made reform a paramount concern for all of Western Christendom. For conciliarists such as John Gerson and Peter d'Ailly, *reformatio in capite et membris* was more practical and political than religious and ethical, with a decided emphasis upon reform *in capite*. The head was seen as the source of the sickness throughout the body. But no agreement was reached as to what shape a general reform should take. In the ensuing struggle for power between the papacy and the conciliarists, the papacy was the ultimate victor.

Although the Renaissance popes each took oaths at the beginning of their pontificates to carry out reform, one was as ineffective as the other. They were lovers of the good life and far too involved in the pursuit of politics to embark on a bold program of reform. Greeted enthusiastically as the dawning of a new age, the V Lateran Council (1512–17) was opened by Giles of Viterbo with a call for a return "to the ancient and original purity;"[32] but all that issued from it was a declaration on the nature of the human soul. The reform program submitted by two Venetian monks, Tommaso Giustiniani and Vincenzo Quirini, occupied the Catholic Church for the next century, but not until it felt itself compelled to do so by Martin Luther and the Protestant Reformation.

From the sixteenth century well into our own, the Catholic Church has been the Church of the Counter-Reformation, a church of reaction. A basic question, though, was how to reform, how to react to the Protestant reformers. One way would have been to take up what was positive in the reformers' challenge; to try to understand their demands and think things out afresh from the original sources; to admit coresponsibility for the schism and seek a reconciliation. Another way of reacting would be to reject utterly the Protestant demands and assume a program of restoration and defensiveness. The first possibility of reacting was exemplified by Cardinal

Gaspare Contarini, who sought a reconciliation with Lutherans at Ratisbon (1541) on the question of justification. He was suspected of heresy and died a year later. The second possible reaction was exemplified by Cardinal Gian Pietro Caraffa, to whom the Roman Inquisition and the Index of Forbidden Books appealed as a more effective means of reform than reconciliatory dialogue. It was Caraffa who eventually became Pope Paul IV (1555–59), and it was his concept of reform as restoration which prevailed.

The initial Catholic response to the Protestant Reformation produced three remarkable documents which deserve mention in any survey of Catholic reform. The first was the Instruction of Pope Adrian VI to his representative Francisco Chiergati at the German Diet at Nuremberg (c. November 25, 1522):

> God has permitted this persecution to be inflicted on his Church because of the sins of men, especially of priests and the Church's prelates. . . . We know that for some years now there have been in this Holy See many abominations, abuses of spiritual matters, misuse of authority. . . . Wherefore, in what touches our office, we promise that we will use all means, that this Curia first of all, from which perhaps all his evil has come, shall be reformed.[33]

Similarly noteworthy was the *Consilium de emendanda Ecclesia.* Under the leadership of Cardinal Contarini, a commission of nine reform-minded cardinals and prelates, including Caraffa, Cervini, Morone, Pole, Sadoleto, and Seripando was charged by Pope Paul III to prepare an assessment of the general state of the Church. The fruit of their deliberations (November 1536 to February 1537) was the charge that the chief blame for all abuses in the Church lay with the Roman Curia and its exaggerated conception of papal authority:

> Teachers come forward to proclaim that the Pope is master of all benefices and, since the master may sell his own property, the pope may not be accused of simony. In like fashion, they taught that the pope's wish, whatever its quality, is the norm for his enterprises and actions. The consequence? Whatever he pleases, he may do. From this source, as from the Trojan horse of old, these many abuses and serious ills have burst forth upon the Church of God.[34]

The third document was the *Eirenikon* authored by Cardinal Pole and delivered to the Council of Trent (January 7, 1546), in which he reminded his fellow bishops: "We, the shepherds, should make ourselves responsible for all the evils now burdening the flock of Christ. The sins of all we should take upon ourselves, not in generosity but in justice; because the truth is that of all these evils we are in great part the cause."[35]

Catholic reform in the sixteenth century drew its initial strength from the reforming efforts of Cardinal Ximenez in Spain and the establishment in Italy of religious orders (the Theatines) and brotherhoods, founded for the sake of renewed pastoral care. The founding of the Society of Jesus (1540) by Ignatius of Loyola provided a force for Catholic restoration numbering some thousand members by 1556 and thirty-five hundred by 1565. The Council of Trent (1545–63), however, was the most important means of Catholic reform. It has been described as *"the most outspoken Reform Council* in all of Church history."[36]

Apart from its doctrinal considerations, Trent's reform efforts centered in its first period around the abuse which was viewed in many ways as the root of all the others, the neglect of required residency by bishops and pastors in their respective dioceses and parishes. The lax practice of dispensations by the Curia permitted not only neglect of residency but also accumulation of such benefices. In its second period the Council prohibited the abuse and sanctioned its prohibition with heavy penalties. Reforms were further decreed for the naming of bishops, the extension of their authority over previously exempt groups, the regular convocation of local synods, the episcopal visitation of churches, and the establishment of seminaries for the education of clergy. The "care of souls" was made the "supreme law" governing all reform, *"salus animarum suprema lex esto."*[37]

The execution of its decrees and the reform of the Curia were tasks which Trent left to the papacy. They were assumed by a series of popes who devoted themselves to carrying out the decrees of Trent vigorously, though with a distinct bias. Assisted by St. Charles Borromeo, the model of a Tridentine bishop, these popes saw reform in terms of an anti-Protestant crusade and the establishment of an even more centralized Roman system. Under Pius V (1566–72), a reformed breviary and missal were prescribed for the entire Catholic Church; the lax dispensation practices of his predecessors were put to an end. Gregory XIII (1572–85) began to employ the system of papal nuncios as an instrument of close papal supervision throughout the Catholic world; with the foundation of the university which bears his name, Rome became a center for theological studies. Sixtus V (1585–90) reorganized the Roman Curia, defining the competences of the various congregations; he established as mandatory the *Visitatio liminum*, whereby the bishops of all dioceses were required to visit Rome regularly to report to the Curia on the condition of the churches entrusted to their care.

Thus within a single lifetime, the face of Catholicism was drastically changed. The flagrant abuses of the Renaissance were reformed and replaced by a Baroque Catholicism proud of its new purity and vigor. The price paid for the welcome reform, however, included such ambiguous measures as the Index of Forbidden Books, the introduction of censorship, and the activities of the Roman Inquisition. For all the good that it accomplished, the sixteenth-century Catholic reform of abuses resulted in an enforced uniformity such as had never existed in the Catholic Church prior to its time.

The reform set into motion by Trent has been criticized as being largely a program of restoration and defense. Its overriding concern was to do battle with Protestantism. Catholic reform looked back with nostalgia to the medieval past and sought to revive it, wherever possible. "It was essentially a bid to restore the *status quo*, and not a *genuine* re-forming." "What everywhere prevailed was a desire simply to conserve and maintain as much as possible of the traditional way of doing things."[38]

The onslaught of Protestantism was soon joined by the Enlightenment, Jansenism, Gallicanism, royal absolutism, the French Revolution, secularism, Napoleon, liberalism, socialism, and any number of other scientific, social, and philosophical revolutions. The Catholic Church felt itself struggling for its very existence and reacted defensively. Forgotten was the tradition of being all things to all men, of pluralism and missionary accommodation. Forgotten was the tradition of criticism within the Church. The Catholic Church retreated into a "splendid isolation" wherein criticism from without was viewed as an enemy's attack and criticism from within was tantamount to treason.

This hypersensitivity to criticism was exemplified strikingly at Vatican I (1869–70). Twenty-one schemas on Church discipline had been prepared;[39] four had been discussed at length, revised, and discussed again; but none reached finalization. The preparatory work was one-sidedly Roman and hardly representative of the entire Church. Too much attention was paid to secondary questions of detail rather than to essentials.[40] Criticism of the Roman posture and system, even the discussion of certain points, was resented by Pope Piux IX and the Roman Curia as an outrage to the dignity of the Holy See.[41]

The defensive attitude of Pius IX (1846–78), exemplified by his Syllabus of Errors (1864), was modified considerably by Leo XIII (1878–1903). In sharp contrast to his predecessors, Leo had a basically positive view of the modern world that had grown up around the Church. Defensiveness returned, though, with his successor, the saintly Pope Pius X (1903–1914), as witnessed by the blanket, undifferentiating condemnations of the modernist theology of A. Loisy and G. Tyrrell (*Lamentabili*, 1907; *Pascen-*

di, 1907). Pius wished to be regarded as a reform pope, however, and he made this clear at his first allocution, when he expressed the desire summed up in his motto *Instaurare omnia in Christo*, "To restore all things in Christ." His reform program was indeed restorative. And like his predecessors since the time of Gregory VII, he regarded law as the most expedient means for effecting it. In 1904 he established a commission for the reform and codification of Canon Law, a reform he is said to have decided upon the very first night after his election.[42] He initiated a *reformatio in capite* by means of a thoroughgoing reorganization of the Roman Curia (*Sapienti Consilio*, 1908), simplifying its structure and removing a number of abuses. Abuses in Church music were reformed by restoring Gregorian chant to a place of prominence (*Musica Sacra*, 1903). His successor, Benedict XV (1914–22), concluded the reform of Canon Law and promulgated the New Code (May 1917).

The reform of abuses, inaugurated by Trent and executed ever since by reforming popes to our own century, did not serve to heal the breach between Catholics and Protestants. The reason why is clear: Adrian VI and Cardinal Pole notwithstanding, it was not the need for reform of morals or abuses in the Church which led to the break with Rome. Luther was not a moral reformer.

> Luther was no Donatist, and any interpretation of the Reformation on this basis fails to strike at the core of the problem. Moral conditions in the Roman Church after Trent were not what they had been in the heyday of the Renaissance, and it is neither fair nor honest to describe them as though they were. Nor dare the Protestant observer forget that the moral level of the Reformation often left much to be desired. . . . It was not moral degradation that brought on Luther's protest and the split, and no amount of moral improvement would have healed the split.[43]

But if it was not a reform of persons or a reform of abuses which might have prevented the Catholic-Protestant schism, what kind of Catholic reform might have? To the mind of Y. Congar, only a reform of life.

Reform of Life

In the same year that Pope Pius XII served warning to the *Nouvelle Théologie* for its liberalizing trends (*Humani Generis*, 1950), Yves Congar published his book *Vraie et fausse réforme dans l'Église*. In it he considered the interior, personal reform advocated by Bishop Keppler and A.M.

Weiss as well as the reform of abuses executed by the Catholic Church since the time of Trent. He found both types of reform wanting. Granted, there were moral failings and abuses in pre-Reformation Catholicism, but there was vitality as well; more than a return to canonical regulations and the restoration of good order were required. A nominalist theology, the kind of preaching which emphasized externals, questionable devotional practices, the manner in which papal and episcopal authority were exercised—these were the things that called for reform, in short, not simply a number of abuses but the *état de choses* (p. 188). A profound return to sources was called for, a reform of life which looked to the needs of the times. And what was true for the sixteenth-century Church holds true likewise for today. Because of its stability, the ancient world valued tradition over change. But in a world as dynamic as our own, it is not sin in the Church that scandalizes so much as immobility, a narrowness which renders the Church incomprehensible (pp. 67–68). "Our times are less interested in the *moral* sins of men in the Church than in its faults and failings as regards the requirements of the times."[44]

A reform of life confronts the fact that too often "our Christianity appears like a ritualism which does not change anything of the lives of those who practice it."[45] Congar laid the blame for this on antiquated historical forms, insufficient for the demands of our day. "It is an often verified fact that the external forms of the Church in our day comprise for many a screen not only in front of the gospel and of God but in front of the mystery of the Church itself: the Christian world constitutes a screen in front of Christianity" (pp. 55–56). True fidelity to Christianity, both to its origins and future, involves going deeper, beyond the mere external, historical form (p. 599). Christianity is eternal, but not the forms in which it realizes itself. These are conditioned by a particular state of development, and to invest them with the same permanence is to absolutize the relative (pp. 177–78). As examples of these forms open to reform Congar offered Christian civilization, the concrete organization and administration of the Church, exterior forms of worship, the style of catechetics and preaching, and the education of seminarians (pp. 55, 177). These are sometimes referred to as the structures of the Church, a term Congar found vague and misleading (p. 57n50), precisely because it is apt to become confused with that in the Church which is above reform, namely, the structure of the Church.

Whereas the life of the Church and its external forms are open to reform according to Congar, not so its structure, not so its dogma, sacraments, or hierarchical structure. These are interior to the Church and constitutive of its essence, infallible and irreformable in that they share in the infallibility and holiness of God himself. Here there can be no question of narrowness, no question of obsolescence or inadaptation (pp. 103–5, 456). And here, to Congar's mind, lay precisely the error of Luther and Calvin, the failing which vitiated their reform and rendered it false. They went beyond reforming the life of the Church and attacked its dogmas, sacraments, and hierarchical structure (p. 366). For Congar, *Ecclesia semper reformanda* could be applied to the life of the Church, but not to its structure (p. 466). The exercise and living of Christianity are our domain, but the foundation and structure are the domain of Christ (p. 477). "We affirm the infallibility and irreformability of the institution in its elements of foundation or structure, because *in them* the Lord is engaged and involved" (pp. 478–79). "In no case could a Catholic reform claim to change the essential structure, the traditional form, received and transmitted since the time of Christ and the apostles" (pp. 366–67).

Congar admitted that it is not always easy to distinguish between the dogmatic, sacramental, hierarchic structure of the Church and the concrete forms in which that structure is realized. The line between them is narrow, and for this reason the Catholic Church has not always heard the call for a reform of life, fearing that it would involve a tampering with the structure of the Church (p. 358). Adaptation has been identified with novelty, and novelty in religious life is often synonymous with error. Even St. Jerome was accused of unsettling the foundations of faith with his new translation of the Bible (p. 178). Congar's observation was well justified. Despite his oft-repeated insistence that a reform of the external forms of the Church need not affect its structure, his call for a reform of life in the Church was seen nonetheless as a threat to that structure. Congar had already been under suspicion by the Vatican for his earlier book, *Chrétiens désunis*. The announcement of an Italian translation of *Vraie et fausse réforme dans l'Église* brought him a prohibition from the Vatican, forbidding him to allow either a new French edition of the book or any translation. From that time on, he was required to submit all his writings to Rome for examination prior to their publication.[46]

Vatican reaction to Congar's book was not without precedent. Congar was calling for a reform of the Church in terms of updating and accommodation. This could only mean a break with some of the traditional forms of the past as well as a certain amount of innovation. Few values in Church history have been prized so highly as tradition, or few risks so hesitatingly taken as innovation.

Adaptation was certainly not unknown to the early Church. One need witness only the translation of Christianity from a Jewish sect to a world religion; the opening up of the Church to the Gentiles; the successful struggle of Paul over conservative Judaizing Christians who wished to absolutize the Law. Witness the accommodation of Christianity by the Church Fathers from Jewish to Greek thought-patterns; the adaptation of the liturgy to changing circumstances, resulting in the subsequent plurality of its forms. Witness the translation of the Bible from the original languages into the vernacular Latin; the accommodations successfully employed by Christian missionaries like SS. Cyril and Methodius.

In its struggle with hellenistic enthusiasm and Gnosticism, however, the Church came quickly to set a premium upon apostolic tradition. It assumed the values of Greek philosophy and culture, values which included the conviction of eternal verities and principles. This could result only in the attitude expressed by Pope Stephen I (254–57) in his celebrated dictum: "*Nihil innovetur nisi quod traditum est.*" For Tertullian, discipline could admit of corrections but the *regula fidei* was immobile and irreformable. In the struggle against heresy, antiquity became the decisive criterion. *Novitas* was seen as a threat and understood only *in malam partem.* This appears most clearly in the *Commonitorium* of Vincent of Lerins, for whom the canon of faith was universality, antiquity, and consent, with the emphasis upon antiquity. If one expresses something in a new manner, let him beware lest he express a new thing: *Ut cum dicas nove, non dicas nova.*

The conservatism of the Vincentian canon was re-enforced by the relative stability of the medieval world it helped create. It was a conservatism in no way rejected by the early Protestant reformers. "In the early sixteenth century there was . . . no call for the reform of the Church through *aggiornamento.* As a matter of fact, it is hard to imagine an intellectual atmosphere in which reform through a program of bringing things up-to-date would have received a more startled and uncomprehending hearing."[47] The sixteenth century was convinced that its age was the most corrupt of any prior age. "What was needed was not to change the Church in the direction of making it more viable in the contemporary world, but to change the contemporary world by bringing it into conformity with the Church, i.e., with the authentic Church of the past."[48] The question, of course, was what constituted the authentic Church of the past. When attacked for having founded a new church, Luther countered by accusing the Catholic Church of innovation: "What if I should prove that we hold to the true, real old Church; nay, that we are the real, old Church, that you have become apostates from us, that is from the old Church, and erected a new Church against the old Church" (*Werke* 51:478). Calvin likewise accused Roman Catholicism of confecting new articles of faith (*Institutes,*

IV, 8.10), convinced that what stems from human inventiveness corrupts religion (*Institutes*, I, 5.12).

Under the impact of the Enlightenment and subsequent philosophical and political revolutions of the eighteenth and nineteenth centuries, the Catholic Church intensified the defensiveness of the Counter-Reformation. Innovation was suspect of error and for that reason rejected. The 1864 Syllabus of Errors of Pius IX provides a ready symbol of the Catholic siege mentality with its catalogue of proscribed isms, concluding with the proposition: If anyone says "the Roman Pontiff can and should reconcile himself and come to terms with progress, with liberalism, and with modern civilization," let him be anathema (Denz. #2980). The attitude was to persist on into the twentieth century, at least with regard to modernism. A change was in the offing, though; without being acceptable in theory, reform of life in terms of adaptation did gradually begin to appear in practice.

The siege mentality of the Catholic Church relaxed noticeably under Pope Leo XIII (1878–1903). In sharp contrast to his predecessors, Leo took a basically positive view of the modern world. Resistance to innovation and anathemas gave way to flexibility and a willingness to meet the new age halfway. He threw open the doors of the Vatican archives for scholarly research with the expressed wish that nothing of the truth be hidden. He referred to Protestants not as heretics but as "beloved brothers." His encyclicals gave support to the political framework of the modern state and came to terms with democracy. Leo's openness to social issues resulted in the encyclical *Rerum Novarum* (1891), which upheld the basic rights and dignity of the working classes. The Pope's openness did not extend to "higher criticism" of the Bible or to the exegetical work of non-Catholic scholars, but Catholic biblical studies were encouraged (*Providentissimus Deus*, 1893), and plans were laid for a Pontifical Biblical Institute. In 1897 perhaps the first significant step was taken toward reforming the life and worship of the Church once again in terms of adaptation: the ban was lifted forbidding translations of the Roman missal into the vernacular. In an excessive reaction against Protestantism, Pope Alexander VII had prohibited under pain of excommunication the publication of any translation of the Latin Mass (1661), a ban which was renewed by Pius IX (1857). With the turn of the century Catholics were permitted at least to follow the Latin Mass with missals in their own language.

The moderateness of Leo XIII, in comparison to Pius IX, encouraged a number of disconnected reform movements throughout Europe, especially in Germany. They were given the blanket designation of *Re-*

formkatholizismus,[49] a term coined by Joseph Müller in a book under the same name (1898). Included under this description were movements opposed to Roman centralism, mandatory celibacy for clergy, and neo-Scholasticism as the exclusive philosophy for the Catholic Church. Other movements fostered reform of seminary training, liturgical pluralism, a greater openness to contemporary science and culture, and Catholic involvement in social issues. Among the more prominent exponents of Reform Catholicism were university professors F.X. Kraus, A. Ehrhard, and especially H. Schell, who fought against superstitious and vulgarized forms of Catholic piety. Rome was not quite ready, however, for such independent critical thinking. Several of Schell's writings were placed upon the Index of Forbidden Books (1898). Although Reform Catholicism was quite distinct from Modernism, which existed at the same time, the differentiation was not always made, and the proponents of Reform Catholicism came to suffer the same fate as the Modernists.

Despite the thoroughness of the anti-Modernist purge under Pius X, some steps were taken toward adaptation in practice. Children were permitted to receive the Eucharist once they reached the age of reason (1905); daily reception of Holy Communion was encouraged (1905); the Roman Breviary was reformed (1911, 1913); in the light of changing social conditions, the number of Holy Days of Obligation was reduced (1911). Benedict XV directed his energies toward peace and the alleviation of misery after World War I. His successor, Pius XI (1922–39), continued Catholic social teaching by upholding the rights of workers to collective bargaining (*Quadragesimo Anno,* 1931). In his support of Catholic Action, he encouraged laymen to take a more active part in the life and mission of the Church.

Moderating, somewhat, the anti-Modernist posture, Pius XII (1939–58) gave encouragement to the Catholic biblical movement by approving the use of modern methods of critical historical exegesis (*Divino Afflante Spiritu,* 1943). With *Mediator Dei* (1947) he gave impetus to the liturgical movement and encouraged lay participation in the Mass through singing and the recitation of the Latin responses. Other reforms in the direction of accommodation likewise centered around the liturgy. The Easter Vigil was restored (1951), and shortly thereafter the entire Holy Week liturgy reformed (1955). A relaxation of the rules governing the Eucharistic fast (1953, 1957) did more to encourage frequent reception of Holy Communion than any prior number of papal exhortations. In recognition of changed circumstances of modern living, the practice of evening Masses was introduced (1953), and a reform of rubrics (1955) advanced the modernizing trend toward liturgical simplification.

Although in practice he often acted otherwise, Pius XII (Address to the International Catholic Press Congress, Rome, 1950) admitted in theory the need for critical public opinion in the Church, "within those areas, of course, where there is room for free discussion."[50] With Pope John XXIII (1958–63), however, and the Second Vatican Council (1962–65), reform of life in terms of adaptation became a program. In his official convocation of the Council, Pope John designated as its objectives not only growth in faith and the restoration of sound morals but also an "appropriate adaptation of Church discipline to the needs and conditions of our times" (*Ad Petri Cathedram*, 1959). That "appropriate adaptation" was described as an *aggiornamento* (*Osservatore Romano*, November 1, 1959), a reform program whereby the Church could "show herself better and better fitted to solve the problems of men of this age" (*Humanae Salutis*, 1961). This confidence was repeated by Pope John in his celebrated opening speech to the Council (October 11, 1962): "By bringing herself up-to-date where required, and by the wise organization of mutual cooperation, the Church will make men, families, peoples really turn their minds to heavenly things."

If there had been doubt prior to Vatican II, the first session of the Council dispelled it: the Counter-Reformation was over.[51] Gone was the conditioned reflex against criticism, the reaction against Protestantism. The Council was set upon reform. As it could never be, interior, personal reform was not forgotten:

> The Church, embracing sinners in her bosom, is at the same time holy and always in need of being purified, and incessantly pursues the path of penance and renewal. [CE, #8]

> She [the Church] exhorts her sons to purify and renew themselves so that the sign of Christ may shine more brightly over the face of the Church. [CE, #15]

> Every renewal of the Church essentially consists in an increase of fidelity to her own calling. [DOe, #6].

Recognizing that the Catholic Church had not always been as faithful to that calling as it should have, Vatican II admitted the Catholic share of guilt in the sins against Christian unity and asked non-Catholic Christians for pardon (DOe, #7). It admitted that believers often conceal rather than reveal the authentic face of God and religion, so that they share in the responsibility for the widespread extent of atheism in our time (CEMT, #19).

Most characteristic of Vatican II, however, was its call for reform in terms of adaptation. This was the leitmotif which ran through the Council from its opening Message to Humanity to the final days in which adaptation was designated as "the law of all evangelization."

> In this assembly under the guidance of the Holy Spirit, we wish to inquire how we ought to renew ourselves, so that we may be found increasingly faithful to the gospel of Christ. We shall take pains so to present to the men of this age God's truth in its integrity and purity that they may understand it and gladly assent to it. [Message to Humanity]
>
> Her [the Church's] purpose has been to adapt the gospel to the grasp of all. . . . Indeed, this accommodated preaching of the revealed Word ought to remain the law of all evangelization. For thus each nation develops the ability to express Christ's message in its own way. [CEMT, #44]

It was in terms of Christian unity, however, that the Church, its discipline, and even its doctrinal formulations were most explicitly described as open to reform:

> Christ summons the Church, as she goes her pilgrim way, to that continual reformation of which she always has need, insofar as she is an institution of men here on earth. Therefore, if the influence of events or of the times has led to deficiencies in conduct, in Church discipline, or even in the formulation of doctrine (which must be carefully distinguished from the deposit itself of faith), these should be appropriately rectified at the proper moment. [DOe, #6]

Vatican II not only spoke of reform, but served to inaugurate it, for example, the undefensive, affirmative stance taken toward non-Catholic churches, non-Christian religions, and the secular world; the updating of liturgy through simplification of forms and introduction of the vernacular; the emphasis upon collegiality, upon shared responsibility and decision-making at all levels of church government; the updating of clerical and religious life and education; the missionary adaptation of Christianity to local cultures; the more positive, unpolemical presentations of Catholic teaching on the nature of the Church, revelation, the relation of Scripture to tradition, the ministry, and religious freedom. The evaluation of Vatican II made by Karl Barth sums it up accurately: "It was a reform council, if there ever was one."[52]

Pope John's call for an *aggiornamento* was echoed more widely and loudly than Congar's or any other theologian's could ever have been. It would be impossible to cite here all the literature on reform of life and adaptation of forms that has appeared since the first announcement of Vatican II. The most significant affirmation, however, must be mentioned, namely, that of his successor, Pope Paul VI. If there had been any doubts that he would reconvene the second session of Vatican II, Pope Paul dispelled them by embracing both the Council and its aims, including that of adapting of forms. From the very first months of his pontificate, however, one notices emphases upon the limits of reform, upon eternal truths, essential traditions, and exoneration of the past. A fear is evidenced that the timeless might be sacrificed to the transitory. Even before the second session of the Council, Pope Paul expressed fears of fads and evil days:

> It [*aggiornamento*] is a word which might appear to give servile honor to capricious and fleeting fads, to an existentialism that does not believe in transcendent objective values, and to hunger only for the fullness of the momentary and subjective. Rather it assigns due importance to the rapid, inexorable passing of phenomena in which our life develops and seeks to correspond to the celebrated recommendation of the Apostle: "Make the most of your time, because the days are evil."[53]

In his opening address to the second session of the Vatican Council (September 29, 1963), Pope Paul expressed fears that reform might be taken to imply a break with the past:

> The question of the Church's renewal is most certainly of great concern to this Council. But the expression of this desire must not be interpreted as an admission of guilt on the part of the Catholic Church of our day for having falsified the mind of her founder in a matter of grave moment. . . . Hence the renewal with which the Church is concerned must not be thought of as a repudiation of the present life of the Church or a break with essential and time-honored traditions. She shows her reverence for tradition by rejecting forms which are spurious or moribund, and by wishing to make them genuine and fruitful.[54]

In his first encyclical, *Ecclesiam Suam*, August 6, 1964, Paul repeated once again that Pope John's *aggiornamento* expressed the aim and object of his own pontificate (#50), but he took pains to define carefully the limits and nature of that reform.[55] It was becoming clear that for Pope Paul reform was primarily interior, personal, and moral.

> Obviously, there can be no question of reforming the essential nature of the Church or its basic and necessary structure. To use the word reform in that context would be to misuse it completely. We cannot brand the holy and beloved Church of God with the mark of infidelity. [#46]

We must strengthen these convictions [of the Church's holiness and splendor] in ourselves if we also are to avoid another danger which the desire for reform can produce, not so much in us pastors, . . . as in many of the faithful, who think that the reform of the Church should consist principally in adapting its way of thinking and acting to the customs and temper of the secular world. . . . Those who are not deeply rooted in the faith and in the observance of the Church's laws readily imagine that the time is ripe to adjust themselves to worldly standards of living, on the assumption that these are the best and only possible ones for a Christian to adopt. [#48]

The Church will rediscover its youthful vitality not so much by changing its external legislation, as by submitting to the obedience of Christ and observing the laws which the Church lays upon itself with the intention of following in Christ's footsteps. [#51]

The completion of Vatican II concluded neither the call for Catholic reform nor the efforts to attain it. But differences of opinion became increasingly apparent regarding the nature of that reform, the acceptable limits of adaptation, and the areas to which reform could be justifiably applied. The momentum created by Catholic self-criticism and the desire to update began to extend to areas held by many to be sacrosanct and above criticism. Catholic reform efforts, to Pope Paul's mind, were becoming too radical. He began using words like *revolution,* reformation of *structures,* and the *Protestant* spirit of reform, all as part of a worldwide phenomenon of transformation:

The present generation, in fact, is intoxicated, as it were, by this transformation. It calls it progress and takes part in it, collaborates with it forcefully and enthusiastically, often without any reserve: the past is forgotten, tradition interrupted, habits abandoned. . . . People want the transformation to be general and they think it is necessary, beneficial, liberating in every case. Thus they are always talking about revolution; thus they are introducing contestation into every field today, though both its cause and its purpose are often unjustified. The new, the new! Everything is questioned, everything must be in crisis. . . . [Man today] is seized by a frenzy, a giddy exaltation, sometimes a madness urging him to overturn everything.

In particular, there has been, and still is, a great deal of talk about the "structure"of the Church, with intentions that are not always aware of the reasons justifying them and of the dangers that would arise if they were changed or destroyed. It should be noted that interest in renewal has in many cases taken the form of insistence on the exterior and impersonal transformation of the ecclesiastical edifice, and of acceptance of the forms and spirit of the Protestant Reformation, rather than the essential and principal renewal desired by the Council: moral, personal and inner renewal.[56]

There is reason for the claim that reform is a word with "a solid foundation in Catholic tradition." *Ecclesia semper reformanda* is hardly exclusive to Protestantism. But is this what Tillich meant by the Protestant principle—reform of persons, abuses, external historical forms? The presentation of his ecclesiology shows that it is not. The chief characteristic of the Protestant principle is precisely its radicality, its protest against the absolutization of any Church structure. And here Catholicism seems to draw the line. Dogmas, sacraments, and the hierarchic structure of the Church were, for Congar, above reform. His view enjoys widespread Catholic support. For example, P. Wacker: "The central word of faith, the substance of the sacraments, and the hierarchic structure of the Church, insofar as it was instituted by Christ, are not in need of reform. Rather they are the starting point, the standard, and the power source for any renewal;"[57] J.A. Fichtner: "History corroborates the fact that the Church has always accepted the so-called Calvinistic principle of continual reform, though it has been wary of applying it either too radically or too superficially."[58]

Is it here then that Catholicism rejects the Protestant principle, on the question of radicality? In the view of several Protestant commentators, it would seem so. R. McAfee Brown says, "This is perhaps the ultimate issue dividing Protestantism and Roman Catholicism. . . . When the judgment turns to a radical judgment *upon the church*, the Roman Catholic would have to demur. He would have to insist that the church does not need reformation in any basic sense, that by its very nature it is irreformable, and that its dogmas are infallible."[59] Visser 't Hooft: "The fact that the *ex cathedra* decisions of the Pope are irreformable means that the whole life of the Church is dominated by a principle of irreformability and that the forces of renewal, while they may go in many and important directions, can never touch the life of the Church as a whole."[60] U. Valeske: So long as the line of reform is drawn at dogma, sacraments, and hierarchic structure, no illusions should be harbored for a union among Catholics and Protestants. "As much as one welcomes a confession of guilt, like that of Adrian VI's regarding the sins of the Church's leaders, yet alone it can do little to prepare the way for Church unity."[61]

All these Protestant criticisms were written before the conclusion of the Second Vatican Council, before the development of post-conciliar Catholic theology. The warnings cited above from Pope Paul indicate that there exists within the Catholic Church today reform thinking which goes beyond the limits set by Congar. But how far beyond? Far enough to be called radical? Radical enough to regard dogmas as reformable? Radical enough to affect sacramental and hierarchic structures? And if so, how Catholic, how universal, how representative of post-conciliar Catholic theology? Are just a few theologians involved, a small insignificant coterie? And what reasons are being proposed by Catholics for a more radical reform? Here is the critical point in our consideration. If it is claimed that the Protestant principle can be found within the Catholic Church today, it must be shown to exist in all its radicality—protesting the absolutization of dogma, sacrament, and hierarchic structure.

12

Post-Conciliar Catholicism and Radical Reform

History compels us to fasten on abiding issues, and rescues us from the temporary and transient.
Lord Acton, Essays on Freedom and Power

The dogmatic, sacramental, and hierarchic structures of the Church stand above radical criticism and reform, according to Congar, and he is not alone in the opinion. Congar bases his restriction on a real distinction between life and structure in the Church, between form and essence. This distinction follows from distinguishing between a fallible, sinful Church, viewed as a community of men, and an infallible, sinless Church, viewed as a divine institution. Congar's distinctions have not been without their critics. Rahner has criticized the separation of the Church from its members in such a way that the Church is absolved of sin though not of sinners, in his view a highly questionable idealist notion of the Church.[1] Küng has criticized the attempt to make a real distinction between the life of the Church and its structure, "dividing things which in reality cannot be divided." Although life and structure can be distinguished logically, "there can be no faith, sacraments and offices, nothing of an institutional nature, without men."[2] This means that "what is changing and what is unchanging cannot be neatly divided up; while there are permanent factors, there are no absolutely irreformable areas."

Life and structure in the Church, according to Küng, cannot be separated any more than form and essence can. "There is not and never was, in fact, an essence of the Church by itself, separate, chemically pure, distilled from the stream of historical forms."[3] This is not to say that essence and form are identical. A conceptual distinction must be maintained, since "no form of the Church, not even that in the New Testament, mirrors the Church's essence perfectly and exhaustively."[4] No aspect of the Church, however, neither dogma, nor sacraments, nor Church offices, is above criticism and reform.

> It is clear that we cannot simply speak of "irreformable areas" of the Church, as though there were two stories of a building, one on top of the other, of which one was reformable and the other irreformable; as though it were possible adequately to separate off the irreformable essence of the Church's institutions, as established by God, from the concrete working out of them in the living structure given to them by men in the history of the Church. It is rather that the essence is embedded in the human working out in history somewhat as the plan, and the permanent principles of architecture and engineering, enter into the actual concrete building. Every part of the building, even the innermost room in it, or the most important or the most valuable, is, basically, liable to need renewing and can therefore be reformed and renewed. Only the plan as expressed in any particular part of the building, and the laws of construction, as they apply to it, must not be set aside; no part of the building must become simply something else, or collapse altogether. Every institution, even the very holiest (the celebration of the Eucharist, or the preaching of the Gospel), every aspect of organization (even the primacy of Rome, or the episcopal government of the Church) can, through the historical process of formation and deformation, come to need renewal, and must then be reformed and renewed; only the basic irreformable pattern given by God through Christ must not be set aside.[5]

An irreformable pattern, but no irreformable parts: is this radical enough for Tillich's Protestant principle? Tillich himself admitted certain constants in the Church: for example, accepting Jesus as the Christ; the New Testament "picture" of Jesus as a medium of New Being; the Church itself as a medium of New Being; the priestly and prophetic elements in the Church. If Küng's assessment regarding "no absolutely irreformable areas" in the Church is not identical with Tillich's, it certainly comes very close. But how Catholic is Küng's assessment? Is he alone in making it, or do a significant and representative number of Catholic theologians come to the same conclusion? A study of post-conciliar Catholic theology gives compelling evidence that the Protestant principle is not only present in the Catholic Church but widespread in all its radicality.

It would hardly be possible to present here a detailed survey of all the work that Catholic theology has done since Vatican II in the areas of dogma, sacraments, and hierarchic structure. The material is too voluminous and mounts continuously. But it is possible to be selective and still indicate several of the main lines that Catholic theology is taking. Since the reformability of dogma lies at the base of the reformability of sacraments and Church offices, it is reasonable to concentrate primarily on dogma. On the basis of dogma, claims are made for irreformable, divinely established sacramental and hierarchic structures. A de-absolutization of the dogmatic structure *ipso facto* de-absolutizes the sacramental and hierarchic structures. Even with this limitation, the thinking of all the Catholic theologians who have written since Vatican II on dogmatic reform cannot be presented here, but several of the more prominent exponents can be surveyed. They represent not only systematic theology but also philosophy and exegesis, and exemplify theological thinking in North America, France, Germany, and Holland. No claim can be made that theirs is the only direction that Catholic theology is taking. But it is certainly a leading direction, one which exerts a powerful influence on all the Catholic Church today. But more important than their numbers and influence are their arguments. They, even more than their exponents, do not permit either of casual dismissal or easy answers.

Catholic Dogma and Radical Reform

Following in the direction indicated by Vatican I (Denz., #3011), manuals of Catholic theology prior to Vatican II were wont to describe dogma as a truth immediately and formally revealed by God, proposed as such by the Church's magisterium for faith. The condemnations against Modernism taught that a dogma is an expression of an objective truth, the content of which is unchangeable (Denz, #3422, #3481–83). In 1950 (*Humani Generis*), Pius XII rejected as dogmatic relativism the notion that dogmas should be expressed in the philosophical ideas of a particular age and thus included in the stream of philosophical development: "This concept makes dogma to be a reed, driven every which way by the wind" (AAS42:567). Catholic Neo-Scholastic theology, confronted with the history of dogma, was compelled to admit a development of doctrine already recognized by Vatican I (Denz., #3016, 3020). But only accidental and homogeneous development was considered acceptable, a process whereby truths believed materially come to be defined formally, whereby truths believed implicitly come to be known and believed explicitly.

At first glance it would seem that Vatican II simply reconfirmed the rigid stance taken by Vatican I on the question of infallible, irreformable dogmas: "His [the Pope's] definitions, of themselves, and not from the consent of the Church, are justly styled irreformable, for they are pronounced with the assistance of the Holy Spirit..." (CE, #25). A closer inspection of the text, though, reveals that irreformability is here contrasted with the requirement of consent by the rest of the Church. As a matter of fact, a rigid, absolutizing approach to dogma was relativized considerably by Vatican II. In his opening speech to the Council, Pope John spoke in favor of a magisterium "which is predominantly pastoral in character," penetrating doctrines through methods of research, expounding them through literary forms of modern thought. This implies the distinction which Pope John made then and which has since become celebrated: "The substance of the ancient doctrine of the deposit of faith is one thing, and the way in which it is presented is another."[6] The distinction was confirmed later by the Council itself, when it affirmed the legitimacy of a plurality of dogmatic formulations and admitted the possibility of correcting such formulations:

> While preserving unity in essentials, let all members of the Church... preserve a proper freedom... even in the theological elaborations of revealed truth. [DOe, #4]

> If the influence of events or of the times has led to deficiencies... even in the formulation of doctrine (which must be carefully distinguished from the deposit of faith itself), these should be appropriately rectified at the proper moment. [DOe, #6]

Likewise significant was the admission at Vatican II that "in Catholic teaching there exists an order or 'hierarchy' of truths, since they vary in their relationship to the foundation of the Christian Faith" (DOe, #11). The implication is that Catholic teaching regarding Church offices or indulgences is not as central as that regarding Jesus as the Christ. The question arises whether divergence in interpreting Christian truths actually divides the Church into separate Catholic, Protestant, and Orthodox churches, or simply constitutes differing schools of theology.[7]

Vatican II was not the only factor which contributed to a less absolutistic understanding of dogma. *Humani Generis* taught that the sources of revealed doctrine contain so many treasures of truth that they can never be exhausted (Denz., #3886). Furthermore, the formulation of doctrine is not constant; progress and change are possible in the verbal and conceptual formulations of the truths of faith (Denz., #3883). All human understanding of divine mysteries is analogous, with the implication that our understanding is more dissimilar to the mysteries than similar. The 1963 Instruction of the Pontifical Biblical Commission constituted an important shift of emphasis with the admission that exegesis has the task not only of indicating the biblical basis for dogmas but also of interpreting the Church's teaching in the light of Scripture.[8] Rahner demonstrated that a dogma can be true and still be hasty, presumptuous, ambiguous, even dangerous;[9] dogmas are means not ends, beginnings not conclusions.[10] All this—together with the reinterpretation of individual dogmas taking place today—has given impetus to a Catholic reevaluation of the nature and function of dogma. A survey of the main lines of that reevaluation provokes questions as much as it provokes answers.

Gregory Baum: Profound Doctrinal Reform

For Canadian theologian Gregory Baum, Vatican II has proved to be the beginning of a "profound doctrinal reform in the Catholic Church." "Doctrinal positions, which at a time not so far away had been regarded as irreconcilable with the Catholic faith, were adopted by the Vatican Council as doctrinal expressions of the Church's new self-understanding."[11] This was true not only of social, ethical issues, such as religious liberty, but also of dogma. A significant example of the latter is the Catholic teaching of no salvation outside the Church, defined solemnly at the Council of Florence (Denz., #1351). Although it retains the formula *extra ecclesia nulla salus*, Vatican II clearly no longer teaches it in the same sense that the Council of Florence did. Vatican II recognizes a great deal of salvation outside the Church. Although the formula remains unchanged, nonetheless a development has taken place, by no means a homogeneous development from the implicit to the explicit or an organic unfolding from truth to greater truth. On the contrary, development in this instance is better described as a "conversion," a "change of heart," a matter of a "death and resurrection," "the acknowledgement that we must abandon a position of the past and pass on to a new insight created in us by the living Gospel."[12]

Confronted with this and other doctrinal reforms, Baum feels compelled to criticize the traditional Catholic notion of infallibility. In his article "Doctrinal Renewal," he decries as dangerous the exaggerated veneration for teaching authority which leads to myths. When expectations prove to be unjustified, the reality is apt to be abandoned along with the myth. Baum is particularly critical of the extension of infallibility after Vatican I to ordinary papal magisterium. He condemns as well the confusion of authoritative teaching with infallible teaching, whereby almost everything that is derived from the Gospel is regarded as infallible, for example, theological conclusions, the canonization of saints, natural and social morality. "Such an understanding of the Church's infallibility is fantastic!! There is not a shred of evidence for it in Catholic doctrine" (p. 373). The proper object for the Church's infallibility is not "all of human wisdom" but rather "the Gospel and its meaning for human life" (p. 369). It is the gift of the Gospel that is protected by infallibility, thanks to Scripture and the Holy Spirit (p. 366). As to defining what exactly this "gift of the Gospel" includes, Baum limits himself to a "nucleus of teaching," announcing the Gospel and in certain concrete historical situations defending and explaining it. Beyond this central core, authoritative teaching is not infallible or irreformable.

> By confusing and identifying the Church's authoritative teaching with her infallible magisterium, the theological trend after Vatican I has created the legend of the inerrant Church. By extending the subject of infallibility and by widening its object, they have produced a mythical understanding of the papacy. [P. 374]

> Despite the Church's infallibility in teaching the Gospel, it is meaningful to speak of the blindness and fallibility of the Church and assert confidently that God's merciful action, always present within her, will open her eyes. [P. 377]

> The magisterium which announces and, at certain historical moments, defends and explains the Gospel infallibly is not an inerrant magisterium; it is the teaching authority of a pilgrim people, walking not by sight but by faith, which eagerly listens to God's Word and continues to be taught by it. In this context it is possible to assert that the magisterium has made mistakes. This is the Christian reality revealed in Christ which must be carefully distinguished from the myth of an omniscient teaching authority. [P. 378]

In "The Magisterium in a Changing Church," Baum develops his thinking by distinguishing between the Church's continuous magisterium and intermittent magisterium. Through the Church's continuous magisterium, its liturgy and preparation for it, the risen Christ continues today to teach people, to reveal and communicate himself.

> The Gospel is handed on in the Church, not as a series of teaching but as so many ways in which the living Word addresses himself to us and enters into fellowship with us. In other words, the tradition of faith is not simply doctrinal tradition; it includes the entire life of the community . . . It is to this living tradition of the Gospel in the Church, protected as it is by the Spirit, that Catholic teaching regarding the indefectibility and infallibility of the Church has its first and foremost application. This tradition of faith is indefectible in the sense that it will never disappear from this earth; it is called

infallible in the sense that it communicates unfailingly the message of salvation. While this divinely protected tradition may historically exist in greater or lesser clarity, Christ never ceases to communicate himself in this traditioning of the Gospel. The infallibility *in credendo* and *in decendo* has here its primary application. [P. 72]

Since Jesus Christ is a living person and his self-communication takes place, not simply through doctrinal statements but through the proclamation of the Good News in the community, it cannot be taken for granted that the continuity of the infallible magisterium necessarily implies the immutability of Christian doctrine. [P. 75]

The intermittent magisterium consists of creedal statements or formulas such as those found in the New Testament. Although often necessary to sum up the Gospel or settle doctrinal controversy, such formulas are not the first meaning of the Church's magisterium. Even though authoritative, not all such formulas are infallible, since infallibility applies only to proposing the revealed Gospel (primary object) and to issues which are absolutely necessary for the preservation of the Gospel.

It would seem, therefore, that the Church cannot always tell whether a particular teaching is held infallibly or not. The notion of universal ordinary magisterium is still too vague and the object of infallibility can be circumscribed only abstractly. The Church often does not know what she knows. [P. 78]

Catholic theology today is willing tentatively to engage in inquiries whose conclusions do not agree with the apparent meaning of dogmatic conciliar statements, for it is difficult to estimate the degree to which doctrinal decisions of the past bind today. As in the case of Vatican II, we are capable of being led again from a state of blindness to seeing.

The ecclesiastical magisterium, though equipped with the gift of infallibility, is again and again led to acknowledge its blindness on certain issues, to confess that while God had spoken, it had not really listened. [P. 79]

In *The Credibility of the Church Today*, Baum explains the doctrinal reform of Vatican II as a "quantum leap," resulting from a "re-focusing" of the Gospel. Finding itself in a new situation, the Church today does not simply translate its preaching but re-focuses it, replying to new questions and proclaiming the Gospel to people who experience the value of life in a new way. This is not just an intellectual process but a new listening to God's word, a discovery in faith of the meaning of the Gospel for the dilemmas

229

and problems of a new generation (pp. 152–56). Although their methods of investigation differ greatly, Baum admits that his conclusions agree substantially with those of Leslie Dewart (p. 174). For Dewart, however, "re-focusing" is termed "re-conceptualizing," and the fundamental reform needed by the Church today is the "dehellenization of dogma."

Leslie Dewart: Dehellenization of Dogma

In *The Future of Belief*,[13] subtitled *Theism in a World Come of Age*, Canadian philosopher Leslie Dewart confronts the problems of integrating Christian faith with the everyday experiences of contemporary man (p. 7). His primary concern is with the Church's doctrine of God, but he finds it necessary to confront the entire question of dogma and its development. As a philosopher, Dewart considers inadequate the classical Greek notion of truth assumed by the early Church and maintained ever since. He regards it as the root of a dogmatic underdevelopment in the Church. Confronted by a certain incongruity between Christianity and the contemporary world, he sees the Church today as needing not only a demythologization of Scripture but also a comprehensive dehellenization of dogma.

Although the hellenization of Christianity is an accepted historical fact, its interpretation has long been a source of disagreement.[14] Some historians, like Harnack, have seen it as a substantial change in Christianity, involving the substitution of hellenistic elements for the original elements of the apostolic Church. Others stress substantial continuity by regarding the hellenization as affecting only the "expressions" of Christian truth, not the eternal, necessary core. Dewart criticizes both views for their common premise, itself rooted in Greek thought, namely, that the nature of truth demands the constancy of substantially unchanging human knowledge.

To the hellenistic mind, truth was seen as conformity of the human intellect to its object, which increases either by an accumulation of new objects or by a better, more complex way of knowing an object already known. Christianity adopted this notion of truth, and, in doing so, was compelled to admit a development of its doctrine only in the latter sense, since it believes revelation to be complete in Jesus Christ. Dewart criticizes this concept of truth as deficient; it presumes we can conceive and understand knowledge from outside (p. 95). In going out to the Gentile world of its day, the apostolic Church necessarily became hellenistic. Unfortunately, however, "hellenization introduced into Christianity the ideals of immutability, stability, and impassability as perfections that all

Christians and Christianity as a whole should strive for . . ." (p. 134). This led the Church to the conviction that it should not develop further or transcend its hellenistic form. The "universal" culture of the Greco-Roman world, however, was just as contingent and provincial as that of the Jewish world which the Church had already transcended. It cannot be presumed to have eternal validity or adequacy for all time. Dewart feels it legitimate, therefore, since Christianity maintains no revealed theory of truth, to propose a different one, a theory which sees both truth and its development in terms not of knowledge but of consciousness.

Consciousness is the process whereby the being of a man emerges, whereby he becomes present to himself by self-differentiating himself from the totality of being. "It is the coming-into-being of mind, soul, and man. There is no real difference, therefore, between the development of *consciousness* and the development of *self-consciousness*" (p. 91). Viewed within this framework of consciousness, truth is seen not as the conformity of a mental faculty to things but rather as the adequacy of our conscious existence, the fidelity of consciousness to being.

> Conformity is a relation toward another which is owing to another by reason of the other's nature. *Fidelity* is a relation towards another which one owes to one-self by reason of one's own nature. Conformity obligates from the outside. Fidelity, like nobility, obligates from within. [P. 96]

Truth, therefore, may be called an adequation of man not to things but to reality, but only in the sense of adjustment, usefulness, expediency; not conformity, likeness, or similarity (p. 110). Seen in this light, truth not only can develop but does so necessarily, for it is the very nature of consciousness to develop. "The only valid 'criterion' of truth is that it create the possibility of more truth. And the most reliable sign that we are coming to the truth is that we are dissatisfied with it" (p. 111). This pragmatic approach to truth has obvious implications for understanding dogma and its development.

> Like all other concepts, the concepts of Christian belief are not true because of their effectiveness in representing objects. They are true because of their effectiveness in relating (by a relation of truth) man's reality to the reality of that-in-which-he-believes. . . . Truth, therefore, is attributable to Christian belief by reason of the latter's character as religious experience. . . . This means, as I have suggested, that the concepts in which Christian belief are cast are true, not in virtue of their representative adequacy, but in virtue of their efficacious adequacy as generative forms of the truth of religious experience. [Pp. 112–13]

The truth of Christianity is a historical, not an eternal one. Christianity has a contingent, factual, temporal truth, because contingency, factuality and temporality are the notes of God's historical presence and self-revelation to man. [P. 121]

With the foregoing as premises, Dewart concludes that Christian dogmas can evolve.

They can, and in the normal course of events ought to, transform themselves culturally as their concepts undergo cultural evolution. This process can be properly called a transformation, because it is precisely the form that changes. It can be properly called an evolution, because the emergent form cannot be reduced to the act of the potentiality of the original form. [P. 118]

Dewart understands the development of dogma as the historical transformation and evolution of the conceptualization of the Christian faith. What is needed today, therefore, is a re-conceptualization of Christian dogma. This means more than simply translating creeds and doctrinal formulas into new cultural and philosophical language. Rather, it is the response of the Church to the Christian revelation as it is addressed to it in the present. It is a new self-consciousness.

To master a foreign language is to acquire a new conceptual system; it is not simply to learn new verbal signs for the same concepts. It is, therefore, a genuine expansion of experience, in the sense that the later stage of experience grows out of the earlier but is not reducible to it. [P. 107]

To master the "language" of contemporary experience is in reality to think in contemporary concepts—and to think in new concepts is to develop one's original experience. [P. 109]

Dewart's understanding of infallibility follows logically from the preceding. Dogmas are not infallible, in the sense of being eternally valid propositions. What is radically infallible is the faith of the Church.

We believe that the faith of the Church is privileged in that it shall not suffer ultimate failure, a privilege which, of course, no individual believer ever has. We would misunderstand this privilege if we so construed it as to render impossible every inadequacy short of the failure to the faith of the Church, or of its teaching by the magisterium. . . . Essentially, it can only be the assurance of the *ultimately* unfailing nature of the Christian faith in and through the establishment of a legitimate teaching authority for the benefit of the faith of the Church as a whole. The "privilege" of infallibility is thus essentially related to the *eschatological* nature of the Church as a *believing commu-*

nity . . . the magisterium's infallibility is not in the service of the truth of eternally valid propositions; it exists for the sake of the believing Church. Infallibility, thus, can hardly mean that the teaching of the magisterium is always as adequate as it could be—it only means that it is not less adequate than it absolutely must be if the Christian faith is to survive. [Pp. 127–28]

Georges Dejaifve:Dogmatic Diversity

Whereas Baum and Dewart speak of dogma in terms of refocusing and reconceptualizing, Jesuit Georges Dejaifve does so in terms of dogmatic plurality and diversity. In his article, *"Diversité dogmatique et unité de la Révélation,"*[15] Dejaifve singles out Vatican II's affirmation of freedom "in theological elaborations of revealed truth" (DOe, #4). This admission of a legitimate plurality in theology is of immense consequence, as was the Council's attitude toward doctrinal differences between the Catholic West and Orthodox East, the fact that they are "often to be considered as complementary rather than conflicting" (DOe, #17). The Council of Florence provided an excellent sample of precisely this, when it accepted the Greek formula regarding the procession of the Holy Spirit "from the Father through the Son" as corresponding to the same reality represented in the West by "from the Father and the Son" (pp. 16–17). According to Vatican II, what has been revealed and communicated to us is not a collection of truths but God himself and his will for the salvation of men (CR, #6). This revelation is communicated through human witness and therefore allows for legitimate diversity both in comprehending revelation and in expressing it, a legitimate diversity, therefore, in dogma (p. 19).

Dejaifve supports his thesis with several arguments. For one, there is the New Testament itself, in which the one mystery of Christ receives not only diverse treatment but diverse interpretation as well, from a variety of viewpoints. The one Gospel of Jesus Christ is presented according to four different evangelists, each with his own distinct comprehension and expression, and the theology of Paul regarding faith and works is certainly not that of James (p. 20). But this should not come as a surprise. The mystery revealed in Christ infinitely transcends the capacity of the human spirit to express it. For this reason, a diversity of witness is required, precisely to express its plenitude. Second, there is Vatican II's affirmation of legitimate diversity in theology and traditions among different cultures and ethnic groups. If a diversity in theology is admitted, there is no reason why a diversity could not be admitted in dogmatic statements as well (pp. 21–22). Third, there is the close relationship between dogmatic formulas and spiritual experience. Dogma is not simply the result of reasoning upon revelation, as if revelation were simply a collection of doctrines. Dogma results from a community experience of a divine reality, an experience that is conditioned and stamped by the thought and language that experiences it (pp. 22–23). Last, one should remember that, as conceived by the early Church, dogma is a "liturgical statement," and that liturgy itself has doctrinal implications. Diversity in dogma need not prejudice the unity of faith any more than diversity in worship prejudices the unity of the priesthood (p. 23).

Defending himself against the possible charge of dogmatic relativism, Dejaifve distinguishes between dogmatic formulas and that which they signify, a reality which can never be exhausted. Diverse representations are able to signify the same mystery from different perspectives, without being either mutually exclusive or super-imposable. This is not to say that every dogmatic formula of a Christian community is legitimate. There is always the possibility of a church breaking with the apostolic tradition on one point or another, especially when it lacks the guarantee of an authentic magisterium. To the extent, however, that the great Christian confessions are attached to the deposit of faith, at least by their fidelity to Scripture and a certain continuity with apostolic tradition, they may well possess valid expressions of the Christian mystery which are admissible by all. To verify this, the churches would have to compare together their various formulas with the authentic apostolic faith (p. 24). All Christian churches need to realize the limitations of their dogmatic formulas and to recognize the possibility and legitimacy of dogmatic expressions different from their own. They need not deny their past or pull up roots for the sake of a new confession of faith which would serve as an abstract common denominator. Without prejudice to the unity of faith, a variety of charisms in giving witness to Christ can be legitimately ascribed to churches as well as to individuals (p. 25).

Avery Dulles: The Survival of Dogma

For American theologian Avery Dulles in his book, *The Survival of Dogma*,[16] the notion that there could be revealed doctrines immune to historical limitations and capable of being imposed by the sheer weight of extrinsic authority reflects the non-historical, juridical thinking which prevailed in the Catholic Church during the Counter-Reformation. The roots of this absolutistic view of dogma go back to Greek intellectualism and

Roman legalism, but its proximate cause was the Catholic theology of a rationalistic era. To ward off naturalistic rationalism, Catholic theology adopted a supernaturalistic rationalism in which revelation was conceived of as a divinely imparted system of universal and timeless truths (p. 155).

Without explicitly rejecting this rationalistic concept of dogma, Vatican II (*Dei Verbum*) depicted revelation primarily as a vital interpersonal communion between God and men. In doing so, the council paved the way for a reconsideration of dogma that calls into question at least four important features of the absolutistic view: the identity of dogma with revelation; its conceptual objectivity; its immutability; and its universality.

1. Dogmas cannot be simply identified with revelation. They serve an important and in some ways an indispensable function in bringing men into contact with God's revelation of himself. "But revelation itself cannot be limited to spoken or written words, nor do such words of themselves constitute revelation" (p. 155).

2. Dogmas do not enjoy any supposed conceptual objectivity which permits them to circumscribe the content they affirm. Like the early Christian confessions from which they arise, creedal and dogmatic statements are doxological in character, combining elements of repentance, faith, worship, and witness. Dogmas speak of eschatological realities which transcend our present experience and power of conceptualization; hence they speak provisionally, metaphorically, with approximative imagery. It is futile to treat dogmas as if they were intended to be descriptive or scientific statements. Dogmatic language is "mystagogical," almost sacramental, in that it transmits not the idea but the reality of God's presence and generous self-outpouring (pp. 157–58).

3. Dogmas are not above change. The meanings of words change according to varying circumstances of time and place, and the Church may be forced to reformulate its dogmas to convey what they originally intended. But changing words is not enough. Revelation comes to us within some definite sociocultural situation. The modern believer cannot be asked to accept the world view of ancient or medieval Christians. To the extent that dogmas are conditioned by such world views, they must be reinterpreted and reconceptualized (pp. 158–60).

4. Dogmas need not be universal. Before the conversion of Constantine, when Christianity became part of the law of the Empire, local churches possessed their own local creeds, and the recitation of identical creedal formulas was not considered essential to Christian fellowship. The Council of Florence acknowledged that conceptually diverse formulations

may coexist in different sections of the Church. The mere fact that a formula may be true does not mean it should be imposed as a test upon all members of the Church (pp. 162–63).

For Dulles, therefore, all doctrinal statements are historically relative (p. 173). Even in its infallible definitions, the Church is subject to human and historical limitations. Infallibility, as currently understood, means the entire Church cannot be definitively committed to error (p. 197). If formulated for the first time today, the definition of infallibility would probably sound very different. "Perhaps even the word 'infallibility' would not be used; almost certainly the confusing term 'irreformable' would be omitted" (p. 198). Like a skyscraper that sways with the wind or an ocean liner that bends with the waves, the Church must be flexible in order to survive. Precisely because it has a mission to every time and culture, the Church must be able to adapt its message and its structures (p. 203).

Jean-Pierre Jossua: Restructuring Dogma

Jean-Pierre Jossua, "Immutabilité, Progrès ou Structurations Multiples des Doctrines Chrétiennes?"[17] insists, like Baum, that history simply does not permit a theory of homogeneous development of dogma. One need consider only the many doctrines which in their own time enjoyed not only universal recognition but also the sanction of the magisterium. Consider the wide divergence between Vatican II and prior Catholic teaching on religious liberty or on the relationship between Church and State. Consider the divergences between Vatican II and the statements of the Pontifical Biblical Commission earlier in this century. An apologetic view of homogeneous development is simply another form of naive fixism which denies development altogether by ignoring history (pp. 195–96).

It is not the notion of a "homogeneous" development that Jossua finds objectionable so much as that of "development" in the singular. The history of dogma has been one of developments, in the plural. The discontinuities have been much more pronounced than any continuity. And this should come as no surprise. Theology has not produced a continuous, irreversible progress. It has been much more abundant than that, much more productive of multiple approximations and diverse directions (pp. 196–97). The history of dogma indicates not only progression but regression as well, not only discovery but also forgetting and rediscovery (p. 175). It records in more than one instance the supplanting of one world view by another. What results is described by Jossua in terms not unlike those of Baum and

Dewart; for Jossua, however, the process is not one of refocusing or reconceptualizing but restructuring.

A dogmatic structure, according to Jossua, is the conjoining of the fundamental elements of Christianity with structuring elements issuing from a given cultural context. It is the conjoining of the kerygma with the inevitable questions which arise in any age (p. 177). The variations within the structuring elements—the variations in philosophy, culture, in the questions addressed to this kerygma—all serve as the primary factor in the variation and mutability of dogma. Although there is a certain permanence and coherence among them, there is also discontinuity. Structures do not cease to evolve, to disintegrate, and to renew themselves again, marking the same reality in every instance with differing accents. In a certain measure, the rational framework of Christianity is modified in every epoch (pp. 178–79).

The Church today needs to recognize the contingent character, the relativity of every doctrinal structure. The kerygma is distinct and superior to any structure given to it, including that given it in Scripture. The biblical formulation was but the first of a series of "structurations" it was to receive. It is this kerygma, the fundamental, structured element in Christianity, that the Church must take today and restructure, reinterpreting it, even selecting from it. Restructuring, admittedly, requires taking a risk, but it is a risk which can be assumed with faith that the Holy Spirit will not permit the Church to perish (p. 182).

In restructuring the kerygma found within Scripture, the Church does not neglect to see it at the same time within a living tradition of subsequent structures. Although comparing theological structures cannot give us an absolute criterion for discerning between the kerygma and the more relative structuring elements, it does give us "rules of structural equilibrium" as proportional principles (p. 184). Dogmas of the past may have lost their full value by ceasing to signify what they once did. But they still maintain a certain permanent value as models. Only a knowledge of the past enables us to appreciate the originality of the options which present themselves to us today. Although such knowledge of the past relativizes all dogmas, it does so without depreciating them (pp. 185–86). And it gives us both the courage and impetus to set upon the task of restructuring the Christian message for our own age.

> It is time in many areas to put aside, in their incoherent survival, the debris of the grand synthesis of the past. As ingenious as the ancient structures may have been, as precious as the lessons may be which they have yet to teach us,

their artificial survival is procured only with great harm. . . . The schizoid
tendency of a certain speculative theology is an all too evident sign that it
cannot become the real intellectual act of any contemporary man as such. [P.
186]

Walter Kasper: Dogma under the Word of God

For German theologian Walter Kasper, so long as one has a correct
understanding of what dogma is and what dogmatic truth means, dogmas
can never be regarded as absolute or irreformable. In his book, *Dogma
unter dem Wort Gottes,* as well as in other writings, Kasper insists that
dogmas, like the Church, stand under Scripture and are to be interpreted
by Scripture. They should never be seen as a *non plus ultra.* On the other
hand, neither should they be regarded as opposed to the Gospel. Kasper
argues his case by making a biblical and historical study of the meaning of
Gospel, dogma, and theological truths.

From Erasmus to Harnack, dogma has often been considered as
standing in opposition to the Gospel (pp. 7–19). Because of the intolerance
dogma has frequently occasioned, it has been accused of being the very
perversion of the Gospel of freedom. Behind the accusation lies the fact
that Protestant orthodoxy identified the Gospel with Scripture, while
Roman Catholicism identified the Gospel with its tradition and therefore
its defined doctrine. Historical-critical theology has shown both viewpoints
to be wrong. The Gospel cannot be identified with Scripture, since the
Gospel receives the witness of Scripture, which is itself the crystallization
of a multifaceted, tension-filled process of tradition. And neither can the
Gospel be identified with this tradition of dogmas (pp. 24, 84), since the
Gospel is not letter but spirit (2 Cor. 3:6). Originally the word *Gospel*
signified the living proclamation of the Church. Only later did it come to
mean a book or four books or a report about Jesus' life, death, and resurrection. Its real meaning is "the power of the risen Lord in and over the
Church through his living word. The Gospel, therefore, is not an historical
entity but a present power which expresses itself ever new in the confession
and witness of the Church, without ever becoming exhausted in this
confession" (p. 24).

Dogma has come to be understood in the narrow sense of the revelation of God defined by the Church as revealed. The description of Vatican I
was by no means a comprehensive theological definition of dogma.[18]
Looking at the history of the word shows how considerably its meaning has
changed over two thousand years (pp. 28–36). Dogma first came to receive

its present meaning in the eighteenth century, and only in the nineteenth century did this newer, narrower meaning enter into the official language of the Church (p. 37). In the Middle Ages, dogma was a much broader term, involving subjective as well as objective faith, *fides qua* as well as *fides quae creditur*. This broader concept of dogma did not permit the two to be separated. There was no isolating dogma from its living understanding and from the act whereby the Church receives it. The danger of the newer, narrower understanding is that one attempts to capture faith into objective statements and then isolates those statements from the whole of faith. The content of faith, though, is always more than a formulated statement (pp. 41–42).

Quite different from a conformity of the intellect to its object, as the Greeks would have it, is the biblical notion of truth (pp. 71–80). For Scripture, truth is "that which proves itself in history to be what it claims, that which proves itself trustworthy and constant *(treu)* in praxis, in word and work" (p. 71). It is a self-identification, therefore, a self-verification which becomes apparent only in history. The confirmation of a promise, that is, proven fidelity, constitutes the center of the Bible's understanding of truth. It involves a remembrance of God's salvific action in the past and expectation of the eschatological fulfillment he promised for the future. "Within history the truth always remains promise. It cannot be caught up adequately into statements but is open to the ever-greater future of God" (p. 80).[19]

Taking the biblical notion of truth for our own means that we must interpret the truth of dogmas historically, dynamically, prophetically (p. 84). Such interpretation recognizes both the identity and difference between teaching and fulfillment, caught up in the tension between letter and spirit, between already and not-yet (pp. 104–5). Seen from this perspective, dogma is a "dynamic functional concept" (p. 108). It is the result of the Church's experience of the Gospel and an anticipation of further experience, for which the Church must leave itself open.

The Gospel, as an ever-present power in the Church, is not historical or past but an ever-new manifestation of the divine Spirit in the Church. The New Testament writers gave a qualified witness to the Gospel in and for their particular situation (pp. 114–15). Dogmas provide the same kind of witness to the Gospel but for different situations. Although these Church decisions enjoy the assistance of the Holy Spirit, there is no question of their being put on the same level as Scripture (p. 115). On the contrary, both the Church and its dogma stand under Scripture.[20]

Dogma is the historically pre-given statement of the question under which we read the Scripture. Dogma is that about which we question the Scripture. [P. 116]

Dogma is the result of an historical hearing of the Scripture; it presents a point of convergence of various witnesses found in Scripture and builds a horizon under which the Scripture should be understood and questioned. But this is a horizon which changes with the process of understanding, a horizon which is open and can be widened, without one having to give it up. [P. 125]

In emphasizing that Scripture is to be the soul of theology, Vatican II (CR, #24) viewed the relationship between Scripture and dogma as two-directional (pp. 118–19).

It is no longer a question of interpreting Scripture in the light of tradition and dogma, but the biblical scholar is now rather expected to make his contribution to the Church's judgment. This means that the process may be inverted so that dogma must be understood in the light of Scripture.[21]

In the correct interpretation of Scripture, dogma renders valuable service in many instances; it provides the proper emphasis and clears up simple misunderstandings. But Scripture is not to be utilized within the framework of the Church's teaching; on the contrary, the teaching of the Church must be presented within the framework of the Scripture's testimony. This means not only that dogma must further the interpretation of Scripture, but also that the interpretation of dogma must proceed from Scripture.[22]

The Church in establishing the canon of Scripture recognized certain writings as the original witness of the Gospel. All other witnesses are derived from this original witness and are to be understood in its light (p. 118). Dogma does not constitute a fixed entity to which the exegete must subject himself. The exegete has the task of interpreting dogma to determine in the light of Scripture what a dogma says and what it cannot be made to say. "Any progress made in exegetical knowledge is at the same time progress in the interpretation of dogmas" (p. 120).

It is not enough to read and interpret the Scripture from the standpoint of the later dogmas. Dogma contains only a partial aspect of the whole, usually because of a historical contingent, often polemical narrowing down of that whole. Such a partial aspect can be correctly seen and its proper proportions maintained only from the standpoint of the whole. Dogma therefore can and must be completed, deepened, and carried on by the Scripture.[23]

The biblical notion of truth leads Kasper to conclude that a dogma can never be regarded as absolute. Grounded upon an eschatological event, the Church and its preaching are eschatological as well (pp. 126–30). The fullness of truth present to the Church in the person of the risen Christ is present precisely as an anticipation of a future, greater fulfillment. Dogmas therefore are not conclusions but beginnings, witnesses for a Gospel which extends beyond them. Insofar as they participate in the final chapter of Christian revelation, they are final.[24] But they are also provisional, signs of the "fragmentary" nature of our faith and the promise of future fulfillment (p. 140).

> Dogma can only be regarded as a relative, historical reality of purely functional significance. Dogma is relative *insofar* as it serves and points to the pristine Word of God, and *insofar* as it is tied up with the questioning process of a given era, contributing to the proper understanding of the Gospel in wholly concrete situations.[25]

> The truth of the formulae of faith is . . . always at the same time decisive and provisional; it is always imperfect (1 Cor. 13:9,12) because it will only be manifest in the end, eschatologically.[26]

In view of this eschatological understanding of dogmatic truth, infallibility can be understood as the perseverance of Christ's glory within history, the protection whereby the Church does not commit itself definitively to error and trusts infallibly that it will not be disavowed (p. 127). As for individual dogmas, clarification is always possible. For example: "It is thoroughly possible that the real meaning of the two Marian dogmas of 1854 and 1950 will be fully clarified only in the future" (p. 132).

A third conclusion Kasper draws is the same as that of G. Dejaifve, the need for a plurality of dogmatic forms. Both Scripture and dogma are witnesses to the one Gospel, but neither exhaust it. In its own way, every writing of the New Testament, every dogma of the Church, witnesses to the Gospel within a particular situation (pp. 97–98).

> There is a legitimate multiplicity of creeds and ideologies, and integration within this multiplicity is possible.[27]

> What is needed is a multiplicity of formulae, of viewpoints and of concepts, so that men can draw near to the Word of God in its many-sided reality. Each age, each culture, each way of looking at things, will have its own peculiar problems, its own ideas and prejudices with which it confronts the Gospel message. Each of these is a limited category, but each of them in its own way reveals a new aspect of the eternal mystery of God which is hidden in Christ Jesus (Eph. 1:9).[28]

Thus, neither Scripture nor dogma constitute rigid boundaries. Dogma should not lead beyond Scripture quantitatively but rather lead into Scripture more profoundly. The Church's association with the Bible is an inner historical process that is never ended (p. 126).

> The transcendence and universal validity of the Word of God forbid us to confine it within historically fixed and developed forms and formulae. No formulation, no matter how true it is or may be, is a *non plus ultra;* it is rather a simple beginning, a signpost, which directs us out beyond itself into the eternal mystery of God himself.[29]

Hans Küng: Nemo Infallibilis Nisi Deus Ipse

Swiss theologian Hans Küng, from the beginning of his theological career, has been concerned with de-absolutizing dogmas. Because he has written at greater length on the subject than most current theologians, his celebrated theories will be examined in greater detail. In his first book, *Justification*[30], Küng emphasizes that dogmas, for all their dignity and value, are no more than human accounts of divine revelation (p. 111), that they are not "rigid and frozen formulations, but rather . . . living signposts for continued research into the inexhaustible riches of the revelation of Jesus Christ" (p. 101). Dogmas are to be taken seriously, "with the same sense of devotion and reverence" (Denz., #1501) as Scripture, but only insofar as they revolve around and gravitate toward Scripture (p. 114). It is Scripture which enjoys the "absolute precedence" (p. 111), "valid for all times and places, . . . inexhaustible . . . the theologian's primary norm . . ." (p. 112).

In *Structures of the Church*, Küng expresses the conviction shared by others already mentioned regarding the diversity of dogmatic formulation (pp. 385–94). The distinction between faith and formula is fundamental: Scripture indicates that the same Lord can be described in terms of lowliness or sublimity; that the same Eucharist can be recounted with different words of institution. The Council of Nicaea presupposed one hypostasis in God; I Constantinople and Chalcedon presupposed three hypostases in God. The Council of Florence admitted the procession of the Holy Spirit both "from the Father through the Son" and "from the Father and the Son." The only conclusion possible is that the "Christian faith has a historical character and is expressed in ever-new formulations" (p. 386). "The faith can be the same, the formulations different, indeed contradictory" (p. 387). It is paramount to realize the imperfection, incompleteness, and fragmentary character of all formulations of faith (p. 388). Regarding development of dogma, Küng emphasizes that progress cannot be either indefinite or one-directional. Development may not go beyond revelation.

> No popular piety and no *sensus fidelium* can procure a new revelation for the Church; if this were so the Council herself would become a revelation to herself and thereby call into question the revelation that has been concluded for all time. [P. 391]

The polemical orientation of dogma renders it particularly susceptible to the limitations of all human statements, especially that of bordering on error (pp. 392–94). To assert that any statement in its verbal formulation must be either true or false is a simplification of truth. A statement can be both (p. 394). Truth and error are the counterparts of every human truth (p. 392). There is a tendency for polemically oriented dogma so to emphasize the error of a half-truth that the dogma itself becomes a half-truth.

> A truth pronounced for polemical reasons borders particularly on error, since it is directed against a specific error which it is attempting to destroy. Since every error, no matter how great, contains the kernel of some truth, a polemically oriented utterance is in danger of striking not only at the error but also at the error's kernel of truth: namely, at the erroneous opinion's legitimate demand. [Pp. 392–93]

In *Structures of the Church*, Küng, prompted by ecumenical considerations, also begins to develop his thinking on the nature of infallibility. "Nowhere else do the enormous difficulties blocking the way to a reunion of separated Christians seem to be more difficult to overcome than on this very point" (p. 353). As Calvin asserted, the infallibility of an ecumenical council does not follow necessarily from the biblical doctrine that the Church is the pillar and mainstay of truth. Does the statement that Peter is the foundation of the Church necessarily imply that Peter must be infallible? Would not the victory of grace be more complete if he could err in faith and still remain the foundation (p. 359)? Even though designated as the Body of Christ, the Church is still capable of sin. If not immune from sin, then why from error? If the Church can be holy in its essence and yet sinful in its members, can it not be infallible in its essence and yet err in all of its members (pp. 378–79)? Does the infallibility of the Church, its continuance in truth and indestructability, necessitate the infallibility of particular statements (p. 381)?

The questions Küng raises in *Structures*, he begins to answer in *The Church*. He describes infallibility as "fundamental remaining in the truth, which is not disturbed by individual errors" (p. 342).

The Church will not yield to untruth; it is undeceivable. God has promised and granted to it infallibility. Despite its errors and misunderstandings, God will preserve it in the truth. [P. 342]

This is the understanding Scripture has of infallibility. It was never questioned by the reformers. Not so, however, the infallibility of particular statements, a distinction with which Vatican I never really came to grips. The a priori, unquestionable, and verifiable infallibility of particular statements is not directly demonstrable from the New Testament (p. 342). This does not mean that such Church statements do not enjoy authority. They certainly enjoy a higher value and binding force than those made by individuals (p. 343). But it is problematic as to whether the infallibility of the Church protects individual dogmas from error (p. 343). This in substance is what Küng reaffirms in *Truthfulness: the Future of the Church.* The infallibility of the pope is to be understood within the context of the infallibility of the Church. As for the infallibility of the Church: insofar as it is obedient to the word of God, the Church shares in the truth of God, who will not permit it to perish.

> Anyone whose trust in God and in his Spirit is not superficial or rationalistic, but profoundly Christian, believes unshakeably that the Spirit of God will maintain the Church in the truth of the Gospel, in *spite* of all error and *through* all errors. This is the great miracle . . . that the Church, in spite of her defection from God, is never dropped by God, never abandoned by God. [P. 136]

Unlike most Catholic theologians, Küng has been forthright in asserting that the Catholic Church has made errors in its teaching office. He is willing to speak explicitly of dogmas being reformable. Dogmas have been reformed and corrected in the past; they are open to reform and correction in the future:

> As human and historical formulations, it is of the very nature of the definitions of the Church to be *open to correction* and to stand *in need of correction.*[31] In doctrines as elsewhere we have to distinguish between what is given, *irreformably,* by God through Jesus Christ in the Holy Spirit, and what comes, *reformably,* from men . . . the reformable and the irreformable cannot be adequately represented as being on two separate levels. *Every* dogma of the Church expresses at the same time both the irreformable divine revelation and what is human and reformable. There are, indeed, in the Church's dogmas certain abiding constants which remain in every possible formula . . . but there are not, properly speaking, any irreformable *areas* in what is of human, ecclesiastical formulation.[32]

In speaking forthrightly of correcting and reforming dogmas Küng is not without precedent. He appeals to St. Augustine, who did not shrink from using the word *correct (emendare)* precisely in this connection.

> But who can fail to be aware that the Councils themselves, which are held in the several districts and provinces, must yield, beyond all possibility of doubt, to the authority of the universal Councils that are formed for the whole Christian world; and that even of the universal Councils, the earlier are often corrected by those which follow them, when, by some actual experiment, things are brought to light which were before concealed, and that is known which previously lay hid *(De bapt. contra Donatistae).* [33]

Küng is able to call Cardinal Newman to his support as well. In 1871, shortly after Vatican I, Newman wrote:

> Let us have a little faith in her [the Church] I say. Pius is not the last of the popes. The fourth Council modified the third, the fifth the fourth. . . . The late definition does not so much need to be undone, as to be completed. . . . Let us be patient, let us have faith, and a new Pope, and a reassembled Council may trim the boat. [34]

Küng does not hesitate to cite specific historical examples of dogmas being subsequently reformed by the Church. The Council of Chalcedon corrected the Christological teachings of the Council of Ephesus. [35] Even though the Council of Florence, in its doctrinal decree for the Armenian Union, taught that the substance of priestly ordination consisted in the handing over of the chalice and paten, Pius XII ruled that the substance of orders was exclusively the imposition of hands. [36] As for the authority to administer confirmation, Küng in *The Church* says, "Vatican II specifically corrected the Tridentine definition. (p. 430). Trent defined: "Whoever says that the ordinary minister of holy confirmation is not the bishop alone, but any simple priest, let him be anathema" (Denz., #1630). Vatican II, however, replaced the decisive word and instead of "ordinary minister" speaks only of the "original minister." This leaves open the possibility that the "simple priest" too can be the "ordinary minister" of confirmation, as has always been the case in the Eastern Churches and has been permitted for parish priests in the Western Church in case of need since 1946 (p. 419).

On the divine institution of the Church's hierarchy, Küng credits exegetical and historical research for "an explicit correction of a canon of the Council of Trent" (p. 418) by Vatican II. Trent declared: "Whoever says that there is in the Catholic Church no hierarchy established by divine ordinance, consisting of bishops, presbyters, and deacons, let him be anathema " (Denz., #1776). Vatican II (CE, #28) makes obvious reference to this canon and reforms it in three ways: 1. Trent uses the unbiblical word *hierarchy;* Vatican II speaks of *ecclesiastical ministry.* 2. Trent refers to the distinction between bishops, presbyters, and deacons as being of "divine ordinance"; Vatican II applies the words *divinely established* solely to ecclesiastical ministry as such. 3. Trent speaks of a "hierarchy established by divine ordinance, consisting of *(constat)* bishops, presbyters, and deacons"; Vatican II says only that the ministry is exercised on different levels by those who from antiquity (hence not from the very beginning) have been called bishops, presbyters, and deacons. "The Tridentine proposition, if strictly interpreted, does not agree with historical realities, but the proposition of Vatican II does" (p. 418).

The conclusions regarding the dogmas of the Council of Trent in this regard cannot help but apply to the doctrinal decisions of any council or any pope:

> The decisions of the Council of Trent (or of other councils) cannot be regarded as binding definitions where they concern questions which are being put differently today in the light of completely different problems. The Fathers of those days could not decide upon matters they did not know about. This applies particularly to new exegetical and historical problems, which only arose in recent times and need new solutions. No council is granted a fresh revelation; its solutions are tied to the capacities of the theology of its time. This does not mean, of course, that the conclusions of the Council of Trent on this subject are irrelevant for us today. . . . But it does mean that Trent . . . cannot dispense us from the task of asking these questions again and finding new answers to them, in the light of modern exegetical, historical and systematic research and scholarship. [p. 419]

The most comprehensive presentation of Küng's thought on the reformability of dogma is in his book *Infallible? An Inquiry.* Here he asserts once again that the Church's teaching office has made many serious errors (p. 29). Küng has been distinctive from those Catholic theologians who hesitate to apply the word *error* to dogma, who are willing to admit only that dogmas are relative and inadequate, historically finite and therefore open to misunderstanding. For Küng, inadequacy and openness to misunderstanding in the concrete cannot be so sharply separated from error.[37]

Along the lines indicated in his earlier writing, Küng demonstrates with close historical analysis that Vatican II in its statements on infallibility was fully dependent on Vatican I (p. 62). But Vatican I did not provide proof either from Scripture or from commonly accepted tradition to substantiate a claim for the infallibility of statements (pp. 96–111). Catholic tradition holds rather for the infallibility of the Church as such, not of particular officeholders (p. 163) or statements. Küng points to the rationalistic, Cartesian origins of a theology which sees the clear and distinct idea as an ideal for all truth and attempts to achieve clarity for faith by way of definitive statements (pp. 146–52).

Küng does not question the truth of statements but their infallibility. He affirms that statements and therefore dogmas can be both true and binding (p. 126). He affirms as well that the Church requires statements to summarize its faith in confessions and creeds; the Church rightfully defines and defends its faith with dogmas that polemically differentiate that which is Christian from that which is not (p. 129). But it has not been proved that Christian faith requires statements that are a priori infallible. On this, the decisive point in question, Vatican I simply presumed that infallible statements were possible. It did not see the deeper, more complex problem and therefore could not go into it. What a council did not see as a problem, it also has not decided (p. 140).

In virtue of the promise of Christ and the guidance of the Holy Spirit, the Church is assured that it will not perish in error. The infallibility of the Church, in short, is a fundamental perseverance in the truth in spite of all possible errors (p. 158). Because the word *infallibility* can be easily confused with freedom from moral failing or falsely applied to statements, Küng suggests that a better word would be *indefectibility* or *perpetuity* in the truth (p. 163). Catholic theology has been wont to apply these terms to the very being of the Church rather than to the truth in the Church, but, in this instance at least, being and truth cannot be separated. To err is human; because it is human, the Church can err. Neither councils, bishops, nor popes (not even the Bible, when it is taken as a "paper pope") can make infallible statements. Only God is infallible. *Nemo infallibilis nisi Deus ipse.*

The reaction created in theological circles by Küng's *Inquiry* has been considerable, to say the least. The books, articles, and reviews responding to his position pro and con number in the hundreds.[38] The most publicized criticism has been that of Karl Rahner, in which he attacked the thesis that the infallibility, or better indefectibility, of truth in the Church does not require a priori infallible statements.[39] Rahner's dissent together with articles of other theologians taking issue with Küng were published in a collection edited by Rahner entitled *Zum Problem Unfehlbarkeit.* Küng, joined by several prominent defenders, responded with a similar work entitled *Fehlbar?* in which he answered his critics and marshalled further support for his position in a lengthy article, "Eine Bilanz der Unfehlbarkeitsdebatte." Without asserting anything substantially new in the article, Küng goes to great lengths to clarify his position. He does not deny the possibility or reality of true statements, open a posteriori to verification. He does not deny the possibility or necessity of binding statements, of creeds, of symbols or dogmas to communicate, recapitulate, or defend the Church's faith. But he does deny the possibility of statements, whether dogmas, decrees, formulas, or creeds, which claim, on the basis of the assistance of the Holy Spirit, hence a priori, to be guaranteed *infallibly true* (p. 379).

Küng, taking the collection of criticisms edited by Rahner as representative of the best of the lot, expresses himself as more justified than ever in his position. "Not one single theologian in the debate up to this time has been able to present a proof for the possibility of guaranteed infallible statements" (p. 383). With good reason: neither Scripture nor the great ancient Catholic tradition provides a foundation for an assumption of such statements. In fact, the most recent historical research into the role of Peter in the early Church, into the authority claimed by the earliest ecumenical councils, and into the question of the historical origins of the doctrine of papal infallibility points to quite the contrary (pp. 403–27). As a consequence, the existence of divinely guaranteed infallible statements can no longer be simply presumed within Catholic theology. They are no longer *in possessione.*

After examining the differing positions of both his critics and apologists, Küng sees emerging from the debate a fundamental consensus among Catholic theologians on at least three issues: 1) Even among Küng's sharpest opponents, there is arising a general recognition that the Church's highest teaching authorities have *de facto* erred in the past. 2) A general skepticism is developing not only about the exercise of infallibility but also about the intelligibility and usefulness of the very concept. 3) A general agreement is emerging regarding Küng's positive thesis which sees the indefectibility of the Church in the sense of its abiding in the truth despite all errors (pp. 367–73).

For those who see his position as threatening the very existence of Catholicism, Küng goes on to show how the Church can live with error and survive, even as it has done in the past. Persevering in the truth despite errors is more a matter of orthopraxy than orthodoxy, more a matter of individuals and individual communities within the Church than of institutions, more a matter of the "common people" than of hierarchs and theologians. Errors perpetrated by the Church's teaching authorities are a serious matter, but they do not threaten the existence of the Church, for the object of the Church's faith is not truths or statements. The object of Christian faith is God himself, and the revelation of God in Jesus Christ. Such a faith cannot be destroyed even by doctrinal errors.

Piet Schoonenberg: The Historical Nature of Dogma

For Dutch theologian Piet Schoonenberg, the contingency of dogmas is a necessary consequence of their historical nature, the historical stamp they bear because of their origin in history. In *Die Interpretation des Dogmas,* he describes the task of interpretation as one of "understanding dogmas out of their own historical situation and translating them into our own situation" (p. 59). What this implies, Schoonenberg develops by way of nine theses.

> 1. A dogma is a statement of faith formulated as a doctrine, taught by the Magisterium as a defence against heresy. [P. 59]

Because they are essentially polemic and defensive, it is difficult to establish the boundary lines of dogmas. For this reason, dogmas should not be overrated (p. 62).

> 2. The interpretation of dogma is the erection of a bridge from that situation in which the dogma originated to our own situation. [P. 62]

The difference between the two situations can be a matter not only of time but also of culture, thought, life, and feeling. Interpretation is the bridging over of two different worlds. This requires knowing the world from which a dogma originates, coming to it with questions but not presuppositions, so as to learn what the dogma wants to say. It means that interpretation must be preceded by commentary.

> 3. The first task of interpretation is to find that which is proper to the text. [P. 65]

Interpretation requires determining the statement of the question for which the dogma was sought as an answer. It also requires distinguishing the dogma from its thought-world and presuppositions. Essential implications bind faith as strongly as the dogmatic statement itself. But dogma must be dissociated from mere presuppositions originating from the world view of the historical situation in which it arose.

249

> 4. There are many grounds why a relative difference can be made between that which a dogmatic statement intends to say and the means or form in which the statement is made. [P. 69]

Although content and form cannot be separated, every translation presumes a certain relative difference between them. The meanings of words change. *Person* means something else for us from what it did for the Eastern Church when it defined the doctrine of the Trinity. *Substance* means something else today from what it did when medieval theology coined the term *transubstantiation.* In the course of time, dogmas can acquire different meanings, emphasizing what may have been important for an earlier world view but obscuring the faith for our own. For these reasons, a dogma should not be seen as a law in the sense of *nomos,* but rather in the sense of a *canon,* a rule or guide. Dogmas point out certain directions without eliminating others. They are not intended to serve as a single exclusive rendering of faith. As canons, dogmas maintain a historical value and deserve our respect. They guide us in our own formulations of faith.

> 5. The post-biblical tradition, and dogma within it, interprets Scripture. But it is itself also interpreted by Scripture. Furthermore, both must be understood in the light of the gospel or kerygma, i.e., the kernel of the Christian message. [P. 76]

By rendering Scripture for a particular age, dogmas interpret it. But the witness of Scripture is much broader than any formula, and this means that Scripture must interpret dogma as well. Schoonenberg adds his name to those Catholic theologians who hold that Scripture contains the substance of the whole Christian revelation. The post-biblical tradition does not add new factors to the biblical message. It simply says the same thing in other words and concepts. Dogmas are logical interpretations of Scripture. Nicaea did not intend to say more than was already contained in the prologue of John's gospel. The article of the creed confessing Jesus as "conceived by the Holy Spirit, born of the Virgin Mary" does not intend to say more than Luke and Matthew did. From this it follows that questions of exegesis are not solved by dogmatic answers. Quite the contrary. If dogmas are no more than logical interpretations of Scripture, then questions of exegesis automatically become questions of interpreting dogma (p. 78). Both scripture and dogma are to be interpreted by the Gospel or kerygma, which is, above all, the event whereby God's communication of salvation addresses us in the person of Christ. The kerygma is the beginning of every didache, including the several streams of didache seen in the New Testament. Some of these streams, like adoptionistic Christology, have not been developed as much as others, for example, incarnational. These unused traditions within Scripture need to be brought into a similar development, so that their truth content will not be lost (p. 79).

> 6. There is an order of rank or "hierarchy" of truths within Church teaching, each with a different kind of relationship to the foundation of the Christian faith. [P. 80]

While there are some truths which pertain to our goal, others pertain to the means for attaining that goal. To the first category belong the Church doctrines on God in his relationship to man, creation, Christ, redemption, and the Holy Spirit. To the second category belong doctrines regarding Mary, the Church, and morality. The Marian dogmas are to be interpreted Christologically, that is, according to Scripture, so that they say no more than Scripture. The Mary of the dogma is a "type of the Church," and is to be distinguished from the historical Mary. Therefore, it is possible that the Marian dogmas of the Immaculate Conception and Assumption are not only chiefly but even, when necessary, exclusively to be understood typologically, paradigmatically (pp. 83–84). When it comes to doctrines concerning the organization of the Church, it may be said that the Holy Spirit guided the development of certain hierarchical structures and arrangements in particular historical situations. But this does not mean that these arrangements necessarily have to last for all time. Our concepts of divine right and institution need to be re-thought. The same Spirit can introduce a further development of the structures already at hand as well as a change of these structures (p. 86). The division, transformation, or even disappearance of certain offices is not out of the question. When it comes to moral questions, moral norms must always be interpreted in terms of their presuppositions. Concrete morality is always an expression of an experience that later shows itself to be historically contingent.

> 7. The historical character of dogmatic statements is not abolished by their infallibility. Rather, infallibility must itself be interpreted in the light of this historical character. [P. 88]

Only God is true in the full sense of the word. Only his guidance is free of errors and failings. There is a profound difference, therefore, between divine infallibility and the human infallibility given to the Church. The Church's infallibility is that of a creature, of something at the same time quite fallible, because it is constantly developing (p. 90). Infallibility is a gift of God; it is not something over which the Church has disposal. It is always limited, sharing in the victory of grace over sin and error, yet still assailed by sin and error (p. 91). As there is a great difference between the infallibility of God and the Church, so also is there between the infallibility of the Church and of texts. The infallibility of a text is always a conditional and limited reflection of the Church's infallible view of faith, an inadequate objectifying of the infallible guidance of the Holy Spirit (p. 92). The way dogmas are expressed can be changed; under certain circumstances, a translation of all dogmas can be required. When it comes to peripheral dogmas, not only their expression but even their contents are tied up with time, so that a revision may be necessary (p. 93).

No council has yet taught what constitutes the nature of infallibility. Vatican I simply presupposed it, defining that it existed and who its bearers are. Like those who ascribe inerrancy to Scripture only in terms of its totality, Schoonenberg suggests that individual dogmas may be considered as relatively infallible, that is, infallible only to the extent that they contribute to an infallible whole (p. 94). "The inerrancy or 'infallibility' of dogmas is given precisely in their connection with one another and their gradual building up of a growing interpretation of faith" (p. 95). In the process of that growing interpretation, there is a place not only for infallible statements but also for statements that err. The Holy Spirit "leads us through searching and temptation, hence through unrefined insights, through whole and half truths, and hence also through whole and half errors" (p. 96).

> 8. Dogmas are interpreted by expressing their meaning in contemporary thought without eliminating anything from their meaning. [P. 97]

Interpretation of dogma completes the task of commentary. It is itself a never-ending task, always incomplete, taking many and varied forms. If faith is to be intelligible to various streams of thought and language (p. 101), a community of faith requires a plurality of dogmatic expression.

> 9. The function performed by dogmas in the Church will indeed continue. But it can be exercised in a way other than that of dogma, and it probably will be. [P. 104]

There will always be expressions of faith. In fact, a real need exists today for a contemporary, intelligible, short formula of faith. But a Church without dogma is a distinct possibility for the future. The Church existed from Pentecost until Nicaea without proclaiming any dogmas, and Vatican II preached the Christian faith without proposing any dogmatic definitions. Whether dogmas can perform their defensive task any longer is debatable, since they are no longer denied so much as simply ignored. Defense of the faith today depends more on preaching than on formulating dogmas. Defense through anathema must be replaced by defense through dialogue (p. 109). The Church's preaching to today's world should not consist of individual dogmas but of the entire Christian tradition, especially of Scripture. "In the interpretation of dogmas, it is really Scripture that is to be interpreted" (p. 110). Even more than Scripture, however, the Church must preach Christ today, not dogmas.

Excursus: Sacraments, Church Offices, and Radical Reform

To appreciate the openness to radical reform within post-conciliar Catholicism, there is good reason to concentrate on dogma. Both sacramental and hierarchic structures rest on the foundation of dogmatic structure. If dogmas can be reformed or corrected, this cannot help but affect absolute dogmatic claims made in behalf of the divine institution of seven sacraments, the papacy, or the episcopate. If dogmas can be reformed, so can sacraments and Church offices. In these areas too, Catholic theology since Vatican II has begun to open avenues and pursue directions which would permit radical reform in both Catholic thinking and practice. Only a brief outline of these directions need be sketched here.

The *sacramental structure* of the Catholic Church was dogmatically defined at Trent as consisting of seven sacraments, "no more or less," all instituted by Christ (Denz., #1601). Branded as a Modernist error (*Lamentabili*, 1907) was the opinion that the sacraments took their origin from the apostles and their successors under the force of circumstances (Denz., #3440). Neo-Scholastic theologians regarded as *sententia certa* that Jesus instituted all the sacraments personally and immediately, including the substance of the sacramental rites.[40] It was conceded that the Church had the right to modify and reform ceremonies and prayers surrounding the sacraments, but, in accordance with Trent, not the substance itself (Denz., #1728), since this substance is of divine institution. But what is this substance? How specific is it? Did Christ determine the matter and form of each sacramental rite? Theologians disagree. Certainly the matter and form of certain sacraments, for example, Confirmation and Holy Orders, have been modified in the course of history. Examination of their history has served to modify absolute claims made in behalf of seven divinely instituted sacraments.

The word *sacramentum,* up to the twelfth century, had a much broader meaning than it does today. It translated the Greek word *mysterion,* which in the New Testament referred to God's secret plan for man's salvation. Neither *sacramentum* nor *mysterion* originally meant a liturgical rite. One of the earliest meanings of *sacramentum,* though, was the oath of allegiance given by recruits going into the army. Tertullian was the first theologian to use the term as a designation for Baptism, whereby allegiance is sworn to Christ. St. Cyprian (third century) referred to Baptism as the "sacrament of salvation" and to the Eucharist as the "*mysterion* of the Lord's passion and our redemption." St. Ambrose described as sacraments not only the Church's rites but also its feasts and doctrines. For St. Augustine a sacrament was a *signum sacrum,* a sign of a sacred reality; he applied the term to such rituals as the sign of the cross, exorcisms, and the recitation of the Lord's Prayer at Baptism. Although he spent much time and effort expounding on the symbolism of the number seven, Augustine never dreamed of limiting the number of sacraments to seven. In the same vein, St. Peter Damian (eleventh-century) enumerated twelve sacraments. St. Bernard (twelfth-century) mentioned ten sacraments. Hugh of St. Victor enumerated as many as thirty sacraments. Various listings appeared including among their enumerations the ordination of abbots, the anointing of kings, the consecration of altars, funeral rites, and the washing of feet. Peter Lombard, however, listed the sacraments as seven, and the influence of his *Sentences* was such as to impress all subsequent theology in the Middle Ages. It was seen as appropriate that the sacraments be seven in number. The official magisterium accepted the listing and taught it formally, first at the Council of Florence ("Decree for the Armenians," 1439), and then at the Council of Trent. While defining authoritatively that Christ had instituted seven sacraments, Trent did not determine if he did so immediately himself or mediately, through the instrumentality of the subsequent Church. Thomas Aquinas held for immediate institution, but St. Bonaventure, Alexander of Hales, Hugh of St. Victor, and Peter Lombard held for mediate institution of at least some of the sacraments.

Drawing conclusions from the historical evolution of the meaning and enumeration of sacraments, theologians have modified the positions assumed by Neo-Scholasticism prior to Vatican II. The following are selected examples of their thinking.

Yves Congar[41] points out that the Middle Ages easily accepted the idea of the sacraments as being only indirectly of divine institution. He accords a position of privilege to Baptism and the Eucharist, seeing them as "principle," "major," or "fundamental" sacraments. There is a grading among sacraments even as there is among dogmas and councils. The sacraments can be generalized only in an analogical way.

Jacques Dournes,[42] basing himself on Thomas Aquinas, insists on a oneness of the sacraments (*Summa Theol,* III, q. 72, a. 1). Their seven-ness is simply a matter *de convenientia,* by analogy with bodily life (*Summa Theol,* III, q. 65, a. 1). Seven is symbolic of totality, a union of three and four, of odd and even, the open and closed, the visible and invisible. Seven symbolizes the plenitude of the divine gift. It is not a matter of arithmetic, since there is but one capital sacrament, and that is Jesus Christ. The seven concrete signs do not exhaust the gift of the Spirit but rather signify the full range of its application.

Josef Finkenzeller[43] agrees that the mystical interpretation of the number seven influenced the enumeration of the sacraments. It could have been otherwise, without leaving any out or adding any others. Baptism and Confirmation could be considered as different steps within one sacrament of initiation. Penance and Anointing of the Sick could likewise be considered as aspects of one sacramental rite. In a similar vein, both Baptism and the Eucharist have been seen as pluriform sacraments, embracing a variety of sacramental rites. The Orthodox Church, since the second half of the thirteenth century, took over the notion of seven sacraments from the West. For them too, however, the notion of seven was simply one of congruence and convenience.

Karl Rahner[44] maintains that the institution by Christ himself, of Confirmation, Anointing of the Sick, Matrimony, and Holy Orders simply cannot be demonstrated historically. We have no word of Jesus about them. Their institution, however, is implicit in the institution of the Church. The sacraments are the basic acts of the Church, which is itself the *Ursakrament.* Such a basic act, which really belongs to the essence of the Church and flows from it, is *eo ipso* a sacrament. The institution of a sacrament can result simply from this: that Christ has founded the Church with its nature as *Ursakrament.* This does not imply that every prayer of the Church for grace is a sacrament since many official acts of the Church are not directed toward individuals or do not engage the Church fully. The treatise on the sacraments is but a part of the treatise on the Church.

Hans Meyer,[45] in the light of contemporary Catholic liturgical re-form, confronts the question: What in the sacramental structure is above reform? He answers that the basic cast of Baptism and the Eucharist is obligatory and immutable. For the other sacraments, though, few substantive elements can be regarded as unchangeable in practice, and these must be demonstrated, not simply taken for granted. The historically attested changes which have taken place have been so profound that we would hardly have the courage to take responsibility for initiating some of them today.

Specific lines of comparison between contemporary Catholic theology and Tillich's thought on sacraments do not need to be made here, but the question to be asked is: Does the Catholic Church indicate in its thinking today an openness to radical reform? Despite its brevity, the above survey indicates that with sacraments, as with dogma, Catholic theology today sees much less as absolute or above reform than was earlier surmised. While there are permanent factors, absolutely irreformable areas are not apparent. The sevenfold nature of the sacraments does not appear any more absolute than the substance of the sacraments, outside of Baptism and the Eucharist. And even here history indicates variation and change.

What further modifications of the sacraments are possible? This is one of the more complex questions facing Catholic theology and practice today. Certainly it would be irresponsible for the Church to lose sight of its past. The Church of tomorrow, despite any and all external change of form, must be recognizable as the Church which began with Jesus and the apostles. Unity, historical identity and continuity are values not to be treated lightly. Even with this in mind, Catholic theology is coming to regard the sacraments as rites not so much divinely instituted as determined by concrete historical situations. This does not mean that the sacraments can be changed arbitrarily. But it does imply a pragmatic approach to the suitability of liturgical rites, even with respect to the substance of the sacraments, not entirely dissimilar from the position Tillich took on the sacraments. On these same pragmatic grounds Tillich was willing to accept the authority of offices within the Church, whether that of pope, councils, or episcopate. Here too, contemporary Catholic thinking, in view of the historical development of the Church's hierarchic structures, appears open to the possibility of a reform much more radical than would have been allowed prior to Vatican II.

The *hierarchic structure* of the Catholic Church was dogmatically defined at Trent as instituted by divine ordinance and consisting of bishops, presbyters, and deacons (Denz., #1776). Bishops were defined as superior to presbyters, in that presbyters were denied the power to confirm and ordain; those without ordination and canonical delegation were rejected as legitimate ministers of the Word and Sacraments (Denz., #1777). *Lamentabili* (1907) branded as error the modernist position that the Church's hierarchy is the result of a gradual historical development (Denz., #3454). Neo-Scholastic theologians taught as *de fide* that the powers conferred upon the apostles have been passed on to the bishops of the Church, who are the successors to the apostles (Denz., #3061). The distinctions between layman and presbyter, between presbyter and bishop were regarded as of divine institution and for that reason irreformable.

With the Church's hierarchic structure, as with dogma and the sacraments, history has served to modify absolutistic claims to divine institution. Critical historical exegesis of the New Testament has led Catholic theologians to accept the historical fact that authority structures in the Church have changed. Once again, the volume of material written on Church offices since Vatican II prohibits anything but a brief survey of several leading lines of thought. But they suffice to indicate here too an openness within Catholic thought to radical reform.

Gregory Baum[46] holds that no Christian church can demonstrate the exclusive apostolic origins of its ecclesiastical structure. This includes the hierarchic system of the Catholic Church. The apostolic ministry in the early Church was manifold and enjoyed an "extraordinary flexibility." Only gradually did it develop into its present form. That form was adapted in the past to the needs of the people and to the changing conditions of culture. It is an adaptation which is able to move ahead today as well.

Yves Congar[47] emphasizes that the apostolic succession of bishops is to be understood within the context of the apostolic succession of the entire Church. And this in turn is inseparable from the profession of the apostolic faith.

Bernard Dupuy[48] points to the tradition, going back to St. Jerome, which stresses the equality between bishops and presbyters in one single priesthood. The distinction between them is a development based simply on ecclesiastical law. Neither Christ nor the apostles provided a normative structure for the ministry, fixed definitively for all time. Christ willed simply the ministry of the Church. The three-fold division is a product of development. Scripture and history prevent the affirmation of anything like a rigorously dogmatic difference between the episcopate and presbyterate. It is a difference established by human law, neither absolute nor immutable. Priests have the same power as bishops, a *potestas ordinis*, but it is bound, a *potestas ligata*.

Joseph Duss-von Werdt[49] points out that the New Testament makes no distinction between priests and laymen. Rather, it deliberately avoided using the term *priest* to describe the Church's ministers. The undisputed Pauline epistles make no reference to ordination, and, since the Pauline churches were charismatic, an ordination should not be presumed. Thus, to assert that an ordained priest always celebrated the Eucharist in Paul's absence requires a burden of proof awkward to carry in the light of the Pauline epistles. It cannot be determined a priori what a layman can or cannot do without an ordained priest. In principle laymen can do anything an ordained priest can, but they ought not to, because this would introduce an unbiblical anarchy into Church order.

Antonio Javierre[50] emphasizes that the differences between the apostles and bishops are such that an identification between them is impossible. The idea of bishops serving as successors to the apostles rests solely on analogy.

Hans Küng[51] summarizes the meaning of apostolic succession in eight points: 1) The whole Church and each individual member shares in apostolic succession. 2) This consists essentially in cohesion with the apostolic witness and apostolic service. 3) Within the apostolic succession of the Church as a whole, there is an apostolic succession of various pastoral ministries. 4) Among these pastoral ministries those of presbyter, bishop, and deacon acquired increasing importance in the post-apostolic period. 5) But those who have succeeded to the prophets and teachers of the New Testament likewise enjoy a special apostolic succession. 6) Succession in the pastoral ministry is neither automatic nor mechanical with the imposition of hands. It must be tested by the faithful for possible error or failure. 7) The apostolic succession of pastors implies service to the Church and world; this in turn implies the cooperation of both pastors and community. 8) In the light of Pauline church order, other ways of entry into pastoral service (besides the imposition of hands) remain open. Church order today can be open in principle to all the possibilities which existed in the New Testament Church. The institutional order which was determined mainly by the Palestinian tradition and developed into the present organization of offices must not be absolutized.

John L. McKenzie[52] agrees that Jesus left no instructions on how the Church is to be governed. Neither absolute authority nor its absolute use can be reconciled with the New Testament. The structure of the early Church was tolerant of variation in both form and function. Hence, the structure of the Church today is not sacred; both office and function can be modified. Authority in the New Testament should not be viewed as absolute but, if anything, as democratic.

Wilhelm Pesch[53] insists that the New Testament is the critical judge of the Church, providing examples of legitimate forms of ministry which did not develop but are still open possibilities, for example, a local church led by a college of bishops. The development which led to a priestly office is not the only possibility. The New Testament foundations offer wide possibilities of further development.

Is the Protestant principle present within the Catholic Church today? The foregoing makes it clear that it is very much present, operative, and widespread throughout the Catholic world. Not only does *Ecclesia semper reformanda* have "a solid foundation in Catholic tradition," but it is applied radically to dogmatic, sacramental, and hierarchic structures. The authors cited above cannot be dismissed as an exceptional or fringe phenomenon. They are both serious scholars who command considerable respect and highly representative; the foregoing survey is hardly exhaustive. The point has been made conclusively, it would seem, that a major and leading part of post-conciliar Catholic theology is open to the radical reformability of the Church.

In no way, however, is it a contention here that openness to radical reform has found its way into official Catholic teaching or into the pastoral practice of the Catholic hierarchy at high levels. On the contrary, the direction taken by post-conciliar theology has more than once become a cause for alarm to the Vatican and its Sacred Congregation for the Doctrine of the Faith. Attempts have been made to restrict the activity and influence of theologians who depart too far beyond what is deemed the pale of acceptable Catholic opinion. The most prominent example is the case of Hans Küng.

In June 1973, the Congregation published a declaration entitled *Mysterium Ecclesiae*, "concerning Catholic doctrine on the Church against certain errors of the present day."[54] Without mentioning Küng by name, the declaration repeats the teaching of Vatican I and clearly rejects his interpretation of infallibility: "the faithful are in no way permitted to see in the Church merely a fundamental permanence in truth which, as some assert, could be reconciled with errors contained here and there in the propositions that the Church's magisterium teaches to be held irrevocably." The declaration of the Congregation has not gone without its critics, among them Karl Rahner.[55] But for the first time in any official Catholic pronouncement, there is in this declaration an admission that dogmas are historically conditioned, sometimes incomplete (though not false), and affected by the changeable conceptions of a given epoch. Rahner himself has asked, Where does the truth of incomplete, historically conditioned dogmatic formulations leave off and where does error begin?[56] Given this significant, albeit grudging, admission of the historical nature of dogma, it is difficult to see how the Congregation for Doctrine or any other institution within the Catholic Church can prevent the logical conclusions from being drawn from that admission, conclusions such as those drawn by the above authors.

Ever since Rahner compared Küng's position on infallibility to that of a liberal Protestant,[57] questions have been raised regarding Hans Küng's Catholicism.[58] As shown above, however, he is not exceptional in his radical approach and critical historical interpretation of dogmas. If this makes Küng a liberal Protestant, then he is joined by a considerable number of his colleagues. Nolens volens, Rahner himself has not been above the accusation of unorthodoxy even after Vatican II.[59] If Küng's Catholicism is open to question, then so is that of Gregory Baum, Avery Dulles, Walter Kasper, Piet Schoonenberg et al. The supposition does not merit serious consideration.

On February 15, 1975, the Congregation for the Doctrine of the Faith issued a monitum to Küng, in which he was admonished to desist teaching his opinions on a number of areas, among them infallibility.[60] Given the fact that severe disciplinary measures might have been applied and that Küng was not even asked to recant the theses in question, the monitum is popularly seen as a gentle slap on the wrist and a virtual victory for Küng.[61] How long that victory will last, however, is something else again, for it is unlikely that either the Congregation or Küng have seen the last of each other.

The position of systematic theologians like Küng and those treated above parallels closely that of Catholic biblical scholars who only a generation ago were under similar suspicion for applying the same critical historical principles to Scripture as these men do to dogmas. There is reason for confidence that the same historical scholarship which brought about the demise of an uncritical biblicism in the Catholic Church will bring about the same demise of dogmatism. The critical study of the New Testament and of subsequent church history exerts a powerfully relativizing influence upon all claims to absolute validity, whether in a formula or a structure. Despite any alarmist attempts to contain the activity or negate the influence of theologians such as the above, it can be argued compellingly that the future of Catholic thought and practice lies on their side. Certainly anyone who would deny their conclusions assumes the burden of answering the same questions and facing the same historical problems they did. The enemy of dogmatism within the Catholic Church is not so much the spirit of the times, as time itself.

Tillich's primary objection to the Catholic Church was that it made itself, its dogmas, sacraments, and hierarchic structures into absolutes. Doubtless he would have been amazed and gratified at the openness to radical reform within the Catholic Church today. But, if dogmas, sacraments, and Church offices are not above criticism, neither is Tillich himself, or his theology of the Church. Now the other side of the polarity, Catholic substance, must be considered. How truly catholic was Tillich in his theology of the Church? Is the Protestant principle the corrective that Tillich claimed it to be? Does it merely complement Catholic substance in his theology? Does Tillich really maintain a polar tension between Catholic substance and the Protestant principle? And, more important, if the Catholic Church no longer absolutizes itself and its structures, what would constitute the essential difference today between Catholic and Protestant churches? Does that difference justify the division existing between Catholics and Protestants? These are the questions still remaining. Since this is a Catholic appraisal of Tillich's theology of the Church, a Catholic protest against protest on principle now becomes necessary.

13

A Catholic Protest against Protest on Principle

*The life of Protestantism depends on the survival of that
against which it protests.*
T.S. *Eliot,* Notes toward a Definition of Culture

"No one who reads Tillich can fail to learn from him."[1] As
in other areas, so too in the theology of the Church, Tillich brought insight
and illumination. Where he did not answer questions, he helped to clarify
them. Where he did not solve problems, he helped to indicate where the
real issues lie. In translating the Christian message for our time, he broke
through the crust of traditional formulations and revealed the meaning that
lies within. His thought evokes a sense of liberation not only from Protestant readers but Catholic as well. A Catholic reading Tillich finds much that
is congenial and familiar, as well as provocative.

Much in Tillich's theology of the Church recommends it to Catholics
today. The concept of latent and manifest Spiritual Community merits
attention, and not only from missionaries; in today's pluralistic society all
Christians work and live among people who may not believe that Jesus is
the Christ but who nevertheless are not without God and his grace. Tillich's
distinction between the necessary functions of the Church and the institutions which serve those functions can prove useful to those charged with
the responsibility of reform within the Church. Partisans of political theology can learn from Tillich's writing on religious socialism, in particular from
his insistence on the Church's maintaining both religious obligation to the
world and religious reserve. A Catholic who reads Tillich can learn to

appreciate better his own Catholicism—the meaning of sacraments, the value of tradition as a source of theology after the Bible, the significance of the Church as a *complexio oppositorum.*

Traditionally Catholics have been inclined to develop a theology of the Church based almost exclusively on the Acts of the Apostles and the Pastoral epistles, to the neglect of St. Paul, especially his epistles to the Corinthians. Catholic theology can be grateful to Tillich for drawing attention to important elements of Pauline ecclesiology, not only to Spiritual Community but also to the charismatic nature of ministry in the Church. Tillich pointed out some of the implications of charismatic, factual authority typified by John the Baptist as opposed to established authority in principle, exemplified by the Jewish scribes. We can be grateful to Tillich too for his translation into the Protestant principle of many central Pauline concerns—the meaning of the cross, justification by grace through faith, the prohibition of the first commandment against idolatry. The cross was St. Paul's primary means of resistance against the Judaizers at Galatia, who wished to absolutize the Law, and against the enthusiasts at Corinth, who believed that the kingdom of God had already come in all its fullness. In terms of Tillich's Protestant principle, the cross can still serve as a judgment against traditionalists who wish to absolutize the status quo and revolutionaries caught up in the enthusiasm of an imminent utopia. The Protestant principle reminds us compellingly both of Jesus' attitude toward law and St. Paul's emphasis upon freedom.

With all its strengths, though, Tillich's theology of the Church is not without weaknesses as well. It is not above criticism, as Tillich assuredly would have agreed. Tillich ended his theological career dreaming of a new system. He would have been the last to regard the theology he wrote as in any way final. But to criticize his theology for not being sufficiently dialectical—could any objection be less fair? If any theologian in our day stood on the boundary, straining to strike a balance between polarities, it was Tillich. The undialectical no was as primitive and unproductive for him as the undialectical yes. How un-Lutheran he was in his Christian Socialism or in his attempt to mediate the tension between faith and works with a theology of love. How un-Calvinistic he was in his insistence upon the necessity of symbols and sacraments in the Church. How un-Protestant he was in his affirmation and development of a theology of Catholic substance. Walking the tightrope between Catholic substance and the Protestant principle, Tillich performed with as much virtuosity as he did balancing his many other boundaries. He merits admiration and applause merely for attempting the feat. Standing with the pedestrians on the Catholic side of the boundary, however, it appears to an observer that Tillich at times leaned too far to one side to keep from falling. The objection may be accused of Catholic bias, but, from this vantage point at least, Tillich was not always as dialectical in practice as he apparently strived to be.

Protest on Principle

With all his emphasis upon the universality of revelation and grace, of Spiritual Presence and Spiritual Community in general, Tillich had little to say about visible community in particular, except that it is ambiguous. He held that latent Spiritual Community is but a preparation for reception of Jesus as the Christ and subsequent transition into the manifest Church; yet Tillich emphasized the ambiguities of the manifest Church to such an extent that it is difficult to find in his theology a significant advantage for making the transition. In a similar vein, the horizontal relationship of Christians to one another received neither the attention nor emphasis Tillich gave to the vertical. His earlier writing in Germany on Christian Socialism expressed a strong sense of the horizontal dimension. But his later, more systematic, and by far more influential works produced in America betray a distinct bias in the direction of individualism. His leaning is understandable enough in the light of Tillich's deep-seated fear of heteronomy, but regrettable nonetheless, when one considers the loneliness and uprootedness of today's autonomous man and his need for meaningful community.

His tendency to emphasize the universal at the expense of the particular becomes apparent likewise in Tillich's discussion of the marks of the Church. Noticeably omitted from the traditional listing taken from the Nicene Creed is the mark of apostolicity. This is understandable as a rejection of Roman Catholic claims to exclusive apostolic succession. Within the polarity of tradition and reformation, however, it results in a marked leaning toward reformation and relevance over tradition and identity. With Tillich, I agree that both sides of the polarity need to be kept in mind. But, unlike Tillich, if compelled to incline slightly toward one direction over the other, I would prefer identity. A crisis of relevance can be confronted where there is already a healthy sense of tradition, identity, and continuity. But no amount of relevance will succeed in resolving an identity crisis either for an individual or for a church where there is not a strong awareness of historical roots.

In this same vein, one wonders if Tillich did not give too little consideration to the Jesus of history to be found within the Synoptic gospels. Certainly he was correct in insisting that faith cannot rest upon the latest findings of critical biblical scholarship. But Tillich also admitted that Jesus as a historical person or his life as a historical event must not be lost sight of if Christianity is to avoid the risk of docetic-gnosticism. It was the Jesus of history who became the Christ of faith, the bearer of the New Being, and it is from the Jesus of history that the Church takes its origins. Even within the context of the Pauline Spirit-Christology which Tillich took for his own, it does make a difference to the Church, its faith and practice, that Jesus was not an Essene, a Pharisee, or a Zealot. It makes a difference to the Church that Jesus associated with the poor, with publicans and sinners. It makes a difference to the Church that Jesus put people and human considerations above the law. It makes a difference to the Church that Jesus died outside the walls of the establishment as a disturber of the peace and a threat to law and order. The truth of faith cannot be demonstrated with historical probabilities. But neither can Christian faith afford to ignore its historical roots. Ecclesiology must take its origins from Christology. And even a Spirit-Christology must take its origins from the historical Jesus. Unless the Church maintains a clear awareness of the Jesus of history as its foundation, it runs the danger of becoming a mystery cult creating a myth out of a cosmic Christ.

With sacraments as with community, Tillich had much to say about symbolism and sacramentalism in general, but almost nothing about the Church's sacraments in particular, whether seven or two. His silence is all the more remarkable, seeing that he regarded worship and prayer among the constitutive functions of the Church. Tillich excused this omission of the sacraments in his *Systematic Theology* with the claim that it is a system and not a summa. But, with the exception of one early essay, one searches in vain for a detailed consideration of the sacraments in any of Tillich's writings. The deficiency is difficult to reconcile with his avowed alarm at the disappearance of sacramental thinking from Protestantism and his fear that this would lead to the demise of the Protestant churches.

For a Catholic at least, the absence of a consideration of the Eucharist is a particularly glaring deficiency in Tillich's theology. One does not expect Tillich to accord it the centrality that a Catholic would. But neither is the sacrament of the Lord's Supper peripheral. Leading Protestant exegetes have expressed the opinion that the Last Supper should be considered as the essential founding act of the Church.[2] Even if he would not agree to this or to the constitutive character of the Eucharist, its significance should warrant much more recognition than Tillich seems willing to grant. Tillich spoke of some of the sacramental symbols as irreplaceable, especially because of their historical context.[3] Does this include the Eucharist? How does this modify and interpret his apparent sacramental maximalism, his insistence on "the freedom of the Church from and for every sacramental action"? Tillich makes allusions to the sacraments often enough to raise questions but not enough to answer them.

Despite Tillich's insistence upon sacraments as constitutive of the Church, upon the priestly as prior to the prophetic, upon the polarity between Catholic substance and the Protestant principle, a Catholic is compelled to question: how much polar tension actuality existed for him between Catholic substance and the Protestant principle? Are word and sacrament really complementary? Is the "already," the sacramental, and immanent aspect of the kingdom of God as evident in Tillich's theology as the "not yet," the prophetic, and transcendent? Is the Protestant principle really simply a corrective for Tillich, or does it become itself constitutive? Offering a Catholic appraisal, I cannot help but incline to the opinion that often the gentleman "doth protest too much."

Tillich's interpretation of Protestantism has been criticized more than once by his fellow Protestants as being too negative. Barth wished that the word *Protestant* would disappear altogether in favor of *evangelical*.[4] Others prefer to interpret Protestantism positively as a profession of the Gospel, as a protest for rather than a protest against. The criticism of negativism is not altogether fair, when one considers that Tillich's denials are the by-products of his affirmations. He had a prophet's abhorrence for idols, insisting that God alone is absolute; his interpretation of Protestantism affirms the finiteness of man, justification by grace alone, and the centrality of the cross. Certainly this is not mere negativism.

There is some difficulty, though, with Tillich's Protestant principle. Not because it is negative, or because it protests, but because it is so central that it becomes for Tillich the essence of Protestantism and hence, it would seem, of what he would consider the best in Christianity; not simply a principle, but an overriding and even, at times, exclusive principle, *the* principle which governed his theology as a whole, particularly his theology of the Church.

The polarity between Catholic substance and the Protestant principle arises out of Tillich's understanding of analogy or religious symbolism. We have accused him of not being sufficiently dialectical in that he emphasized the Protestant principle in practice far more than Catholic substance. It is a bias to which Tillich himself admitted in a response to G. Weigel:

A Catholic Protest against Protest on Principle

> I believe you are right when you say that my understanding of analogia is more negative-protesting than positive-affirming. I am more worried about the idolic character of traditional theology and popular beliefs about God than you are. [OW, p. 24]

Tillich's struggle for personal autonomy was a painful one. His sensitivity to all that would threaten that autonomy, his crusade against the Grand Inquisitor, his preoccupation with the Protestant principle—all obviously sprang from deep, personal concerns. Without denying the validity or seriousness of those concerns, we are led to question nevertheless: Does protest deserve the centrality Tillich accords it?

Tillich regarded the Protestant principle as the essence of Protestantism (PE, p. vii). If it is the essence and not simply the specific difference, it would seem that protest has become the very substance of Protestantism, with the unpleasant implication that it depends for its meaning and survival on the existence of that against which it protests, that is, the existence of Roman Catholicism. One is led furthermore to ask: In those churches where protest has been not merely operative but central, has it served as a principle of edification? Has it served as a source of vitality in faith, charity, unity, or service? Perhaps G. Weigel was somewhat unfair in his triumphalism, but he touched a sensitive nerve with his question: "Is not Tillich's half-hearted recognition of the fact that Catholicism has better preserved the substance of Christianity than Protestantism a protest against unlimited protest"?[5]

To be quite clear here in my criticism, it is not Tillich's crusade against idolatrous absolutes that I find objectionable. I am not against prophetic protest or the concept of radical reformability within the Church. My criticism is against protest on principle, against protest as central. Tillich described the Protestant principle as a corrective which simply complements the constitutive element of Catholic substance. *De facto,* however, at least in several significant parts of his theology, the Protestant principle is much more dominant than Catholic substance. In questions traditionally disputed between Catholics and Protestants, protest has become substantive, the corrective has become constitutive. I cannot help, therefore, but ask: Is this truly the essence of Christianity, the heart of the Gospel message? Certainly flexibility and openness to change, development, and reform were characteristics of the New Testament Church; but they were hardly focal points. Indeed, is the Protestant principle, with its insistence that God alone is absolute, really so distinctive of Christianity? Is

267

not the fear of idols much more characteristic of Judaism and Islam, what with their aversion for images altogether? It comes as no surprise that Tillich expressed not only an "enthusiasm" for the Old Testament but admitted that it had shaped his life and thought (OB, p. 49).

The danger of making protest central to the extent he did becomes most evident in Tillich's discussion of the Church and the world religions. Tillich attributed the uniqueness and superiority of Christianity to the fact that it has the cross as its central symbol. The cross symbolizes the conquest by Jesus of the demonic temptation to self-elevation, upholding God alone as ultimate, and judging all other claims to ultimacy as idolatrous. The Church has a superior criterion with which to judge itself along with all finite realities. Yet Tillich admitted, along with Calvin, that the human mind is a working factory of idolatry; so much so that even the cross itself can become an idol. The implication could be drawn, therefore, and indeed no matter how strenuously Tillich might object to it, the implication has been drawn, that for Tillich there was no significant difference between Christianity and other religions.[6] The cross, it would seem, is not necessarily a foolproof defense against idolatry. It is simply a less likely candidate for idolatry than other possible religious symbols such as Vishnu or Buddha.

This is reductionism, of course. But is not reductionism the inevitable result of attempting to establish any symbol or doctrine, any aspect of Christianity, as its essence? The difficulty is not new with Tillich. It has been a problem with which Protestantism has had to contend from its very beginning. Reductionism and undialectical overemphases invariably result as soon as one selects a doctrine, no matter how important, and raises it up as the *articulus stantis et cadentis Ecclesiae.*

Protestant Principles and Reductionism

For the Protestant reformers, especially for Luther, the doctrine of justification by grace through faith was not simply one biblical teaching alongside the others. More than the chief article of faith, it was regarded as the category which determines all of Christian life, the measure by which all else can be judged as evangelical or not, the article by which the Church stands or falls. From the Pauline doctrine of justification, Luther became convinced that much in the tradition and practice of the Catholic Church lacked scriptural foundation and, in some instances, contradicted the Bible. To *sola gratia, sola fide* was joined *sola scriptura* as a Protestant watchword. To offset the possibility of exaggerated anthropocentrism,

Calvin added *soli Deo gloria* to the litany of principles by which the Reformation systematized and evaluated all other aspects of Christian faith.

Recent Catholic scholarship has demonstrated compellingly that these hallmarks of the Protestant Reformation have their roots deep in Catholic tradition.[7] They are susceptible of a thoroughly Catholic interpretation. But in the heat of confessional controversy, they were also open to one-sided interpretation. The *sola* in each of the formulations can be justified by Catholic traditions that go back long before Luther. Emphasis came to be placed upon the word *alone* to such an extent, however, that there arose exaggerations and misinterpretations in every sphere—grace, faith, and Scripture. To these overemphases was added the neglect by the reformers of much within Catholic tradition that was thoroughly biblical, much within the New Testament that is genuinely Catholic.

By means of *sola gratia, sola fide, sola scriptura*, the Protestant Reformation simplified Christianity considerably. In great measure the attractiveness and vigor of the Reformation and the impact which it exerted on the sixteenth century can be attributed to this simplification. Congar pointed out that "the great reformers are generally simplifiers" (VFR, p. 248). This bent toward simplification has remained with Protestantism throughout its history. In recent years it has been exemplified by the discussion regarding a canon within the Canon.[8] Originally, the reformers had accused the Catholic Church of the Middle Ages of distorting the purity of the Gospel message. After closer historical consideration, the distortion was pushed further back, first to the ancient councils and then to the period of Constantine, back into the post-apostolic period and finally into the New Testament itself. Luke and Acts, the Pastoral epistles and 2 Peter have become designated as exponents of "early Catholicism" and then set up over and against Paul. But even within the genuine Pauline epistles one can see the roots of early Catholicism in his teaching on sacraments and realized eschatology.[9] The result is that Paul is set up over and against Paul. A canon is established within the Canon, a formal principle of interpretation for the rest of the New Testament.

Undoubtedly, it is possible and even necessary to discriminate among the many witnesses in the New Testament, to subordinate some of its doctrines to others. There is much within the biblical Canon that is peripheral rather than central to the Christian message. Not everything in the Bible, not everything in the New Testament, can be put on the same level; it is by no means illegitimate to look for a center in Scripture.

Vatican II recognized an order or "hierarchy" of truths with respect to doctrines, since they vary in their relationship to the foundation of the

Christian faith (DOe, #11). For the same reason we must also recognize an order or hierarchy among the books of the Bible. A Christian does not view the Old Testament the same way a Jew does but measures and evaluates it in the light of the New Testament. It is not the law of Moses which determines a Christian way of life but the Sermon on the Mount.

The same differentiation must be made within the New Testament itself. It is the product of a long and complex history of some one hundred years and comprises a plurality of witnesses to the Christ-Event and to the acceptance and interpretation of that event by the apostolic Church. One perceives within the New Testament a fundamental unity of faith. But there are also distinct differences of perspective, emphasis, theology, and approach. The New Testament reflects differences among the individual writers, differences in their theologies, differences in the missionary situations for which they wrote, differences in the traditions from which they drew. A critical historical approach to the Bible does not permit leveling down all these differences to a common denominator or indiscriminately harmonizing the tensions among them. On the contrary, it means taking the New Testament as a whole with all its differences, with all its tensions, divergencies, and nuances. It is possible, and in some instances even necessary, to differentiate between primary and secondary witnesses in the New Testament on the basis of chronology, authenticity, and that which is distinctively Christian.[10]

Although all the writings of the New Testament have a normative value, that value is not the same for all of them. They do not all have equal importance. Jesus' preaching of God's kingdom is more basic to Christianity than the enigmatic images of the Apocalypse. The epistle to the Galatians, written by an eyewitness, provides a more accurate description of certain historical events than does the book of Acts, written from secondhand information many years later. The epistle to the Romans, written by an apostle, deserves more serious consideration than the derived witness of 2 Peter, written long after the passing of the first generation of Christians. The epistles to the Corinthians were actually written by St. Paul; the epistles to Timothy were not. Paul's understanding of faith as total commitment is more profound than the intellectualistic concept of faith expressed in the epistle of James. The theology of John is deeper and more comprehensive than that of Luke. St. Paul's teaching on service and charisms is more distinctively Christian and more important as a criterion for the Church today than the natural, rather commonsense admonitions for Church order and government to be found in the Pastoral epistles. The epistle to the Philippians is more valuable than that to Philemon.

Approaching the New Testament historically and critically, the Church cannot help but listen to some voices in the New Testament over others. But among all the voices there, the one to which the Church must be most attuned is, of course, that of Jesus himself. Jesus' words, actions, and destiny, his life, death, and resurrection, as critical scholarship permits us to know them, constitute the normative origins of the Church, the beginning of the Gospel, the center of Scripture.

There is a hierarchy of value within the Scriptures. Discriminating among the New Testament witnesses, however, and subordinating some of its doctrines to others is one thing. Abstracting essences and establishing a canon within the Canon is another. Formal principles of interpretation tend in practice to become material principles of selection and thereby exclusion. Concentration upon a canon, principle, or essence leads in practice to the neglect of that outside it. Such selection constitutes precisely the meaning of heresy.[11]

It was the heresy of Marcion in the second century to simplify Christianity by reducing it to Paulinism. A similar temptation has plagued Protestantism for much of its history, resulting in a multiplicity of Protestant churches and sects. Protestant churches no longer omit certain books from the Canon as Marcion did. But there is still a tendency among many Protestants to focus on certain books of the Bible to the all but complete neglect of the others. Hence the tendency of some Lutherans to concentrate almost exclusively upon St. Paul, especially his epistle to the Romans; Pentecostal, Spirit-centered churches tend to concentrate similarly on the Acts of the Apostles, especially chapter two; liberal Christians and proponents of the Social Gospel tend to concentrate on the Synoptics, especially the Sermon on the Mount. While it is legitimate to emphasize central teachings within the New Testament, formalizing a Protestant principle or a canon within the Canon runs the risk of neglecting the rest of the Canon and thereby the fullness of Christianity.

> Each protest-making selection from the New Testament refutes all the other ones and is refuted by them in turn. A *false* understanding of *sola scriptura* leads to *sola pars scripturae* and this again to *sola pars Ecclesiae;* in short, to a devastating chaos in preaching and doctrine and a progressive fragmentation of Protestantism.[12]

Lest the impression of self-righteous triumphalism be given, the fact that reductionism has been a failing not only of Protestantism but of Roman Catholics as well should be immediately pointed out. Certainly Matthew 16:18 and the Pastoral epistles have been much more central to

271

the Catholic Church than Paul's teaching on charisms or justification by faith. The Catholic Church has often been more Roman than catholic, without recognizing a contradiction implicit in the very conjoining of those two words. Catholicism has often been just as particularist and selective in its emphases as Protestantism. But Catholicism has not canonized emphases into essences. Without always striving in practice to be as open and universal as it should be, the Catholic Church has at least held up before itself in principle the ideal of being catholic, of being open to the entire legitimate development of Christian tradition, and therefore of being open to the whole New Testament. The Catholic Church has not always lived up to its name, but at least catholicity has remained enough of an ideal to provoke a troubled conscience.

The criticism raised here against the Protestant tendency to create principles has been raised by Catholic theologians before. J. A. Möhler accused Protestantism of so concentrating on one or another of the contraries within Christianity that they become contradictories.[13] Congar similarly has accused Protestantism of unilateralism and unitraditionalism (VFR, pp. 248, 280). R. Knox made a similar point: "It is an excellent thing to abandon yourself, without reserve, into God's hands; if your own rhetoric leads you into fantastic expressions of the idea, there is no great harm done. But teach on principle that it is an infidelity to wonder whether you are saved or not, and you have overweighed your whole devotional structure; you have ruled out a whole type of religious expression."[14]

H. Küng agrees: "It is highly dubious procedure to reduce all the disputed points to some one theological principle and then build up a theological system . . . on *that* rather than on Revelation as a whole."[15]

Not only Catholics but Protestants have recognized how questionable this selection of principles can be. It was precisely protest as a principle in Protestantism that Kierkegaard saw as a problem: "Surely Protestantism, Lutheranism, is really a corrective; and the result of having made Protestantism into the regulative has caused great confusion."[16] J. Dillenberger has denied altogether that Protestantism can be summed up in a principle: "One cannot define it by a single religious concept."[17] Selection of principles results in a one-sidedness which Friedrich Heiler found particularly objectionable:

> Because it [Protestant theology] is always one-sided and fragmentary, it cries out for completion and correction.[18]
>
> One-sidedness is often necessary for the re-establishing of a balance that had been disturbed. In the light of the degeneracy of the Church at the

end of the 15th century, one-sidedness was necessary. All prophetism is one-sided and must be one-sided in its concentration upon an aspect of religious faith and life that had been neglected, weakened, or deformed. But within Protestantism the one-sidedness, which is a relative and temporary need, became a constant. Or perhaps better: the pressure toward self-correction of a particular one-sidedness has led to ever new forms of one-sidedness within the history of Protestantism. For Luther the forgiveness of sins was the central issue. For Calvin it was the glory of God. For the Baptists it is the holy community; for Methodists, the experience of conversion. For Spiritualists it is the pure, spiritual experience of the eternal Christ; for Rationalists, the worship of a reasonable morality. Such one-sidedness is reflected in the interpretation of Scripture. The Bible itself is infinitely manifold; the New Testament raises a variety of voices, the Synoptics, Paul, John, James. Protestant exegesis, however, reads into Scripture whatever happens to be the dominant fundamental principle at the time. As with exegesis, so too with faith in Christ; first Christ appears as the Savior from sin, then as King and Lord, for a time as a model of holiness and then as the teacher of truth and morality or as an inner light. The history of Protestant piety and theology is one of one-sided, fragmentary interpretations, conflicting and replacing one another, first in one direction then another, often turning an about-face from one extreme to another.[19]

If the Catholic Church has been a *complexio oppositorum*, it is because the New Testament is a *complexio oppositorum*. I reject, therefore, the Protestant penchant for selecting centers out of the New Testament and canonizing them into principles of exclusion. The Catholic response to the reformers' *sola scriptura* is an appeal for serious consideration of the *tota scriptura*.[20] To be sure, it is hardly possible to maintain constantly a perfect balance among all the contrasts and tensions present within the New Testament and the traditions built upon it. Emphases and leanings are inevitable. No great harm is done, though, so long as an emphasis is not crystallized into an essence; so long as leanings are not formalized into principles of exclusion; so long as contraries are not permitted to become contradictories. My objection is not against the existence of emphases or against the subordination of some parts of the Bible to others. Both are necessary. Catholics object, however, to making a part into the whole, taking one book and making it the Bible.

This then is my response to Tillich's Protestant principle and to any other principles abstracted from the New Testament. With all the above distinctions that need to be made, consideration needs to be given to the *tota scriptura*, accepting its points of emphasis but avoiding any principles of exclusion. As fundamental as the protest against idolatry may be, the first commandment is not the entire decalogue. As significant as it is, Paul's preaching on justification is not the whole of the New Testament. As central as it is to Christianity, even the cross loses its proper proportion when abstracted from the life of Jesus or seen apart from the Resurrection. The contents of revelation are too complex, the aspects of faith too many-splendored, the voices of the New Testament too varied for Christianity to be formalized or distilled into any one principle or essence.

This is not to deny the usefulness, indeed, the necessity of formulas and doctrines to intellectualize and summarize Christian faith. The New Testament contains a plurality of them along with a plurality of theological principles. But there is no single *articulus stantis et cadentis ecclesiae*. There is no formula, no doctrine, no principle that can define the essence of Christianity. No formula, no doctrine, no principle can assume the centrality which belongs to God alone, the God revealed in Jesus Christ. Christianity is not a principle but a person: it is Jesus and the rich, variegated response he evoked in those who accepted him as the Christ. Christianity did not begin with the incarnation of an idea but with an event, with the life of one who healed estrangement, imparted new depth and meaning to life, and inspired in turn a new way of life. To attempt to reduce it to a principle or an essence may simplify Christianity greatly but the result is impoverishment.

My critique of Tillich's theology of the Church comes down then to accusing Tillich of being more Protestant than Catholic, more negative-protesting than positive-affirming. Despite the priority he gave the priestly element in theory, in practice his emphasis lay decidedly on the prophetic. But, Tillich would probably answer, could it have been otherwise? Given our finite condition and our situation of ambiguity in time and space, no perfect balance between the priestly and prophetic is ever possible. One aspect of religion invariably outweighs the other. Could Catholic theology in Tillich's day or Catholic institutional practice today claim to be any more dialectical, any more balanced? Catholicism has its own one-sidedness.

The Catholic "And"; the Protestant "Alone"

In distinction to Protestantism with its will for purity and simplification, Catholicism has been characterized as a search for plenitude.[21] I have objected that simplification leads to reduction, that concentration upon the Protestant "alone" leads to impoverishment. Hence my rejection of protest on principle or of any essence or principle for Christianity. I appeal instead for greater Protestant concern for catholicity, plurality, fullness, openness, wholeness, the *tota scriptura*. This does not mean that Catholicism has always been catholic; I have already pointed out how selective the Catholic Church can also be in its reading of the New Testament. But neither does the Catholic hold up fullness or plenitude undialectically as a Christian ideal.

Catholic plenitude is no less a mixed blessing than Protestant purity. The undialectical yes is as primitive and unproductive as the undialectical no. Just as the Protestant "alone" can lead to reductionism if not in polar tension with the Catholic "and," so too the Catholic "and," unless maintained in tension with the Protestant "alone," can lead to syncretism. There is an enrichment which can become simply the excuse to introduce foreign elements into Christian faith and practice. There is a plurality which can be promiscuity, a breadth which can be mere shallowness, a *complexio* which can be simply a disguise for confusion.

If Protestant churches are prone to a *peccatum per defectum*, the Catholic temptation is toward a *peccatum per excessum*. The only way to avoid both extremes is to conjoin the Catholic "and" with the Protestant "alone" in dialectical tension. If they are not to remain simply at odds with one another, a deeper unity must be found, a synthesis which preserves both Catholic plenitude and Protestant purity in their basic meaning and intent, while resolving at the same time any contradictions between them.

A resolution of contradictions between the Catholic "and" and the Protestant "alone" is possible, I believe, but only when one is grounded firmly in the other, only when the Catholic "and" is grounded firmly in the Protestant "alone." Plenitude must be measured and evaluated in terms of purity. The notion of "faith and works" must be grounded in the biblical teaching of "grace alone" and "faith alone," an expression of the fact that man is incapable of self-justification: all is giving on God's part (grace), and receiving on man's part (faith), but a receiving, a faith, that is active in works, "working through love" (Gal. 5:6). One may speak of cooperation between "God and man" only if "God alone" is first recognized as the initiator and source and therefore the foundation for any relationship between God and man. The same must be said for the relationship of Scripture to tradition. One may speak of "Scripture and tradition" only if tradition is first seen as grounded in "Scripture alone," the original Christian tradition which alone serves as the norm for all subsequent tradition. The fullness of tradition must be measured and evaluated by the criterion of Scripture.

The question of the relationship between Scripture and tradition is far too complicated to discuss here at any length. A call for conjoining Catholic plenitude and Protestant purity cannot avoid it altogether, however, since it is precisely in the name of tradition that one appeals for the Catholic "and"; it is in the name of Scripture that one insists on the Protestant "alone." Fortunately, recent theology has clarified much of the confusion which characterized earlier Protestant-Catholic controversy on the question. Today it is more clearly recognized than in the sixteenth century that Scripture and tradition cannot be dissociated. On the contrary, there is an organic unity between them. Scripture springs from tradition; it records the apostolic preaching which constituted the Church's earliest oral tradition. At the same time, post-apostolic tradition is based on Scripture; it circles around the original record, explaining it, interpreting it, applying it to changing circumstances and to new historical situations.

When the Council of Trent taught that the truth of the Gospel is contained in written books "and" in unwritten traditions, its intention was not to teach that revealed truth is found "partly" in Scripture and "partly" in tradition. Indeed, such an interpretation was expressly rejected by Trent. There is an ever-growing consensus among Catholic theologians that all evangelical truths are found in Scripture, that tradition is but their living interpretation. This view was held by Cardinal Newman and J.A. Möhler in the last century and is shared more recently by Y. Congar, H. Küng, K. Rahner, J. Ratzinger, M. Schmaus, L. Scheffczyk et al.

If tradition interprets Scripture, however, the question arises: How normative are the interpretations of Scripture contained in tradition? Undoubtedly they are of great significance for the Church and its theology today. But tradition includes a variety of interpretations, many contradictory to others. Tradition contains not only orthodoxy but also heterodoxy, not only progress but also regress, not only development but also deterioration and decline. Although it has a normative value, post-biblical tradition, including the teaching of ecumenical councils, constitutes a witness to the revelation first recorded in Scripture. Both tradition and the magisterium are secondary sources and guides. Their testimony is derived and stands under Scripture, which alone serves as the primary witness to Christian revelation and enjoys a priority over all other forms of witness. Tradition constitutes a *norma normans* for the Church today but also a *norma normata*. Scripture, on the other hand, is a norm which judges both tradition and the magisterium, determining whether or not any teaching merits the designation Christian. Scripture alone is the *norma normans non normata*.

The Church is built upon the witness of the apostles, a unique witness that cannot be reproduced. When the Church established the Canon of the

Scriptures, it thereby declared implicitly that all other traditions stood under the criterion of that apostolic witness, set down in the canonical Scriptures. The Church established the Canon at a time when any number of claims were being made for secret apostolic traditions, claims made precisely by the Gnostics. Their gospels, acts of the apostles, and epistles were rejected by the Church as apocryphal and erroneous. To be sure, Jesus and the apostles said and did more than the New Testament tells us; the writings in the New Testament canon were for the most part occasioned by particular questions and situations; there was no intention of recording all the tradition of the first-century Church; the oral tradition of the apostolic Church included much more than is contained in the New Testament. But the books of the New Testament are the only witness which the early Church recognized as its original tradition and accepted as truly apostolic. Except for the New Testament, there is no other way of determining whether or not a teaching or practice goes back to the apostles.

At the origin of the Church there stands a historical person, a historical event, and a historical community. What we know of them is based on certain historical documents. Jesus and the historical community which first received him as the Christ constitute not only the origins of the Christian Church but also the criterion for all subsequent development within the Church. History makes clear that not every development in the Church, its teaching, worship, and discipline can be justified by the New Testament. There is no harm done if such a development stands outside the Gospel, so long as it is not absolutized. But if a development stands in contradiction to the Gospel, it obviously must be rejected. The Church is not a law unto itself. It stands in submission to the person of Jesus and his teaching as received from the apostles. Fidelity to its founder, therefore, requires of the Church a constant return to its origins and to the documents which have recorded them. Fidelity to the Christ requires a constant return to and reflection upon the witness and teaching of the New Testament.

If Protestants have often been guilty of the sin of Marcion, wanting to reduce Christianity to Paulinism, to a pure "gospel" or principle, Catholics have sinned in the direction of the Gnostics, opening Christianity up to any number of extra-evangelical elements in the name of development or unwritten tradition. Both extremes are unsatisfactory and ultimately contradict the attitude of the early Church, which combined catholicity with "evangelical concentration." Catholicity requires openness to the *tota scriptura* and to all the developments in tradition which can be justified by the New Testament, including the secondary witnesses to be found within

277

it. Evangelical concentration requires measuring and evaluating the Church today and its tradition in terms of Scripture, hearing the Gospel as it is presented even by its secondary witnesses, but subordinating those secondary witnesses and interpreting them by witnesses more primary. In this way the Catholic "and" is maintained in proper tension with the Protestant "alone," upon which it is grounded. Catholic plenitude does not become promiscuity, and Protestant purity does not become reductionism. The Church, rather, opens itself up to the fullness of the tradition of the past and to all possible developments in the future, testing all tradition and all development by the standard of Scripture.

And what if such were to be the case? What if the Catholic Church would officially open itself up to the concept of radical reformability? What if Catholics would no longer absolutize their dogmas, sacraments, or hierarchic structure? What if the Catholic Church would live up to its name, if it would see Matthew 16:18 and the Pastoral epistles within the *tota scriptura* and therefore within the broader, more distinctly Christian framework of service and charism? And, on the other hand, what if Protestant churches would not absolutize the corrections and sometimes one-sidedness, which characterized the reformers' response to their historically relative circumstances? What if Protestants stopped making protest into a principle? What if Protestant churches would accept the *tota scriptura* and therefore take seriously the "early Catholicism" of the New Testament? What then would constitute the specific difference between Catholics and Protestants?

In chapter 9, I pointed out the Protestant consensus that the fundamental difference between Catholics and Protestants consists of the Protestant no to Catholic absolutes. I tend to see another difference consisting of the Protestant reduction of Christianity to one or another principle, in violence to a catholicity rooted in the *tota scriptura*. But if both Catholics and Protestants would see God as absolute; if Catholics would take seriously Paul's teaching on justification, freedom, and the charismatic nature of the Church; and if Protestants would stop selecting principles and take seriously the *tota scriptura* including the "early Catholicism" of the New Testament—what difference then? It would be hard to provide any answer other than differences of emphasis, differences in theology, differences of perspective and approach; there would certainly not be enough differences to warrant the division of Christians into separate Catholic and Protestant churches.[22]

Differences of emphasis, cultural as well as theological, will ever remain among the Christian churches. There will always be schools of theology at variance with one another. Roman Catholic tradition will favor the values of unity and order symbolized by Peter. Eastern Orthodox tradition will hold up the mysticism of John. Protestant tradition will incline toward Paul. But, as in the parable by V. Solovyov, all three traditions, as all three apostles, will recognize the central issue to be simply the revelation of God in Jesus as Christ and Lord. Despite the tensions among them, the differences of emphasis within the Church of the New Testament were not sufficient to disrupt its unity. They were not sufficient to prevent the New Testament canon from being accepted as one entity. They were not sufficient to prevent intercommunion between Jerusalem and Corinth, Antioch and Rome. The differences between Jewish and Gentile Christians, between James and Paul, considerable as they were, did not necessitate a break.

"Overemphasis upon one favorite point is an occupational disease of theology."[23] Be that as it may, a hazard for theology need not become formalized into a principle or normalized into a church, at least not into a church formally divided from other Christian churches. An evangelical catholicism, such as envisioned by Tillich, requires both the *tota* and the *sola*, the "and" together with the "alone," plenitude together with purity. As in the churches of the New Testament, this will undoubtedly require living with a loose unity amid the broadest diversity, together with the tensions that invariably accrue to such a situation. Tension, however, is the existential price of striving for any dialectic. Tension is the price of living on any boundary.

POSTSCRIPT

This then was the vision of Paul Tillich—a Church without idols: not without scriptures or symbols, not without dogmas, creeds, offices, or authorities, but without the biblicism, dogmatism, or authoritarianism that raises these human realities into irreformable absolutes.

Tillich's ideal is not easily achieved. The temptation to raise idolatrous claims for itself or its structures is ever present for the Church, in an attempt to attain security against the transience, contingency, and relativity characterizing all human existence. For Protestants the temptation lies in the direction of an inerrant, literally interpreted Bible; for Catholics, infallible dogmas; for Eastern Orthodox Christians, an uncritical acceptance of the tradition of the church fathers and early councils. Essentially, however, the temptation is the same: to find safety against impermanence in something else besides God.

The alternative to ascribing absolute validity and value to finite forms is the Church's willingness to subject its symbols, structures, and institutions, like all else finite, to reinterpretation, revision, and reform. Openness to radical reform invariably arouses fear and objections of anarchy, infidelity, and upheaval. Such objections can be answered, however, with the reminder that a yes to God, to Jesus as the Christ, and to Spiritual Presence within the Church need not require a similar yes to ecclesiastical structures or institutions. The Church places its faith not in forms or formulas but in the God revealed by Jesus.

Obviously the Church requires tradition; it must constantly refer to the singular event upon which it is based. That event constitutes the measure against which the Church of any era must gauge itself. Adherence to its scriptural origins and pastoral accommodation to the exigencies of its present situation constitute the two norms by which the Church maintains both its identity and vitality, testing everything and holding fast to what is good.

The consequence of such a stance is not anarchy but the freedom and flexibility which prevent structures from becoming anachronistic and ultimately inert. Not openness to reform but intransigence inevitably leads to upheaval. Precisely the refusal to reform provides the tinder for revolutions. The twin crises of identity and change which have confronted the Catholic Church in the last generation are not unlike those which confronted Protestantism in the Enlightenment and Judaism once it was permitted to leave the ghetto. Because the Catholic Church has barricaded itself for so long against criticism and contamination from a changing world, the crises with which Protestants and Jews have had to cope over the past two hundred years have now become concentrated for it. The crises, challenges, and questions came rushing in all at once, and, for that reason, they are all the more acute.

For the Church to become open to radical reform implies, therefore, not infidelity but faith, a faith not in traditional forms and formulas but in the God to whom they point; not anarchy but firm rootedness in its biblical origins, in the critical testing of its traditions, in the translation of its symbols, and in a pragmatic, pastoral adaptation of its structures; not destructive upheaval but the freedom and flexibility which alone can prevent it.

To be willing to reassess critically and continually all aspects of the Church is no little thing. To forego the time honored and familiar or the comfortable security they provide is not easy. It takes courage, like that of Abraham, willing to leave Ur of the Chaldees in quest of a promise, the courage to face uncertainty. It takes maturity, the refusal to fixate at an early stage of development, the ability to say no to the temptation to recreate childhood and live in the past. One can admire and appreciate Byzantine mosaics, Gothic arches, Renaissance frescoes, and Baroque statuary without slavishly reproducing them.

Tillich was aware of the difficulty of living on the boundary between the priestly and prophetic, the difficulty of saying yes to tradition and authority but no to any absolute claims made on their behalf. But such is the challenge to faith, courage, and maturity posed by Paul Tillich's theology of the Church. Catholic, Protestant, or Orthodox, it is a challenge no church can refuse to take up, except at its own risk.

NOTES

Key to abbreviations of frequently cited works. Full bibliographical information is listed in the bibliography.

AAS *Acta Apostolicae Sedis*
BR Tillich,*Biblical Religion and the Search for Ultimate Reality*
CB Tillich,*The Courage to Be*
CE *Constitutio de Ecclesia* of Vatican II
CEMT *Constitutio de Ecclesia in Mundo huius Temporis* of Vatican II
CEWR Tillich,*Christianity and the Encounter of the World Religions*
CR *Constitutio de Revelatione* of Vatican II
Denz Denzinger, *Enchiridion Symbolorum*
DF Tillich, *Dynamics of Faith*
DOe *Decretum de Oecumenismo* of Vatican II
EN Tillich,*The Eternal Now*
FR Tillich,*The Future of Religions*
GW Tillich,*Gesammelte Werke*
HCT Tillich,*A History of Christian Thought*
IH Tillich,*The Interpretation of History*
JR *Journal of Religion*
KB Kegley and Bretall, *eds., The Theology of Paul Tillich*
LPJ Tillich, *Love, Power, Justice*
LThK *Lexikon für Theologie und Kirche*, 2d ed.
NB, Tillich,*The New Being*
OB Tillich,*On the Boundary*
OW O'Meara and Weisser, eds., *Paul Tillich in Catholic Thought*
PE Tillich,*The Protestant Era*
PL *Patrologia Latina*, J.P. Migne, ed.
PPT Tillich, *Perspectives on 19th and 20th Century Protestant Theology*
RGG *Die Religion in Geschichte und Gegenwart*
RS Tillich,*The Religious Situation*
SA Tillich,*My Search for Absolutes*

SF Tillich,*The Shaking of the Foundations*
ST Tillich,*Systematic Theology*
TC Tillich,*The Theology of Culture*
ThBl *Theologische Blätter*
ThSt *Theological Studies*
UC Tillich,*Ultimate Concern*
VFR Congar, *Vraie et fausse réforme dans l'Église*
WS Tillich,*The World Situation*
ZThK *Zeitschrift für Theologie und Kirche*

Introduction

1. *Dogmatics in Outline*, p. 141.
2. McKelway, *The Systematic Theology of Paul Tillich*, p. 269.

Chapter 1

1. Nels F.S. Ferré, KB, p. 248.
2. Ulrich Neuenschwander, in *Werk und Werken Paul Tillichs*, p. 103.
3. "Existential Aspects of Modern Art," p. 145. Here Tillich gives further indication of the centrality which the idea of symbol holds in his theology. In it he claimed that he did not learn as much from any theology book as he did from the great modern artists who were able to break through the surface form of reality and descend into the depth where symbols are born. How early Tillich developed his thought on symbolism is evidenced in "Das Religiöse Symbol," published in his *Religiöse Verwirklichung* in 1930. See GW 5: 196–212.
4. HCT, p. 12. It is difficult to see how Hamilton can accuse Tillich of disguising an "experience theology" by substituting "awareness" for "experience," *System and Gospel*, pp. 112–15. Tillich did not hesitate in the least to make the equation. See *My Search for Absolutes*, pp. 127–28.
5. DF, p. 78. This is not to imply that revelation for Tillich is only experience. "Revelation is more than religious experience. It is the divine criticism and transformation of religious experience. But the material of revelation ... is religious experience. Without the historical process of religion there would not have been the event of revelation, nor the prophetic criticism and transformation of a pagan tribe into the people of God and the church of Christ." "Natural and Revealed Religion," p. 165.
6. John H. Randall, Jr., in James Lyons, ed., *The Intellectual Legacy of Paul Tillich*, p. 21.
7. Translated by Louis Macneice, p. 160.
8. Some of the more important titles are: Rhein, *Paul Tillich: Philosophie und Theologie;* Rowe, *Religious Symbols and God;* Schmitz, *Die Apologestische Theologie Paul Tillichs;* Thomas, *Paul Tillich: An Appraisal*, as well as the following articles, L. Ford, "Tillich and Thomas"; G. McLean, "Symbol and Analogy" in OW, pp. 145–83; G. Weigel, "Paul Tillich: An Impression," in OW, pp. 25–41.
9. ST 1: 128—41. Tillich rejected Barth's criticism of analogy by holding it as a necessary vehicle for speaking about God. He stood with Barth in rejecting analogy of being as a basis for creating a natural theology. It is not a method of discovering truth about God but rather constitutes the form in which every knowledge of revelation must be expressed.
10. A. McKelway, p. 33. There is a difference between Tillich and St. Thomas regarding the ontological foundation required for analogy or symbol. But there is such a broad area of agreement that we may speak of them as functionally interchangeable. Methodological differences do exist but they are not decisive for philosophical theology. See Ford, "Tillich and Thomas," JR 46 (1966): 229–45.

11. TC, pp. 54–56; DF, pp. 41–43; "Existential Analyses and Religious Symbols," p. 54.
12. "Rejoinder," JR 46: 188.
13. "The Meaning and Justification of Religious Symbols," in *Religious Experience and Truth*, p. 5.
14. Tillich regularly described symbols as being transparent to the absolute. He was criticized for doing so, however, in that transparency seemed to be too passive a concept. Tillich admitted toward the end of his career (1966) that translucency might be a better metaphor. Transparency permits things to be seen clearly, whereas translucency implies that the medium contributes something of itself. Thus clear glass is transparent, but stained glass is translucent. "The light that shines through the stained glass window is, taken as a metaphor, the unapproachable divine mystery. The colors and forms are the contributions of the medium which makes seeing of the invisible possible." "Rejoinder," p. 187.
15. For Tillich the ultimacy encountered in a religious symbol is the ontologically ultimate. Every experience of what is phenomenologically ultimate was for him an experience of what is ontologically ultimate. See Rowe, *Religious Symbols and God*, pp. 166–68.
16. Sanderson, who regards this as the controlling thought in Tillich's theology, has pointed out the explicit connection between Tillich's and Plotinus' description of God: "The One is not Mind but something higher still; Mind is still a being, but the One is no being but the ground of all being. It cannot be a being, for a being has what we may call the shape of its reality, but the One is without shape, even intellectual shape." *Ennead* 6. 9.3. Cited in Sanderson, "Historical Fact or Symbol?" pt. 2, p. 71.
17. ST 1:244–45. Tillich has been accused of pantheism and of denying the personhood of God because of this understanding of God in terms of *esse ipsum*. Tillich countered the criticism of pantheism by maintaining that God is the power of being, not the sum of all beings. He admitted the aptness of person as a symbol for God, since God is not an "it," i.e., God is not sub-personal. But neither is God *a* person, in the sense of being a being. Rather, he is trans-personal, supra-personal. "The God who is *a* being is transcended by the God who is Being itself, the ground and abyss of every being. And the God who is *a* person is transcended by the God who is the Personal-itself, the ground and abyss of every person." BR, pp. 82–83.
18. CB, p. 179. In adopting Schelling's notion of God as *das Unbedingte*, Tillich was not proposing that this become a substitute for the name of God but rather a key to opening "the closed door of the Holy of Holies of the name 'God.'" He held that the present situation does not permit us to use the name of God as if it could still mediate directly the power once associated with it. Once the term *Unconditional* or *Absolute* served to open the meaning of the name "God," then it could be discarded. "Antwort," THBl 2(1923): 296. In the meantime it serves to characterize the Holy not only as entirely other but also as that other which is of decisive importance, from which we cannot withdraw ourselves. See "Die Kategorie des 'Heiligen' bei Rudolf Otto," THBl 2:12.
19. How strongly Tillich felt this is indicated by his conviction that to worship a God who is a being alongside other beings is tantamount to idolatry. He believed that idolatry could be found not only in polytheism but monotheism as well. "Neu Sein," *Eranos* 23: 262.
20. See John Dillenberger, in Ferré, *Paul Tillich, Retrospect and Future*, p. 31.
21. SF, p. 131. Tillich exemplified the impossibility of genuine atheism with Nietzsche's *Thus Spoke Zarathrustra*: After he has murdered God, the ugliest man subjects himself to Zarathrustra, because Zarathrustra has looked into his depth with understanding. Hence the murderer of God finds God in man. He has not succeeded in killing God at all. God has returned in the person of Zarathrustra. God is always revived in somebody or something. He cannot be murdered. The story of every atheism is the same. SF, p. 54.
22. "Der Begriff des Dämonischen," ThBl 5 (1926): 32.
23. "Die Idee der Offenbarung," pp. 408–9; "Die Kategorie des 'Heiligen' bei Rudolf Otto" p. 12.

Chapter 2

1. ST 2: 98. Tillich criticized putting together the words *Jesus Christ* in such a way that the title *Christ* becomes no more than a second name for Jesus. Christ is a title and expresses reception of Jesus as inaugurator of the new eon. For this reason Tillich preferred to speak of "Jesus as the Christ" or "Jesus the Christ," to emphasize both aspects of the Christ-event equally, both the fact and the reception. See UC, p. 67.
2. Martin Kähler, *Der sogenannte historische Jesus und der geschichtliche biblische Christus* (1892). Tillich considered the book of singular significance and was instrumental in its translation and publication in English with title: *The So-called Historical Jesus and the Historic Biblical Christ* (Philadelphia, 1964).
3. "Reply," OW, p. 309; UC, pp. 86–89. This was Tillich's answer to those who accused him of minimizing historical elements in the gospels, or of contradicting his theology of Jesus as the concrete, historical embodiment of New Being. See J. Livingston in Ferré, *Paul Tillich, Retrospect and Future*, pp. 42–50, and Dulles in OW. Although he admitted in private that he was personally conservative when it came to biblical criticism, Tillich refused to base the risk of faith upon the risk of historical error. Christian faith can simply guarantee that the NT picture of Jesus is an expression of a bearer of the Spirit and hence healing, the New Being. "It is the bearer of the Spirit who through the Spirit has created the church and the picture of himself in the New Testament in mutual dependence. In this sense the Christian faith guarantees directly his foundation." "Rejoinder," JR46: 194.
4. "A Reinterpretation of the Doctrine of the Incarnation," p. 139.
5. Ibid., p. 144. Tillich's understanding of the Incarnation is far too broad and complex to be examined here. His Christology has been considered in detail by Tavard, *Paul Tillich and the Christian Message*; Thomas, *Paul Tillich: An Appraisal*; Hamilton, *The System and the Gospel*; Killen, *The Ontological Theology of Paul Tillich*; and Weigel, "Contemporaneous Protestantism and Paul Tillich." It is controverted as to whether Tillich's Christology stands within the classical dogmas. Mollegen believes it does. KB, pp. 230–45. Tavard has tried vigorously to show that it does not.
6. "A Reinterpretation," p. 147.
7. CEWR, pp. 28–31; Tillich pointed out that the attitude of the Christian Church toward other religions is not to be confused with its attitude toward heretics, especially in the late Middle Ages. The cruelty with which heretics were treated contrasts with the relative mildness shown to other religions.
8. CEWR, pp. 44–46. Tillich believed that Barth and his followers have given up the classical Logos doctrine in which Christian universalism is most clearly expressed. For Tillich the term *religion* is unavoidable because religion is an empirical reality. There is a great similarity in all religions, including Christianity. If the word *religion* were dropped, another word would have to be substituted for it. See PPT, p. 108.
9. "Reply," OW, p. 305.
10. Tillich has been credited by Carl Braaten as being the only modern theologian to integrate the Logos doctrine into his theological system. PPT, pp. xix–xx.
11. "Reply," OW, p. 305.
12. ST1:137. Critics who accuse Tillich of relativizing Christianity would do well to pay closer attention to this aspect of his theology. It is the reason why philosophers at the opposite pole of criticism accuse Tillich of never really transcending the "parochial limits" of Christianity and deny he was really a philosopher. See Fox, "Tillich's Ontology and God," *Anglican Review* 43: 260.

Chapter 3

1. Leibrecht, *Religion and Culture*, p. 19.
2. PPT, p. 21. See UC, p. 114; HCT, pp. 230–31.

3. Tillich regularly used the term *the Spiritual Community*, but Maurice Schepers rightly suggests omitting the definite article and referring simply to *Spiritual Community* in order to keep in mind Tillich's insistence that Spiritual Community is not a separate community but rather the dynamic essence of all religious communities. OW, p. 239.
4. Armbruster, *The Vision of Paul Tillich*, p. 216.
5. ST3:163. Tillich admitted to making a studied effort in the *Systematic Theology* to avoid using the term *the Church* (with a capital *C*). He used the term *the church* (with a small *c*) as an equivalent of Spiritual Community, and *the churches* as referring to concrete Christian assemblies which manifest not only the characteristics of Spiritual Community but also the ambiguities of religion. In his other writings, however, Tillich did use the term *the Church*, and he admitted that the terminology, although helpful in one respect, may be confusing in another. Because Tillich used the term *the Church* in his other writings and because confusion is an all too real possibility, I will use the term *the Church* (with a capital *C*) to refer to the Church universal. I will use *the churches* (with a small *c*) to refer to individual local churches, and *Spiritual Community* to refer to the Spiritual essence of both the Church and the churches. The only exceptions are direct quotations, in which the original typography is used. In these cases, the context makes clear enough the meaning desired to be conveyed.
6. PPT, p. 200; GW 3:34.
7. "Missions and World History," pp. 281, 285.
8. ST3:189. The importance of this distinction can be readily seen in Tillich's approach to authority within the Church.

Chapter 4

1. PE, p. xiii. Besides *kairos*, such Tillichian concepts as the Protestant principle, the demonic, Gestalt of grace, and the trio of heteronomy, autonomy, and theonomy were worked out at this time for the sake of a new interpretation of history. See Braaten, PPT, p. xviii.
2. Tavard sees this shift from *kairos* to New Being as a sign of Tillich's shift from history to ontology. D. Hopper sees it rather as a shift from an almost exclusive concern with the corporate-historical aspects of human existence to a point of view more inclusive of individualistic dimensions. Tillich never gave up history as a primary concern. See Hopper, *Tillich: A Theological Portrait*, pp. 97, 101.
3. *An Essay on the Development of Christian Doctrine*, p. 35.
4. Cited by Nels F. S. Ferré in KB, p. 249.
5. GW 10: 167; IH, p. 280; "The Kingdom of God and History," p. 119.
6. PE, p. 23; "Die Staatslehre Augustins nach De Civitate Dei," p. 84.
7. "The Kingdom of God and History," p. 118.
8. ST3:369. Tillich was led to make a sharp distinction between revelation and *kairos*, between primary and secondary *kairoi*, when Emanuel Hirsch began canonizing National Socialism in 1934 by means of the *kairos* doctrine, hailing Nazism as a *kairos* for Evangelical Christianity. Tillich criticized Hirsch strongly for using the eschatological *kairos* teaching to consecrate a contemporaneous political situation. See "Die Theologie des Kairos"; "Um was es geht."
9. Tillich emphasized the kingdom of God as a "breaking in" or "breakthrough" into our midst in opposition to A. Ritschl's notion of the kingdom as simply an ideal or a beginning. The kingdom stands not only at the end of history and therefore conditioned by history. It is already a reality as well, standing above history. It is the presence of God. It is grace. "Albrecht Ritschl," p. 53.
10. "Reply," KB, p. 345.
11. Ibid., p. 348.
12. "Missions and World History," p. 282.

13. "Reply," OW, p. 311.
14. "Die Theologie des Kairos," p. 327.

Chapter 5

1. HCT, pp. 155, 236; RS, p. 213; GW 3: 112.
2. PE, pp. xix, 111. See also PPT, p. 147; *The Recovery of the Prophetic Tradition*, p. 27.
3. PE, pp. 94, 109; OB, p. 73. Tillich's concern expressed itself in his close association with the Evangelische Michaelsbrüderschaft (Evangelical Brotherhood of St. Michael), and the liturgical renewal in the Evangelical Church in Germany. Cf. Wendland, "Was Bedeuten Tillichs Thesen," p. 202.
4. PE, p. 108; PPT, p. 147; ST3:121.
5. In his autobiographies Tillich displayed a strong affinity for nature. He saw it as the finite expression of the infinite ground of all things and criticized the attitude which views nature only as something to be controlled technically. Rudolf Otto's *Idea of the Holy* made a great impression upon Tillich, giving him a deeper insight into the sacramental implications of the holy and motivating him to participate in movements for liturgical renewal. See OB, pp. 17–18; "Autobiographical Reflections," KB, pp. 4, 6; SA, pp. 25–26, 29.
6. GW 3: 158; PE, pp. 102, 109.
7. Cited in Walter Hartmann, "Kritik und Gestaltung," p. 333.
8. "Reply," KB, p. 349.
9. PE, pp. 95–98. This essay regarding nature and sacrament appeared originally in 1930 in *Religiöse Verwirklichung*, hence quite early in Tillich's career. He wrote no detailed treatment of sacraments subsequent to it.
10. Weigel, "Contemporaneous Protestantism and Paul Tillich," ThSt11:185–87.
11. Tavard, OW, p. 89.
12. OB, p. 48. See also PE, p. ix. The development of Tillich's concept of the Protestant principle can be seen in his earlier writings: in 1922, "Die Überwindung des Religionsbegriffs in der Religionsphilosophie" (GW 1:367), and in 1924, the lecture "Rechtfertigung und Zweifel." In the article "The Permanent Significance of the Catholic Church for Protestantism" (1941), Tillich related the Protestant principle to Catholic substance. *Protestant Digest* 3: 23–31; also GW 7: 124–32.
13. HCT, pp. 203–4, 214–15. To eliminate the possibility of *sola fide* being interpreted as a good act which merits grace, Tillich insists that the principle of justification be properly formulated as "justification by grace through faith."
14. *The Recovery of the Prophetic Tradition*, p. 3. See "The Problem of Theological Method," 252–53; *Hegel und Goethe*, p. 44.
15. *The Recovery of the Prophetic Tradition*, p. 2.
16. Ibid., p. 6.
17. HCT, pp. 263–64; GW 10: 132.
18. Cited by Tillich in *Hegel und Goethe*, pp. 43, 47.
19. PPT, p. 66; "Albrecht Ritschl," in ThBl 1:51.
20. "Ernst Troeltsch," *Kant Studien* 29:357.
21. *Morality and Beyond*, p. 35.
22. *Morality and Beyond*, p. 44.
23. Armbruster, *The Vision of Paul Tillich*, p. 307.
24. Tillich credited his American experience for the realization that the name Catholic can be predicated of the Orthodox and Anglican churches as well as the Roman Catholic Church. His writing on these other churches is quite limited, however, and our chief concern here is his attitude toward Roman Catholicism. TC, p. 169.
25. HCT, pp. 211–12, 224; UC, p. 149.
26. *Masse und Geist*, p. 38.
27. PE, p. 194. See also HCT, p. 134.

28. UC, p. 64. See also GW 7:151; HCT, pp. 210–11, 218; RS, p. 186.
29. PPT, pp. 236–37. See also UC, p. 62.
30. PE, pp. vii–viii, 163; GW 7:152; *The Recovery of the Prophetic Tradition*, p. 9.
31. PE, pp. 198–99. Thus Protestantism, for Tillich, meant that we do not have to cover up any part of our human situation but rather have to look at it in its depths of estrangement and despair. For this reason he considered *Guernica* by Picasso as a Protestant religious picture, because it shows the human situation without gloss, the depiction of the saturation bombing of a Basque village in northern Spain, an expression of disruptiveness, emptiness, meaninglessness, and doubt. "Existentialist Aspects of Modern Art," p. 138.
32. "The End of the Protestant Era?" written in 1937, republished in PE, pp. 222–33.
33. PE, p. 220; GW 7:157–58.
34. In *Protestant Digest* 3 (1941): 23–31. Also published in GW 8:124–32.
35. GW 3:151–52, 158. See *Masse und Geist*, pp. 45, 47.
36. Thus Tillich held that one should not claim that up to a certain time, whether 500 or 1500 A.D., there was one church, actual in time and space. Otherwise, one of the churches claims to be *the Church* and regards itself as superior to all other churches. ST 3:378.

Chapter 6

1. J. Heywood Thomas, OB, p. vii; Wilhelm Pauck, FR, p. 24.
2. "Autobiographical Reflections," KB, p. 8; see SA, pp. 32–33.
3. KB, p. 8. Cf. OB, pp. 40–41; IH, p. 80; GW 6:44.
4. *An Essay on the Development of Christian Doctrine*, p. 103.
5. SF, p. 159; see CB, p. 132.
6. ST 1:93; PE, p. 56.
7. TC, p. 136. See GW 3:21; *Morality and Beyond*, p. 24; *Hegel und Goethe*, p. 40.
8. Leibrecht, *Religion and Culture*, p. 17.
9. PE, pp. xii, 46, 47; LPJ, p. 76; GW 1:271–72, 331; OB, p. 41; "Das Recht auf Hoffnung," p. 273; "Theonomie," RGG 5(1930): 1128–29.
10. ST1:149. See also IH, p. 236; HCT, p. 188. Tillich saw the cosmological approach to God of Thomas Aquinas as contributing to the breakdown of medieval theonomy. Augustine and the early Franciscans held for the ontological approach to God, whereby we have a direct, immediate relationship to God in the depth of reason. In Aquinas, God is approached from the outside, through nature, history, and culture. Since such indirect reflections never lead to certainty about God, only probability, outside authority becomes the most important source of certitude. Faith thus becomes subjection to authority. HCT, pp. 160, 201; TC, pp. 10–29.
11. LPJ, pp. 89–90. See TC, p. 140.
12. LPJ, p. 90. See TC, p. 139.
13. HCT, pp. 154, 254; see also RS, p. 193.
14. "The Relevance of the Ministry in Our Time," pp. 21–22.
15. "An Afterword: Appreciation and Reply," OW, p. 304.
16. Ibid.
17. *The Recovery of the Prophetic Tradition*, p. 25.
18. Ibid.
19. "The Problem of Theological Method," p. 245.
20. HCT, p. xiii; UC, p. 88.
21. "An Afterword: Appreciation and Reply," OW, p. 309.
22. NB, pp. 70–71; HCT, pp. xiii, xiv, xv; "Reply," KB, p. 332.
23. OB, pp. 31–32, 51; HCT, p. xvi.
24. "The Problem of Theological Method," p. 246.
25. ST 3:146. Fear of heteronomous subjection led Tillich to object to the World Council of Churches assuming as its creedal basis acceptance of "our Lord Jesus Christ as God and

Savior." Tillich feared that this description raised the historical image of Jesus to the rank of the unconditioned, so that it could become idolatrous. Cf. Sanderson, "Historical Fact or Symbol," p. 164.

Chapter 7

1. TC, pp. 9, 41–42, 51. See also GW 1:320; GW 9:96.
2. RS, pp. 51–52; WS, pp. 2–9.
3. PPT, pp. 95–96, 160, 209; PE, p. ix. Tillich regarded Thomas Aquinas as a mediating theologian par excellence. "He understood, better than anyone else, the mediating function of theology." The question facing Thomas was: How could a world educated in the Augustinian tradition be mediated with the secular system of ideas and meanings in the complete Aristotle that had just been rediscovered? The question facing us is: "How can the scientific revolution since the seventeenth century be mediated with the Christian tradition." HCT, pp. 183–84.
4. "The Problem of Theological Method," pp. 77–78.
5. "Relation of Metaphysics and Theology," p. 58; "Das neue Sein als Zentral begriff," p. 264.
6. "The Relevance of the Ministry in Our Time," p. 26.
7. Ibid., p. 22.
8. When accused of just such a surrender Tillich answered: "I cannot accept criticism as valuable which merely insinuates that I have surrendered the substance of the Christian message because I have used a terminology which consciously deviates from the biblical or ecclesiastical language. Without such deviation, I would not have deemed it worthwhile to develop a theological system for our period." ST 2:viii. The Second Vatican Council regarded accommodation as "the law of all evangelization." CEMT, #44.
9. ST 2:29; PPT, p. 228; WS, p. 44.
10. PE, p. 108; OB, pp. 65–66; EN, pp. 94–95.
11. Helmut Thielicke, in Karl Hennig, ed., Der Spannungsbogen, p. 19.
12. ST 2:27–28; TC, pp. 49, 207; GW 10:180; "Existential Analysis and Religious Symbols," pp. 37–55; Existentialist Aspects of Modern Art," pp. 141–42.
13. "Existential Analysis and Religious Symbols," pp. 49–54; TC, pp. 208–9, 211–12; UC, p. 98; EN, p. 40.
14. GW 10:311–12; TC, p. 213.
15. Tillich's participation in the Religious Socialism Movement was to prove most fruitful for his theology. It underlies much of part 5 of Systematic Theology on the kingdom of God and prompted his thinking regarding kairos, theonomy, and the demonic. When, later in his career, his theology was described as "beyond religious socialism," Tillich objected strongly. "If the prophetic message is true," he answered, "there is nothing beyond religious socialism." "Autobiographical Reflections," KB, pp. 12–13.
16. OB, p. 62. See PE, p. 161; GW 2:118, 160–75; GW 3:117.
17. At the 1937 Oxford Conference, Tillich was chairman of a committee which drew up a statement regarding the relation of the Church to socialism and communism. Subsequently approved by the Conference, that statement admitted the feasibility of God speaking more distinctly through those enemies of religion than through the Church itself. Tillich was proud of the statement, regarding it as a prophetic perception. PPT, p. 236; GW 10:310–11.
18. TC, p. 197; GW 2:13–15, 30; PW, p. 51.
19. PE, p. xx; GW 2:18–20; GW 10:151.
20. GW 10:153–56; WS, p. 16; TC, pp. 50–51; "Kingdom of God and History," p. 136.
21. "The Relevance of the Ministry in Our Time," p. 24.
22. SA, p. 129; FR, pp. 67, 81.
23. GW 3:160, 168–70; "Missions and World History," pp. 287–88.

24. UC, p. 152; FR, pp. 86–87; CEWR, p. 57.
25. "Missions and World History," p. 287.

Chapter 8

1. This is compellingly demonstrated by the ever growing amount of secondary literature on Tillich. The most complete and up-to-date bibliography is available from the "Kreis der Freunde Paul Tillichs, E.V.," Universität Göttingen. Also helpful is the Paul Tillich Archiv, Marburg, and the Paul Tillich Archives of Harvard Divinity School.
2. See Tavard, JR46: 224–26.
3. Hamilton, *The System and the Gospel*, p. 10; also Tavard, in OW, p. 96.
4. Niebuhr, JR46:203.
5. "Autobiographical Reflections," in KB, p. 13.
6. OB, p. 13. For this same reason the festschrift published in honor of his 75th birthday was titled *Der Spannungsbogen*, the "bow of tension."
7. Cooper, *The Roots of Radical Theology*, p. 128.
8. Considered the primary difficulty by Tavard, OW, p. 94.
9. Hamilton, pp. 32–36.
10. McKelway, *The Systematic Theology of Paul Tillich*, p. 60.
11. Braaten, in PPT, p. xv.
12. Leibrecht, *Religion and Culture*, pp. 7–8.
13. Braaten, in PPT, p. xxi. Tillich admitted his preference of Augustine over Aristotle or Aquinas: HCT, pp. 104,111.
14. Tillich, *Hegel und Goethe;* HCT, p. 293; "Albrecht Ritschl," in ThBl 1:49–54.
15. Thomas, in OB, p. xviii.
16. GW 1: Frühe Hauptwerke. See D. O'Hanlon, *The Influence of Schelling on the Thought of Paul Tillich;* Leibrecht, pp. 7–8,25.
17. Tillich, "Ernst Troeltsch."
18. Tillich, "Die Kategorie des Heiligen bei Rudolf Otto."
19. For the limits to which Tillich could be regarded as an existentialist, see PPT, pp. 142–43; Leibrecht, pp. 5–6; McKelway, p. 65.
20. ST 3:4. This is certainly not unexpected of a German theologian; Tillich regarded R. Bultmann as both a colleague and a friend. See Tillich, "Das Neu Sein," p. 263.
21. Weigel, in OW, p. 16.
22. Weigel, in ThStl1: 201.
23. McKelway, p. 35. Also Tavard, in OW, p. 90.
24. Weigel, in ThStl1: 185,199.
25. Thomas, in OB, p. xviii. Hamilton objects most strongly precisely for such an attempt. McKelway criticizes Tillich for approaching the Catholic theology of Vatican I in this regard, pp. 139–41.
26. "Autobiographical Reflections," in KB, p. 10.
27. McKelway, p. 33; see also pp. 103, 112; Leibrecht, p. 355n3.
28. Weigel, "The Multidimensional World of Paul Tillich," p. 70.
29. Harnack, *Aus Wissenschaft und Leben*, 1:97.
30. Weigel, in ThStl1: 195.
31. Cited by Barth, *Protestant Thought from Rousseau to Ritschl*, p. 321.
32. H. Richard Niebuhr, JR46: 204.
33. Reinhold Niebuhr, in KB, p. 217.
34. "Autobiographical Reflections," KB, p. 10. See also UC, p. xiv; Pittenger, in *Anglican Theological Review* 43: 268; Leibrecht, pp. 10:27.
35. Weigel, in ThStl1: 185.
36. H. Lilje, cited in Schmitz, *Die Apologetische Theologie Paul Tillichs*, p. v.
37. Theodore Green, in KB, p. 50.

38. Introduction by the editors, KB, p. xi.
39. Niebuhr, cited in C. Rhein, *Paul Tillich*, p. 195.
40. Dillenberger, in Ferré, *Paul Tillich, Retrospect and Future*, p. 36.
41. Weigel, in *The Christian Scholar*, pp. 43, 67.
42. C. Hartshorne, in Ferré, *Paul Tillich, Retrospect and Future*, p. 28.
43. Hartmann, in H.J. Schultz, ed. *Tendenzen der Theologie*, p. 270.
44. Erich Schmidt, in *Neue Zeitschrift für Systematische Theologie und Religionphilosophie* 5: 97.
45. Walter Horton, in KB, p. 46.
46. Hans J. Baden, in *Friedenspreisträger Paul Tillich*, p. 23.
47. Leibrecht, p. 4.
48. Roger Shinn, in Lyons, *The Intellectual Legacy of Paul Tillich*, pp. 60–61.
49. Introduction by the editors, KB, pp. ix–x.
50. Cited in Van de Pol, *The End of Conventional Christianity*, p. 252.
51. Altizer, *The Gospel of Christian Atheism*, p. 10.
52. H. Lilje, in Hennig, ed., *Der Spannungsbogen*, p. 151. See also Brauer, JR46: 89–91.
53. Nels Ferré, cited in OW, p. 274.
54. Ibid.
55. Christoph Rhein, in *Friedenspreisträger Paul Tillich*, p. 40.
56. Cf. Hamilton, p. 236; McKelway, p. 168; Tavard, *Paul Tillich and the Christian Message*, p. 119; Weigel, ThSt14: 577.
57. Dillenberger, in *The Christian Century* 76: 669. Cited in McKelway, p. 101.
58. Hamilton, pp. 118, 206.
59. Dulles, in OW, p. 129.
60. Tavard, in OW, p. 93; also in JR46: 223.
61. Tavard, *Paul Tillich and the Christian Message*, p. 76.
62. Ibid., p. 162.
63. Ferré, in *Paul Tillich, Retrospect and Future*, p. 7. See also C. Rhein, p. 40.
64. Tavard, p. 51. See also Hamilton, in JR46: 228.
65. Wernsdörfer, *Die Entfremdete Welt*, p. 372.
66. Hamilton, in JR46: 227.
67. Pittenger, in *Anglican Theological Review* 43: 285.
68. Ibid., p. 278.
69. Mollegen, in KB, p. 230.
70. Weigel, in ThSt11: 200.
71. Hartmann, in H.J. Schultz, p. 271.
72. Reprinted in J. Lyons, p. 104.
73. Braaten, in PPT, p. xxxii.
74. Greene, in KB, p. 52.
75. Braaten, in PPT, p. xiv.
76. Ibid.
77. Pittenger, p. 275; Weigel, ThSt11: 189.
78. Pittenger, p. 277. See also his *The Word Incarnate*.
79. Weigel, ThSt11: 193.
80. Mollegen, in KB, p. 243.
81. Cited in Weigel, ThSt11: 201.
82. Weigel, "The Multidimensional World of Paul Tillich," p. 70.
83. Weigel, "Recent Protestant Theology," p. 574.
84. Tavard, in OW, p. 236.
85. Mollegen, in KB, p. 231.
86. C. Kiesling, in OW, p. 272.
87. Weigel, in OW, p. 18.
88. Niebuhr, in KB, pp. 226–27.

Chapter 9

1. Cooper, *The Roots of Radical Theology*, p. 90.
2. Ibid., p. 91.
3. Dee, "Wesen und Wirklichkeit der Kirche," p. 272.
4. Hessen, *Der Absolutheitsanspruch des Christentums*, p. 26.
5. Bolewski, "Zum Verhältnis von manifester und latenter Kirche," p. 230.
6. See Rhein, p. 21; Tavard, JR46: 223.
7. Cited in Rhein, p. 28; ein *"allseitig anwendbarer Grundgedanke."*
8. J. Haroutunian, in Ferré, *Paul Tillich, Retrospect and Future*, p. 51.
9. See Tavard, OW, p. 86. Also Wendland, "Was Bedeuten Tillichs-Thesen," pp. 193–94.
10. Weigel, in ThStl1: 186.
11. Weigel, ThStl1: 192.
12. Ibid., p. 196.
13. *The Spirit of Protestantism*, pp. 40–50.
14. Ibid., p. 40.
15. "Protestantismus," in *Pädagogisches Lexikon*, pp. 749–51.
16. Ibid., p. 751.
17. *Der Freie Protestantismus*, p. 18.
18. *Die Religion des protestantischen Menschen*, p. 163.
19. *Glaube, Kirche, Theologie*, p. 133.
20. Ibid., p. 180.
21. *Der Protestantismus in unserer Zeit*, p. 10.
22. *Das protestantische Wagnis*, pp. 22, 25, 47.
23. Schütte, *Protestantismus*, p. 247.
24. Cullmann, *Message to Catholics and Protestants*, p. 19.
25. Ibid., p. 20.
26. Käsemann, *Jesus Means Freedom*, p. 91.
27. Schütte, p. 151.
28. Ibid., pp. 155, 206.
29. Ibid., p. 164.
30. Ibid., p. 166.
31. Ibid., p. 174.
32. Armbruster, *The Vision of Paul Tillich*, p. 307.
33. R. Lindner, *Grundlegung einer Theologie der Gesellschaft*, cited in Schütte, *Protestantismus*, p. 74.
34. Pelikan, *Obedient Rebels*, p. 23.

Chapter 10

1. GW 3:153. Cf. chapter 5.
2. See Weigel, OW, p. 12.
3. "Reply," KB, p. 348. Although Tillich treats of Spiritual Community in his system before he does the kingdom of God, I have inverted the order; the concept of the kingdom of God is more fundamental and the objection of identification is more frequently voiced.
4. *What Is Christianity?* p. 273.
5. "All the doctrinal errors of Rome come from the direct identification of the Church as an organization institution . . . with the kingdom of God." Iremonger, *William Temple*, p. 420.
6. *The Coming Great Church*, p. 87.
7. For example, Adam, *The Spirit of Catholicism*, p. 15; Journet, *L'Église du Verbe Incarné* 2:997n1; Lambert, *Le Probleme Oecumenique* 1:222.
8. Jackson and Lake, *Beginnings of Christianity* 1:330.

9. For a brief history of the identification and some of its implications, Küng, *The Church*, p. 90; Visser 't Hooft, *The Renewal of the Church*, pp. 57, 95.
10. *Jesus' Proclamation of the Kingdom of God.*
11. *The Quest of the Historical Jesus.*
12. *The Parables of the Kingdom.*
13. For example, Schnackenburg, *God's Rule and Kingdom;* Feuillet, *Introduction.*
14. Fries, "Reich Gottes," in LThK, 8:1118.
15. McKenzie, *The Power and the Wisdom*, p. 69.
16. Feuillet, *Introduction*, p. 756. See also P. Hoffmann, "Reich Gottes," in Fries, ed., *Handbuch Theologischer Grundbegriffe* 2:414.
17. Schnackenburg, *The Church in the New Testament*, p. 188.
18. J. Nelis, in Haag, ed., *Bibel-Lexikon*, p. 1465.
19. Fries, "Reich Gottes," LThK 8:1119.
20. Rahner, *Theological Investigations*, 6:298. See also Rahner-Vorgrimler, *Theological Dictionary*, p. 251.
21. Küng, *The Church*, pp. 92–93.
22. Ibid., p. 74.
23. McKenzie, p. 69.
24. Feuillet, *Introduction*, p. 782. See also McKenzie, p. 69; Küng, pp. 96–104.
25. Küng, p. 96.
26. CE, #6, #7, #14, #48; DOe, #6.
27. Abbot, ed., *The Documents of Vatican II*, p. 17n11.
28. AAS35 (1943):202; the identification is also made in the encyclical *Humani Generis*, AAS42 (1950).
29. *Mystici Corporis* itself recognized this danger and warned against the "insidious growth of a false mysticism which, with its attempt to obliterate the inviolable frontiers between things created and their Creator, falsifies the Sacred Scriptures," AAS35: 197.
30. For surveys and/or literature, cf. Jáki, *Les Tendances Nouvelles de l'Ecclesiologie;* Küng, *The Church;* Schmaus, *Katholische Dogmatik* III/1, as well as the standard lexicons.
31. Published in the *American Ecclesiastical Review* 77 (1952): 307–11.
32. Congar, *Sainte Église*, p. 27.
33. See de Lubac, *Corpus Mysticum;* Ratzinger, *Das Neue Volk Gottes*, p. 83.
34. Ratzinger, p. 234.
35. Ratzinger, "Leib Christi," LThK, 6:911.
36. Ratzinger, *Das Neue Volk Gottes*, pp. 100, 230, 232.
37. The reactions were not only Protestant. See, for example, Congar, *Sainte Église*, p. 29; VFR, p. 482.
38. For example, Käsemann, *Leib und Leib Christi;* Schlier, *Christus und die Kirche im Epheserbrief* (Schlier has since become a Catholic); E. Schweitzer, "Soma," in G. Kittel, *Theological Dictionary to the New Testament.*
39. Protestant theologian H. Diem (*Die Kirche und ihre Praxis* 25n1), has gone so far as to say that the exegetical controversy is "almost boundless. Practically everything here is disputed."
40. Cf. Ratzinger, "Leib Christi," LThK; Küng, *The Church*, and the more recent lexicons and commentaries for summaries and literature.
41. J. de Fraine, "Kirche," in Haag, ed., *Bibel-Lexikon*, p. 951.
42. Cf. Schlier, *Der Brief an die Epheser*, p. 91; Congar, *Sainte Église*, p. 29; J. Fitzmeyer, in R. Brown, ed., *Jerome Biblical Commentary* 2:824, and other recent Catholic literature on Ephesians.
43. Congar, *Sainte Église*, p. 29.
44. Rahner-Vorgrimler, p. 61.
45. Congar, *Sainte Église*, pp. 102–4.
46. Schmaus, *Katholische Dogmatik* III/1:296.

47. Küng, *The Church*, pp. 237–38.
48. Groot, "The Church as Sacrament of the World," pp. 51–52.
49. Semmelroth, *Die Kirche als Ursakrament;* Rahner, *The Church and the Sacraments;* Schillebeeckx, *Christ the Sacrament of the Encounter with God.*
50. Groot, p. 61.
51. Schnackenburg, *The Church in the New Testament*, p. 76.
52. Grillmeyer, LThK12:160.
53. Rahner-Vorgrimler, p. 251.
54. Fries, "Reich Gottes," in LThK 8:1119.
55. Ratzinger, "Leib Christi," in LThK 6:911–12.
56. *Kirche als Ereignis*, p. 28.
57. *Die Kirche als Ursakrament*, p. 166.
58. "Catholic Ecclesiology in Our Time," p. 185.
59. *Christ the Sacrament of the Encounter with God*, p. 50.
60. Baum, *The Credibility of the Church Today*, pp. 48–49. See also Groot, "The Church."
61. LThK, commentary of the Dogmatic Constitution on the Church, p. 317.
62. *The Recovery of the Prophetic Tradition*, p. 6.
63. *Die heilige christliche Kirche—evangelisch gesehen*, p. 9.
64. Cited in Schütte, p. 467.
65. *The Council, Reform, and Reunion*, p. 10.
66. "Ecclesia semper reformanda," p. 240.
67. *Kirche als Ereignis*, p. 26.
68. *In dieser Stunde der Kirche*, p. 26.
69. Address to a general audience, May 7, 1969, reprinted in *The Catholic Voice*, Oakland, Cal., June 4, 1969, p. 5.

Chapter 11

1. Haller, *Papstum und Kirchenreform*, p. 11.
2. Simon, *The Human Element in the Church of Christ*, p. 57.
3. The exact origins of the formula are unknown. As far as can be ascertained, it goes back to Voetius, a Dutch Calvinist theologian at the Synod of Dordrecht. The phrase appears in the writings of two of his friends and disciples. See Barczay, *Ecclesia Semper Reformanda*, p. 19; Congar, K"Comment l'Église Sainte doit se renouveler," p. 332; Visser't Hooft, *The Renewal of the Church*, p. 82.
4. Lortz, *The Reformation, A Problem for Today*, p. 200.
5. McNally, *Reform of the Church*, p. 14.
6. Mourret, *Apologetique* (Paris, 1937), cited in VFR, p. 693.
7. O'Malley, *Giles of Viterbo*, p. 1.
8. For an examination of these related forms of renewal as well as an extensive bibliography, see Ladner, "Erneuerung," in *Reallexikon für Antike und Christentum* 6:240–75.
9. Ladner, *The Idea of Reform*, p. 9. Ladner's book may be considered a standard if not definitive work on the patristic idea of reform.
10. For examples, see VFR, p. 356.
11. Ladner, *The Idea*, p. 3.
12. Ibid., p. 61.
13. See Ladner, p. 61, his article "Erneuerung," and VFR, pp. 80–86.
14. VFR, p. 69
15. Ladner, *The Idea*, p. 281.
16. Ibid., pp. 319–20.
17. Ibid., p. 62.
18. Ibid., p. 277n147.
19. Cited in Haller, *Papstum*, p. 14.

20. Mansi 32:669.
21. Cited in VFR, p. 462.
22. *Die religiöse Gefahr; Lebens- und Gewissensfragen der Gegenwart* 2; *Liberalismus und Christentum.*
23. *Die religiöse Gefahr*, p. 479.
24. Ibid., p. 252.
25. *Lebens- und Gewissensfragen der Gegenwart* 2:60.
26. Ibid., p. 144.
27. *L'Église du Verbe Incarné* 2:904.
28. *Canones Apostolorum et Conciliorum*, H. T. Bruns (Berlin, 1839), 2:139; cited in Ladner, *The Idea*, p. 302.
29. *Canones*, 1:207; cited in Ladner, p. 302.
30. Ladner, p. 277n147.
31. Ullmann, "Pope Gregory VII," *New Catholic Encyclopedia* 6:773.
32. Mansi 32:669.
33. The complete original is in *Deutsche Reichstagsakten* 3:390–99. See McNally, *Reform of the Church*, p. 115, for a partial English translation.
34. Cited in McNally, ibid., p. 120.
35. Translated by V. McNabb, *Dublin Review* 198 (1936): 149–60; cited in McNally, *Reform*, p. 125.
36. Jedin, *Katholische Reformation oder Gegenreformation*, p. 57.
37. Ibid., p. 59.
38. Adolfs, *The Church Is Different*, pp. 107, 108.
39. Mansi 53:721–84.
40. Butler, *The I Vatican Council* 1:220.
41. Cf. Mourret, *Le Concile du Vatican* (Paris, 1919); also VFR, p. 35.
42. Schmidlin, *Papstgeschichte der Neuer Zeit* 3:33.
43. Pelikan, *Obedient Rebels*, p. 23.
44. Congar, "Comment l'Église doit se renouveler," *Irenikon* 34:323.
45. Abbe Michonneau, *Paroisse, Communaute missionaire*, p. 258; cited in VFR, p. 51.
46. Subsequently related by Congar in *Chrétiens en Dialogue*, p. lii.
47. O'Malley, "Historical Thought and the Reform Crisis," in ThSt28:537.
48. O'Malley, *Giles of Viterbo*, p. 2.
49. See the articles on Reformkatholizismus by A. Hagen in LThK and G. Maron in RGG; also Heiler, *Im Ringen um die Kirche.*
50. Herder-Korrespondenz 4 (1950): 316.
51. The phrase is credited to Cardinal Bea. See Robinson, *The New Reformation?* p. 9.
52. *Ad Limina Apostolorum*, p. 59.
53. "Redimentes tempus, quonian dies mali sunt." *The Pope Speaks* 9 (1963):159–60.
54. *The Pope Speaks* 9 (1963): 134.
55. Ibid. 10 (1964–65): 253–92.
56. Address to a general audience, *L'Osservatore Romano*, Eng. ed. (Jan. 23, 1969), 2:1–2.
57. "Ecclesia Semper Reformanda," p. 246.
58. "Reform in the Church," p. 172.
59. *The Spirit of Protestantism*, p. 45.
60. *The Renewal of the Church*, p. 110.
61. *Votum Ecclesiae*, p. 194.

Chapter 12

1. *Kirche der Sünder*, p. 14.
2. Küng, *The Church*, p. 130.
3. Ibid., p. 5.

4. Ibid., p. 6.
5. Küng, *The Council, Reform, and Reunion*, pp. 54–55.
6. "Pope John's Opening Speech to the Council," W. Abbott, ed., *The Documents of Vatican II*, p. 715.
7. See Commentary by J. Feiner, LThK 13:89–90.
8. AAS 56 (1964): 712–18; English text in *Catholic Biblical Quarterly* 26 (1964): 299–312.
9. *Theological Investigations* 4:3–35.
10. Ibid. 1:149–51.
11. *The Credibility of the Church Today*, pp. 12, 94.
12. "Doctrinal Renewal," p. 376.
13. Enlarged upon subsequently in *The Foundations of Belief*.
14. *The Foundations of Belief*, p. 106.
15. In *Nouvelle Revue Théologique* 89: 16–25.
16. (New York, 1971).
17. In *Revue des Sciences Philosophiques et Théologiques* 52: 173–200. See also "Rule of Faith and Orthodoxy," in *Concilium* 51 (1970): 56–67.
18. *Theological Investigations* 5:42–66.
19. See also Kasper, *The Methods of Dogmatic Theology*, pp. 45–65; "The Relationship between Gospel and Dogma," p. 154.
20. "The Church under the Word of God," pp. 87–93.
21. "The Relationship between Gospel and Dogma," p. 166.
22. *The Methods of Dogmatic Theology*, pp. 27–28.
23. "Schrift-Tradition-Verkündigung," p. 37.
24. *The Methods of Dogmatic Theology*, pp. 24–25.
25. Ibid., p. 25.
26. "The Relationship between Gospel and Dogma," p. 157.
27. "The Church under the Word of God," p. 92.
28. Ibid., p. 89.
29. Ibid.
30. (New York, 1964).
31. *The Living Church*, p. 308.
32. *The Council, Reform, and Reunion*, pp. 115–16.
33. Cited by Küng, *Structures of the Church*, p. 202.
34. Letter to Plummer, in F.L. Gross, *John Henry Newman* (London, 1933), p. 170; cited by Küng, *The Council, Reform, and Reunion*, p. 162.
35. *Structures of the Church*, p. 389. See also his *Council, Reform, and Reunion*, p. 114.
36. *Structures of the Church*, p. 205.
37. See also "Im Interesse der Sache, Antwort an Karl Rahner," *Stimmen der Zeit* 187:109.
38. For a listing of the literature on the debate up to 1973, see the bibliography in H. Küng, ed., *Fehlbar?*
39. The debate between Rahner and Küng originally appeared in *Stimmen der Zeit* 186: 361–77; 187: 43–64, 105–22, 145–60; an English translation appeared in the *Homiletic and Pastoral Review* 71 (May–Aug. 1971).
40. Ott, *Fundamentals of Catholic Dogma*, pp. 336–37.
41. "The Idea of 'Major' or 'Principle' Sacraments."
42. "Why Are There Seven Sacraments."
43. "Die Zählung und die Zahl der Sakramente."
44. *Kirche und Sakramente*.
45. "How Much Change Is Permissible in the Liturgy?"
46. *The Credibility of the Church Today*.
47. "Apostolicité de ministère et apostolicité de doctrine."
48. "Is There a Dogmatic Distinction between the Function of Priests and the Function of Bishops?"
49. "What Can the Layman Do without a Priest?"

50. "Notes on the Traditional Teaching on Apostolic Succession."
51. *The Church*, pp. 441–42. See also "What Is the Essence of Apostolic Succession."
52. *Authority in the Church.*
53. "Kirchlicher Dienst und Neues Testament."
54. AAS 65: 396–408; English text in *L'Osservatore Romano*, Eng. ed. (July 19, 1973), 6: 6–8.
55. *Stimmen der Zeit* 191:579–94.
56. Ibid., p. 592.
57. Rahner, *Zum Problem Unfehlbarkeit*, p. 32.
58. Küng's Catholicism has been recognized by Protestants and defended by Catholics too often to require our efforts here. The most significant defense is his own, made on the basis of the seriousness he has always accorded in his theology to the entire Catholic Christian tradition as it is found throughout history and throughout the world. His criticism of the Roman system has been made by leading members of the Catholic hierarchy as well. And he has expressed himself as critically loyal to the concept of the papacy when seen as a primacy of service. See Küng, ed., *Fehlbar?* pp. 337–46.
59. Rahner's orthodoxy on the divinity of Christ was questioned in a public controversy with the Cardinal Archbishop of Cologne. See Küng, ed., *Fehlbar?* pp. 512–14.
60. The Latin and Italian text of the *monitum* is in *L'Osservatore Romano*, Feb. 21, 1975: a French translation is in *La Documentation Catholique*, no. 1672, Mar. 16, 1975, pp. 258–59.
61. See A. Schalk, "Küng's Brush with Rome," *Commonweal* 102 (May 23, 1975): 138–41.

Chapter 13

1. McKelway, *The Systematic Theology of Paul Tillich*, p. 269.
2. A. Schlatter, T. Schmidt, F. Katenbusch. See Ratzinger, *Volk Gottes*, p. 78.
3. "Rejoinder," JR 46:187.
4. *Ad Limina Apostolorum*, p. 17.
5. "Contemporaneous Protestantism," ThSt11:195.
6. See Rowe, *Religious Symbols and God*, p. 242.
7. See Bouyer, *The Spirit and Forms of Protestantism.*
8. See Käsemann, *Essays on New Testament Themes*, pp. 95–107; "Notwendigkeit und Grenze des NT Kanons," ZThK 47 (1950): 277–313; Braun, in *Gesammelte Studien zum NT und seiner Umwelt* (1962), pp. 310–24.
9. Schlier, *Kurze Rechenschaft*, p. 177.
10. Küng, "Die Kirche des Evangeliums."
11. For a detailed Catholic criticism of the Protestant attempt to establish a canon within the Canon, cf. Küng, *The Living Church*, pp. 233–93.
12. Ibid., p. 283.
13. *Die Einheit in der Kirche*, p. 156.
14. *Enthusiasm*, p. 580.
15. *The Council, Reform, and Reunion*, p. 102.
16. *The Journals of Soren Kierkegaard*, p. 509.
17. *Protestant Christianity*, p. 2.
18. *Im Ringen um die Kirche*, p. 284.
19. Ibid., pp. 539–40.
20. Küng, *The Living Church*, p. 283.
21. For example, Jean Guitton, "Difficultes de croire" (Paris, 1948), cited in Congar, "Comment l'Église Sainte doit se renouveler sans cesse," *Irenikon* 34: 343.
22. This is not to minimize non-theological, practical matters which separate Christians, such as historical prejudice or the method of exercising authority; but such issues, important as they are, certainly are not as central as the ones considered here.
23. Pelikan, *Obedient Rebels*, p. 203.

BIBLIOGRAPHY

Only the editions used are listed.

Works by Tillich

"An Afterword: Appreciation and Reply." In O'Meara and Weisser, eds. *Paul Tillich in Catholic Thought*, pp. 301–11.

"Albrecht Ritschl: Zu seinem hundertsten Geburtstag." ThBl 1 (1922): 49–54.

"Autobiographical Reflections." In Kegley and Bretall, eds. *The Theology of Paul Tillich*, pp. 3–21.

"Der Begriff des Dämonischen und seine Bedeutung für die systematische Theologie." ThB1 5 (1926): 32–35.

Biblical Religion and the Search for Ultimate Reality. Chicago, 1964.

Christianity and the Encounter of the World Religions. New York, 1963.

The Courage to Be. London, 1962.

Dynamics of Faith. London, 1957.

"Ernst Troeltsch." *Kant-Studien* 29 (1924): 351–58.

The Eternal Now. London, 1963.

"Existential Analysis and Religious Symbols." In *Contemporary Problems in Religion*, edited by Harold Basilius, pp. 37–55. Detroit, 1956; reprinted in *Four Existential Theologians*, edited by Will Herberg, pp. 277–91. New York, 1958.

"Existentialist Aspects of Modern Art." In *Christianity and the Existentialists*, edited by Carl Michalson, pp. 128–47. New York, 1956.

The Future of Religions. New York, 1966.

Gesammelte Werke. Edited by Renate Albrecht. 14 vols. Stuttgart, 1959–74.

Bibliography

Hegel und Goethe. Tübingen, 1932.

A History of Christian Thought. Edited by Carl E. Braaten. New York, 1968.

"Die Hoffnung der Christen." In *Juden, Christen, Deutsche,* edited by Hans Jurgen Schultz, pp. 258–62. Stuttgart, 1961.

"Die Idee der Offenbarung." ZThK 8 (1927): 403–12.

The Interpretation of History. New York, 1936.

"Die Kategorie des 'Heiligen' bei Rudolf Otto." ThBl 2 (1923): 11–12.

"The Kingdom of God and History." In *The Kingdom of God and History.* The Official Oxford Conference Books 3. New York, 1938.

Love, Power, Justice. New York, 1960.

Masse und Geist. Berlin, 1922.

"The Meaning and Justification of Religious Symbols." In *Religious Experience and Truth,* edited by Sidney Hook, pp. 3–11. New York, 1962.

"Missions and World History." In *The Theology of the Christian Mission,* edited by Gerald H. Anderson, pp. 281–89. New York, 1961.

Morality and Beyond. London, 1964.

My Search for Absolutes. New York, 1967.

"Natural and Revealed Religion." *Christendom* 1 (1935): 159–70.

"Das neue Sein als Zentralbegriff einer christlichen Theologie." *Eranos-Jahrbuch* 23 (1954): 251–74.

The New Being. London, 1956.

"Offenbarung." RGG 4 (1930): 664–69.

On the Boundary. London, 1967.

"The Permanent Significance of the Catholic Church for Protestantism." *The Protestant Digest* 3 (1941): 23–31.

Perspectives on 19th and 20th Century Protestant Theology. Edited by Carl E. Braaten. London, 1967.

"Philosophie und Religion grundsätzlich." RGG 4 (1930): 1227–33.

Political Expectations. Edited by James Luther Adams. New York, 1971.

"The Problem of Theological Method." JR 27 (1947): 16–26.

The Protestant Era. Chicago, 1957.

"Das Recht auf Hoffnung." In *Ernst Bloch zu Ehren,* pp. 265–76. Frankfurt a/M, 1965.

The Recovery of the Prophetic Tradition in the Reformation. Washington, D.C., 1950.

"A Reinterpretation of the Doctrine of the Incarnation." *Church Quarterly Review* 147 (1949): 133–48.

Bibliography

"Rejoinder." JR 46 (1966): 184–96.

"Relation of Metaphysics and Theology." *The Review of Metaphysics* 10 (1956): 57–63.

"The Relevance of the Ministry in Our Time and Its Theological Foundation." In *Making the Ministry Relevant*, edited by Hans Hofmann, pp. 19–35. New York, 1960.

The Religious Situation. New York, 1956.

"Reply." *Gregorianum* 37 (1956): 53–54; reprinted in O'Meara and Weisser, eds. *Paul Tillich in Catholic Thought*, pp. 22–24.

"Reply to Interpretation and Criticism." In Kegley and Bretall, eds. *The Theology of Paul Tillich*, pp. 329–49.

The Shaking of the Foundations. Harmondsworth, Middlesex, Gt. Brit., 1962.

"Die Staatslehre Augustins nach Civitate Dei." ThBl 4 (1925): 77–86.

Systematic Theology. 3 vols. Chicago, 1951–63.

"Die Theologie des Kairos und die gegenwärtige geistige Lage." ThBl 13 (1934): 305–28.

The Theology of Culture. New York, 1959.

"Theonomie." RGG 5 (1930): 1128–39.

Ultimate Concern. Edited by D.M. Brown. London, 1965.

"Um was es geht, Antwort an Emanuel Hirsch." ThBl 14 (1935): 117–20.

"War Aims." *The Protestant Digest* 4 (1942).

The World Situation. Philadelphia, 1965.

Other Works

Abbott, Walter, ed. *The Documents of Vatican II.* New York, 1966.

Acton, Lord. *Essays on Freedom and Power.* Edited by G. Himmelfarb. Boston, 1949.

Adam, Karl. *The Spirit of Catholicism.* Translated by Don Justin McCann. New York, 1954.

Adolfs, Robert. *The Church Is Different.* Translated by Hubert Hoskins. New York, 1964.

Alston, William P. "Tillich on Idolatry." JR 38 (1958): 263–67.

Altizer, Thomas. *The Gospel of Christian Atheism.* Philadelphia, 1966.

Armbruster, Carl J. *The Vision of Paul Tillich.* New York, 1967.

Balthasar, Hans Urs von. *Schleifung der Bastionen.* Einsiedeln, 1952.

Bárczay, Gyula. *Ecclesia Semper Reformanda.* Zurich, 1961.

Barth, Karl. *Ad Limina Apostolorum.* Translated by Keith R. Crim. Richmond, Va., 1968.

―――. *Dogmatics in Outline.* Translated by G.T. Thomson. London, 1966.

―――. *Protestant Thought: From Rousseau to Ritschl.* Translated by Brian Cozens. New York, 1959.

Bibliography

Baum, Gregory. *The Credibility of the Church Today.* New York, 1968.

_____. "Doctrinal Renewal." *Journal of Ecumenical Studies* 2 (1965): 365–81.

_____. "The Magisterium in a Changing Church." *Concilium* 21 (1967): 67–83.

Bolewski, Hans. "Zum Verhältnis von manifester und latenter Kirche." *Pastoraltheologie, Wissenschaft, und Praxis* 55 (1966): 230–42.

Bornkamm, Heinrich. *Die eine heilige christliche Kirche—evangelisch gesehen.* Göttingen, 1961.

Bouyer, Louis. *The Spirit and Forms of Protestantism.* Translated by A.V. Littledale. New York, 1956.

Braaten, Carl E. "Paul Tillich and the Classical Christian Tradition." In Tillich, *Perspectives on 19th and 20th Century Protestant Theology,* pp. xiii–xxxiv.

_____. "Toward a Theology of Hope." *New Theology,* no. 5. New York, 1968.

Brauer, Jerald C. Preface to special supplement in honor of Paul Tillich. JR 46 (1966): 89–91.

Braun, Herbert. *Gesammelte Studien zum NT und seiner Umwelt.* Tübingen, 1962.

Brown, Raymond et al., eds. *The Jerome Biblical Commentary.* New York, 1968.

Brown, Robert McAfee. *The Spirit of Protestantism.* New York, 1961.

_____ and Weigel, Gustave. *An American Dialogue.* New York, 1961.

Butler, Edward Cuthbert. *The Vatican Council.* 2 vols. London, 1936.

Calvin, John. *Institutes of the Christian Religion.* 2 vols. Grand Rapids, Mich., 1966.

Congar, Yves. "Apostolicité de ministère et apostolicité de doctrine." In *Volk Gottes,* edited by Remigius Bräuner and Heimo Dolch. Freiburg, 1967.

_____. *Chrétiens en Dialogue. Unam Sanctam* 50. Paris, 1964.

_____. "Comment l'Église Sainte doit se renouveler sans cesse." *Irenikon* 34 (1961): 322–45.

_____. "The Idea of 'Major' or 'Principle' Sacraments." *Concilium* 31 (1968): 21–32.

_____. *Sainte Église.* Paris, 1964.

_____. *Vraie et fausse réforme dans l'Église.* Paris, 1950.

Cooper, John Charles. *Radical Christianity and Its Sources.* Philadelphia, 1968.

_____. *The Roots of Radical Theology.* Philadelphia, 1967.

Cullmann, Oscar. *The Early Church.* Translated by A.J.B. Higgins and S. Godman. London, 1956.

_____. *Message to Catholics and Protestants.* Translated by Joseph A. Burgess. Grand Rapids, Mich., 1959.

Dee, Helmut. "Wesen und Wirklichkeit der Kirche." *Monatschrift für Pastoraltheologie* 54 (1965): 269–78.

Dejaifve, Georges. "Diversité dogmatique et unité de la Révélation." *Nouvelle Revue Théologique* 89 (1967): 16–25.

Bibliography

De Lubac, Henri. *Corpus Mysticum*. Paris, 1944.

Denzinger, H. *Enchiridion Symbolorum*. 32d ed. Freiburg, 1963.

Deutsche Reichstagsakten. Jüngere Reihe IV. Göttingen, 1963.

Dewart, Leslie. *The Future of Belief*. New York, 1966.

―――. *The Foundations of Belief*. New York, 1969.

Diem, Hermann. *Die Kirche und ihre Praxis*. Munich, 1963.

Dillenberger, John. *Protestant Christianity*. New York, 1955.

Dodd, Charles H. *The Parables of the Kingdom*. London, 1953.

Döpfner, Julius Kardinal. "Reform—Ein Wesenselement der Kirche." In *In dieser Stunde der Kirche*, pp. 26–37. Munich, 1967.

Dournes, Jacques. "Why Are There Seven Sacraments." *Concilium* 31 (1968): 67–86.

Dulles, Avery. *The Dimensions of the Church*. Westminster, 1967.

―――. *The Survival of Dogma*. New York, 1971.

Dupuy, Bernard. "Is There a Dogmatic Distinction between the Function of Priests and the Function of Bishops?" *Concilium* 34 (1968): 76–86.

Duss-von Werdt, Joseph. "What Can the Layman Do Without a Priest?" *Concilium* 34 (1968): 105–14.

Eliot, T.S. *Notes toward a Definition of Culture*. London, 1949.

Ellwein, Theodore. "Protestantismus." *Pädagogisches Lexikon*. Stuttgart, 1961. pp. 749–51.

Evely, Louis. *Gospel without Myths*. Translated by J. F. Bernard. New York, 1971.

Ferré, Nels F. S. "Three Critical Issues in Tillich's Philosophical Theology." *Scottish Journal of Theology* 10 (1957): 225–38.

―――. et al. *Paul Tillich, Retrospect and Future*. Nashville, Tenn., 1966.

Feuillet, A., and Robert A., eds. *Introduction to the New Testament*. Translated by A. Robert from 2nd French ed. New York, 1968.

Fichtner, J.A. "Reform in the Church." *New Catholic Encyclopedia* 12: 169–74.

Finkenzeller, Josef. "Die Zählung und die Zahl der Sakramente." In *Wahrheit und Verkündigung* 2, edited by Leo Scheffczyck et al., pp. 1005–33. Munich, 1967.

Ford, Lewis S. "Tillich and Thomas: The Analogy of Being." *JR* 46 (1966): 229–45.

Fox, Marvin. "Tillich's Ontology and God." *Anglican Theological Review* 43 (1961): 260–67.

Friedenspreisträger Paul Tillich. Stuttgart, 1963.

Fries, Heinrich. *Aspects of the Church*. Translated by Thomas O'Meara. Westminster, Md., 1965.

―――. *Kirche als Ereignis*. Düsseldorf, 1958.

―――. "Reich Gottes," *LThK* 8: 1115–20.

Bibliography

Goethe, Johann Wolfgang von. *Faust.* Part 1, translated by Philip Wayne. New York, 1959; part 2, translated by Louis Macneice. London, 1951.

Grabowski, Stanislaus. *The Church.* London, 1957.

Greene, Theodore. "Paul Tillich and Our Secular Culture." In Kegley and Bretall, eds., *The Theology of Paul Tillich*, pp. 50–66.

Groot, Jan. "The Church as Sacrament of the World." *Concilium* 31 (1968): 51–66.

Guggisberg, Kurt. *Der freie Protestantismus*, 2d ed. Bern-Stuttgart, 1952.

Haag, Herbert, ed. *Bibel-Lexikon.* Einsiedeln, 1968.

Hagen, August. *Der Reformkatholizismus in der Diözese Rottenburg 1902–1920. Stuttgart, 1962.*

Haller, J. Papstum und Kirchenreform. Berlin, 1903.

Hamilton, Kenneth. *The System and the Gospel.* New York, 1963.

Harnack, Adolf von. *Aus Wissenschaft und Leben.* 2 vols. Giessen, 1911.

———. *What Is Christianity?* Translated by Thomas Bailey Saunders. New York, 1957.

Hartmann, Walter. "Kritik und Gestaltung." *Monatschrift für Pastoraltheologie* 52 (1963): 329–40.

———. "Paul Tillich." In *Tendenzen der Theologie im 20. Jahrhundert*, edited by Hans Jürgen Schultz, pp. 270–76. Stuttgart, 1966.

Heiler, Friedrich. *Im Ringen um die Kirche.* Munich, 1931.

Hennig, Karl, ed. *Der Spannungsbogen.* Stuttgart, 1961.

Heschel, Abraham. *God in Search of Man.* New York, 1955.

Hessen, Johannes. *Der Absolutheitsanspruch des Christentums.* Munich, 1963.

Hoffman, P. "Reich Gottes." In *Handbuch theologischer Grundbegriffe*, edited by H. Fries. Munich, 1963.

Hopper, David. *Tillich: A Theological Portrait.* New York, 1968.

Iremonger, F.A. *William Temple, Archbishop of Canterbury, His Life and Letters.* London, 1950.

Jackson, F.J. Foakes, and Lake, K. *The Beginnings of Christianity.* 5 vols. London, 1957.

Jáki, Stanislaus. *Les Tendances nouvelles de l'Ecclesiologie.* Rome, 1957.

Javierre, Antonio, "Notes on the Traditional Teaching on Apostolic Succession." *Concilium* 34 (1968): 16–27.

Jedin, Hubert. *History of the Council of Trent.* Translated by Ernest Graf. London, 1957.

———. *Handbook of Church History.* New York, 1963–.

———. *Katholische Reformation oder Gegenreformation?* Lucerne, 1946.

Jossua, Jean P. "Immutabilité, Progrès ou Structurations Multiples des Doctrines Chrétiennes?" *Revue de Sciences Philosophiques et Théologiques* 52 (1968): 173–200.

_____. "Rule of Faith and Orthodoxy." *Concilium* 51 (1970): 56–67.

Journet, Charles. *L'Église du Verbe Incarné*. 2 vols. Paris, 1951. Vol. 1 translated by A. H. C. Downes as *The Church of the Word Incarnate*. New York, 1955.

Kähler, Martin. *The So-called Historical Jesus and the Historic Biblical Christ*. Philadelphia, 1964.

Käsemann, Ernst. *Essays on New Testament Themes*. London, 1964.

_____. *Leib und Leib Christi*. Tübingen, 1933.

_____. *Jesus Means Freedom*. Philadelphia, 1969.

Kasper, Walter. "The Church under the Word of God." *Concilium* 4 (1965): 87–93.

_____. *Dogma unter dem Wort Gottes*. Mainz, 1965.

_____. *The Methods of Dogmatic Theology*. Translated by John Drury. Glen Rock, New Jersey, 1969.

_____. "The Relationship between Gospel and Dogma: An Historical Approach." *Concilium* 21 (1967): 153–67.

_____. "Schrift-Tradition-Verkündigung." *Umkehr und Erneuerung, Kirche nach dem Konzil* edited by Theodor Filthaut, pp. 13–41. Mainz, 1966.

Kegley, Charles W., and Bretall, Robert W., eds. *The Theology of Paul Tillich*. New York, 1964.

Kelsey, D.H. *The Fabric of Paul Tillich's Theology*. New York, 1967.

Keppler, Paul Wilhelm von. "Wahre und falsche Reform." *Deutsches Volksblatt*. Stuttgart, 1902.

Kierkegaard, Soren. *The Journals of Soren Kierkegaard*. Edited and translated by A. Dru. London, 1938.

Killen, R. Allan. *The Ontological Theology of Paul Tillich*. Kempen, Netherlands, 1956.

Kinder, Ernst. *Was Ist Eigentlich Evangelish*. Stuttgart, 1961.

Knox, Ronald. *Enthusiasm*. Oxford, 1950.

Kümmel, W. G. "Notwendigkeit und Grenze des NT Kanons." ZThK 47 (1950): 277–313.

Küng, Hans. *The Church*. Translated by Ray and Rosaleen Ockenden. London, 1967.

_____. *The Council, Reform, and Reunion*. Translated by Cecily Hastings. New York, 1965.

_____. ed. *Fehlbar? Eine Bilanz*. Zurich, 1973.

_____. "Im Interesse der Sache, Antwort an Karl Rahner." *Stimmen der Zeit* 187 (1971): 46–62, 105–22.

_____. *Infallible? An Inquiry*. New York, 1972.

_____. *Justification*. Translated by Thomas Collins, Edmund E. Tolk, and David Granskou. New York, 1965.

Bibliography

———. "Die Kirche des Evangeliums." *Diskussion um Hans Küng "Die Kirche."* Edited by H. Häring and J. Nolte. Freiburg, 1971.

———. *The Living Church.* Translated by Cecily Hastings and N. D. Smith. New York, 1963.

———. "Reform der Kirche." *Handbuch theologischer Grundbegriffe* I. Edited by H. Fries, pp. 822–27. Munich, 1963.

———. *Structures of the Church.* Translated by Salvator Attanasio. New York, 1964.

———. *Truthfulness: The Future of the Church.* New York, 1968.

———. "What Is the Essence of Apostolic Succession?" *Concilium* 34 (1968): 28–35.

Ladner, Gerhart B. "Erneuerung." *Reallexikon für Antike und Christentum* 6 (1966): 240–75.

———. *The Idea of Reform.* New York, 1967.

Lambert, Bernard. *Ecumenism: Theology and History.* New York, 1967.

Leese, Kurt. *Die Religion des protestantischen Menschen.* Munich, 1948.

Leibrecht, Walter, ed. *Religion and Culture, Essays in Honor of Paul Tillich.* New York, 1959.

Loewenich, Walter von. *Glaube, Kirche, Theologie.* Witten/Ruhr, 1958.

Lortz, Joseph. *The Reformation: A Problem for Today.* Translated by John C. Dwyer. Westminster, 1964.

Luther, Martin: *Werke.* Weimarer Ausgabe.

Lyons, James, ed. *The Intellectual Legacy of Paul Tillich.* Detroit, 1969.

McBrien, Richard. *The Church in the Thought of Bishop Robinson.* Philadelphia, 1966.

McKelway, Alexander J. *The Systematic Theology of Paul Tillich.* Richmond, Va., 1964.

McKenzie, John L. *Authority in the Church.* New York, 1966.

———. *The Power and the Wisdom.* Milwaukee, 1965.

McNally, Robert E. *Reform of the Church.* New York, 1963.

Mansi, J. D., ed. *Sacrorum conciliorum nova et amplissima collectio.* 31 vols. Florence, 1759–98.

May, Rollo. *Paulus.* New York, 1973.

Meyer, Hans. "How Much Change Is Permissible in the Liturgy?" *Concilium* 42 (1969): 37–48.

Möhler, Johann Adam. *Die Einheit in der Kirche.* Tübingen, 1843.

Mollegen, A. T. "Christology and Biblical Criticism in Tillich." In Kegley and Bretall, eds. *The Theology of Paul Tillich*, pp. 230–45.

Mourret, F. *Le Concile du Vatican.* Paris, 1919.

Newman, John Henry, Cardinal. *An Essay on the Development of Christian Doctrine.* New York, 1960.

Bibliography

Niebuhr, H. Richard. "Paul Tillich's Systematic Theology, I: a Review." JR 46 (1966): 203–5.

Niebuhr, Reinhold. "Biblical thought and Ontological Speculation in Tillich's Theology." In Kegley and Bretall, eds. *The Theology of Paul Tillich*, pp. 216–27.

O'Hanlon, Daniel J. "The Influence of Schelling on the Thought of Paul Tillich." S.T.D. dissertation, Gregorian University, 1957.

O'Malley, John W. *Giles of Viterbo on Church and Reform*. Leiden, 1968.

_____. "Historical Thought and the Reform Crisis of the Early 16th Century." ThSt 28 (1967): 531–48.

O'Meara, Thomas A., and Weisser, Celestin D., eds. *Paul Tillich in Catholic Thought*. London, 1965.

Ott, Ludwig, *Fundamentals of Catholic Dogma*. Translated by J.C. Bastible. St. Louis, 1962.

Otto, Rudolf. *The Idea of the Holy*. New York, 1958.

Pelikan, Jaroslav. *Obedient Rebels*. New York, 1964.

Pesch, Wilhelm. "Kirchlicher Dienst und Neues Testament." In *Zum Thema Priesteramt*. Edited by W. Pesch et al. Stuttgart, 1970.

_____. "Priestertum im Neuen Testament." *Trier theologische Zeitschrift* 79 (1970): 65–83.

Piault, Bernard. *Was ist ein Sakrament?* Anschaffenburg, 1964.

Pittenger, W. Norman, "Paul Tillich as a Theologian; An Appreciation." *Anglican Theological Review* 43 (1961): 268–86.

_____. *The Word Incarnate*. New York, 1959.

Prenter, Regin. *Der Protestantismus in unserer Zeit*. Stuttgart, 1959.

Rahner, Karl. *The Church and the Sacraments*. Translated by W.J. O'Hara. New York, 1963.

_____. *Kirche der Sünder*. Freiburg, 1948.

_____. *Theological Investigations*. 11 vols. Baltimore, 1961–.

_____. *Zum Problem Unfehlbarkeit: Antworten auf die Anfrage von Hans Küng*. Freiburg, 1971.

_____. "Zur konziliaren Mariologie." *Stimmen der Zeit* 174 (1963–64): 87–101.

_____ and Vorgrimler, Herbert, eds. *Theological Dictionary*. Translated by Richard Strachan. New York, 1965.

Ratzinger, Josef. "Leib Christi." LThK 6 (1955): 910–12.

_____. *Das Neue Volk Gottes*. Düsseldorf, 1969.

_____. "Das Problem der Mariologie." *Theologische Revue* 61 (1965): 74–82.

Remmers, Johannes. "Apostolic Succession: An Attribute of the Whole Church." *Concilium* 34 (1968): 36–51.

Rhein, Christof. *Paul Tillich: Philosophie und Theologie*. Stuttgart, 1957.

Rigaux, Béda. "The Twelve Apostles." *Concilium* 34 (1968): 5–15.

Bibliography

Robinson, John A.T. *The New Reformation?* London, 1965.

Rowe, William L. *Religious Symbols and God: A Philosophical Study of Tillich's Theology.* Chicago, 1968.

Russell, Jeffrey B. *Dissent and Reform in the Early Middle Ages.* Berkeley, 1965.

Sanderson, John W. "Historical Fact or Symbol? The Philosophies of History of Paul Tillich and Reinhold Niebuhr." *Westminster Theological Journal* 20 (1958): 158–69; 21 (1958): 58–78.

Schillebeeckx, Edward. *Christ the Sacrament of the Encounter with God.* Translated by Paul Barrett. English text revised by Mark Schoof and Lawrence Bright. New York, 1963.

Schlier, Heinrich. *Der Brief an die Epheser, ein Kommentar.* Düsseldorf, 1957.

————. *Christus und die Kirche im Epheserbrief.* Tübingen, 1930.

————. *Die Zeit der Kirche.* Freiburg, 1966.

Schmaus, Michael. *Katholische Dogmatik.* 5 vols. Munich, 1953–58.

Schmidlin, Josef. *Papstgeschichte der neuesten Zeit.* 4 vols. Munich, 1933–39.

Schmidt, Erich. "Gedanken zu Paul Tillichs philosophischer Theologie, eine Apologie." *Neue Zeitschrift für systematische Theologie und Religionsphilosophie* 5 (1963): 97–118.

Schmitz, Josef. *Die Apologetische Theologie Paul Tillichs.* Mainz, 1966.

Schnackenburg, Rudolf. *The Church in the New Testament.* Translated by W. J. O'Hara. New York, 1965.

————. *God's Rule and Kingdom.* Translated by John Murray. New York, 1963.

Schoonenberg, Piet. "Geschichtlichkeit und Interpretation des Dogmas." In *Die Interpretation des Dogmas,* edited by Piet Schoonenberg, pp. 58–110. Düsseldorf, 1969.

Schultz, Hans Jurgen, ed. *Tendenzen der Theologie im 20. Jahrhundert.* Stuttgart, 1966.

Schütte, Heinz. *Protestantismus.* Essen-Werden, 1966.

Schweitzer, Albert. *The Quest of the Historical Jesus.* Translated by W. Montgomery. New York, 1961.

Semmelroth, Otto. *Die Kirche als Ursakrament.* Frankfurt a/M, 1963.

Simon, Paul. *The Human Element in the Church of Christ.* Translated by Meyrick Booth. Westminster, 1954.

Spinka, Matthew. *Advocates of Reform.* London, 1953.

Tavard, George. *Paul Tillich and the Christian Message.* London, 1962.

————. "Paul Tillich's Systematic Theology, III: a Review." JR 46 (1966): 223–26.

Teilhard de Chardin, Pierre. *The Divine Milieu.* New York, 1965.

Thomas, J. Heywood. "Catholic Criticism of Tillich." *Scottish Journal of Theology* 16 (1963): 32–49.

————. *Paul Tillich: An Appraisal.* London, 1965.

Tillich, Hannah. *From Time to Time.* New York, 1973.

Bibliography

Toynbee, Arnold J. *A Study of History.* Vol. 4, *The Breakdown of Civilizations.* London, 1939.

Ullmann, W. "Gregory VII, Pope, St." *New Catholic Encyclopedia* 6:772–75.

Valeske, Ulrich. *Votum Ecclesiae.* Munich, 1962.

Van de Pol, W.H. *The End of Conventional Christianity.* Translated by Theodore Zuydwijk, S.J. New York, 1968.

Visser 't Hooft, W.A. *The Renewal of the Church.* Philadelphia, 1956.

Wacker, Paulus. "Ecclesia semper reformanda, Theologische Grundlegung der kirchlichen Erneuerung." *Theologie und Glaube* 54 (1964): 241–51.

Walz, Hans Herman. *Das protestantische Wagnis.* Stuttgart, 1958.

Wedel, Theodore O. *The Coming Great Church.* London, 1947.

Weigel, Gustave. "Catholic Ecclesiology in Our Time." *Christianity Divided.* Edited by D. Callahan et al, pp. 177–91. London, 1961.

———. "Contemporaneous Protestantism and Paul Tillich." ThSt 11 (1950): 177–202.

———. "The Multidimensional World of Paul Tillich." *The Christian Scholar* 43 (1960): 67–71.

———. "Recent Protestant Theology." ThSt 14 (1953): 568–94.

Weiss, Albert Maria. *Die religiöse Gefahr.* Freiburg, 1904.

———. *Lebens- und Gewissensfragen der Gegenwart* 2. Freiburg, 1911.

———. *Liberalismus und Christentum.* Trier, 1914.

Weiss, Johannes. *Jesus' Proclamation of the Kingdom of God.* Translated by R.H. Hiers and D.L. Holland. Philadelphia, 1971.

Wendland, Heinz-Dietrich. "Was Bedeuten Tillichs Thesen über den Protestantismus." *Neue Zeitschrift für systematische Theologie und Religionsphilosophie* 5 (1963): 192–213.

Werk und Werken Paul Tillichs, Ein Gedenkbuch. Stuttgart, 1967.

Wernsdörfer, Thietmar. *Die entfremdete Welt, Paul Tillich und das Problem der Entfremdung.* Zurich, 1968.

Winkelhofer, Alois. *Kirche in den Sakramenten.* Frankfurt a/M, 1968.

Wolf, Ernst. "Protestantismus." RGG 5(1956): 648–61.

INDEX

Absolutism, 123
Absolutizing. *See* Demonization
Adam, Karl, 191
Adaptation, 82, 213–20.
Adrian VI, pope, 208
Agape, 75. *See also* Love
Alienation. *See* Estrangement
Ambiguity, 35–37, 53, 60–61; in the
    Church, 75–76, 78, 86, 109; history and,
    93–94, 103, 104; of dogmas, 143–44; of
    the ecumenical movement, 127–28
Analogy of being, 27, 166, 266–67
Anti-Christian movements, 70–71
Apologetics, 83, 149–52, 157
Apostolicity, 264
Arianism, 143
Art, religious, 84–85
Asceticism, 88
Atheism, 30
Augustine, saint, 23, 29, 119, 149; Church
    as sacrament, 194, 197; kingdom of God,
    96, 100, 186–87; latent Spiritual Com-
    munity, 68; on the Church as a commu-
    nity of love, 75; on reform, 202, 245;
    universalism, 50
Authoritarianism, 130–32; in the Catholic
    Church, 107, 117, 119, 121. *See also*
    Heteronomy
Authority, 115, 125, 131–35
Autonomy, 122–23, 130, 132–34, 267

Baptism, 111
Barth, Karl: example of particularism, 51;

on: authority, 129; church history, 140;
    Protestantism, 266; revelation, 24; Vati-
    can Council II, 218
Baum, Gregory, 257, 227–30
Bible. *See* Scripture
Biblicism, 139, 142
Being, 29
Bernard of Clairvaux, saint, 206
Body of Christ, 115, 190–93. *See also*
    Spiritual Community
Bonhoeffer, Dietrich, 24, 147
Bornkamm, Heinrich, 197
Bouyer, Louis, 197
Brahmanism, 41
Brown, Robert McAfee, 180, 221
Bucer, Martin, 187
Buddhism, 41

Calvin, John, 112–121; authority in the
    Church, 136; innovation, 214–15; Scrip-
    ture, 139; Spiritual Community, 68
Capitalism, 148, 152–53
Charism, 135
Catholic Church, 89, 117–21; ambiguity
    in, 37, 76, 77, 78, 102; asceticism 88;
    control of art, 85; early Catholicism,
    269; identification with kingdom of God,
    100; identification with Spiritual Com-
    munity, 68; interpretation of history, 94;
    interpretation of Scripture, 141;
    monophysite trends, 116; reductionism
    in, 271–72; significance of, 125–26; Til-

Index

Index

Protestantism, orthodox, 37, 102, 121, 139
Psychology, 109
Puritanism, 88

Quasi-religions: examples of ultimate concern, 26; relationship to Church, 31–32; revelation, 53; world religions, 155, 157

Rahner, Karl, on: Church as sacrament, 194; dogma, 227; infallibility, 247–48, 260; scaraments, 255; sin in the Church, 223
Reaction, 94. *See also* Conservatism
Reform, 81, 200–1; application of Protestant principle, 114–15; in Catholic Church, 120, 198; of: abuses, 205–11; life, 211–20; persons, 201–5
Reform Catholicism, 203–4, 215–16
Reformation, Protestant, 118, 211; ambiguity of, 78, 125; attitude toward sacraments, 107; based on Protestant principle, 113, 121, 197; problem of authority, 136; reductionism in, 268–69
Relativism, 82, 138
Relevance, 264
Religion, 24–25, 32–37; ambiguities, 35–37, 53; attack on, 87; end of, 104; necessity, 32–34; types, 34–35; Spiritual Community, 70. *See also* Quasi-religions; World Religions
Religious Socialism, 66, 95, 98, 152–53
Renaissance, 50
Resurrection, 45
Revelation, 23–24, 25, 32; Christ-event and universality of, 52–53; relation to dogma, 235
Revolution, 94, 103
Ritschl, Albrecht, 113, 187

Sacramentalism, 101, 103–4, 122. *See also* Catholic substance; Priestly element
Sacraments, 80, 107–12, 194, 253–56; Catholic Church and, 107, 125; Church, 194–97; deficiency in Tillich, 265–66
Saints, 116
Salvation, 152
Sartre, Jean-Paul, 31, 41
Scheeben, Matthias, 191
Schelling, Friedrich Wilhelm Joseph, 51
Schillebeeckx, Edward, 194
Schleiermacher, Friedrich, 23, 167, 170
Scholasticism, 30
Schoonenberg, Piet, 249–53

Schütte, Heinz, 181
Schweitzer, Albert, 43, 187
Scientism, 37
Scripture: authority, 138–41; historical criticism, 45; pluralism, 270–71, 273; relationship of dogma to, 240, 250; relationship of tradition to, 275–77
Sectarianism, 68, 78, 102
Secularism, 25; Spiritual Community, 67, 70; Protestantism, 102, 108, 122, 124; problem for ministry, 150; world religions, 155, 157
Security, 122, 123–24
Semmelroth, Otto, 194, 196, 197
Signs, 27. *See also* Symbols
Sin, 152
Skepticism, 133
Skydsgaard, K.E., 182
Social Gospel, 271
Social Justice, 152–55
Socialism, 153
Solovyov, Vladimir, 279
Spirit, 60, 62, 115, 146
Spiritual Community, 64–71, 90, 104; essence of Church, 71
Spiritual Community, latent (Latent Church), 66–71; "Gestalt of grace," 116; kingdom of God and, 99, 102; Catholic parallel, 193
Spiritual Presence, 61–63; evangelism, 83–84; identified with Eternal Life, 104; mediated by sacraments, 107, 109; kingdom of God, 95
Stählin, W., 182
Stoicism, 50
Streck, K.G., 182
Symbols, 27–28, 33, 84
Symbols, religious, 22, 26–29, 56, 266; applied to Incarnation, 47; Church viewed as, 48; interpretation, 85, 148–52; sacraments, 109
Synthesis, 166

Teilhard de Chardin, Pierre, 92
Temple, William, archbishop, 186
Theism, 30
Theology, 85, 143, 149–52
Theonomy, 133–34, 138
Tillich, Paul:
—life: influences on, 125, 129–30, 165; interest in world religions, 156; involvement with Religious Socialism,

313

Ronald Modras, assistant professor of systematic theology at St. John's Seminary, Plymouth, Michigan, has degrees from St. Mary's College, Orchard Lake, Michigan (B.A., 1959), Catholic University of America (S.T.B., 1963), and the University of Tübingen (Ph.D., 1974). He has published in *Concilium* and the *Journal of Ecumenical Studies*, and his *Paths to Unity* was published in 1968.

The manuscript was edited by Marguerite C. Wallace. The book was designed by Don Ross. The typeface for the text is Merganthaler's Linotype Caledonia designed by W.A. Dwiggins about 1938; and the display face is Melior designed by Hermann Zapf about 1952.

The text is printed on International Bookmark paper. The book is bound in Columbia Mills' Llamique cloth over binders' boards. Manufactured in the United States of America.